AF690293

Tom Tabori is a specialist public law barrister, with expertise in human rights law, education law, electoral law, immigration law, equalities law, information rights, and regulatory law. Before becoming a barrister, he worked in Parliament for two MPs and coordinated an all-party group.

A PRACTICAL GUIDE TO ELECTION LAW

A PRACTICAL GUIDE TO ELECTION LAW

TOM TABORI

Barrister, 39 Essex Chambers

Consultant Editor

TIMOTHY STRAKER QC

Barrister, 4-5 Gray's Inn Square

Law Brief Publishing

© Tom Tabori

All rights reserved. No part of this publication may be reproduced, stored in a retrieval system, or transmitted, in any form or by any means, electronic, mechanical, photocopying, recording or otherwise, without the prior permission of the publisher.

Excerpts from judgments and statutes are Crown copyright. Any Crown Copyright material is reproduced with the permission of the Controller of OPSI and the Queen's Printer for Scotland. Some quotations may be licensed under the terms of the Open Government Licence (http://www.nationalarchives.gov.uk/doc/open-government-licence/version/3).

Cover image © iStockphoto.com/claudiodivizia

The information in this book was believed to be correct at the time of writing. All content is for information purposes only and is not intended as legal advice. No liability is accepted by either the publisher or author for any errors or omissions (whether negligent or not) that it may contain. Professional advice should always be obtained before applying any information to particular circumstances. Links to third-party websites are provided in good faith and for information only. The author and publisher disclaim responsibility for the materials contained in any third-party website referenced in this work.

Published 2020 by Law Brief Publishing, an imprint of Law Brief Publishing Ltd
30 The Parks
Minehead
Somerset
TA24 8BT

www.lawbriefpublishing.com

Paperback: 978-1-912687-72-5

PREFACE

This book is no substitute for obtaining legal advice on the complex issues that electoral law may throw up in different contexts, but it does seek to provide candidates, agents, returning officers, regulators, campaigners, and legal practitioners with a practical guide to the framework of electoral law as contained in the main legislation and at common law.

As to scope, this book does not cover Scottish local elections, elections to the Northern Ireland Assembly, nor referendums. It does however cover parliamentary elections ("**PE**"), local elections ("**LE**") in England and Wales, Welsh Assembly elections ("**WAE**"), London Assembly elections ("**LAE**"), and police and crime commissioner elections ("**PCCE**"). It covers returning officer's administration of elections, candidates' contestation of campaigns, the Election Court's trial of petitions, and the Electoral Commission's regulation of political parties, members associations, office-holders, third party campaigners, and donors.

The book also discusses the right to free elections protected by Article 3 of Protocol No.1 to the European Convention on Human Rights ("**A3P1**"). Whilst A3P1 is given its own chapter, it is also discussed throughout the book, where it arises in the scheme of things. This approach seeks to present more clearly the impact of the ECHR on an area of domestic law that is already highly developed.

Lastly, the book looks ahead, to electoral law reform ideas that are presently the subject of heightened debate. This purview is partly a reflection of Law Brief Publishing's interest in law's development, and partly it reflects the moment that electoral law reform is currently having in the attentions of the Law Commission, certain House of Commons select committees, and to a significant extent HM Government. Nonetheless, the book seeks to describe the law as it stands in **mid-June 2020**.

I owe a great debt of gratitude to my consultant editor, Timothy Straker QC. It was an honour for me and to the great enhancement of this book that Timothy should have accepted this role, as it reached its final drafts. Having the input of a practitioner of Timothy's standing and unrivalled experience in this area of law, as both barrister and Election Court commissioner, has inevitably strengthened the scope and analysis of the work. Any errors left in the book are entirely my responsibility.

I am extremely grateful also to Richard Harwood OBE QC and to my neighbour in our currently quiet chambers corridor, Paul Stinchcombe QC, for their generosity with their time, in reading the chapter drafts and blessing the book with their erudite analysis. I am grateful also to another colleague in chambers, Gethin Thomas, for discussions about subjects on which he was well versed as a former researcher on the Law Commission's electoral law reform project, and to Anne Saville and Rory Forbes for invaluable proofreading. Lastly, I want to thank my partner, Jenn, for her patience and support during these past months. I could not have done it without her.

TOM TABORI
June 2020

CONTENTS

CHAPTER 3: ELECTION CAMPAIGNS: AGENTS, EXPENSES AND OFFENCES

CHAPTER 4: RETURNING OFFICERS AND THEIR CONDUCT OF ELECTIONS

CHAPTER 5: ELECTION PETITIONS: PRINCIPLES AND PROCEDURE

TABLE OF CASES

TABLE OF LEGISLATION

STATUTES

STATUTORY INSTRUMENTS

INTERNATIONAL CONVENTIONS AND AGREEMENTS

LIST OF ABBREVIATIONS

ERO: electoral registration officer

GLAER 2007: Greater London Authority Election Rules 2007

GLRO: Greater London returning officer

LAE: London Assembly election

LE: local election

LEPAR 2006: Local Elections (Principal Areas) (England & Wales) Rules 2006

NAWRPO 2007: National Assembly for Wales (Representation of the People) Order 2007

PCCE: police and crime commissioner election

PCCEO 2012: Police and Crime Commissioner Elections Order 2012

PE: Parliamentary election

PO: presiding officer

PPERA 2000: Political Parties, Elections and Referendums Act 2000

PVS: postal voting statement

RO: returning officer

RP: registered party

RPA 1983: Representation of the People Act 1983

RTP: registered third party (campaigner)

UA: unincorporated association

WAE: Welsh Assembly election

LIST OF ABBREVIATIONS

CHAPTER ONE
THE ELECTORAL COMMISSION AND ITS REGULATEES

1.1. Following recommendations for an independent commission in reports by the Select Committee on Home Affairs ("**the Howarth working group**"),[1] the Committee on Standards in Public Life ("**the Neill Committee**"),[2] and the Independent Commission on the Voting System ("**the Jenkins Commission**"),[3] the Electoral Commission ("**the Commission**") was established by the Political Parties, Elections and Representations Act 2000 ("**PPERA 2000**").[4] It is important to note that, though the Commission has general duties to report on the administration of certain elections,[5] and may send representatives to attend proceeding conducted by returning officers or counting officers,[6] the Commission operates within an electoral system in which elections are not run by the Commission. Where the Commission does hold sway is in the registration of political parties and certain other political actors, and in the regulation of their funding.

1.2 The Commission took over a political party registration scheme that had only been in existence since 1998,[7] enacted to solve the problem of misleading descriptions of candidates standing under party labels easily confused with those of major parties, such as 'Conservative', or 'New Labour', or 'Literal Democrat',[8] which the courts had held to be lawful whilst nonetheless inviting Parliament to consider following other jurisdictions by adopting *"a system of registration of political parties and a statutory provision limiting the ability of candidates to use the name of a political party"*.[9] Prior to 1998, political parties did not occupy a distinct legal status. With the introduction of registration in

---

[1]Electoral Law and Administration, Fourth Report, HC 768 1997-8, paras 54 and 156.
[2]Fifth Report of the Committee on Standards in Public Life, 'The Funding of Political Parties in the United Kingdom, vol. 1, October 1998.
[3]Report of the Independent Commission on the Voting System, Cm 4090, October 1998.
[4]S 1 PPERA 2000.
[5]S 5 PPERA 2000. Parliamentary general elections, Scottish Parliamentary general elections, National Assembly for Wales general elections, Northern Ireland Assembly general elections, and ordinary elections of police and crime commissioners.
[6]S 6A PPERA 2000.
[7]Registration of Political Parties Act 1998.
[8]Home Secretary statement on publication of the Registration of Political Parties Bill 188 of 1997-98, Home Office Press Notice 176/98, 14.5.98.
[9]*Sanders v Chichester* [1995] 92(3) LSG 37, [1995] 139 SJLB 15 (DC), p 50, per Dyson and Forbes JJ.

1998 and then the controls on funding in 2000, tightened further in 2009,[10] political parties now exist in as finely worked a regulatory regime as other sectors of public and commercial life.

1.3 This chapter summarises this PPERA 2000 statutory scheme administered by the Commission across the following topics:

A. The Commission and the registers of political parties;

B. Registration;

C. Registered party ("**RP**") regulation;

D. RP members, members associations, and certain elected office-holders ("**regulated donees/participants**");

E. Third party national election campaigners;

F. Unincorporated associations;

G. Enforcement by the Commission;

H. General offences;

I. Incidental powers;

J. Interpreting the legislation; and

K. Judicial review of the Commission.

A. THE COMMISSION AND THE REGISTERS OF POLITICAL PARTIES

1.2 The Commission has a duty to *"maintain"* two registers of political parties: the Great Britain register and the Northern Ireland register.[11]

1.3 Subject to a requirement that the Commission mark the part of Great Britain in respect of which a registered party ("**RP**") is registered and whether it is a 'minor party' (only contesting parish or community elections),[12] the registers may be maintained in such form as the Commission chooses.[13]

1.4 This duty to maintain has been held to entail a power to alter entries in the register.[14] It has also been held to be concerned with content and not form, such that an initially compliant entry may be removed if its substantive meaning

[10]Political Parties and Elections Act 2009.

[11]S 23(1)(a) PPERA 2000.

[12]S 23(3) PPERA 2000.

[13]S 23(1)(b) PPERA 2000.

[14]R *(English Democrats Party) v Electoral Commission* [2018] EWHC 251 (Admin) at 44-45, per Supperstone J.

changes in light of events that put it in breach of, say, requirements as to offensiveness.[15]

B. REGISTRATION

1.5 To field candidates, a political party must be registered with the Commission.[16] The Commission has published guidance on how to do so.[17] Below is a summary of what the law requires.

How to register

1.6 To be registered, a party must send the Commission an application accompanied by a declaration that the party is applying for registration in the GB register, NI register, or both (depending on where it intends to contest elections). Alternatively, the party may accompany its application with a minor party declaration (that it intends only to contest one or more parish or community elections) and is accordingly applying to be registered in the Great Britain register only.[18] The Commission's PEF Online services can be used for registration.

1.7 The application must:

(i) State the party's registered name and address of its headquarters;

(ii) State the name and home address of the leader, nominating officer and treasurer;

(iii) Be accompanied by a copy of the party's constitution (defined as *"the document or documents (of whatever name) by which the structure and organisation of the party is determined"*)[19] and a draft of the financial scheme proposed to be adopted; and

(iv) Be signed by the leader, the nominating officer, the treasurer and (if applicable) the campaigns officer, making clear if someone is signing in two capacities.[20]

---

[15] R *(English Democrats Party) v Electoral Commission* [2018] EWHC 251 (Admin) at 43, Supperstone J rejecting challenge to Commission decision to remove RP's 'England worth fighting for' description in the register ahead of by-election held in the wake of the murder of Jo Cox MP.

[16] S 22 PPERA 2000.

[17] Electoral Commission, 'Introduction to registering a political party' https://www.electoralcommission.org.uk/sites/default/files/pdf_file/intro-registration-rp.pdf.

[18] S 28(2) PPERA 2000.

[19] S 26(9) PPERA 2000.

[20] Para 7 sch 4 PPERA 2000.

1.8 The application may request that the following are also included in the party's entry in the Register:

(i) The name of its campaigns officer, if has one;

(ii) Up to twelve descriptions (to be used on nomination papers or ballot papers, to help voters identify them);[21]

(iii) A joint description with another party;[22] and

(iv) Up to three emblems.[23]

1.9 The Commission may check whether the registration requirements are satisfied, and must apply an objective test when undertaking that check.[24]

Descriptions

1.10 The Commission must register the desired description(s) unless:[25]

(i) It is more than six words long;

(ii) It is the same as an existing RP's description;

(iii) It would likely lead to electors confusing the party with another an existing RP *"already registered in respect of any part of Great Britain in respect of which that party is applying to be registered"*;[26]

(iv) It would be likely to *"(i) to result in an elector being misled as to the effect of his vote, or (ii) to contradict, or hinder an elector's understanding of, any directions for his guidance in voting given on the ballot paper or elsewhere"*;[27]

(v) It is obscene or offensive;

(vi) Its publication would likely amount to commission of an offence; or

(vii) It includes any script other than Roman script.

1.11 This mirrors case law on candidate descriptions, from which guidance may be derived, e.g. *"the Official Byron Ward Conservative"*[28] and *"Literal Democrat"*.[29]

---

[21] S 28A PPERA 2000.

[22] S 28B PPERA 2000.

[23] S 29(1) PPERA 2000.

[24] *Grimes v Electoral Commission* (unreported, 19.7.19, County Court at Central London), at 87, per HHJ Dight; following R *(English Democrats Party) v The Electoral Commission* [2018] EWHC 251 (Admin).

[25] S 28A(2) PPERA 2000.

[26] S 28A(5) PPERA 2000.

[27] S 28A(2)(e) PPERA 2000.

[28] *Jessie Patterson v David Steven Merrick and Michael Hammond*, unreported, 2.11.1988, May and Woolf LLJ. See Chapter 2.

[29] *Sanders v Chichester* [1995] 92(3) LSG 37; [1995] 139 SJLB 15, Dyson and Forbes JJ.

(i) *"The Official Byron Ward Conservative"* former was subject of an injunction granted by the High Court during a LE by-election, and which the court refused to discharge. The Court of Appeal upheld that refusal, May LJ (with whom Woolf LJ agreed) holding *"Clearly the description which this appellant applied to himself in relation to his nomination was capable of confusion with the description applied to herself by the plaintiff and we have no doubt that it was for that reason that the learned judge made the original injunction in October".*[30]

(ii) *"Literal Democrat"* was a description entered on the nomination paper of a candidate for a European Parliamentary election. The acting returning officer ("**RO**") held this was valid as it was good in form and the candidate went on to receive 10,203 votes. The Li<u>b</u>eral Democrat candidate lost by 500 votes and brought a petition challenging the election. He claimed the *"Literal Democrat"* description was intended to confuse and mislead electors. The RO is (and was then) only entitled to hold a nomination paper invalid on narrow formal grounds of *"the particulars of the candidate or the persons subscribing the paper are not as required by law"*, the paper not being *"subscribed as required"*, or the candidate being disqualified.[31] The Court (Dyson and Forbes JJ) held that the particulars of the candidate using the description 'Literal Democrat' were as *"required by law"* and thus the acting RO had not breached their duty in so deciding,[32] as *"the description did not remove the sufficiency of the identification of him given by his full names and home address".*[33]

1.12 It is hard to reconcile these cases, but PPERA 2000 supersedes the issue by making the Commission gatekeeper for descriptions, requiring parties to register with the Commission, and requiring candidates' use of a description to be authorised by a party's nominating officer. The RO is thus spared having to enquire into the correctness of a given description.

Emblems

1.13 The Commission must register a proposed emblem unless one of the grounds for refusing a proposed description are made out (these are the same grounds as

---

[30] *Jessie Patterson v David Steven Merrick v Michael Hammond*, unreported, 2.11.1988, May and Woolf LLJ, p 1.
[31] S 12(2)(a)-(c) RPA 1983.
[32] *Sanders v Chichester* [1995] 92(3) LSG 37; [1995] 139 SJLB 15, Dyson and Forbes JJ, p 48 of transcript.
[33] *Sanders v Chichester* [1995] 92(3) LSG 37; [1995] 139 SJLB 15, Dyson and Forbes JJ, p 23 of transcript.

for descriptions save for the word-length and Roman-script description restrictions).[34]

1.14 If the Commission rejects an emblem, it must notify the party of its reasons.[35]

Financial scheme

1.15 To be registered by the Commission, a party must also adopt a scheme that sets out its arrangements for regulating its financial affairs in compliance with the below financial controls.[36] The scheme also must state whether the party is to be taken to consist of:

(i) A single organisation with no division of responsibility for its financial affairs and transactions for purposes of its accounting requirements; or

(ii) A central organisation with one or more separate accounting units (constituent or affiliated organisations each responsible for its own financial affairs and transactions for purposes of its accounting requirements). If so, then the scheme must state which organisations are to constitute the central organisation and which the accounting units, and the name of each.[37]

1.16 The prospective RP must submit the scheme to the Commission for approval.[38] The Commission may request that the applicant submit a revised scheme,[39] specifying any modifications it considers should be incorporated or matters it thinks should be dealt with.[40]

1.17 The level of scrutiny by the Commission is likely to be greater since *Erlam v Rahman*,[41] where an application for registration had been approved even though *"there was no responsible financial scheme whatsoever"*,[42] leading the Election Court to remark *"that the enquiries into the structures of [the party] cannot have been excessively rigorous"*.[43] That scrutiny must however be exercised with regard to the Commission's *"responsibility for promoting participation in the democratic process"*.[44]

---

[34] S 29(2) PPERA 2000.
[35] S 29(5) PPERA 2000.
[36] S 26(1) PPERA 2000.
[37] S 26(2) and (3) PPERA 2000.
[38] S 26(1) PPERA 2000.
[39] S 26(5) PPERA 2000.
[40] S 26(6) PPERA 2000.
[41] *Erlam v Rahman* [2015] EWHC 1215 (QB).
[42] *Erlam v Rahman* [2015] EWHC 1215 (QB) at 275.
[43] *Erlam v Rahman* [2015] EWHC 1215 (QB) at 274.
[44] Para 23 Explanatory Notes to PPERA 2000.

Party office-holders

1.18 To be registered, a party must also give the name and home address of the persons to be registered as its:

(i) Leader[45] (who must be its overall leader or a person who is the leader of the party for some particular purpose);[46]

(ii) Treasurer[47] (responsible for the party's compliance with PPERA's accounting requirements and control of donations, loans and certain other transactions, plus campaign spending, third party spending, referendums, and financial controls on recall petitions).[48] A RP with accounting units must have a treasurer of the accounting unit and another person as officer of the unit, and the application for party registration must name them;

(iii) Nominating officer,[49] who has responsibility for arranging (a) the submission of lists of candidates for elections; (b) the issuing of a certificates authorising a party description;[50] and (c) the approval of descriptions and emblems used on nomination and ballot papers at elections).[51]

1.19 A RP **may** also register someone as its campaigns officer. If so, this campaigns officer replaces the treasurer as person responsible for compliance with campaign spending, third party spending, and financial controls on recall petitions.[52] This may be its leader or nominating officer, but may not be its treasurer.[53] The campaigns officer may appoint up to twelve deputy campaigns officers.[54]

1.20 A registered treasurer or campaigns officer commits an offence if they register having been convicted in relation to an election offence in the past five years.[55] The offence is triable summarily and the maximum penalty is an unlimited fine.[56] If they commit such an offence after registration, then their appointment terminates.[57]

---

[45]S 24(1)(a) PPERA 2000.
[46]S 24(2) PPERA 2000.
[47]S 24(1)(c) PPERA 2000.
[48]S 24(4) PPERA 2000.
[49]S 24(1)(b) PPERA 2000.
[50]S 22(6) PPERA 2000.
[51]S 24(3) PPERA 2000.
[52]S 25 PPERA 2000.
[53]S 25 PPERA 2000.
[54]S 25(4) PPERA 2000.
[55]Ss 25(3) and 24(8) PPERA 2000.
[56]Sch 20 PPERA 2000.
[57]S 24(9) PPERA 2000.

Registration amendment

1.21 An RP may request its entry be altered.[58] The Commission must refuse if it considers any of the original grounds for refusing to register a description or emblem are present.[59] If an application to amend or substitute a description is granted after the date of publication of the notice of an election that is contested and before the date of the poll, the amendment only takes effect at the subsequent election.[60]

1.22 An RP treasurer must notify the Commission within 28 days (or fourteen if due to death or termination of appointment)[61] if any particulars of its entry in a register cease to be accurate in respect to:

(i) The name or home address of any registered officer of the RP or one of its accounting units;

(ii) *"The address of the party's headquarters (or, if it has no headquarters, the address to which communications to the party may be sent)"*;[62] or

(iii) The name and headquarters address of any accounting unit of the RP.[63]

Ceasing to be registered

1.23 An RP may have its entry in the register removed if: (i) it fails to send notice confirming particulars and constitution or notifying of any changes;[64] or (ii) it applies to have its entry removed, enclosing a declaration, signed by signed by the responsible officers of the party,[65] that it does not intend to have any candidates at any relevant election.[66]

False statement offence

1.24 A person commits an offence if, on behalf of a party or purporting to be on a party's behalf, for purposes of party registration, they knowingly or recklessly make a false statement to the Commission.[67] The offence is triable summarily only and the maximum penalty is a fine at Level 5 on the standard scale (unlimited).[68]

---

[58] S 30(1) PPERA 2000.
[59] S 30(4)-(6) PPERA 2000.
[60] S 30(6A) PPERA 2000.
[61] S 31(4) PPERA 2000.
[62] S 31(2)(c) PPERA 2000.
[63] S 31(1) and (2) PPERA 2000.
[64] S 33(2A) PPERA 2000.
[65] Para 14 sch 4 PPERA 2000.
[66] S 33(2) PPERA 2000.
[67] S 39 PPERA 2000.
[68] Sch 20 PPERA 2000.

C. RP REGULATION

Accounting requirements

1.25 The RP treasurer must keep accounts showing entries showing: (i) all sums of money received and spent by the RP and in respect of what; and (ii) a record of the RP's assets and liabilities.

1.26 Within four months[69] of every financial year end, the treasurer must prepare and deliver to the Commission a statement of accounts, approved by the RP's management committee (or leader if it does not have one).[70] The statement can be submitted via the Commission's PEF Online interactive website[71] or the spreadsheet tools or templates created by the Commission to assist treasurers.[72] The accounts must be kept by the treasurer for six years.[73]

1.27 If the RP has accounting units, each unit need only prepare a statement of accounts where its total income of spending exceeds £25,000 or the Commission requests it.[74]

1.28 If an RP's gross income or total spending in any financial year exceeds £250,000, or it does not but the Commission requests it, that financial year's accounts must be audited by a qualified auditor within six months of the end of the financial year in questions.[75] If the Commission considers the accounts not duly audited in time, it may appoint an auditor to do so.[76] That appointee has a right of access and to request information,[77] misleading response to which is an offence,[78] punishable by an unlimited fine or six months' imprisonment (on summary conviction) or one year's imprisonment (on indictment).[79] Failure to comply with the auditor's request for information is treated as per disobedience to court orders, upon application by the Commission to the High Court.[80]

---

[69]S 45 PPERA 2000.
[70]S 42 PPERA 2000.
[71]https://www.electoralcommission.org.uk/sites/default/files/electoral_commission_pdf_file/PEF-Online-user-guide-creating-and-submitting-your-statement-of-accounts.pdf.
[72]https://www.electoralcommission.org.uk/i-am-a/party-or-campaigner/political-parties/guidance-submitting-your-statements-accounts.
[73]S 42(6) PPERA 2000.
[74]Para 6 sch 5 PPERA 2000.
[75]S 43(1) PPERA 2000.
[76]S 43(4) PPERA 2000.
[77]S 44(1) PPERA 2000.
[78]S 44(4) PPERA 2000.
[79]Sch 20 PPERA 2000.
[80]S 44(3) PPERA 2000.

1.29 The Commission must make these statements of account available for public inspection.[81] They are displayed on the Commission's website.[82]

1.30 If the treasurer fails, without reasonable excuse, to comply with any of these requirements, they commit an offence[83] triable summarily and punishable by unlimited fine.[84]

1.31 After submission of a statement of accounts, the treasurer may revise them[85] and the Commission may raise questions of the treasurer.[86] If the latter, the treasurer must be given at least one month to respond.[87] If no satisfactory response is received, the Commission may apply to the County Court[88] for (i) a declaration that the statement of accounts is non-compliant with prescribed requirements; and (ii) an order that the treasurer prepare a revised version.[89]

Confirmation of registered particulars

1.32 Within six months of the first date by which the RO's annual statement of accounts is to be delivered to the Commission (i.e. within ten months[90] of every financial year end),[91] its treasurer must notify the Commission as to:

(i) Whether the particulars in the RP's entry in the register remain accurate, and if not then apply to alter its entry on the register as necessary;[92] and

(ii) Any change to the RP's constitution occurring since the last confirmation of particulars, or if the first time then since the RP registered.[93]

1.33 If the treasurer fails to do so in time, the Commission must remove the RP's entry from the register.[94]

---

[81]S 46 PPERA 2000.

[82]http://search.electoralcommission.org.uk/Search/Accounts?currentPage=1&rows=10&sort=PublishedDate&order=desc&et=pp&register=gb&register=ni&register=none&regStatus=registered&rptBy=centralparty&rptBy=accountingunits&optCols=PublishedDate&optCols=FinancialYearEnd&optCols=BandName&optCols=SoaType.

[83]S 47 PPERA 2000.

[84]Sch 20 PPERA.

[85]S 48(1) and (2) PPERA 2000.

[86]S 48(3) PPERA 2000.

[87]S 48(4) PPERA 2000.

[88]S 48(5) PPERA 2000.

[89]S 48(6) PPERA 2000.

[90]S 45 PPERA 2000.

[91]S 32(1A) PPERA 2000.

[92]S 32(2) PPERA 2000.

[93]S 32(3) PPERA 2000.

[94]S 33(2A) PPERA 2000.

RP obligations in relation to donations, loans and transactions

Scope

1.34 'Donations' to an RP (but not a minor party)[95] means:

(i) Gifts of money or other property (including where the RP gives consideration in return, if the consideration is less than the value of the money or property), including (a) gifts or transfers to an RP officer, member, trustee or agent in their capacity as such, and not for their own use or benefit;[96] (b) gifts or transfers to an RP indirectly through any third person;[97] and (c) bequests;[98]

(ii) Membership or affiliation fees or subscriptions;[99]

(iii) The discounted provision of any property, services or facilities for the use or benefit of the RP;[100] or

(iv) Money spent directly paying expenses incurred by the RP, or given to the RP to helping it pay those expenses ('sponsorship').[101]

1.35 'Donations' does not include:

(i) Donations up to £500 (but attempts to game this limit by arranging mass sub-£501 gifts may amount to evasion);[102]

(ii) Public grants for security costs at a party conference, applicable to conferences held in the UK for the purposes of an RP that has at least two MPs, or one MP and that received not less than 150,000 votes at the last election, and that is certified by a chief of police;[103]

(iii) Transmission by a broadcaster, free of charge, of a party political broadcast;[104]

(iv) Facilities provided pursuant to candidates' statutory rights an elections;[105]

---

[95]S 50(9) PPERA 2000.
[96]S 50(6) PPERA 2000.
[97]S 50(8) PPERA 2000.
[98]S 50(8) PPERA 2000.
[99]S 50(2)(c) PPERA 2000.
[100]S 50(2)(f) PPERA 2000.
[101]S 50(2)(b) PPERA 2000.
[102]S 52(2)(b) PPERA 2000.
[103]S 52(1)(b) PPERA 2000 and s 170 Criminal Justice and Public Order Act 1994.
[104]S 52(1)(d) PPERA 2000.
[105]S 52(1)(e) PPERA 2000. See Chapter 3.

(v) Assistants to local authority political groups, appointed under s 9 of the Local Government and Housing Act 1989 to assist councillors' discharge of their functions;[106]

(vi) Unpaid, volunteer campaigning (e.g. door-knocking, envelope-stuffing, leafletting);[107]

(vii) Any interest accruing to an RP whilst dealing with an impermissible donation;[108]

(viii) Donations to be included in a return as to election expenses in respect of a candidate at a particular election;[109] or

(ix) Stand hire at party conference.[110]

1.36 Further to this statutory delineation of the scope of 'donation', the Court of Appeal has interpreted the term (albeit in the referendum context) as follows:

(i) Not all donations can be regarded as *"expenses incurred"* by the donor;[111]

(ii) 'Expenses incurred' does not mean the same thing as 'spent'[112] and, equally, 'expenses' *"are not necessarily the same as "spending" or spending"*;[113]

(iii) Expenses are not 'incurred' every time a person's assets are diminished;[114]

(iv) Whilst the same money may be treated both as a donation by one person and as an expense by the recipient, if cannot be treated as an expense by both.[115]

1.37 'Regulated transactions' means: (a) loans to RPs; (b) credit facilities made available to RPs; and (c) the provision of security for a sum owed by an RP.[116]

---

[106] S 52(1)(f) PPERA 2000.
[107] S 52(1)(g) PPERA 2000.
[108] S 52(1)(h) PPERA 2000.
[109] S 52(2)(a) PPERA 2000. See Chapter 3.
[110] S 52(3) PPERA 2000.
[111] R *(Good Law Project) v Electoral Commission* [2019] EWCA Civ 1567, [2020] 1 WLR 1157, at 71.
[112] R *(Good Law Project) v Electoral Commission* [2019] EWCA Civ 1567, [2020] 1 WLR 1157, at 87.
[113] R *(Good Law Project) v Electoral Commission* [2019] EWCA Civ 1567, [2020] 1 WLR 1157, at 87.
[114] R *(Good Law Project) v Electoral Commission* [2019] EWCA Civ 1567, [2020] 1 WLR 1157, at 86.
[115] R *(Good Law Project) v Electoral Commission* [2019] EWCA Civ 1567 at 89. The result of this holding was that one campaign organisation (X) can donate money to another campaign organisation of shared point of view (Y) *(e.g. because X has reached its spending limits and Y has not), for Y to spend to the same ends as X, so long as it is not *"on behalf of"* X.
[116] S 71F PPERA 2000.

1.38 Loans are valued according to the amount lent, credit facilities according to the amount borrowed, and giving security according to the contingent liability under that security.[117]

Permissible donors

1.39 In *R (Electoral Commission) v Westminster Magistrates Court*,[118] Lord Phillips PSC held: *"The primary object [of Chapter II of Part IV of PPERA] is to prevent donations to political parties from foreign sources"*[119] and *"The secondary object of Chapter II of Part IV of the Act is to provide a scheme for achieving the primary object that is easy to apply, easy to police and that contains adequate sanctions for non-compliance"*.[120]

1.40 An RP may not accept a donation if (i) the donor is not a permissible donor; or (ii) the RP is cannot ascertain the identity of the donor.[121]

1.41 The permissible donors are:[122]

(i) Individuals registered in an electoral register;

(ii) Companies registered under the Companies Act 2006 and incorporated within the UK;

(iii) Trade unions entered in the list kept under the Trade Union and Labour Relations (Consolidation) Act 1992 or the Industrial Relations (Northern Ireland) Order 1992;

(iv) A society incorporated under the Building Societies Act 1986;

(v) Limited liability partnerships carrying on business in the UK;

(vi) Registered friendly societies;

(vii) Unincorporated associations (a combination of people with an agreement between them, whether contractual or mere *"tacit understanding"*, as to what they are undertaking),[123] carrying on activities mainly in the UK, and whose main office is also in the UK; and

---

[117] S 71G PPERA 2000.
[118] R *(Electoral Commission) v Westminster Magistrates Court* [2010] UKSC 40.
[119] R *(Electoral Commission) v Westminster Magistrates Court* [2010] UKSC 40, at 25.
[120] R *(Electoral Commission) v Westminster Magistrates Court* [2010] UKSC 40, at 29.
[121] S 54(1) PPERA 2000.
[122] S 54(2) PPERA 2000.
[123] *Grimes v Electoral Commission* (unreported, 19.7.19, County Court at Central London), at 103, per HHJ Dight.

(viii) If received by a Northern Irish RP: an Irish citizen[124] or a body of a type in the foregoing list but registered in the Irish equivalent.[125]

1.42 The following donations are treated as being from permissible donors, even if not from a person on the above list:

(i) Payment out of public funds[126] (e.g. policy development grants, which the Commission distributes equally amongst the eligible parties, or Short or Cranborne Money, which the House of Commons gives to opposition parties);[127]

(ii) Donations to meet qualifying costs of an overseas visit by a RP member or officer (travel to the country and travel, accommodation and subsistence therein), where not exceeding a reasonable amount in respect of those costs.[128]

1.43 RPs must not be party to a regulated transaction, nor derive benefit from a connected transaction, in which one of the parties is not an 'authorised participant'.[129] This has the same meaning as 'permissible donor'.[130] 'Connected transaction' means an arrangement whereby the person with whom the RP agrees a loan or credit facility also enters an arrangement with a third party to give security for the debt owed by the RP.[131]

Donations via agent: information requirements

1.44 Where a donation greater than £500 is provided on behalf of a donor, they must ensure they give the RP all the information the RP will need to be able to record the donation in a quarterly donation report.[132] Failure to do so is an offence, for which the penalty is unlimited fine or six months' imprisonment (on summary conviction) or one year's imprisonment (on indictment).[133]

1.45 The required information is as follows:

(i) Donation by an individual: full name and address, either as shown in an electoral register or home address if different, or if from someone with

---

[124]S 71B(1)(a) PPERA 2000 and art 3 Political Parties, Elections and Referendums Act 2000 (Northern Ireland Political Parties) Order 2007.
[125]S 71B(1)(b) PPERA 2000 and art 4 Political Parties, Elections and Referendums Act 2000 (Northern Ireland Political Parties) Order 2007.
[126]S 55(2) PPERA 2000.
[127]https://www.electoralcommission.org.uk/who-we-are-and-what-we-do/financial-reporting/donations-and-loans/public-funding-political-parties
[128]S 55(3) PPERA 2000.
[129]S 71H PPERA 2000.
[130]S 71H(3) PPERA 2000.
[131]S 71F(4)(b) and (9) PPERA 2001.
[132]S 54(5) and paras 2 and 2A sch 6 PPERA 2000.
[133]S 54(7) PPERA 2000.

an anonymous entry in an electoral register, evidence of the same (to enable the RP to state in a quarterly donation report that it has seen such evidence);

(ii) Company donation: registered name, address of registered office, and number with which it is registered;

(iii) RP donation: registered name and address of registered headquarters;

(iv) Listed trade union: name of the union and address of its head or main office;

(v) Building society: name of the society and address of its principal office;

(vi) Partnership: registered name and address of its registered office;

(vii) Friendly society: name of the society and address of its registered office;

(viii) Unincorporated association: name of the association and address of its main office in the UK;

(ix) Payment of qualifying costs of overseas visit by RP member or official: full name and address of the donor;

(x) Irish donation to Northern Irish recipient: as above, save that it must inform the RP so it can state that the donation is an Irish donation, and be accompanied by a copy of the donor's certified Irish passport, certificate of nationality, or certificate of naturalisation.

Unclear donor: identify checks

1.46 To make sure they do not accept donations from impermissible sources, when an RP receives a donation but it is not immediately clear whether it should accept it, the RP must immediately, without delay, take all reasonable steps to verify or ascertain: (i) the donor's identity; (ii) whether they are a permissible donor; and (iii) the above-listed details required to be given in respect of the donor of a recordable donation.[134]

Impermissible donation: return or forfeit

1.47 If an RP receives an impermissible donation, within 30 days of receipt, it must either: (i) return the donation; (ii) if unable to ascertain the donor's identity, return it to the person who transmitted it, or, if none, then return it to the financial institution who facilitated transmission; or (iii) if neither are possible, send it to the Commission for payment into the Consolidated Fund.[135] Failure

---

[134]S 56 PPERA 2000.

[135]Ss 56(2) and 57(1) PPERA 2000.

to do so is an offence by the RP and its treasurer,[136] punishable on summary conviction by an unlimited fine or six months' imprisonment, or on indictment by a fine or one year's imprisonment.[137]

1.48 If the RP does not take these steps and cannot produce record of the return (or having sent it to the Commission), then: (i) they will be deemed to have accepted the donation;[138] and (ii) a Magistrates' Court may, on an application made by the Commission, if persuaded on the balance of probabilities of the impermissibility and the acceptance, order the forfeiture by the party of an amount equal to the value of the donation[139] or a lesser sum.[140]

1.49 In *R (Electoral Commission) v Westminster Magistrates Court*,[141] the Supreme Court loosened the apparently strict application of the forfeiture provisions. The RP had received 69 donations from an individual entitled to register but not on the electoral register at the time of those donations. The RP was not aware the donor was impermissible. The Magistrates' Court (upheld, ultimately by the Supreme Court) made a forfeiture order only in the value of the donations received by the RP after it became aware the donor was not on the register.[142] Lord Phillips PSC held, allowing the RP's appeal, that:

(i) *"Almost automatic forfeiture of the totality of an impermissible donation is [not] necessary to provide a realistic sanction against non-compliance with the requirements of the Act"*;[143]

(ii) *"Of course the party and the donor should make sure that the donor complies with the statutory requirement of being placed on an electoral register. But if, by inadvertence, or even negligence, they fail to do so, it does not follow that it cannot be disproportionate for the donation to be forfeited. Proportionality will depend on the degree of culpability, the size of the donation and its importance to the party"*;[144]

(iii) *"Parliaments scheme usefully transfers the burden of showing that the donation is not a foreign donation onto the donor and the party. If this burden can be discharged, the primary object of the legislation has not been*

---

[136] S 56(3) and (4) PPERA 2000.
[137] Sch 20 PPERA.
[138] S 56(5)
[139] S 58 PPERA 2000.
[140] R *(Electoral Commission) v Westminster Magistrates Court* [2010] UKSC 40, at 51.
[141] R *(Electoral Commission) v Westminster Magistrates Court* [2010] UKSC 40.
[142] R *(Electoral Commission) v Westminster Magistrates Court* [2010] UKSC 40, at 53.
[143] R *(Electoral Commission) v Westminster Magistrates Court* [2010] UKSC 40, 38.
[144] R *(Electoral Commission) v Westminster Magistrates Court* [2010] UKSC 40, 39.

defeated, and this fact is highly relevant to the issue of whether the power to forfeit should be exercised";[145]

(iv) *"The fact that Parliament has not made ignorance of the impermissibility of the donation a defence is no reason why it should not be a relevant extenuating circumstance when considering whether or not to forfeit the donation"*;[146]

(v) Where the donor is a foreign donor, *"forfeiture is virtually automatic, forfeiture proceedings are unlikely to be protracted"*, but where the donor is not a foreign donor *"the fact that forfeiture is discretionary is likely to involve a significant investigation of the facts"*;[147]

(vi) *"Where it is shown that a political party has accepted a donation from an impermissible source, there should be an initial presumption in favour of forfeiting the donation. ... The onus should be on the party concerned to show why a donation that has been received from an impermissible source should not be forfeited"*;[148]

(vii) *"A first step in discharging this onus will normally be to show that the mischief against which the relevant part of the Act is directed did not occur - that the donation in question was not, in fact, a foreign donation. Where an individual is concerned this should require demonstration that the individual was entitled to be entered on an electoral register. If this cannot be demonstrated, forfeiture should normally follow"*,[149] but *"If it is shown that the donor was in a position to qualify as a permissible donor by registering on an electoral register, the initial presumption in favour of forfeiture will have been rebutted"*.[150]

1.50 In forfeiture appeal proceedings, even if it is unincorporated and therefore has no legal personality independent of its members, the RP must be named in its own right, not that of any member, and the forfeiture must paid out of the central funds of the RP.[151] Appeal lies to the Crown Court against a forfeiture order. The time limit is 30 days. The appeal is by way of a rehearing,[152] in which the court looks at the facts found by the Commission anew, rather than as merely reviewer of the Commission's determination of factual matters.

---

[145] R *(Electoral Commission) v Westminster Magistrates Court* [2010] UKSC 40, 40.
[146] R *(Electoral Commission) v Westminster Magistrates Court* [2010] UKSC 40, 41.
[147] R *(Electoral Commission) v Westminster Magistrates Court* [2010] UKSC 40, 41.
[148] R *(Electoral Commission) v Westminster Magistrates Court* [2010] UKSC 40, 47.
[149] R *(Electoral Commission) v Westminster Magistrates Court* [2010] UKSC 40, 48.
[150] R *(Electoral Commission) v Westminster Magistrates Court* [2010] UKSC 40, 49.
[151] S 60(5)(c) PPERA 2000.
[152] S 59(3) PPERA 2000.

Impermissible transaction: void and repay

1.51 If an RP enters into a regulated transaction with an unauthorised participant or stands to benefit from a connected transaction, then:

(i) The transaction is void and the money paid thereunder must be repaid plus any interest, failing which the Commission may apply to court for an order that the amount owed by the RP be repaid or the security discharged;[153]

(ii) The RP commits an offence (punishable on summary conviction by unlimited fine)[154] if: (a) one of its officers knew or ought to have known that they were unauthorised; or (b) none did, but upon discovering that they were unauthorised fails to repay any money received as soon as practicable;[155] and

(iii) Its treasurer commits an offence if they: (a) knew or ought to have known that they the other participant was unauthorised (punishable by unlimited fine);[156] or (b) did not know and could not reasonably be expected to know, but, upon discovering that they were unauthorised, still failed to repay any money received as soon as practicable (punishable by unlimited fine or one year's imprisonment (on summary conviction) or unlimited fine (on indictment).[157] The treasurer has a defence if they have taken all reasonable steps to prevent the RP entering the transaction or deriving benefit from the connected transaction.[158]

1.52 The transaction is also void if an authorised participant transfers their interest in it to an unauthorised participant.[159]

Evasion offences

1.53 It is an offence, punishable summarily by unlimited fine or six months' imprisonment, or on indictment by a fine or one year's imprisonment,[160] to:

(i) Knowingly enter into or further an arrangement that facilitates (or is likely to facilitate) impermissible donations or transactions, e.g. by concealing or disguising them;[161] or

---

[153]Ss 71I and JPPERA 2000.
[154]Sch 20 PPERA.
[155]S 71L(1), (3), (5) and (7) PPERA 2000.
[156]S 71L(2) and sch 20 PPERA 2000.
[157]S 71L(4) and (6) and sch 20 PPERA 2000.
[158]S 71L(10) and (11) PPERA 2000.
[159]S 71K PPERA 2000.
[160]Sch 20 PPERA.
[161]S 61(1) and 71L(9) PPPERA 2000.

(ii) Knowingly and with intent to deceive give a treasurer any materially false information, or withhold from them any material information, relating to (a) the amount of any donation made to the RP, or (b) the person or body making such a donation.[162]

Quarterly reports

1.54 Once per year, within 30 days of the end of the reporting period to which it relates,[163] the RP's treasurer must prepare and deliver to the Commission a quarterly donations report and a quarterly report of regulated transactions, featuring four reporting periods: January-March, April-June, July-September, and October-December. Failure to deliver a donation report within the time limit is an offence,[164] for which the penalty is an unlimited fine.[165]

1.55 A quarterly donation report must record the following donations:

(i) Each donation accepted from a permissible donor that year, the value of which, either alone or cumulatively with previous donations, exceeded either: (a) £7,500, if the first time donation(s) has reached this amount; or (b) £1,500, if the £7,500 threshold had been crossed previously;[166] and

(ii) Each donation returned to an impermissible donor or, where unidentifiable, returned to the financial institution or Commission.[167]

1.56 A quarterly transactions report must record the following:

(i) Each transaction the RP entered into with an authorised participant, the value of which, either alone or cumulatively with previous transactions, exceeded either: (a) £7,500, if the first time it has exceeded this amount; or (b) £1,500, if the £7,500 threshold had been crossed previously;[168]

(ii) Each transaction entered into with an unauthorised participant where the money generated has then repaid by the RP;[169] and

(iii) Each transaction already recorded that changes in any of the following ways: (a) new authorised participants joins the transaction; (b) change

162 S 61(2) RPA 1983.
163 Ss 65(1) and 71S(1) PPERA 2000.
164 Ss 61(3) and 71S(4) PPERA 2000.
165 Sch 20 PPERA 2000.
166 Ss 62(6) and (6A) PPERA 2000.
167 S 62(9) PPERA 2000.
168 S 71M(6) and (7) PPERA 2000.
169 S 71M(9) PPERA 2000.

in detailed reported previously; (c) the transaction comes to an end,[170] stating how (e.g. loan repaid or debt released).[171]

1.57 If no such recordable donations or transactions have been received, the respective report must state this.[172] After four such nil returns in a row, the RP is exempt from preparing quarterly reports until it receives another recordable donation or transaction.[173]

1.58 In each report, the treasurer must make a declaration that, to the best of their knowledge and belief:

(i) All the donations or transactions recorded as having been accepted by or entered into are from permissible donors or authorised participants; and

(ii) During the reporting period, no other recordable donations or transactions have been accepted or entered into, nor transaction changes.[174]

1.59 The Commission has produced template quarterly donation reports[175] and quarterly transactions reports,[176] which specify the prescribed information and the declaration,[177] and a template statement of nil return.[178]

1.60 Where the RP has accounting units, this quarterly report obligation applies both to the central organisation of the RP and to each of its accounting units.[179] However, in the case of accounting units, the threshold at which a transaction or aggregate transactions must first be reported is £1,500 rather than £7,500.[180]

Weekly donation reports (during election periods)

1.61 Within seven days of the date on which Parliament is dissolved (which marks the start of the general election period)[181] and every seven days thereafter,[182] an RP's treasurer must prepare a report recording every donation or transaction the

---

170 S 71N(1) PPERA 2000.
171 S 71N(2) PPERA 2000.
172 S 62(10) and 71M(10) PPERA 2000.
173 Ss 62A and 71P(1) PPERA 2000.
174 Ss 66 and 71T(2) PPERA 2000.
175 Form RP10 - Quarterly donation return by a registered political party.
176 Form RP10b - Quarterly return of regulated transactions.
177 Schs 6 and 6A PPERA 2000.
178 Form RP10QN Quarterly report of donations to a political party: statement of nil return.
179 S 62(11) PPERA 2000.
180 S 62(11) and 71M(11) PPERA 2000.
181 S 63(6) PPERA. See Chapter 3.
182 Ss 65(2) and 71Q(1) PPERA 2000.

value of which is greater than £7,500 and received by the RP within the preceding seven days, including a nil receipt return if applicable.[183]

1.62 There is a detailed prescription as to what information the weekly report should include,[184] made easier by the Commission's PEF Online database system,[185] via which reports may be made, and by a nil returns form.[186]

1.63 The report must contain the same treasurer's declaration as the quarterly reports.[187]

Reporting offences and enforcement

1.64 The treasurer commits an offence, punishable on summary conviction by an unlimited fine or six months' imprisonment or, on indictment, by a fine or one year's imprisonment,[188] if:

(i) They fail to deliver the quarterly or weekly reports within the relevant time period, and have no reasonable excuse;[189]

(ii) The quarterly or weekly donation report does not contain the requisite information;[190]

(iii) They knowingly or recklessly makes a false declaration that, to the best of their knowledge and belief, all the donations recorded as accepted are from permissible donors, and during the reporting period no other recordable donations have been accepted, nor any impermissible donations.[191]

1.65 An over-inclusive return has been held not to be a false return, so long as the return contains a statement of all payments made.[192]

1.66 Whether or not prosecution is brought by the CPS in respect to these offence, the Commission may apply to the Magistrates' Court for an order that the RP repay the donation or loan (or other order restoring the pre-transaction position). The Court may so order if satisfied on the balance of probabilities[193]

---

[183]Ss 63 and 71Q(3) PPERA 2000.
[184]Schs 6 and 6A PPERA 2000.
[185]https://pefonline.electoralcommission.org.uk/Default.aspx.
[186]https://www.electoralcommission.org.uk/sites/default/files/2019-10/Weekly%20nil%20return%20form%20PE%20political%20parties%20GB%202019.pdf.
[187]Ss 66 and 71T PPERA 2000.
[188]Sch 20 PPERA 2000.
[189]Ss 65(3) and 71S(4) PPERA 2000.
[190]S 65(3) and 71S(5)PPERA 2000.
[191]S 66 PPERA 2000.
[192] *Grimes v Electoral Commission* (unreported, 19.7.19, County Court at Central London), at 93, per HHJ Dight.
[193]S 65(7)(a) PPERA 2000.

that a failure to comply with reporting requirements was attributable to an intention to conceal the existence or true amount of the donation.[194]

Register of donations and transactions

1.67 The Commission must maintain a register of all donations and transactions reported to them pursuant to the above obligations,[195] stating the amount or value, date, whether it is in the form of sponsorship, all prescribed information that the report provided, but not, if a donation from or transaction entered into with an individual, their home address.[196]

RP campaign expenses

Scope

1.68 'Campaign expenditure' comprises expenditure on:

(i) Party political broadcasts;[197]

(ii) Advertising of any nature;[198]

(iii) Unsolicited material addressed to electors;[199]

(iv) Any manifesto;[200]

(v) Market research or canvassing;[201]

(vi) The provision of services during dealings with the media, e.g. press conferences;[202]

(vii) Transporting people with a view to gaining publicity[203] (the Commission's draft statutory code of practice states this includes: (a) the cost of transporting campaigners around, to and from the electoral area or a rally; (b) the cost of tickets, fuel and parking; (c) costs paid by a third party but reimbursed by the RP; and (d) a portion of office accommodation, business rates, electricity, phone rental and internet

[194]S 65(6) and 71S(7)PPERA 2000.
[195]S 69(1) PPERA 2000; https://www.electoralcommission.org.uk/who-we-are-and-what-we-do/financial-reporting/donations-and-loans/view-donations-and-loans.
[196]Ss 69(2) and 71V(3) PPERA 2000.
[197]Para 1(1) sch 8 PPERA 2000.
[198]Para 1(2) sch 8 PPERA 2000.
[199]Para 1(3) sch 8 PPERA 2000.
[200]Para 1(4) sch 8 PPERA 2000.
[201]Para 1(5) sch 8 PPERA 2000.
[202]Para 1(6) sch 8 PPERA 2000.
[203]Para 1(7) sch 8 PPERA 2000.

access where used to plan or book transport, or to design a promotion for the side of a bus);[204]

(viii) Rallies and public meetings (but not party conferences).[205]

1.69 Notional campaign spending, namely an amount reasonably attributable to the use made of property, services or facilities falling within the above categories and transferred to the RP for free or at a discount.[206]

1.70 Expenditure on the following is excluded from the definition of campaign spending:

(i) RP newsletters or similar publications;[207]

(ii) Unsolicited material addressed to party members;[208]

(iii) Property, services or facilities paid for out of public funds;[209]

(iv) Payments to RP staff;[210] or

(v) Travelling and accommodation expenses paid from an individual's own resources.[211]

1.71 The Commission has submitted a draft code to the Minister for the Cabinet Office that will, if approved by the minister and not rejected by Parliament when laid before it, give further guidance on the kind of expenses that do or do not fall within the scope of 'campaign spending'.[212]

1.72 Campaign spending is subject to the below regulation if incurred during the 'relevant period'. For a Parliamentary election ("**PE**"), the relevant period is the year before polling day (or less if two elections are held less than a year apart).[213] For Welsh Assembly elections ("**WAE**"), the relevant period is the four months before polling day for an ordinary general election, and, for an extraordinary general election, from the date proposed by the Secretary of State until polling day.[214] Where a PE is 'pending' (i.e. the 25 working days between dissolution

---

[204]Electoral Commission, 'Code of Practice on qualifying expenses for political parties' (draft), paras 7.1-7.5.
[205]Para 1(8) sch 8 PPERA 2000.
[206]S 73 PPERA 2000.
[207]Para 2(1)(a) sch 8 PPERA 2000.
[208]Para 2(1)(b) sch 8 PPERA 2000.
[209]Para 2(1)(c) sch 8 PPERA 2000.
[210]Para 2(1)(d) sch 8 PPERA 2000.
[211]Para 2(1)(e) sch 8 PPERA 2000.
[212]Para 3 sch 8 PPERA 2000; Draft Code of Practice on qualifying expenses for political parties 2019.
[213]Para 3(7) sch 9 PPERA 2000.
[214]Paras 6(4) and (5) sch 9 PPERA 2000.

of Parliament and polling day)[215] during any part of another the relevant period of another election, the relevant period for that other election changes to either of the following:

(i) If the PE takes place at the same time as the other election or later: the relevant period is the PE relevant period;[216] or

(ii) If the PE takes place before the other election: the relevant period runs from the start of the PE relevant period until the date of the other election.[217]

Authorisation

1.73 An RP must not incur campaign spending, nor make any payment towards it, unless it is authorised by: (i) its treasurer, (ii) one of the up to twelve deputy treasurers whom the treasurer may appoint by notification to the Commission, or (iii) a person authorised in writing by the treasurer or a deputy treasurer.[218]

1.74 Unauthorised campaign spending by or on behalf of an RP is an offence,[219] subject to unlimited fine,[220] and shall not count towards the limits on the RP's campaign spending.[221]

Notification and claims

1.75 If greater than £200, campaign spending must be notified to the treasurer with supporting invoice or receipt.[222] Failure to do so is an offence,[223] punishable by unlimited fine.[224]

1.76 To be payable, claims must be sent to the treasurer, deputy, or authorised person within 30 days of polling day, which represents the end of the relevant campaign period.[225] Such claims must then be paid within 60 days of polling day.[226] It is an offence (punishable by unlimited fine)[227] to pay, without reasonable excuse or court order,[228] a claim sent outside the 30 days, or paying any claim outside

[215] S 3(1) Fixed-term Parliaments Act 2011; para 1(3) sch 9 PPERA 2000.
[216] Para 9(4)(a) sch 9 PPERA 2000.
[217] Para 9(4)(b) sch 9 PPERA 2000.
[218] Ss 75(1) and 76 PPERA 2000.
[219] S 75(2) PPERA 2000.
[220] Sch 20 PPERA 2000.
[221] S 75(3) PPERA 2000.
[222] S 76(2) and (3) PPERA 2000.
[223] S 76(4) PPERA 2000.
[224] Sch 20 PPERA 2000.
[225] S 77(1) PPERA 2000.
[226] S 77(2) PPERA 2000.
[227] Sch 20 PPERA 2000.
[228] S 77(4) PPERA 2000.

the 60 days.[229] RP non-payment and refusal to pay a claim made within the 30 days entitles the claimant to bring an action for this disputed claim.[230]

Financial limits

1.77 PE: in each part of the UK (England, Wales, Scotland, Northern Ireland), an RP must not incur campaign spending in excess of £30,000 multiplied by the number of constituencies it is contesting in that part of the UK.[231] If that figure is less than £810,000 in England, £120,000 in Scotland, or £60,000 in Wales, then these figures become the financial limit.[232] There is no substitute limit for spending in Northern Ireland.[233]

1.78 WAE: the limit is £10,000 for each constituency contested by the RP, plus £40,000 for each region it contests.[234]

1.79 Where a PE relevant period is pending during the relevant period of another election, the spending limit is the aggregate of usual limit at a PE and the usual limit at that other election.[235]

1.80 An RP commits an offence (punishable by unlimited fine)[236] if its campaign spending exceeds these limits, as does its treasurer if they authorised that spending and knew or ought reasonably to have known that it would exceed the relevant limit.[237] When the Commission's draft statutory code of practice is finalised, a defence will lie if the person charged (i) complied with that code when determining the items and amounts to include in the return; and (ii) applying the code, the limit would not have been exceeded.[238]

1.81 When calculating the RP's spending:

(i) If the RP receives targeted spending by a registered third party campaigner ("**RTP**"),[239] and the RP authorises the RTP to exceed the RTP's spending limit,[240] that amount in excess counts towards the RP's spending limit;[241]

---

229 S 77(3) PPERA 2000.
230 S 78 PPERA 2000.
231 Para 3(2) sch 9 PPERA 2000.
232 Para 3(2) sch 9 PPERA 2000.
233 Para 3(3) sch 9 PPERA 2000.
234 Para 6 sch 9 PPERA 2000.
235 Para 9 sch 9 PPERA 2000.
236 Sch 20 PPERA 2000.
237 S 79(2) PPERA 2000.
238 S 79(3) PPERA 2000.
239 As to RTPs, see Section E below.
240 See below.
241 S 79(3A) PPERA 2000.

(ii) If, before the relevant period, the RP incurs expenses on property, services or facilities, but uses them during the relevant period, a proportion of that spending *"reasonably attributable"* to the use is to be counted towards the RP's spending limit.[242]

Return

1.82 Within three months of the end of the relevant period,[243] the treasurer must send the Commission a return containing statements of all payments made, all disputed claims, and all unpaid claims,[244] accompanied by: all invoices and receipts, and the following declarations by its treasurer:

(i) A declaration as to the amount attributed to any notional spending exceeding £200;[245]

(ii) Where the RP authorises an RTP to exceed its targeted spending limit, the amount of any controlled spending targeted at the RP by the RTP and the amount of such spending that exceeds the RTP's targeted spending limit;[246]

(iii) A declaration that the treasurer has examined the return and, to the best of their knowledge and belief, (a) it is complete and correct; (b) all expenses shown have been paid by them, a deputy treasurer, or person they have authorised.[247] Knowingly or recklessly making this declaration falsely is an offence.[248]

1.83 If the total is more than £250,000, the deadline is six months instead of three, and it must be accompanied by an auditor's report on the return.[249]

1.84 The Commission must make a copy of the return and its accompanying documents available for inspection.[250]

1.85 If, out of an abundance of caution, the individual includes the requisite information but also extraneous matters, it has been held that this will not amount to a false statement of expenses.[251]

---

[242] S 79(4) and (5) PPERA 2000.
[243] S 82(2) PPERA 2000.
[244] S 80(3) PPERA 2000.
[245] S 80(4)(b) PPERA 2000.
[246] S 80(4)(c). As to RTP spending, see below.
[247] S 83 PPERA 2000.
[248] S 83(3) PPERA 2000.
[249] S 81 PPERA 2000.
[250] S 84 PPERA 2000.
[251] *Grimes v Electoral Commission* (unreported, 19.7.19, County Court at Central London), at 93, per HHJ Dight.

D. RP MEMBERS, MEMBERS ASSOCIATIONS, AND CERTAIN ELECTED OFFICE-HOLDERS ("REGULATED DONEES/PARTICIPANTS")

1.86 As well as RPs, the Commission regulates RP members, members association, or the holder of a relevant elective office (who may also be an RP member), collectively termed '**regulated donees**' in relation donations and 'regulated participants' in relation to regulated transactions.

Members associations

1.87 A 'members association' is an organisation whose membership consists wholly or mainly of members of an RP, but not an RP itself, its central organisation, nor one of its accounting units (if so structured).[252] Guidance as to the Commission's view on the degree of connectedness to an RP is the example in its guidance for regulated donees of *"An organisation comprised of members of the Big Party (which is registered with the Electoral Commission) has a specific policy interest in welfare issues, and calls itself the Big Party Welfare Society"*.[253] The Commission has found the organisation Momentum to be a members association.[254] The Society of Conservative Lawyers or the Society of Labour Lawyers would come within the definition, or the Fabian Society. A magazine like the New Statesman would fall outside the definition,[255] as would any constituency parties, RP student wings, or affiliated councillor organisations whose registration as accounting units has been approved by the RP's central organisation.[256]

1.88 Reporting requirements imposed on member associations are to be performed by the association's '**responsible person**', which is either its treasurer or, if it does not have one, someone it appoints as its responsible person by notifying the Commission. If the members association receives a donation that it must report or return, unless it has already appointed one, it must appoint one within 30 days of accepting the donation (if it may) or receiving (if it may not).[257] Failure to do so in time, without reasonable excuse, is an offence,[258] triable

---

[252]Para 1(6) sch 7 PPERA 2000.

[253]Electoral Commission, 'Donations and loans: guidance for regulated donees in Great Britain', September 2006 (Revised version January 2010), para 2.6.

[254]Electoral Commission, Investigation: Momentum, 6.3.19

[255]House of Commons, Official Report from Standing Committee G, February 1, 2000, cols 208 onwards.

[256]Para 1(6)(b) sch 7 PPERA 2000.

[257]Para 1A sch 7 PPERA 2000.

[258]Para 1B sch 7 PPERA 2000.

summarily and punishable by an unlimited fine.[259] The notice lasts for twelve months and can be renewed.[260]

Office-holders

1.89 'Holder of relevant office' means: MP, MSP, member of the National Assembly for Wales, member of the Northern Ireland Assembly, police and crime commissioner, member of any local authority (except parish or community council), member of the Greater London Assembly, or an elected mayor.[261]

1.90 An office-holder may appoint a **compliance officer**,[262] by notice to the Commission.[263] If so, the compliance officer may discharge the office-holder's donation reporting duties and it is an offence to give the compliance officer materially false information as to the amount or source of a donation.[264] The notice lapses after twelve months but can be renewed.[265]

1.91 MPs are subject to the parallel reporting regime of the House of Commons and must report permissible donations they accept to the Register of Members Interests instead of the Commission.[266] In relation to impermissible donations or transactions, however, they are subject to the same requirement to report to the Commission as other regulated donees.[267]

Donations to regulated donees

Scope

1.92 The regulation of donations to regulated donees applies to what are termed '**controlled donations**'. A controlled donation has the following elements:

(i) It is a donation (whether gifts of money or other property, sponsorship, money spent in directly paying any expenses incurred, discount provision of any property, services or facilities, or (if to a members association) any affiliation or membership fee);

(ii) It is received by a regulated donee;

---

[259] Sch 20 PPERA 2000.
[260] Para 1A(4) and (5) sch 7 PPERA 2000.
[261] Para 1(8) sch 7A PPERA 2000.
[262] Para 17 sch 7 and para 18 sch 7A PPERA 2000.
[263] Para 18 sch 7 and para 18 sch 7A PPERA 2000. Form CO1 and explanatory notes – Notice of appointment of a compliance officer by a holder of relevant elective office.
[264] Para 17 sch 7 and para 18 sch 7A PPERA 2000.
[265] Para 18 sch 7 PPERA 2000.
[266] Para 15A sch 7 and para 16 sch 7A PPERA 2000; House of Commons, 'The Code of Conduct together with The Guide to the Rules relating to the Conduct of Members', 18.3.15.
[267] Para 15A sch 7 and para 16 sch 7A PPERA 2000.

(iii) It is accepted and retained, or merely offered (whether or not accepted and retained);[268]

(iv) It is accepted and retained, or offered, for the purpose of being used in connection with or benefitting any of the regulated donee's 'political activities' (defined in the next paragraph);[269]

(v) It does not fall into any of the following excluded categories: (a) donations of £500 or less; (b) donations falling to be included in a candidate's return as to election expenses; (c) facilities provided in pursuance of any right conferred on candidates or a party at an election by any enactment;[270] (d) council members services; (e) voluntary service (e.g. campaigners giving their time freely); (f) interest accruing to an RP whilst dealing with an impermissible donation; (g) public funding of personal security of the regulated donee, who is an individual; (h) local authority employee remuneration allowed in respect of time off permitted by the employer for qualifying business; (i) salary or allowances paid to the holder of a relevant elective office in their capacity as such.[271]

1.93 'Political activities' is undefined (and is therefore broad in compass) for office-holders,[272] but, for RP members and members associations, is defined as:

(i) Promoting or procuring the election of any person (including the person doing the promoting or procuring) to any position in, or to any committee of, the RP;

(ii) Promoting or procuring the selection of any person (including the person doing the promoting or procuring) as the party's candidate for election to a relevant elective office; or

---

[268]Para 1(3) sch 7 PPERA 2000.

[269]Para 1(4) sch 7 PPERA 2000. Cf Electoral Commission, 'Donations and loans: guidance for regulated donees in Great Britain', September 2006 (Revised version January 2010), paras 2.11-17.

[270]See election campaign chapter.

[271]Para 4 sch 7 PPERA 2000.

[272]Applying therefore to all the office-holders' political activities. The Commission's example are (a) a donation given to a Welsh Assembly Member hosting a meeting to bring together stakeholders from their constituency; (b) an invitation from a political party in another country to councillors in the UK, to visit as its guests to learn about local government in that country: Electoral Commission, 'Donations and loans: guidance for regulated donees in Great Britain', Jan 2010, p 10.

(iii) Promoting or developing policies with a view to their adoption by the RP.[273]

Regulation

1.94 Regulated donees are subject to the same prohibition on accepting donations from impermissible or unidentifiable donors, or entering into controlled transactions with unauthorised participants, as RPs.[274]

1.95 The same definition of 'permissible donor' is adopted[275] and the sources of income that must be regarded as such.[276]

1.96 The same rules on acceptance and return of donations also apply, but with the duties in relation to dealing with impermissible donations held by the donee or, if to a members association, then by its responsible person, instead of a treasurer.[277]

1.97 The evasion offence also applies,[278] carrying a maximum penalty of unlimited fine or six months' imprisonment (on summary conviction), or, on indictment, a fine or one year's imprisonment.[279]

1.98 Instead of quarterly election once per year with additional weekly reports during elections, regulated donees must deliver a 'donation report' within 30 days[280] of each:

(i) Acceptance of a permissible donation greater than £7,500 (where the donee is a members association) or £1,500 (where they are not), alone or cumulatively with previous donations;[281]

(ii) Receipt of an impermissible donation.[282]

1.99 The information to be recorded in the form is largely the same as for quarterly donation reports (see above),[283] though regulated donees who are holders of elective office must specify their office.[284]

---

[273]Para 1(4) sch 7 PPERA 2000. Cf Electoral Commission, 'Donations and loans: guidance for regulated donees in Great Britain', September 2006 (Revised version January 2010), paras 2.11-17.
[274]Para 6 sch 7 and paras 4 and 8 sch 7A PPERA 2000.
[275]Para 6 sch 7 PPERA 2000.
[276]Para 7 sch 7 PPERA 2000.
[277]Para 8 sch 7 PPERA 2000.
[278]Para 9 sch 7 PPERA 2000.
[279]Sch 20 PPERA 2000.
[280]Para 10(2) sch 7 PPERA 2000.
[281]Para 10(1A) sch 7 PPERA 2000.
[282]Para 11(1) sch 7 PPERA 2000.
[283]Paras 11(3) and (4) and 13 sch 7 PPERA 2000.
[284]Paras 10(4) and 11(2) sch 7 PPERA 2000.

1.100 As with RPs, failing to deliver such a donation report in time, or without the requisite information (without reasonable excuse) is an offence (if the regulated donee is a member association, both the association and the responsible person).[285] Whether or not proceedings are brought, if the Commission can satisfy a Magistrates' Court that the failure was due to intent to conceal the existence or true amount of the donation, the Court makes a forfeiture order.[286]

Transactions

Scope

1.101 In relation to transactions, RP members, members associations, and holders of relevant elective officer are termed '**regulated participants**'.[287]

1.102 The definition of 'transaction' is the same as in relation to RPs (loan of money or provision of credit facility greater than £500 and excluding candidate election expenses),[288] save that:

(i) They are called '**controlled transactions**' rather than 'regulated transactions';[289] and

(ii) To come within the definition, a '**use condition**' must also be satisfied, namely that that the regulated participant intends at the time of entry into the controlled transaction to use any money or benefit obtained in connection with 'relevant political activities', namely those conducted in that role.[290]

1.103 The valuation of controlled transactions is the same as with RPs (loans: total amount to be lent; credit facilities: maximum amount that can be borrowed; security: contingent liability thereunder).[291]

Regulation of transactions to regulated participants

1.104 The same transactions restrictions to which RPs are subject also apply to regulated participants:

(i) Regulated participants may not be parties to, nor derive benefit from, controlled transactions featuring a person who is not an authorised

---

285 Para 12(1) and (2) sch 7 PPERA 2000.
286 Para 12(4) sch 7 PPERA 2000.
287 Para 1(5) sch 7A PPERA 2000.
288 Para 2(1), (2) and (4 sch 7A PPERA 2000.
289 Para 2(1) sch 7A PPERA 2000.
290 Para 2(8) sch 7A PPERA 2000.
291 Para 3 sch 7A PPERA 2000.

participant.[292] 'Authorised 'participant has the same meaning as 'permissible donor';[293]

(ii) If this prohibition is breached: the transaction is void, any money received must be repaid with any interest accrued, failing which the Commission may apply to the County Court[294] for an order,[295] and the regulated participant commits an offence if they knew or ought to have known the other participant was unauthorised or, upon learning of this fact, failed to take all reasonable steps to repay any money received.[296] In relation to members associations, it is the responsible person who is liable for this offence, but has a defence if they can prove that they took all reasonable steps to prevent the members association entering into or benefitting from the transaction.[297] The offence is punishable by unlimited fine or one year's imprisonment.[298]

1.105 If the regulated participant is party to a transaction with an authorised participant and the latter transfers their interest to an unauthorised participant, the transfer is of no effect.[299]

1.106 It is an offence to knowingly enter into any arrangement likely to facilitate participation by a regulated participant into a transaction with an unauthorised participant, e.g. by concealment or disguise.[300] The offence is punishable by unlimited fine or one year's imprisonment.[301]

1.107 Similar reporting requirements apply to regulated participants as apply to RPs. In relation to transactions entered into with authorised participants:

(i) They must prepare a transaction report for each transaction that either: (a) exceeds £7,500 (members association) or £1,500 (RP member or office-holder); or (b) that takes the aggregate value of benefits accruing from donation or transactions from the same person in the same calendar year over those thresholds;[302]

(ii) The report must state the regulated participant's name and address, and office if an office-holder, the date of entry into the transaction or of any

[292]Para 4(1) sch 7A PPERA 2000.
[293]Para 4(3) sch 7A PPERA 2000.
[294]Para 17(2)(a) sch 7A PPERA 2000.
[295]Para 5 sch 7A PPERA 2000.
[296]Para 8 sch 7A PPERA 2000.
[297]Para 8(10) and (11) sch 7A PPERA 2000.
[298]Sch 20 PPERA 2000.
[299]Para 7 sch 7A PPERA 2000.
[300]Para 8(9) sch 7A PPERA 2000.
[301]Sch 20 PPERA 2000.
[302]Para 9(1) and (2) sch 7A PPERA 2000.

variation, plus the information that RP transaction reports must contain;[303]

(iii) The report must be delivered to[304] the Commission within 30 days of entry into the transaction or the £7,500 or £1,500 threshold being exceeded;

(iv) The report must contain a declaration that, to the best of the declarant's knowledge and belief, the transaction was entered into with an authorised participant;[305]

(v) Within 30 days of another participant (authorised or unauthorised) becoming party to an already reported transaction, any change in the details already reported, or the transaction coming to an end, the regulated participant must deliver a further report to the Commission, giving details as to the new participant and of the change.[306]

1.108 In relation to transaction entered into with unauthorised participants, the regulated participant must prepare a report, deliver it to the Commission within 30 days of the date on which they returned any money accrued from it, giving their name and address, that of the unauthorised participant, plus the nature, value and date of the transaction,[307] and containing a declaration that, to the best of the declarant's knowledge and belief, the transaction has been repaid. Office-holders must also state their office in the report.

1.109 In relation to transactions entered into with both authorised and unauthorised participants, the regulated participant (or their responsible person if a members association) commits an offence if:

(i) They fail without reasonable excuse to deliver the relevant transaction report on time;[308] or

(ii) They knowingly or recklessly make a false declaration.[309]

Register

1.110 The Commission maintains a public register of donations and transactions to regulated donees.[310]

---

303 Para 9(9) and (9B) sch 7A PPERA 2000.
304 Para 9(7) sch 7A PPERA 2000.
305 Para 13(2) sch 7A PPERA 2000.
306 Para 11 sch 7A PPERA 2000.
307 Para 10 sch 7A PPERA 2000.
308 Para 12 sch 7A PPERA 2000.
309 Para 13(4) sch 7A PPERA 2000.
310 Para 15 sch 7 and para 15 sch 7A PPERA 2000; https://www.electoralcommission.org.uk/who-we-are-and-what-we-do/financial-

E. THIRD PARTY NATIONAL ELECTION CAMPAIGNERS

1.111 Certain organisations that are not RPs become subject to the following regulation of spending during the election period.[311]

Scope

Who does it apply to?

1.112 The regulation applies to 'third parties' and regulated third parties ("**RTPs**"). Third parties are person or bodies of persons that are not an RP.[312] RTPs are third parties who: (a) have sent the requisite notification[313] to the Commission; (b) are on the Commission's register of such notifications;[314] (c) whose notice is still extant; and (d) fall into one of the categories of permissible donor.[315]

What does it apply to?

1.113 The regulation applies only to 'controlled expenditure', namely: (a) spending that can reasonably be regarded as intended (whether or not it has other purposes too) to promote the success at any relevant election for one or more specific RPs, RPs supporting particular policies, or candidates supporting particular policies or holding particular opinions;[316] or (b) expenses incurred in:

(i) The production or publication of election material;

(ii) Canvassing or market research;

---

reporting/donations-and-loans/view-donations-and-loans/donations-and-loans-regulated-individuals.

[311]Part VI PPERA 2000.

[312]S 85(8) and (9) PPERA 2000.

[313]'Form TP1 – Application to register as a non-party campaigner', available here: https://www.electoralcommission.org.uk/sites/default/files/2019-11/TP1%20Revised%20November%202019%203_0.pdf; or through online notification via the Commission's website.

[314]S 89 PPERA 2000; http://search.electoralcommission.org.uk/Search/Registrations?currentPage=1&rows=20&sort=RegulatedEntityName&order=asc&open=filter&et=tp&register=none&regStatus=registered&optCols=EntityStatusName

[315]S 88(2) PPERA 2000. (i) An individual resident in the UK or registered in an electoral register (who is not the responsible person in relation to another third party); (ii) an RP (e.g. a minor party); (iii) a company registered under the Companies Act 2006, incorporated in the UK, and carrying on business in the UK; (iv) a listed trade union;
(v) a building society; (vi) an LLP carrying on business in the UK; (vii) a friendly society or registered cooperative society; (viii) an unincorporated association of two or more persons not falling within any of the other categories and carrying on business or other activities wholly or mainly in the UK and whose main office is there; (ix) body incorporated by Royal Charter; or (x) a charitable incorporated organisation.

[316]S 85(2) PPERA 2000.

(iii) Media events organised by or on behalf of the third party, e.g. press conferences;

(iv) Transport to places with a view to obtaining publicity, including hire costs; or

(v) Public events such as rallies, other than annual conferences.[317]

1.114 Excluded from the definition are:

(i) Spending incurred by or on behalf of an RP;[318]

(ii) Expenses included in a candidate's expenses return under RPA 1983;[319] and

(iii) Expenses included in a recall petition return.[320]

When does it apply?

1.115 The regulation applies to controlled spending during the year (PE)[321] or four months (WAE)[322] prior to the relevant election ("**the regulated period**").[323]

1.116 If expenses are incurred before the regulated period on property, services or facilities then used after it starts, a proportion reasonably attributable to the use made after the start of the regulated period is treated as incurred during the regulated period.[324]

Regulation of third parties that are not RTPs

1.117 If, during a regulated period, a person or body of persons that has not registered with the Commission as an RTP incurs controlled spending in excess of the following limits, then they are guilty of an offence if they knew or ought reasonably have known that the spending would exceed these limits:

(i) Total spend in England: £20,000;[325]

---

[317]S 85(2) and part 1 sch 8A PPERA 2000.
[318]Unless the RTP exceeds a targeted expenditure limit but not the cap specified in its authorisation by the targeted RP. In that case, the authorised amount is treated as incurred by the RP): ss and 87(3) and 94F PPERA 2000.
[319]C.f. election campaign chapter.
[320]S 87(1) PPERA 2000.
[321]Ss 94(10)(a) and para 3(3) sch 10 PPERA 2000. Nb. The regulated period is less than a year if the election is held less a year after the previous election.
[322]Ss 94(10)(a) and para 6(4) sch 10 PPERA 2000.
[323]S 94(10)(a) PPERA 2000.
[324]S 94(8) and (9) PPERA 2000.
[325]S 94(3(a)(i), (4) and (5) PPERA 2000.

(ii) Total spend in Wales, Scotland or Northern Ireland: £10,000 in each;[326]

(iii) Total spend in each constituency: 0.05% of the £50,000 total of the maximum campaign spending limits in England, Scotland, Wales and Northern Ireland (i.e. £250).[327]

1.118 If a third party incurs spending in a particular territory of the UK or constituency and it is part of an arrangement with another third party intended to achieve a common purpose (of promoting the electoral success of a particular RP, or category of RP or candidate), then that spending is treated as also occurring in the other third party's part of the UK and constituency. [328]

Regulation of RTPs

Responsible person authorisation of spending

1.119 Third parties who have registered as RTPs per the above described process[329] must not incur controlled spending unless authorised by its responsible person or someone the responsible person has authorised in writing.[330] The responsible person is:

(i) Where the RTP is an individual: that individual;

(ii) Otherwise: the person stated in the notification to the Commission as being the person who will be responsible for compliance with the RTP's regulatory duties.[331]

1.120 All payments of controlled spending incurred or to be incurred by or on behalf of a RTP must be:

(i) Made by the responsible person or someone they have authorised in writing (and if the latter they must notify the former and send them the supporting invoice or receipt); and

(ii) Supported by an invoice or a receipt, if more than £200.[332]

1.121 It is an offence to contravene either of these prohibitions, subject to a reasonable excuse defence.[333]

---

[326] S 94(3(a)(i), (4) and (5) PPERA 2000.
[327] S 94(3(a)(ii), (4) and (5ZA) PPERA 2000.
[328] S 94(6) and (7) PPERA 2000.
[329] See above 'Who does it apply to?': para 1.114.
[330] S 90(1) and (2) PPERA 2000.
[331] Ss 85(7) and 88(3) PPERA 2000.
[332] S 90(1) and 91(2) PPERA 2000.
[333] S 90(2) and 91(4) PPERA 2000.

Timing of payments

1.122 Claims for payment of controlled spending incurred by or on behalf of a RTP during a regulated period prior to the poll):

(i) Must not be paid unless sent to the responsible person within 30 days of polling day (absent court permission)[334] or someone they have authorised to incur the spending;[335] and

(ii) Must be paid within 60 days of polling day.[336]

Spending limits

1.123 RTPs must not exceed the following limits on controlled spending during the regulated period.

(i) PE: Spending in England, Scotland, Wales and Northern Ireland: 2% of the maximum RP campaign spending in that part of the UK,[337] based on an RP that contests all the constituencies in that part (i.e. 533 in England, 59 in Scotland, 40 in Wales, and 18 in Northern Ireland),[338] plus £20,000 for spending in Scotland, Wales and Northern Ireland.[339] This equates to the following limits for each UK area:

a. England: £319,800;[340]

b. Scotland: £55,400;[341]

c. Wales: £44,000;[342]

d. Northern Ireland: £30,800;[343]

e. Spending in each constituency: 0.05% of the total maximum campaign spending limits in England, Scotland, Wales, and Northern Ireland,[344] equating to £9,750;[345]

(ii) WAE: £30,000;[346]

---

334 S 92(4) PPERA 2000.
335 S 92(1) PPERA 2000.
336 S 92(2) PPERA 2000.
337 Para 3 sch 10 PPERA 2000.
338 S 94(10)(e) PPERA 2000.
339 Para 3 sch 10 PPERA 2000.
340 £30,000 x 533, x 2% = £319,800.
341 £30,000 x 59, x 2%, + £20,000 = £55,400.
342 £30,000 x 40, x 2%, +£20,000 = £44,000.
343 £30,000 x 18, x 2%, +£20,000 = £30,800.
344 Para 3(2A) sch 10 PPERA 2000.
345 £30,000 x 650 constituencies, x 0.05% = £9,750.
346 Para 6(2) sch 10 PPERA 2000.

(iii) Where a PE is pending during the regulated period for a WAE: the aggregate amount of the spending limits for the two elections.[347]

1.124 If an RTP incurs spending in a particular part of the UK or constituency and that spending is part of an *"arrangement or plan"* with another third party (whether or not an RTP), by which they share a common purpose of promoting the electoral success of a particular RP, or a particular category of RPs or candidates, then that spending is treated as also occurring in that other third party's part of the UK and constituency.[348]

1.125 The effects of this double counting can be avoided if, during the regulated period, the RTP sends a notice[349] to the Commission stating that it is party to such an arrangement, undertaking to be lead campaigner in that arrangement, identifying the other parties to it and stating that they have undertaken to be the minor campaigner(s) in that arrangement.[350] Once registered by the Commission, any controlled spending subsequently incurred by the minor campaigner(s) will be disregarded in determining whether a spending limit is exceeded,[351] so long as the minor campaigner's total spending outside the arrangement and during the regulated period does not exceed the normal RTP spending limits for each part of the UK (£319,800 for England, £55,400 for Scotland, £44,000 for Wales, £30,800 for Northern Ireland).[352]

1.126 If an RTP exceeds these spending limits, they commit an offence, as does their responsible person if they authorised the spending and knew or ought reasonably to have known that it would exceed the relevant limit.[353]

Targeted spending limits

1.127 Controlled expenditure that can reasonably be regarded as intended to benefit a particular RP or its candidates, and no others, is termed 'targeted spending'.[354] Targeted spending is subject to the following limits during a regulated period:

(i) PE: the targeted spending limit is 0.2% of the maximum PE campaign spending limit in that part of the UK,[355] i.e.:

a. England: £31,980;[356]

---

[347]Para 9(3) sch 10 PPERA 2000.
[348]S 94(6) PPERA 2000.
[349]Form TP7 - Notification of a lead campaigner.
[350]S 94A(1) PPERA 2000.
[351]S 94B(3) PPERA 2000.
[352]S 94B(6) PPERA 2000.
[353]S 94(2)-(4) PPERA 2000.
[354]S 94D(1) PPERA 2000.
[355]S 94D(4) PPERA 2000.
[356]£30,000 x 533, x 0.2% = £31,980.

b. Scotland: £3,540;[357]

c. Wales: £2,400;[358]

d. Northern Ireland: £1,080.[359]

(ii) At any other elections, the targeted spending limit is a proportion of the PE targeted expenditure limit (paragraph immediately above), calculated by dividing the number of days in the regulated period by the number of days in a PE regulated period (365 or less if PEs held less than a year apart).[360]

1.128 A RP that receives targeted spending may authorise the RTP to exceed this limit.[361] To do so, the authorisation must be in writing, signed by the treasurer or deputy treasurer, and specify the part of the UK to which it relates, with a copy given to the Commission.[362] The authorisation may also specify a cap on the additional amount of spending authorised.[363] The RP treasurer must also make a declaration of the amount of targeted spending it receives.[364] If so authorised and the RTP proceeds to incur targeted controlled spending in excess of the targeted spending limit, the amount in excess counts as RP campaign spending not the RTP's, so long as the authorised amount is not also exceeded.[365]

1.129 If an RTP exceeds this spending limit, it is guilty of an offence, as is its responsible person if they knew or ought reasonably to have known that the spending would be in excess and cannot show that, applying any code published by the Commission, the spending would not have exceed the limit.[366]

Donations to RTPs

1.130 Subject to minor modifications, donations to RTPs for the purpose of its controlled spending are subject to the same controls as donations to RPs.

1.131 The scope of the definition of 'donation' is the same as in relation to donations to RPs save that it includes money lent other than on commercial terms. The categories are therefore: gifts of money or property, sponsorship, paying the RTP's expenses, money lent or property, services or facilities provided other

---

[357] £30,000 x 59, x 0.2%, +£20,000 = £3,540.
[358] £30,000 x 40, x 0.2% = £2,400.
[359] £30,000 x 18, x 0.2% = £1,080.
[360] S 94D(4) and para 3(3) sch 10 PPERA 2000.
[361] S 94G(1) PPERA 2000.
[362] 94G(2) and (4) PPERA 2000.
[363] S 94G(2)(d) PPERA 2000.
[364] S 94
[365] S 94F(2) PPERA 2000
[366] S 94(4) and (4A) PPERA 2000.

than on commercial terms, or membership fees).[367] The exclusions are the same: donations of £500 or less, volunteering, and interest accrued before an impermissible donation is returned.[368]

1.132 Donations are valued in the same way: (i) property is valued according to its market value; (ii) that which is provided at below market rate is valued according to the difference; and (iii) if conferring a protracted benefit over a period of time, then the value of the donation is the total benefit accruing over that period.[369]

1.133 Similar acceptance restrictions apply to RTPs as to RPs: donations that are not from permissible donors (defined the same way) or whose donor cannot be ascertained must be returned (or sent to the Commission if donor unidentifiable and donation was not transmitted by person or financial facility) within 30 days, failing which the Commission may apply for a forfeiture order.[370]

1.134 The same evasion offence applies: i.e. knowingly entering into or doing anything to further any arrangement likely to facilitate impermissible donations (e.g. through concealment or disguise).[371]

1.135 Between the date on which Parliament is dissolved and the date of the election,[372] for every week within that period, the RTP's responsible person must deliver to the Commission a weekly donation report, detailing every relevant donation greater than £7,500 in value received by the RTP that week.[373] Those details are: (i) all known details as to the name and address of the donor; (ii) the amount of the donation, or if not in money then its value; and (iii) the date received.[374] The report must be delivered to the Commission within seven days of each week period to which it relates[375]. These can be reported using PEF Online or Commission has produced a template form for these weekly returns.[376]

1.136 Within 30 days of the end of the regulated period (i.e. within 30 days of election day), RTPs must prepare and send the Commission a quarterly donation report of donations received between the first day of the regulated period and the day before Parliament is dissolved ("**the pre-dissolution period**"), and divided into

---

[367]Para 2 sch 11 PPERA 2000.
[368]Para 4 sch 11 PPEPR.
[369]Para 5 sch 11 PPERA 2000.
[370]Paras 6 and 7 sch 11 PPERA 2000.
[371]Para 8 sch 11 PPERA 2000.
[372]S 95B(1)-(3) PPERA 2000.
[373]S 95B(5) and (6) PPERA 2000.
[374]Para 7 sch 11A PPERA 2000.
[375]S 95B(7) PPERA 2000.
[376]Pre-poll weekly donation report TP6(ii).

three-month periods.[377] This quarterly report must contain (i) a statement of reportable donations accepted during the reporting period;[378] and (ii) a statement of reportable donations from impermissible or unidentifiable donors dealt with during reporting period.[379]

1.137 If, during the regulated period, the RTP incurs controlled spending in excess of £20,000 in England or £10,000 in other parts of the UK,[380] then, within six months[381] of that period, the RTP's responsible person must prepare and send the Commission a spending return,[382] accompanied by all relevant invoices or receipts.[383] The return must state:[384]

(i) The poll or polls that took place;

(ii) All payments made in respect of controlled spending incurred;

(iii) Each constituency in which the controlled spending incurred exceeded 0.04% of the total of the maximum campaign spending limits in England, Scotland, Wales and Northern Ireland (£200);

(iv) For each constituency: all the RTP's payments of controlled spending incurred by or on behalf of the third party during that period in that constituency;

(v) All disputed claims of which the responsible person is aware;[385]

(vi) Any unpaid claims of which the responsible person is aware in respect of which an application has been made, or is about to be made, to a court for permission to pay out of time; and

(vii) A statement of relevant donations received, stating: (a) accepted donations exceeding £7,500 (alone or cumulatively with previous donations by the same donor), recording its amount (if money) or nature and value (in anything else), date accepted, the donor's name and address; (b) accepted donations less than £7,500: the total value of these donations; (c) donations from impermissible donors: the donor's name and address (if identifiable) or how the donation was

---

[377] S 95A sch 11 PPERA 2000.
[378] Paras 2(1)(a) and 3 sch 11A PPERA 2000.
[379] Paras 2(1)(b) and 5 sch 11A PPERA 2000.
[380] S 94(3(a)(i), (4) and (5) and 96(1) PPERA 2000.
[381] S 98 PPERA 2000.
[382] S 96(1A) PPERA 2000.
[383] S 96(3)(a) PPERA 2000.
[384] S 96(2) PPERA 2000.
[385] S 93 PPERA 2000.

made (if unidentifiable), the amount (if money) or nature and value (if anything else), date received.[386]

1.138 The return need only cover the period after which the RTP became so registered with the Commission, but the return must be accompanied by a declaration of the total value of donations received before the third party became a RTP.[387]

1.139 The weekly and quarterly reports, and spending returns, must be accompanied by a declaration from the RTP's responsible person, stating that to the best of their knowledge and belief:

(i) Weekly reports: no relevant donation greater than £7,500 has been received that is not in the report;[388] or

(ii) Quarterly reports: all the donations reported as accepted were from permissible donors and the report does not omit any impermissible donations;[389]

(iii) Return: the responsible person has examined the return and to the best of their knowledge and belief it is complete and correct, all expenses shown as paid were paid by the responsible person, and all the donations reported as accepted were from permissible donors and the report does not omit any impermissible donations.[390]

1.140 It is an offence to knowingly or recklessly make a false declaration.[391]

1.141 The information reported must be made available for inspection by the Commission[392] for two years.[393]

1.142 On application by the Commission, if the magistrates' court is satisfied that a RTP's failure to deliver in time a compliant quarterly or weekly donations report was due to intent to conceal the amount or fact of a donation, the court may make a forfeiture order.[394]

---

[386]S 96(2)(d) PPERA 2000.
[387]S 96(5) PPERA 2000.
[388]S 95B(8) PPERA 2000.
[389]S 95A(9) sch 11 PPERA 2000.
[390]S 99 PPERA 2000.
[391]Ss 95C(2) and 99(4) PPERA 2000.
[392]S 95F(1) PPERA 2000.
[393]Ss 95F(3) and 100 PPERA 2000.
[394]S 95D PPERA 2000.

Statement of accounts

1.143 Where a return must be submitted by an RTP following a PE, unless the RTP is an individual,[395] within 6 months of the regulated period,[396] the responsible person must also prepare a statement of account including statements of the RTP's (i) income and spending for the regulated period; and (ii) assets and liabilities at the end of the period.[397]

1.144 The responsible person must also enclose a statement that they have examined the statement of accounts and, to the best of their knowledge and belief it is complete and correct statement of accounts as required by law.[398] Failure to do so without reasonable excuse is an offence, as is knowingly or recklessly making a false declaration.[399]

F. UNINCORPORATED ASSOCIATIONS

1.145 An unincorporated association ("**UA**") that contributes more than £25,000 to an RP or regulated donee in one calendar year, whether by donation, loan, or discharging a liability,[400] must notify the Commission within 30 days of the contribution that takes the total over the £25,000 threshold[401] ("**the contribution date**").[402] Only contributions greater than £500 count towards the total.[403]

1.146 Within 60 days of the contribution date, the UA must then send the Commission a report either specifying every gift[404] greater than £7,500 it has received in the previous calendar year, or, if none, stating that no such gifts were received.

1.147 The UA must then send further reports within 30 days of every subsequent quarter (i.e. within 30 days of 31st March, 30th June, 30th September or 31st December) for that quarter.[405]

1.148 A gift is also treated as being greater than £7,500 (and therefore reportable) if:

---

395 S 96A(8) PPERA 2000.
396 S 98(4) PPERA 2000.
397 S 96A PPERA 2000.
398 S 99A(2) PPERA 2000.
399 S 99A(3) PPERA 2000.
400 Para 2 sch 19A PPERA 2000.
401 S 140A and para 1 sch 19A PPERA 2000.
402 Para 2(1) sch 19A PPERA 2000.
403 Para 3 sch 19A PPERA 2000.
404 Para 9 sch 19A PPERA 2000.
405 Para 2(3) sch 19A PPERA 2000.

(i) It is one of two gifts (each greater than £500) from the same person and cumulatively exceeding £7,500;[406] or

(ii) It is greater than £1,500 and from a person who in the same calendar year gave the UA a gift greater than £7,500.[407]

1.149 The report must state the date the gift was received, the amount, the form it took, and the name and address of the donor and any intermediaries (if known).[408]

1.150 The notification and the reports must include a declaration as to the report's accuracy and comprehensiveness[409] and give prescribed details as to the UA and the declarant.[410]

1.151 A UA commits an offence if it fails without reasonable excuse to (i) send the requisite notification or report in time,[411] or (ii) send one that fails to contain the requisite information. The individual whom the UA authorises to make the declarations commits an offence if they do so falsely and with intent or recklessness.

1.152 The Commission will publish a register of all notifications made and gifts reported.[412] This must exclude information that would identify the giver or their intermediary, unless the Commission has first (i) notified them that it proposes to include this information; (ii) waited 45 days for a response; (iii) upon considering any response, decided to include the information and notified the person(s) it identifies.[413]

G. ENFORCEMENT BY THE COMMISSION

Commission monitoring and compliance duty

1.153 The Commission has a duty to *"monitor, and take all reasonable steps to ensure compliance with"*[414] PPERA 2000 requirements and, even though it does not administer elections, also RPA 1983 requirements in so far as they relate to candidates' election expenses and donations.[415]

---

[406]Para 2(5) sch 19A PPERA 2000.
[407]Para 2(6) sch 19A PPERA 2000.
[408]Para 3 sch 19A PPERA 2000.
[409]Para 4 and 5 sch 19A PPERA 2000.
[410]Para 5 sch 19A PPERA 2000.
[411]Para 6(1) sch 19A PPERA 2000.
[412]Para 7 sch 19A PPERA 2000A.
[413]Para 8 sch 19A PPERA 2000.
[414]S 145 PPERA 2000.
[415]S 145 PPERA 2000.

1.154 The enforcement powers at the Commission's disposal *"form part of a package of enforcement functions conferred on the Commission"* and must be read together.[416]

Investigatory powers

1.155 The Commission has the following investigatory powers:[417]

(i) To give a **disclosure notice**, requiring production of documents which *"relate to the income and spending of the organisation or individual in question"* or an explanation of the same, as long as the documents or explanation are *"reasonably required by the Commission for the purposes of carrying out their functions"*.[418]

(ii) To apply for an **inspection warrant** (to enter premises and inspect documents) on the conditions that: (a) *"there are reasonable grounds for believing that on those premises there are documents relating to the income and spending of the organisation or individual"*, (b) *"the Commission need to inspect the documents for the purposes of carrying out functions of the Commission other than investigatory functions"*, and (c) *"permission to inspect the documents on the premises has been requested by the Commission and has been unreasonably refused"*.[419]

(iii) If the Commission has reasonable grounds to suspect someone has committed an offence or contravened a PPERA restriction, power to require them to (a) produce documents by a deadline specified in the notice (which must be a reasonable period of time) or an explanation, or (b) to attend the Commission's offices to answer questions.[420] Upon non-compliance, the paragraph immediately below is engaged.

(iv) If the Commission's document production notice or explanation request notice goes unanswered: power to apply to the High Court for a **document-disclosure order**[421] or **information-disclosure order**[422] on grounds that (a) there are reasonable grounds to suspect that someone has committed an offence under PPERA 2000 or contravened one of its restrictions/requirements; and (b) documents requested by the

---

[416] R *(Vote Leave Ltd) v Electoral Commission* [2019] EWCA Civ 1938 at 23.
[417] S 146 and sch 19B PPERA 2000.
[418] Para 1 sch 19B PPERA 2000.
[419] Para 2 sch 19B PPERA 2000.
[420] Para 3 sch 19B PPERA 2000.
[421] Para 4 sch 19B PPERA 2000. One application for a documents and information disclosure order has been made in the past four years, and withdrawn following receipt of documents and information from the party under investigation: Electoral Commission, 'Annual Report & Accounts 2016–17', HC 223 ECL/2017/01, p 36.
[422] Para 5 sch 19B PPERA 2000.

Commission in a disclosure notice have not been produced, are reasonably required by the Commission for the purposes of investigating the offence or contravention, and the documents are in the possession of the respondent or the respondent is able to provide the explanation.[423] If the court makes such an order, failure to comply may amount to contempt of court.[424] Statements made in compliance with a Commission request are admissible (the privilege against self-incrimination does not apply), but cannot be relied on in criminal proceedings or those brought by the Commission in exercise of its civil sanction powers (see next section), save for perjury or the offence of knowingly or recklessly providing false information in purported compliance with a Commission request under schs 19B or C.[425]

(v) The Commission then has power to (a) retain documents for three months, or longer if criminal or civil sanction proceedings are then brought within that three-month period;[426] (b) make copies or records of information contained in documents or explanation provided.[427]

1.156 The Commission cannot inspect, take possession of or request anything covered by legal professional privilege.[428]

1.157 It is an offence to fail to comply with a Commission disclosure or inspection notice (subject to 'reasonable excuse' defence), or to provide false information *"in purported compliance"*, or to intentionally obstruct someone authorised to do something under sch 19B.[429]

No private law right action where documents retained during investigation

1.158 For as long as the Commission has not concluded its investigation, the Commission does not have to return an expenses return and associated documents, for as long as it is considering the information there contained.[430] Not doing so does not give rise to a private law right of action for breach of statutory duty or conversion.[431] This is despite the treasurer's statutory right,

---

[423] Paras 4 and 5 sch 19B PPERA 2000.
[424] Paras 4 and 5 sch 19B PPERA 2000.
[425] Para 12 sch 19B PPERA 2000.
[426] Para 6 sch 19B PPERA 2000.
[427] Para 7 sch 19B PPERA 2000.
[428] Para 11 sch 19B PPERA 2000.
[429] Para 13 sch 19B PPERA 2000.
[430] *Murphy v Electoral Commission* [2019] EWHC 2762 (QB) at 39 (nb this was in the referendum context).
[431] *Murphy v Electoral Commission* [2019] EWHC 2762 (QB).

two years after the Commission receives a return and accompanying documents, to request their return.[432]

Offence

1.159 It is an offence to alter, conceal or destroy (cause or permit the same) any document which is or is liable to be required to be produced for inspection, if done so with the intent to falsify that document or enabling evasion any of the provisions of PPERA 2000.[433]

S 147 and sch 19C: civil sanctions regime

1.160 The Commission has the following *"quasi-judicial"*[434] civil sanction powers, to avoid them having to bring criminal proceedings for commission of PPERA offences or contravention of its requirements:[435]

(i) 'Fixed monetary penalties' ("**FMPs**"), which are *"a requirement to pay to the Commission a penalty of a prescribed amount"*,[436] currently set at £200.[437] Where the FMP is imposed because of the commission of an offence and that offence is triable summarily and punishable by a fine, the FMP may not exceed the maximum amount of that fine;[438]

(ii) A '**discretionary requirement**', namely a requirement to either: (a) pay a '**variable monetary penalty**' (a fine) to the Commission of such amount as the Commission may determine, the maximum being £20,000,[439] unless the FMP is imposed because of the commission of an offence triable summarily and punishable by a fine, in which case the variable monetary penalty may not exceed the maximum amount of that fine; or (b) take such steps as the Commission may specify, within such period as they may specify, to secure that the offence or contravention does not continue or recur, or to secure that the position is, so far as possible, restored to what it would have been if the offence or contravention had not happened ("**non-monetary discretionary requirement**");[440]

---

432 S 84(2)(b) PPERA 2000.
433 S 148 PPERA.
434 R *(Vote Leave Ltd) v Electoral Commission* [2019] EWCA Civ 1938 at 24.
435 S 147 and sch 19C PPERA 2000.
436 Para 1(5) sch 19C PPERA 2000.
437 Para 1 of sch 1 Political Parties, Elections and Referendums (Civil Sanctions) Order 2010.
438 Para 1(6) sch 19C PPERA 2000.
439 Para 5 sch 1 Political Parties, Elections and Referendums (Civil Sanctions) Order 2010.
440 Para 5(5) sch 19C PPERA 2000.

(iii) '**Stop notices**', prohibiting the person on whom it is served from carrying on the activity specified in the notice until the person has taken the steps specified in the notice;[441]

(iv) '**Enforcement undertakings**', whereby a person offers to undertake action to secure that (a) the offence or contravention does not continue or recur, or (b) the position is, so far as possible, restored to what it would have been if the offence or contravention had not happened, and the Commission accepts the undertaking.[442]

Whom the civil penalties may be imposed upon

1.161 The Commission may by notice impose an FMP, or discretionary requirement on: person (individuals or corporate), RPs, and RTPs.[443]

Burden of proof

1.162 If an individual makes a positive case in defence of proposed sanction, the Commission must ask itself whether it has sufficient evidence to reject that case, not whether there is sufficient evidence to support the regulatee's case.[444]

Standard of proof

1.163 To impose an FMP or discretionary requirement, the Commission must be satisfied *"beyond reasonable doubt"* that the person has committed a PPERA offence or contravened one of restrictions or requirements.[445] This is an objective standard.[446]

1.164 To impose a stop notice, the Commission must *"reasonably believe"* that an activity being carried out or likely to be carried out:

(i) Involves or is likely to involve, or will involve or will likely involve, the person committing an PPERA offence, or contravening a PPERA restriction or requirement; and

(ii) The activity is or will be *"seriously damaging public confidence in the effectiveness of the controls in [PPERA] on the income and spending of*

---

[441]Para 10(1) sch 19C PPERA 2000.
[442]Para 15 sch 19C PPERA 2000.
[443]Paras 1 and 5 sch 19C PPERA 2000.
[444] *Grimes v Electoral Commission* (unreported, 19.7.19, County Court at Central London), at 107, per HHJ Dight.
[445]Paras 1 and 5 sch 19C PPERA 2000.
[446] *Grimes v Electoral Commission* (unreported, 19.7.19, County Court at Central London), at 62, per HHJ Dight.

registered parties and others", or presents or will present *"a significant risk of doing so"*.[447]

1.165 To agree to an enforcement undertaking, the Commission must have *"reasonable grounds to suspect"* that a person has committed a PPERA offence or contravened a PPERA requirement or restriction.[448]

Notice requirements

1.166 Where the Commission proposes to impose an FMP or discretionary requirement on a person, the Commission must first serve a notice stating:

(i) What is proposed;[449]

(ii) Offering them an opportunity to discharge their liability for the FMP by paying the prescribed sum,[450] currently set at £200;[451]

(iii) The grounds for the proposal to impose the FMP;[452]

(iv) *"The effect of payment of the sum"*,[453] and how long they have to do so[454] (which will be a maximum of 28 days from receiving the notice);[455]

(v) That they have the right to make representations and objections, and the deadline for doing so[456] (which will be a maximum of 28 days from receiving the notice);[457]

(vi) *"The circumstances in which the Commission may not impose the [FMP]"*,[458] namely: that they are no longer satisfied beyond reasonable doubt that the person has committed the offence or contravened the restriction or requirement.[459]

---

447 Para 10(2) and (3) sch 19C PPERA 2000.
448 Para 15 sch 19C PPERA 2000.
449 Para 2(1) and 6(1) sch 19C PPERA 2000.
450 Para 2(2) sch 19C PPERA 2000.
451 Para 2 of sch 1 Political Parties, Elections and Referendums (Civil Sanctions) Order 2010/2860.
452 Para 3(1)(a) and 7(1)(a) sch 19C.
453 Para 3(1)(b) sch 19C.
454 Para 3(2)(b) sch 19C.
455 Para 3(2) sch 19C.
456 Para 3(2)(b) and 7(1)(b) sch 19C PPERA 2000.
457 Para 3(2) and 7(1)(b) sch 19C PPERA 2000.
458 Para 3(1)(d) sch 19C PPERA 2000.
459 Para 2(5) sch 19C PPERA 2000.

1.167 In the case of stop notices, the information that must be included is the grounds for serving the notice, rights of appeal, and the consequences of not complying with the notice.[460]

Effect of notice: exclusion of criminal proceedings and conviction

1.168 If the Commission issues a notice proposing an FMP, criminal proceedings may not be brought against the recipient in respect of the act or omission to which the notice relates, either (i) during the period for payment;[461] or (ii) if the FMP is paid, at any time.[462]

Final decision

1.169 After the end of the period for making representations and objections, the Commission must decide whether it is still satisfied that the offence has been committed or the requirement contravened, taking into account any matter raised. If so, then it must serve on the person a final notice imposing the penalty (in the case of an FMP)[463] or specifying what the requirement is (in the case of a discretionary requirement).[464]

1.170 The final notice must state:

(i) The grounds for imposing the discretionary requirement;

(ii) Rights of appeal;

(iii) The consequences of non-compliance;

(iv) For FMPs and where the discretionary requirement is a variable monetary penalty: (a) how payment may be made; (b) the period within which payment must be made; and (c) any early payment discounts or late payment penalties.[465]

Exclusion of conviction

1.171 If an FMP or discretionary requirement is imposed on a person, then they cannot also be convicted of an offence in relation to the act or omission giving rise to that FMP.[466]

---

[460]Para 11 sch 19C PPERA 2000.
[461]Para 4(1)(a) sch 19C PPERA 2000.
[462]Para 4(1)(b) sch 19C PPERA 2000.
[463]Para 2(4) sch 19C PPERA 2000.
[464]Para 6(5) sch 19C PPERA 2000.
[465]Paras 3(3) and 7(3) sch 19C PPERA 2000.
[466]Para 4(2) sch 19C PPERA 2000.

1.172 The exception is non-monetary discretionary requirements, non-compliance with which may yet lead to conviction for an offence in relation to the same act or omission as gave rise to the non-monetary discretionary requirement.[467]

Deadline for payment of FMPs and effect of late payment

1.173 A person on whom a FMP or variable monetary penalty is imposed has 28 days from receipt of the final notice to pay.[468]

1.174 If payment is not made within the 28 days of receipt of the final notice (or determination or withdrawal of the appeal),[469] the amount payable is increased by 25%.[470] If still not paid within 56 days of receipt of the final notice (or determination or withdrawal of the appeal),[471] the amount payable is the original sum plus 50%.[472]

Completion certificates

1.175 Once the person has complied with a discretionary requirement (compliance notice or restoration notice), stop notice, or enforcement undertaking, they may apply to the Commission for a certificate stating that they are satisfied that the person has taken the steps specified in the notice.[473]

1.176 If so, the Commission must decide within 14 days (for stop notices)[474] or 28 days (for compliance notices, restoration notices, or enforcement undertakings)[475] whether they are satisfied that the person has so complied. If so, the notice ceases to have effect.

1.177 If they are, they must issue a certificate to that effect.[476]

---

[467]Para 8(2) sch 19C PPERA 2000.

[468]Paras 3, 4 and 9 sch 1 Political Parties, Elections and Referendums (Civil Sanctions) Order 2010/2860.

[469]Paras 4(4) and 9(2) sch 1 Political Parties, Elections and Referendums (Civil Sanctions) Order 2010/2860.

[470]Para 4(2) sch 1 Political Parties, Elections and Referendums (Civil Sanctions) Order 2010/2860.

[471]Paras 4(5) sch 1 Political Parties, Elections and Referendums (Civil Sanctions) Order 2010/2860.

[472]Para 4(3) and 9(5) sch 1 Political Parties, Elections and Referendums (Civil Sanctions) Order 2010/2860.

[473]Para 6(3), 12(3) and 17(3) sch 1 Political Parties, Elections and Referendums (Civil Sanctions) Order 2010/2860.

[474]Para 12(3) sch 19C PPERA 2000.

[475]Para 6(3) sch 1 Political Parties, Elections and Referendums (Civil Sanctions) Order 2010/2860.

[476]Para 6(1) sch 1 Political Parties, Elections and Referendums (Civil Sanctions) Order 2010/2860.

1.178 If they are not, they must inform the applicant of the grounds for so deciding and of their right of appeal to the County Court.[477] Such appeal must be lodged within 28 days and must be on ground of error of fact or law, unfairness, or unreasonableness.[478]

1.179 The Commission may revoke a completion certificate if granted on the basis of incomplete or misleading information.[479]

Effect of non-compliance with discretionary requirements, stop notice, or enforcement undertaking

1.180 Non-compliance with discretionary requirement empowers the Commission to impose a monetary penalty.[480] There is right of appeal to the County Court on grounds of error of fact or law, unfairness, or unreasonableness.[481]

1.181 Non-compliance with a stop notice is an offence.[482]

1.182 Non-compliance with an enforcement undertaking waives the immunity that agreement of the undertaking otherwise confers (immunity from conviction, FMP or discretionary requirement being imposed in relation to the act or omission that gave rise to the enforcement undertaking).[483]

Appeal

1.183 A person on whom a FMP, discretionary requirement, or stop notice is imposed has 28 days from receipt of the final notice[484] to appeal to the County Court against the decision to impose it,[485] and may do so on the grounds that:

(i) It was based on an error of fact;

(ii) It was wrong in law;

(iii) It was unreasonable;[486]

---

[477]Para 6(5),13(3) and 15(5) sch 1 Political Parties, Elections and Referendums (Civil Sanctions) Order 2010/2860.

[478]Paras 8 and 13(2) sch 1 Political Parties, Elections and Referendums (Civil Sanctions) Order 2010/2860.

[479]Paras 6(6), 11 and 15(6) sch 19C PPERA 2000.

[480]Para 9 sch 19C PPERA 2000.

[481]Para 9(3) and (4) sch 19C PPERA 2000.

[482]Para 14 sch 19C PPERA 2000.

[483]Para 15(2) sch 19C PPERA 2000.

[484]Paras 3 and 7 sch 1 Political Parties, Elections and Referendums (Civil Sanctions) Order 2010/2860.

[485]Paras 2(7) and 6(7) sch 19C PPERA 2000.

[486]Paras 2(6), 6(6) and 13(1)(a)-(c) sch 19C PPERA 2000.

(iv) In the case of discretionary requirements or stop notices: that the nature of the requirement is unreasonable;[487]

(v) In the case of stop notices: that the person on whom it was served: (a) has not acted in a way that involves or is likely to involve, or will involve or will likely involve, them committing a PPERA offence, or contravening a PPERA restriction or requirement, and (b) would not have done so even if the stop notice had not been served.[488]

1.184 Despite one of the set grounds being 'error of fact', the *"test is whether the appellant has shown that it was not open to the Electoral Commission to reach the relevant factual finding, to the criminal standard, on the material available to the Electoral Commission at the time"*.[489] The appeal takes the form of a review of the Commission's decision to issue the final notice imposing the civil sanction, and of the findings of fact that led the Commission to that decision, rather than a rehearing in which the Court may remake those findings of fact.[490] Accordingly, the general position will be that the appellant will not be able to rely on fresh evidence that was not before the Commission's decision-maker at the time of the decision, nor cross-examine Commission witnesses on how the decision was made.[491] The

1.185 In an appeal on grounds of 'unreasonableness', it is the decision to impose the sanction that must be shown to be unreasonable, not the decision-making process which proceeds it.[492]

1.186 An appeal suspends the time for payment of the FMP,[493] but, if the FMP is upheld or varied, or the appeal withdrawn, then the FMP must be paid within 28 days[494] or the amount payable is increased by 25%.[495] If still not paid within

---

[487] Paras 6(6) and 13(1)(d) sch 19C PPERA 2000.

[488] Para 13(1)(e) sch 19C PPERA 2000.

[489] *Grimes v Electoral Commission* (unreported, 19.7.19, County Court at Central London), at 64, per HHJ Dight.

[490] *Leave.EU v The Electoral Commission* (unreported, 21.3.19, County Court at Central London), at 17-19, per HHJ Dight; *Grimes v Electoral Commission* (unreported, 19.7.19, County Court at Central London), at 62, per HHJ Dight.

[491] *Grimes v Electoral Commission* (unreported, 19.7.19, County Court at Central London), at 65, per HHJ Dight.

[492] *Grimes v Electoral Commission* (unreported, 19.7.19, County Court at Central London), at 111, per HHJ Dight.

[493] Paras 3 and 7 sch 19C PPERA 2000.

[494] Paras 4(4) sch 1 Political Parties, Elections and Referendums (Civil Sanctions) Order 2010/2860.

[495] Para 4(2) sch 1 Political Parties, Elections and Referendums (Civil Sanctions) Order 2010/2860.

56 days of receipt of the determination or withdrawal of the appeal,[496] then the amount payable is the original sum plus 50%.[497]

Standard of interventionism

1.187 The Commission was required to issue guidance on the circumstances in which it will exercise these powers, the action it might take, and the circumstances in which it might take action,[498] and did so on 5.4.16 by issuing policy guidance titled '**Enforcement Policy**'.[499] The Commission is required to have regard to the Enforcement Policy in exercising its functions.[500]

1.188 The Enforcement Policy states that the Commission's *"approach to [its] enforcement activity"* is that it will:

(i) *"Regulate in a way that is effective, proportionate and fair"*;

(ii) *"Use advice and guidance proactively in order secure compliance and to give those we regulate a clear understanding of their regulatory requirements"*;

(iii) *"Undertake supervisory work to ensure that regulated organisations and individuals meet their legal requirements"*;

(iv) *"Take enforcement action, including using investigatory powers and sanctions, where it is necessary and proportionate to do so in order to meet our enforcement aim and objectives"*;

(v) *"Take the facts of each situation into account."*[501]

1.189 In *R (Electoral Commission) v Westminster Magistrates Court*, Lord Phillips PSC held:

> "Of course the party and the donor should make sure that the donor complies with the statutory requirement of being placed on an electoral register. But if, by inadvertence, or even negligence, they fail to do so, it does not follow that it cannot be disproportionate for the donation to be forfeited. Proportionality will depend on the degree of culpability, the size of the donation and its importance to the party."

---

[496] Para 4(5) sch 1 Political Parties, Elections and Referendums (Civil Sanctions) Order 2010/2860.

[497] Para 4(3) sch 1 Political Parties, Elections and Referendums (Civil Sanctions) Order 2010/2860.

[498] Para 14(1) sch 19B and para 25(1) sch 19C PPERA 2000.

[499] Electoral Commission, 'Enforcement Policy', 5.4.16; https://www.electoralcommission.org.uk/sites/default/files/pdf_file/April-2016-Enforcement-Policy.pdf.

[500] Para 14(4) sch 19B and para 25(8) sch 19C PPERA 2000.

[501] Electoral Commission, 'Enforcement Policy', 5.4.16, para 2.3.

Power to publish investigation report setting out offences found and fines imposed

1.190 The Commission has a power, incidental to its s 145 duty to take all reasonable steps to *"secure compliance with"* various requirements of PPERA 2000,[502] to publish a report setting out its account of its investigation under sch 19B PPERA 2000,[503] including:

(i) Whether the offence or contravention was established;

(ii) Whether a sanction was issued, and the nature of the sanction;

(iii) The subject of the investigation and the offence or contravention;

(iv) A brief summary of the reasons for the imposition of any sanction or the decision not to impose a sanction;

(v) The level of any penalty imposed;

(vi) Whether the sanction is the subject of any appeal;

(vii) For monetary penalties, when they were paid; and

(viii) For compliance notices, whether and when a completion certificate was issued.[504]

1.191 Notably, in finding the Commission to have this incidental power, the Court rejected the submission that the fact that returning officers do not possess implied powers[505] should also apply to the Commission,[506] marking a limit to the relevance of the law of the conduct of election to the PPERA 2000 scheme administered by the Commission.

1.192 Whilst the Commission's power to publish is established, a decision to do so is amenable to judicial review.

H. GENERAL OFFENCES

1.193 If the RP treasurer, responsible person within a members association, or RTP requests from one of its office-holders, candidates or that candidate's agent[507] information reasonably required to comply with a regulatory requirement, then it is an offence, punishable by unlimited fine or six months' (on summary

---

[502] R *(Vote Leave Ltd) v Electoral Commission* [2019] EWCA Civ 1938 at 23.
[503] R *(Vote Leave Ltd) v Electoral Commission* [2019] EWCA Civ 1938
[504] Electoral Commission, 'Enforcement Policy', 5.4.16, para B.14.
[505] R *(De Beer) v Returning Officer for Harrow LBC* [2002] EWHC 670; *Begum v Returning Officer for Tower Hamlets LBC* [2006] EWCA Civ 733.
[506] R *(Vote Leave Ltd) v Electoral Commission* [2019] EWCA Civ 1938 at 22.
[507] S 148(5) PPERA 2000.

conviction) or one year's (on indictment) imprisonment,[508] for the office-holder, candidate or agent, to:

(i) Fail, without reasonable excuse, to supply that information as soon as reasonably practicable;[509]

(ii) Provide information which is false in a material particular (only applicable to the office-holder);[510]

(iii) Withhold that information.[511]

I. INCIDENTAL POWERS

1.194 Besides the express powers provided to it by Parliament in PPERA 2000, as is common in statutes creating regulatory bodies, PPERA also provides the Commission with the power to *"do anything (except borrow money) which is calculated to facilitate, or is incidental or conducive to, the carrying out of any of their functions"*.[512]

J. INTERPRETING THE LEGISLATION

1.195 PPERA 2000's words and phrases should be given their natural meaning as a matter of ordinary language, though any ambiguity may be resolved by construing the terms according to their policy aims.[513]

1.196 The draftsman is presumed to use words consistently in a statute.[514]

1.197 In *R (Good Law Project) and The Electoral Commission*,[515] the Court of Appeal listed the following further principles of statutory construction in the PPERA context:

(i) Concepts derived from contract or equity *"are far removed from those with which electoral law is concerned"*;[516]

(ii) Where the PPERA provisions under being construed are ones which create potential criminal liability on the part of individuals, the

---

[508] Sch 20 PPERA 2000.
[509] S 148(1) and (3) PPERA 2000.
[510] S 148(2) PPERA 2000.
[511] S 148(3) PPERA 2000.
[512] Para 2 sch 1 PPERA 2000.
[513] R *(Vote Leave Ltd) v Electoral Commission* [2019] EWCA Civ 1938, at 24. For the definitive guide to statutory interpretation, the reader is directed to 'Bennion on Statutory Interpretation', 7th ed (LexiNexis Butterworths, 2019).
[514] R *(English Democrats Party) v Electoral Commission* [2018] EWHC 251 (Admin) at 44.
[515] R *(Vote Leave Ltd) v Electoral Commission* [2019] EWCA Civ 1938.
[516] R *(Vote Leave Ltd) v Electoral Commission* [2019] EWCA Civ 1938, at 77.

statutory principle against "doubtful penalisation" is engaged and must be given sufficient weight;[517]

(iii) *"[L]egislation needs to be read and given effect in a way which can be applied in a practical way by all those concerned"*;[518]

(iv) *"[W]hen Parliament wished to enact specific provisions for circumstances in which it might otherwise be said that limits on spending could be circumvented, it expressly said so. Where Parliament has chosen not to do so, either generally or because the specific provisions relating to common plans do not apply (as was the presumed basis of fact on which the Divisional Court proceeded), the courts should not interpret legislation in effect to create further circumstances in which the donor can also be regarded as having incurred expenses which potentially exceed the statutory limit on spending by that person"*.[519]

1.198 In the context of publication of investigation reports, the Court of Appeal has confirmed the relevance of the public interest in the exercise of the Commission's powers, applying the principle that public bodies with an investigatory function should be as open as possible about enquiries they have conducted.[520] Describing the public interest in making inquiries such as that conducted by the Commission as open as possible, Singh LJ stated:

> "This is important not only in cases such as this, where an investigation led to the imposition of fines, but would be equally important in cases where the Commission does not find a breach of the rules or no sanction is imposed. In such cases the public would still have an important interest in knowing that the Commission had gone about its work properly and conscientiously."[521]

1.199 The term 'public interest' is used in the Commission's Enforcement Policy, which states that one of the factors the Commission will consider in deciding whether to investigate or sanction it is in the public interest to do so.[522] Though it is the Commission's prerogative to decide whether a given course is **in** the public interest, it does not decide what constitutes **a** public interest. That is a political judgment for the legislature, reflected in PPERA 2000 and to be interpreted by the courts,[523] which have generated principles as to what is in the

---

[517] R *(Vote Leave Ltd) v Electoral Commission* [2019] EWCA Civ 1938, at 78.
[518] R *(Vote Leave Ltd) v Electoral Commission* [2019] EWCA Civ 1938, at 79.
[519] At 80.
[520] R *(Vote Leave Ltd) v Electoral Commission* [2019] EWCA Civ 1938 at 24, applying *Kennedy v Charity Commission* [2014] UKSC 20, [2015] AC 455 at 488-489.
[521] R *(Vote Leave Ltd) v Electoral Commission* [2019] EWCA Civ 1938 at 38.
[522] Enforcement Policy, para 6.9 and 7.3.
[523] *Attorney-General v Jonathan Cape Ltd* [1976] QB 752, at 770, per Lord Widgery LCJ.

public interest in respect to regulatory conduct.[524] Because PPERA 2000 does not expressly mention 'public interest' or define it, the scope for judicial interpretation, in particular in relation to incidental powers, is the greater.

K. JUDICIAL REVIEW OF THE COMMISSION

1.200 The proper means of challenging a decision of the Commission is a public law claim by way of judicial review, not a civil claim for, say, abuse of process.[525] Abuse of process may however be a ground of judicial review. The grounds and procedure for judicial review lie outside the scope of this work.[526]

---

[524] R *(Breckland DC) v Electoral Commission Boundary Committee for England* [2009] EWCA Civ 239, at 104 (public interest in good administration); R *(English Democrats Party) v Electoral Commission* [2018] EWHC 251 (Admin), at 57 (public interest in urgency); R *(Vote Leave Ltd) v Electoral Commission* [2019] EWCA Civ 1938 at 24 (public interest in publication of detailed investigation reports).

[525] *Murphy v Electoral Commission* [2019] EWHC 2762 (QB).

[526] The interested reader is referred to Auburn, Moffett, and Sharland, 'Judicial Review: Principles and Procedure' (OUP: Oxford, 2013).

CHAPTER TWO
THE RIGHT TO VOTE AND REGISTRATION

2.1 This chapter discusses the following issues:

A. The right to registration;

B. The electoral registration officer ("**ERO**") and the registers;

C. Applications to register;

D. Absent voting (proxy and postal);

E. Alteration of the register;

F. Registration appeals; and

G. Errors in the registers.

A. THE RIGHT TO REGISTRATION

2.2 The right to vote is a basic or constitutional right.[1] However, it is not a universal right but permits derogation by Parliament. In *Moohan v Lord Advocate*,[2] Lord Hodge (with whom Lord Neuberger agreed) held:

> "I do not think that the common law has been developed so as to recognise a right of universal and equal suffrage from which any derogation must be provided for by law and must be proportionate. … The UK Parliament through its legislation has controlled and controls the modalities of the expression of democracy."[3]

2.3 In *Hipperson v Electoral Registration Officer for the District of Newbury*,[4] Sir John Donaldson MR commented:

> "Voting rights lie at the root of parliamentary democracy. Indeed many would regard them as a basic human right. Nevertheless they are not like the air we breathe. They do not just happen. They have to be conferred, or at least defined and the categories of citizen who enjoy

---

[1] *Watkins v SSHD* [2006] 2 AC 395, at 25, per Lord Bingham, and at 61, per Lord Rodger; *Moohan v Lord Advocate* [2014] UKSC 67, at 33, per Lord Hodge.

[2] *Moohan v Lord Advocate* [2014] UKSC 67.

[3] *Moohan v Lord Advocate* [2014] UKSC 67, at 34, per Lord Hodge.

[4] *Hipperson v Electoral Registration Officer for the District of Newbury* [1985] QB 1060.

them have also to be defined. Thus no one would expect a new born baby to have voting rights or that citizens could vote in all constituencies or in that of their unfettered choice."[5]

2.4 Discussed in Chapter 6, the right to vote is additionally guaranteed by article 3 of Protocol 1 to the European Convention on Human Rights ("**A3P1**"). As at common law, A3P1 permits limitations, though they are not expressed in the text of A3P1. The legislature may therefore make the right subject to conditions and have a wide margin of appreciation in which to do so, *"provided that they do not impair the very substance of the right and render it wholly ineffective"*.[6] Those conditions are as follows.

2.5 A person has a right to vote in an election if, on the date of the election, they are:

(i) Registered in the relevant register, namely: the register of parliamentary electors for that constituency ("**PE register**")[7] (PE), the register of local government electors ("**LE register**") for that electoral area (LE, LAE, WAE and PCCE);[8]

(ii) 18 years or over,[9] or 16 years for WAE;[10]

(iii) Not subject to any legal incapacity to vote,[11] by being a convicted person serving a term of imprisonment[12] or detained subject to a hospital order under the Mental Health Act 1983;[13]

(iv) Either a Commonwealth citizen (British, Irish, or a person who does not require leave under the Immigration Act 1971 to enter or remain in the UK)[14] or a citizen of the Republic of Ireland (not an 'alien').[15]

---

[5] *Hipperson v Electoral Registration Officer for the District of Newbury* [1985] QB 1060, p 1070G.
[6] *Benkaddour v France* (51685/99), 18.11.03 [Section II].
[7] S 1 Representation of the People Act 1983 ("**RPA 1983**").
[8] S 2(1)(a) RPA 1983; s 17 Greater London Authority Act 1999; s 12(1) Government of Wales Act 2006; s 52(1) Police Reform and Social Responsibility Act 2011.
[9] Ss 1(1)(d) and 2(1)(d) RPA 1983; s 52(1) Police Reform and Social Responsibility Act 2011.
[10] S 12(1A) Government of Wales Act 2006 (applicable to the first WAE poll after 5.4.21).
[11] Ss 1(1)(b) and 2(1)(b) RPA 1983.
[12] S 3(1) RPA 1983.
[13] S 3A RPA 1983.
[14] S 4(6) RPA 1983. S 37(1) British Nationality Act 1981 defines 'Commonwealth citizen' as a status enjoyed by British citizens, British Overseas Territory citizens, British Overseas citizens, British subjects, and citizens of independent Commonwealth countries listed in sch 3 British Nationality Act 1981.
[15] S 1(1)(c) and 2(1)(c).

2.6 A person has a right to be in the PE register for any constituency, or the LE register for any electoral area, if on the date they apply[16] they are:[17]

(i) Resident in the parliamentary constituency (PE), electoral area (LE), or Wales (WAE);

(ii) Not subject to any legal incapacity to vote (imprisonment, disqualification, or detention in mental health hospital under hospital order issued by the Crown Court or magistrates' court, interim hospital order, or committal by the Magistrates' Court);

(iii) Either a qualifying Commonwealth citizen or a UK or Irish citizen; and

(iv) 18 years or over,[18] or 16 for WAE.[19]

2.7 EU citizens are currently entitled to register in LE registers.[20] The legislation so entitling them has not yet been amended. The Withdrawal Agreement did not cover citizens' voting rights.[21] LE: the UK is forming reciprocal agreements with EU countries on a bilateral basis.[22] WAE: EU citizens will be able to vote in pursuant to a declaration of local connection.[23]

Residence

2.8 Determination as to whether a person is 'resident' at a particular address involves regard to the purpose of their presence or absence at the address on the date they apply for registration, whilst having regard to the following rules.

2.9 A person staying at an address other than on a permanent basis may still be resident there if they have no home elsewhere, but they will not be resident there if they do have a home elsewhere.[24]

2.10 A person may be resident at two addresses and choose which address to vote at: students are the classic example.[25] On the other hand, second homes for non-

[16]S 4(6) RPA 1983.
[17]Ss 4 and 5 RPA 1983.
[18]NB. s 2 Local Government and Elections (Wales) Bill [as introduced] (GB/20/2019) would reduce LE voting age to 16 in Wales.
[19]S 12(1A) Government of Wales Act 2006 (applicable to the first WAE poll after 5.4.21).
[20]S 2(1)(c) RPA 1983.
[21]Agreement on the withdrawal of the United Kingdom of Great Britain and Northern Ireland from the European Union and the European Atomic Energy Community, 19.10.19.
[22]Bilateral Voting Rights: Written statements: HCWS1257, 21.1.19 (Spain); HCWS1614, 12.6.19 (Portugal); HCWS1633, 18.6.19 (Luxembourg).
[23]Ss 7B(3)(e) and 203(1) RPA 1983; s 12(1B) Government of Wales Act 2006 (applicable to the first WAE poll after 5.4.21).
[24]S 5(2) RPA 1983.
[25]*Fox v Stirk* [1970] 2 QB 463, 475F-G, per Lord Denning MR.

students are likely to lack the degree of permanence required where the person has another address.[26]

2.11 Temporary absence by reason of attendance at university,[27] or in performance of any duty of service, employment or office, does not mean a person is not resident at the address.[28]

2.12 Detention in legal custody does not establish residence in the place of custody.[29]

2.13 A person resident in a mental health hospital, detained on remand, or detained pursuant to committal is treated as resident there[30] if they are likely to be there for sufficient period, unless:

(i) Their detention is pursuant to a hospital order (issued by the Crown Court or Magistrates' Court), interim hospital order, or committal by the Magistrates' Court, after conviction for an offence, or after a finding in criminal proceedings that they did the act or omission charged;[31] or

(ii) They seek to register elsewhere pursuant to residence there or pursuant to a declaration of local connection there (on which, see below).[32]

2.14 An unlawful residence may nonetheless constitute 'residence' for purposes of registering to vote,[33] e.g. protesters camped outside a military base.[34]

2.15 In *Simmons v Khan*,[35] Election Court commissioner Richard Mawbrey QC stated:

> "[I]n order for an elector lawfully to vote at a local election for a particular local authority ward, he must meet the eligibility criteria and have a "residence" within the boundaries of the Ward. A temporary visitor cannot lawfully register and vote. Similarly someone who, in the words of s 5 has "a home elsewhere" cannot put himself on the register of a ward for the purposes of an election without residing in that ward.

---

[26] S 5(2) RPA 1983.
[27] S 5(5) RPA 1983.
[28] S 5(3) RPA 1983.
[29] S 5(6) RPA 1983.
[30] S 7(1) and 7A(1) RPA 1983.
[31] Ss 7(1) and 7A(1) RPA 1983.
[32] Ss 7(5) and 7B RPA 1983.
[33] *Hipperson v Electoral Registration Officer for the District of Newbury* [1985] QB 1060, at p 71H, per Sir John Donaldson MR: *"We do not consider that Parliament can have intended to cast upon an electoral registration officer the duty of deciding which residential breaches of the criminal law should disqualify an aspiring voter and which should not. Accordingly we reject the submission that the franchise is affected by the fact that the qualifying residence is illegal or, a fortiori, unlawful."*
[34] *Hipperson v Electoral Registration Officer for the District of Newbury* [1985] QB 1060 (protestors camped outside Greenham Common Airfield, sleeping in tents, vehicles or in the open air, committing offences under byelaws).
[35] *Simmons v Khan* [2008] EWHC B4 (QB)

Relatives from abroad who are over in England for a short holiday cannot lawfully register and vote."[36]

Declaration of local connection

2.16 A 'declaration of local connection' is an alternative means of satisfying the residence requirement for registration to vote.[37] It is available to persons of no fixed address at the relevant time (at application for registration). In this category are: (i) patients in mental health hospital who are not detained offenders or on remand; (ii) persons remanded in custody (other than after conviction or finding that they did the act charged); or (iii) homeless persons (defined as a person *"who is not... resident at any address in the [UK]"*).[38]

2.17 The online application to register and the registration form for someone of no fixed address requires:[39]

(i) The declarant's name;[40]

(ii) An address to which the ERO may correspond, or that the declarant is willing to collect correspondence periodically from the ERO's office;[41]

(iii) The date of the declaration;[42]

(iv) That they fall into one of the categories of person who may make a declaration of local connection, specifying which category, and, if resident or detained in a mental hospital, then the hospital address;[43]

(v) The 'required address', namely:

a. If detained or resident in a mental hospital, then the address they would be residing at but for their residence or detention,[44] or, if unable to give such an address, then an address at which they have resided; [45] or

b. If homeless, then the address of, or nearest to, a place in the UK where they *"commonly spend a substantial part of their time*

---

[36] *Simmons v Khan* [2008] EWHC B4 (QB) at 73.
[37] S 7C(1) RPA 1983.
[38] S 7B(2) RPA 1983.
[39] https://assets.publishing.service.gov.uk/government/uploads/system/uploads/attachment_data/file/711758/Register-to-vote-if-you-havent-got-a-fixed-or-permanent-address-England-and-Wales.pdf.
[40] S 7B(3)(a) RPA 1983.
[41] S 7B(3)(a)(i) and (ii) RPA 1983.
[42] S 7B(3)(b) and (10) RPA 1983.
[43] S 7B(3)(c) RPA 1983.
[44] S 7B(3)(d) and (4)(a)(i) RPA 1983.
[45] S 7B(3)(d) and (4)(a)(ii) RPA 1983.

(whether during the day or night)",[46] adding that this has been for the past three months if applying to register in a by-election.[47]

2.18 Registration pursuant to a declaration of local connection lasts for twelve months,[48] but must be removed by the ERO if cancelled by the declarant[49] or the declarant registers elsewhere.[50]

2.19 Disqualified peers may give a declaration of local connection solely for one register (namely: the LE register).[51]

Service declaration

2.20 A further means of satisfying the residence requirement is by way of the 'service declaration'.[52] This is available from the time of leaving to the time of returning to the UK to: (i) members of the forces;[53] (ii) people employed in the service of the Crown in a post outside the UK who are required to devote their whole working time to the duties of that post and whose remuneration is paid wholly out of money provided by Parliament;[54] (iii) people employed by the British Council in a post outside the UK; and (d) their spouse or civil partner if residing outside the UK to be with them.[55]

2.21 The effect is to enable such persons to be treated as resident at the address given in the declaration.[56] The declaration must be attested,[57] must be received within three months of the date of the declaration,[58] and must give certain prescribed information.[59]

---

[46]S 7B(4)(d) RPA 1983.
[47]S 7B(6) RPA 1983.
[48]S 7C(2) RPA 1983.
[49]S 7B(9) RPA 1983.
[50]S 7C(2)(c) RPA 1983.
[51]S 7B(7) RPA 1983.
[52]S 15(1)
[53]Defined by s 59(1) as meaning *"a person serving on full pay as a member of any of the naval, military or air*
forces of the Crown raised in the United Kingdom", to the exclusion of *"(i) a person serving only as a member of a reserve or auxiliary force except in so far as regulations provide that it shall include persons so serving during a period of emergency, or (ii) a member of the regular army whose terms of service are such that, except for the purpose of training, he is required to serve only in Northern Ireland"*.
[54]Reg 14 RP (E&W) Regs 12 2001.
[55]S 14(1) RPA 1983.
[56]S 17 RPA 1983.
[57]S 16(1) RPA 1983.
[58]S 15(8) RPA 1983.
[59]S 16(1) and reg 15 RP (E&W) Regulations 2001.

2.22 Again, registration pursuant to service declaration lasts for twelve months,[60] or sooner if the voter cancels the declaration,[61] another registration takes effect,[62] or the ERO determines that the registration was improperly obtained.[63]

Overseas voters declaration

2.23 Persons not resident in the UK when they apply for registration may register as an overseas elector pursuant to an overseas elector's declaration.[64] To qualify, the applicant must have been registered at an address in the constituency for which they wish to register within the past 15 years (and not registered elsewhere subsequently),[65] or would have been registered in that constituency but were too young.[66]

2.24 Again, registration lasts for twelve months, or sooner if the declaration is revoked or if the ERO determines that the person was not entitled to be registered.[67]

2.25 The 15-year rule has been held compatible with A3P1.[68]

Offences as to declarations

2.26 It is an offence to make or attest a declaration of local connection or a service declaration, or to apply for anonymous registration, when:

(i) Not entitled to do so;

(ii) Subject to a legal incapacity to vote; or

(iii) Knowing that the declaration contains a false statement.[69]

---

[60] S 15(2)(a). This may be replaced by longer period on order made by the Minister for the Cabinet Office: s 15(9)-(12) and 199ZA.

[61] S 15(2)(b) and (7) RPA 1983.

[62] S 15(2)(c) RPA 1983.

[63] S 15(2)(aa) or (ab)

[64] S 2 RPA 1985. Incorporated into the online registration application or available as a separate document here: https://assets.publishing.service.gov.uk/government/uploads/system/uploads/attachment_data/file/711683/Register-to-vote-as-an-overseas-voter-orginally-resident-England-or-Wales.pdf.

[65] S 1(3) RPA 1985.

[66] S 1(4) RPA 1985.

[67] S 2(2) RPA 1985.

[68] *Doyle v UK* (admissibility) (30158/06) [2007] 45 EHRR SE3, p 27; *Shindler v UK* (19840/09) [2014] 58 EHRR 5, at 105.

[69] S 62(1) and (1A) RPA 1983.

Reminders

2.27 Nine to ten months after registration pursuant to a local connection or service declaration, the RO must send the voter a reminder of the need to make a fresh declaration to remain registered, and a second reminder 21-28 days' thereafter.[70]

Legal capacity

2.28 A convicted prisoner detained in prison is legally incapable of voting in Parliamentary or local elections.[71] This blanket restriction on all convicted prisoners in prison has been held incompatible with A3P1[72] but not art 10 ECHR (freedom of expression).[73] The matter is now for Parliament and the courts have refused to issue further declarations of incompatibility.[74]

Age

2.29 The applicant for registration must be 18 years or over.[75] A 16-17 year-old who will turn 18 within the year prior to the next 1st December also satisfies the age criterion,[76] but the ERO must ensure their entry gives the date on which they become 18.

2.30 The imposition of a minimum age has been held compatible with A3P1.[77]

B. THE ERO AND THE REGISTERS

The ERO

2.31 The registration of voters is performed by EROs, who must be appointed by the council of every district and London borough (England), and every county or county borough (in Wales).[78]

The registers

2.32 The PE and LE registers are distinct,[79] but, *"so far as practicable"*, they must be combined, indicating where a voter is registered for only one or the other.[80]

---

[70]Reg 25 RP (E&W) Regulations 2001
[71]S 3 RPA 1983.
[72]*Hirst v UK (no. 2)* (74025/01) [2006] 42 EHRR 41 (GC), at 82.
[73]*Hirst v UK (no. 2)* (74025/01) [2006] 42 EHRR 41 (GC), at 89.
[74]R *(Chester) v Secretary of State for Justice* [2013] UKSC 63, [2014] AC 271.
[75]Ss 1(1)(d) and 2(1)(d) RPA 1983.. In Scotland: 16 or over to register in the RLGE.
[76]S 4(5) RPA 1983.
[77]*Hirst v UK (no. 2)* (74025/01) (2006) 42 EHRR 41 (GC), at 62.
[78]S 8 RPA 1983.
[79]S 9(1) RPA 1983.
[80]S 9(5) RPA 1983.

2.33 The registers must state:

(i) The names of those who have made a successful application for registration;[81]

(ii) Their qualifying addresses[82] (*"the address in respect of which he is entitled to be so registered"*);[83] and

(iii) Their electoral number (as allocated by the ERO, consecutive to the previous allocated).[84]

2.34 Mismanagement of the register so that it omits to mention some registered voters and allows multi-registration of others may affect voters' rights and therefore candidates' right to stand, so breaching A3P1.[85]

The edited register

2.35 The edited register is identical to the full register save that it must omit the name and address of any registered voter who requests the same,[86] including those with anonymous entries.[87] By omitting this personal data, the 'edited register' can be sold and supplied without disclosing the details of a person who wishes to be anonymous.

Misuse of register: offences

2.36 It is an offence for the ERO or their deputy to use, supply or disclose a register other than as permitted by legislation,[88] or for anyone to whom the ERO supplies a register to do so for a purpose other than the purpose for which the register was supplied to them.[89] It is also an offence for anyone granted a request to inspect a register to make copies of it or record it other than by handwritten notes.[90]

ERO's duty to register voters

2.37 The ERO must take all steps necessary to secure that, so far as is reasonably practicable, those *"who are entitled to be registered in a register (and no others) are*

---

[81] S 9(2)(a) RPA 1983.
[82] S 9(2)(b) RPA 1983.
[83] S 9(8)(b) RPA 1983.
[84] S 9(2)(c), (3) and (4) RPA 1983.
[85] *Georgian Labour Party v Georgia* (9103/04) [2009] 48 EHRR 14, at 82-83.
[86] Ss 93 and 93A RP (E&W) Regs 2001.
[87] S 93A(3) RP (E&W) Regs 2001.
[88] Regs 94(3) and 115(1) and (2) RP (E&W) Regs 2001.
[89] Reg 115(1) and (2) RP (E&W) Regs 2001.
[90] Reg 115(1) and (2) RP (E&W) Regs 2001.

registered in it",[91] by (i) conducting an annual canvass of the ERO's area, in order to find out the names and addresses of those entitled to register to vote but not yet registered,[92] and (ii) by taking other prescribed steps deemed necessary by Parliament to secure the overall aim of ensuring those entitled to be registered are registered. Each is explained below.

Annual canvass

2.38 The ERO must attempt to make contact with those at a residential address in the area for which the ERO is responsible and who are eligible, or may be eligible, to be registered in the PE or LE registers.[93]

2.39 Before conducting the annual canvass, '**annual canvass data matching**' must be performed.[94] This requires the ERO to disclose to the Minister for the Cabinet Office, by means notified by the Minister to the ERO, the names, date of birth, address, and unique property reference number (if known) of persons on the ERO's registers,[95] plus any other data specified by the Minister ("**the matching data**"). The Minister may share the matching data with the Secretary of State for Work and Pensions, for comparison with social security databases, before being disclosed back to the ERO. This enables the ERO to determine, without having to canvass, whether the registered persons are still resident at the address and should not be removed from the register and whether an addition to the register is required for that address.[96] Information disclosed to the ERO for purposes of the annual canvass data matching must not be disclosed to any other person or for any other purpose (save legal proceedings).[97] Breach of that prohibition is an offence, for which the guilty is liable to two years' imprisonment for conviction on indictment or one year on summary conviction, or in either case a fine, or both.[98]

2.40 The annual canvass must be conducted as follows:

(i) The ERO must attempt to make contact with those at a residential address in their area and who are eligible, or may be eligible, to be registered in the PE or LE register.[99] They must do so by either (a) sending the paper canvass communication to the address, or (b) visiting

---

[91]S 9A(1) RPA 1983.
[92]S 9D(1) and (2) RPA 1983.
[93]Regs 32ZBA and 32ZBD(1) RP (E&W) Regs 2001.
[94]S 32ZBB RPA 1983.
[95] Only English LE registers, not Welsh.
[96]Regs 32ZBA(4) and 32ZBB(1) RP (E&W) Regs 2001.
[97]Reg 32ZBC(1) RP (E&W) Regs 2001.
[98]Reg 32ZBC(1) RP (E&W) Regs 2001.
[99]Regs 32ZBA and 32ZBD(1) RP (E&W) Regs 2001.

the address in order to obtain the information required by the canvass form;[100]

(ii) If no information in response is received within a reasonable time, the ERO must make a further attempt to make contact with at least one person at the address, in order to obtain the information required by the canvass form;[101]

(iii) The ERO must repeat this attempt if, within a further reasonable time, still no information in response is received;[102]

(iv) These follow-up attempts may be performed by: (a) sending a paper communication to the address, as per the original attempt; (b) making a telephone call or email to each registered voter whom the ERO believes are resident at that address and for whom the ERO holds a telephone number or email address (though only one person at the address needs to be telephoned if that person provides the information required by the canvass form, or if the ERO holds the same number for each perceived resident);[103] or (c) by visiting the address;[104]

(v) In the second follow-up attempt to make contact, if the ERO has not already sent a paper communication or the canvass form, or made a telephone call, they must do so on this second attempt. If the canvass form had not already been sent, it must be sent rather than the paper communication;[105]

(vi) The canvass form that is sent out must be accompanied by prepaid return envelope[106] and, if possible, be pre-populated with: (a) any information that it requires and that the ERO already holds; (b) the full name and nationality of registered voters believed to be at the address; (c) (for persons on the LE register voters in Wales who are aged 16 or over) their date of birth.[107]

2.41 The ERO does not have to canvass an address in their area in the following two cases:

(i) Where the ERO (a) already knows the name of the person registered at that address, based on the ERO's own registration and alteration data,

---

[100]Reg 32ZBD(1) RP (E&W) Regs 2001. The canvass communication and form have been designed by the Commission are available on its website.
[101]Reg 32ZBD(2) RP (E&W) Regs 2001.
[102]Reg 32ZBD(3) RP (E&W) Regs 2001.
[103]Reg 32ZBD(8) RP (E&W) Regs 2001.
[104]Reg 32ZBD(4) RP (E&W) Regs 2001.
[105]Reg 32ZBD(5)-(7) RP (E&W) Regs 2001.
[106]Reg 32ZBD(9)(b) RP (E&W) Regs 2001.
[107]Reg 32ZBD(9)(a) RP (E&W) Regs 2001.

and data provided by the Minister pursuant to data matching; (b) is satisfied that is not necessary to remove the person's name from the register; (c) has *"no reason to believe"* that an addition to the register is required for that address; and (d) remains of that view after conducting the canvass in the wider electoral area;[108]

(ii) Where (a) the address is a registered care home,[109] property at which care home services are situated,[110] house in multiple occupation,[111] student hall of residence,[112] hostel, or property to which the ERO has attempted to deliver a document in the previous 18 months but was unable and that property was one where people who do not form a single household reside together, and (b) the ERO can identify a person from whom they may request information as to residents' names, nationality and whether they are aged 76, who lawfully holds or has access to this information and may lawfully disclose it to the ERO ("**the responsible person**").[113] If the requested information is not returned, however, the ERO must revert to the annual canvass method.[114]

2.42 In relation to properties where either of these two exceptions apply, the ERO may nonetheless conduct an alternative form of annual canvass, by sending each address:

(i) A 'canvass communication A' (a Commission-designed document),[115] pre-populated with the individual's name and nationality;[116] and

(ii) If the ERO holds an email address for any person at the address: an email requesting (a) confirmation that the information in the email is correct; (b) the name and nationality over every person aged 16 years or over residing at the address and eligible to register, as well as confirmation as to whether they are aged 76 or over.[117]

2.43 The ERO must conduct the mandatory annual canvass of that address if this discretionary canvass returns information leading the ERO to believe that (i) a person who resides there may be entitled to be registered, but the ERO remain

---

[108]Reg 32ZBA(4) RP (E&W) Regs 2001.
[109]Under Part 2 Care Standards Act 2000.
[110]Under the Regulation and Inspection of Social Care (Wales) Act 2016.
[111]Within the meaning of s 254 Housing Act 2004.
[112]Within the meaning of para 4 sch 14 Housing Act 2004.
[113]Reg 32ZBF RP (E&W) Regs 2001.
[114]Reg 32ZBF(7) RP (E&W) Regs 2001.
[115]https://www.electoralcommission.org.uk/registration-forms-and-letters [accessed 4.6.2020].
[116]Reg 32ZBE(6) RP (E&W) Regs 2001.
[117]Reg 32ZBE(3)(b) and (4) RP (E&W) Regs 2001.

unaware of their name; or (ii) it may after all be necessary to remove a person registered at that address from a register.[118]

Other necessary steps

2.44 In addition to the annual canvass and in part to support it, the ERO must also do the following:

(i) Contact those not registered by any means the ERO thinks appropriate;[119]

(ii) Inspect any records the ERO is entitled to inspect;

(iii) Train staff to assist in the carrying out of the ERO's duty;[120]

(iv) Make multiple attempts to contact persons by telephone;[121]

(v) LE: send the canvass form more than once;[122]

(vi) Make multiple house to house inquiries,[123] for instance: (a) to obtain information before sending out the canvass form or communication; (b) LE: to obtain the information required by the canvass form; (c) to supplement information provided on the canvass form; or (d) where no canvass form is returned.[124]

Invitation and requirement to apply for registration

2.45 If the ERO becomes aware of a person who is not registered in a register that the ERO maintains, whom the ERO has reason to believe may be entitled to be so registered, and the ERO is aware of their name and address, then, within 28 days of becoming so aware,[125] the ERO must **invite** them to apply for registration.[126] The invitation must be in the form designed by the Commission[127] and may be emailed, delivered in person, or posted to the person in question.[128] If not emailed, it must be accompanied by pre-paid return envelope.[129]

---

[118] Reg 32ZBE(7) RP (E&W) Regs 2001.
[119] S 9A(2)(c) RPA 1983.
[120] S 9A(2) RPA 1983.
[121] S 9A(2)(ba) RPA 1983.
[122] S 9A(2)(a) RPA 1983.
[123] S 9A(2)(b) RPA 1983. In relation to LE voters in Wales, the ERO is not required to perform house to house inquiries in relation to any person under the age of 16: s 9A(2A) RPA 1983.
[124] S 9D(5) RPA 1983.
[125] Reg 32ZC(3)(a) RP (E&W) Regs 2001.
[126] S 9E(1) RPA 1983.
[127] Reg 32ZC(3)(b) RP (E&W) Regs 2001.
[128] Reg 32ZC(3)(za) RP (E&W) Regs 2001.
[129] Reg 32ZC(3)(d) RP (E&W) Regs 2001.

2.46 If the person invited has not applied to register upon three ERO invitations to do so, the ERO may then send the person a **requirement to register** by a specified date.[130] If so, the ERO must give the invitee notice (i) of the deadline for applying; (ii) that the ERO may impose a civil penalty if no response; (iii) of the amount of civil penalty (£80)[131] and interest rate if not paid on time (8%);[132] (iv) that they may make representations as to why a penalty should be imposed; and (v) that they must inform the ERO if they are not in fact eligible to register and why, or that they are already registered at another address and what that address is.[133] When so notifying, the ERO must also provide the prescribed paper application form for applying to register, if possible with the person's name and address already filled in.[134]

2.47 The ERO must cancel the requirement to register if: (a) satisfied that they are not eligible to register or are registered at a different address; or (b) realising any of the steps prior to requiring a person to register have not been completed (i.e. three invitations sent to a confirmed address, at least one received, the and the invitee informed of how to apply and of the civil penalty consequence of non-application).[135]

2.48 Where the ERO exercises their discretion to impose a civil penalty, they must give the recipient notice in writing, specifying: the reason(s), the amount due, how to pay, the rate of interest payable for late payment, that they must apply to register or pay the penalty within 28 days (by which payment they would cease to be liable), or request a review of the decision within fourteen days.[136]

2.49 The ERO must cancel the penalty if: (a) the invitee applies for registration; (b) the ERO is satisfied that they are not after all entitled to register at the address to which the invitations were sent, or are registered elsewhere; or (c) they realise any of the preconditions to issuing the requirement to register were not met.[137] The ERO also has a residual discretion to cancel the penalty.[138]

2.50 If within fourteen days the invitee requests a review of the decision to impose a penalty, the ERO must acknowledge the request within seven days, notifying the person that they may make representations and submit evidence within fourteen days of the notice. After that fourteen days, the ERO must carry out the review, either uphold the decision or cancel the penalty, and inform the

---

[130] S 9E(4) RPA 1983; reg 32E RPA 1983.
[131] Reg 32ZF(1) RP (E&W) Regs 2001.
[132] Reg 32ZG(3) RP (E&W) Regs 2001.
[133] Reg 32ZE(3) RP (E&W) Regs 2001.
[134] Reg 32ZE(4) RP (E&W) Regs 2001.
[135] Reg 32ZE(5) RP (E&W) Regs 2001.
[136] Reg 32ZF(2)-(4) RP (E&W) Regs 2001.
[137] Reg 32ZF(5) RP (E&W) Regs 2001.
[138] Reg 32ZF(6) RP (E&W) Regs 2001.

person of the outcome.[139] If the decision is upheld, the ERO must also notify the person that (a) they may appeal against the decision and the review to the First-tier Tribunal (General Regulatory Chamber) and how, but (b) irrespective of any appeal, they must pay the penalty within 28 days.[140] The Tribunal may uphold the decision or cancel the penalty.[141]

2.51 The ERO may enforce the penalty and interest by applying for an order from the County Court.[142]

C. APPLICATIONS TO REGISTER

The application process

2.52 The ERO must enter a person in the registers if: (a) they apply; (b) they appear to the ERO to be entitled to be registered; and (c) they meet any application requirements.[143]

2.53 The Commission has designed an application form that requires the necessary information and declarations.[144] The ERO must supply individuals wishing to apply to register with application forms and may not charge for them.[145]

2.54 In determining an application for registration, the ERO:

(i) May ask the applicant to give further information,[146] but only the information required for purposes of the ERO's duties, not for information to determine whether they are whom they say they are.[147] If the applicant does not provide the information, they are liable to a fine (currently capped at £1,000);

(ii) May ask for evidence of age or nationality;[148] and

---

139 Reg 32ZF(6) RP (E&W) Regs 2001.
140 Reg 32ZF(7) RP (E&W) Regs 2001.
141 Reg 32ZI(2) RP (E&W) Regs 2001.
142 Reg 32ZF(4) RP (E&W) Regs 2001.
143 S 10ZC RPA 1983.
144 Reg 26 RPA (England and Wales) Regulations 2001; https://www.gov.uk/register-to-vote and for printing: https://assets.publishing.service.gov.uk/government/uploads/system/uploads/attachment_data/file/711618/Register_to_vote_if_you_re_living_in_England_or_Wales.pdf
145 Reg 4 Representation of the People (England and Wales) Regulations 2001.
146 Reg 29(3) RP (E&W) Regs 2001.
147 Reg 23 RP (E&W) Regs 2001.
148 Regs 24 and 26 RP (E&W) Regs 2001.

(iii) Must consider any objection made by another person, if it complies with requirements for objection[149] and is made by someone else on the same register.[150]

2.55 If no objection is made to the application to register within five days of its entry by the ERO in the list of applications, the ERO may allow an application.[151]

Anonymous registration

2.56 When applying for registration, an application may also be made for the entry in the registers to be anonymous.[152] The ERO must be satisfied that the safety of the applicant or that of any other person of the same household would be at risk if their name register or address were published in the registers.[153] Victims of domestic violence are the main example. To satisfy the ERO of this test, the application must be accompanied by evidence consisting of relevant court orders or injunctions,[154] or an attestation certifying that the safety of the applicant or person with whom they live would be at risk if their name were on the register.[155]

2.57 If the application for anonymous registration is successful, then (i) the entry shows the individual's electoral number together with the letter 'N';[156] (ii) anything previously held must be removed;[157] and (iii) any communication sent by the ERO to the anonymous voter must be sent in an envelope or other form of covering.[158]

2.58 An anonymous entry lasts for twelve months, or less if the voter cancels the declaration that they made when applying for the anonymity.[159]

---

149 Reg 27 RP (E&W) Regs 2001.
150 S 10ZC(2) RPA 1983.
151 Reg 29(4) RP (E&W) Regs 2001.
152 S 9B(1) RPA 1983.
153 S 9B(2) and (10) RPA 1983.
154 Regs 31G and 31I RP (E&W) Regs 2001. In partnership with Women's Aid, the Commission has issued guidance about supporting survivors of domestic abuse to register to vote (March 2018).
155 Reg s 31G and 31J RP (E&W) Regs 2001.
156 S 9B(3) and 41A RP (E&W) Regs 2001.
157 S 9B(5) RPA 1983.
158 S 9B(8) RPA 1983.
159 S 9C(1) RPA 1983.

Provision of false information offence

2.59 Anyone who provides false information to an ERO is guilty of an offence[160] and an illegal practice.[161] That includes a fake signature.[162] Not knowing and having no reason to suspect that the information was false is a defence.[163]

2.60 *Simmons v Khan*,[164] *Ali v Bashir*[165] and *Erlam v Rahman*,[166] are examples of petitions in which the Election Court found false registration. The names of real and made up persons not resident in the respective wards were registered at addresses in the wards, and those names subsequently used to obtain and cast postal votes. The offence was found irrespective of whether those persons consented to or participated in the process.[167] As some of the names caused to be entered on the register may not have existed at all, they were termed 'ghost voters'.[168]

Electoral identity cards

2.61 In Northern Ireland, electoral identity cards show: (a) the voter's full name and date of birth; (b) their photograph; (c) when the card ceases to be current; and (d) such other information and be in such form as the Chief Electoral Officer shall determine.[169] The Chief Electoral Officer determines application for electoral identity cards.[170] They expire after ten years.[171]

2.62 Providing false information in an application for an identity card is an offence.[172] Not knowing and having no reason to suspect the information provided to be false is a defence.[173]

---

160 S 13D(1) RPA 1983.
161 *Ali v Bashir* [2013] EWHC 2572 (QB) at 273(iii)(a).
162 S 13D(3) RPA 1983.
163 S 13D(4) and (5) RPA 1983.
164 *Simmons v Khan* [2008] EWHC B4 (QB) (the Slough Election case).
165 *Ali v Bashir* [2013] EWHC 2572 (QB).
166 *Erlam v Rahman* [2015] EWHC 1215 (QB).
167 *Simmons v Khan* [2008] EWHC B4 (QB) at 150 and 328.
168 *Simmons v Khan* [2008] EWHC B4 (QB) at 150 and 328; *Ali v Bashir* [2013] EWHC 2572 (QB). *Erlam v Rahman* [2015] EWHC 1215 (QB), at 334.
169 S 13C RPA 1983.
170 S 13C RPA 1983.
171 S 13C RPA 1983.
172 S 13CZA RPA 1983.
173 S 13CZA RPA 1983.

D. ABSENT VOTING (PROXY AND POSTAL)

Application for a proxy vote

2.63 A voter who is unable to vote in person on polling day can appoint someone else to do so on their behalf. That person is their proxy. An application for a proxy vote may be made for a specific type of election or all, for an indefinite period or a specific period.[174] This may be altered subsequently.[175] A voter may have only one proxy at one time.[176]

2.64 Eligibility for a proxy vote for a particular elections arises when a voter's circumstances on polling day are likely to mean they cannot reasonably be expected to vote in person at the polling station likely to be allotted to them.[177]

2.65 Eligibility for a proxy vote for an indefinite or definite period is afforded to the following:

(i) Those registered pursuant to a service declaration or overseas elector's declaration;

(ii) Those with an anonymous entry in the register;

(iii) Those who cannot reasonably be expected to go in person to their allotted polling station or to vote unaided by reason of disability, the nature of their occupation, or by reason of attendance on an education course (university students);

(iv) Those who could not vote in person without making a journey by air or sea.[178]

2.66 An ERO will grant an application to vote by proxy if they are satisfied that the applicant: (a) is eligible; (b) is or will be registered to vote; and (c) had made a compliant application.[179] A compliant application features a statement that the proposed proxy is capable of being appointed and is willing to be so appointed,[180] whether they have applied for anonymous entry,[181] and:

(i) If applying for a proxy vote for an indefinite or definite period (rather than a particular election), the application must be attested and signed by a healthcare professional, who must state where they are treating or

---

[174]Reg 51(4) and (5) RP (E&W) Regs 2001.
[175]Para 3(6), sch 4, RPA 2000.
[176]Para 6(2), sch 4, RPA 2000.
[177]Para 4, sch 4, RPA 2000.
[178]Para 3(3), sch 4, RPA 2000; art 8(2) NAWRPO 2007.
[179]Paras 3 and 4, sch 4, RPA 2000.
[180]Reg 52RP (E&W) Regs 12 2001.
[181]Reg 51 RP (E&W) Regs 12 2001.

caring for the applicant in respect to their disability (if a doctor or nurse), that the applicant has the disability mentioned in their application form and cannot be reasonably be expected to go to their allotted polling station or vote unaided;[182]

(ii) If applying for a proxy vote for a particular election: the circumstances prevailing on the day of the election that mean they cannot reasonably be expected to vote in person at their allotted polling station (unless they have an anonymous entry).[183]

2.67 It is an offence to make a knowingly false declaration or attestation, or knowingly attest without the purported authority.[184]

Deadline

2.68 An application to vote by proxy, whether for a particular election or a definite period or indefinitely, must reach the ERO before 5pm six days before polling day.[185] If the relevant grounds for eligibility arose thereafter, the deadline is 5pm on polling day.[186]

Restrictions on proxies

2.69 A proxy must be 18 or over by polling day (16 for Welsh Assembly elections), themselves registered to vote in the type of election for which they are to act as proxy, and not subject to any legal incapacity.[187]

2.70 A person may not vote as proxy in one constituency, electoral area, or Assembly constituency for more than two voters of whom they are not the spouse, civil partner, parent, grandparent, brother, sister, child or grandchild.[188]

Application for a postal vote

2.71 An ERO will grant an application to vote by post at a particular election, for a definite period or indefinitely, if satisfied that (i) the applicant is registered to vote, and (ii) their application is in writing, dated, and states the applicant's name and registered address, address to which the ballot paper should be sent, and whether they have applied for anonymous entry.[189]

---

[182]Para 3, sch 4, RPA 2000; reg 53 RP (E&W) Regs 12 2001.
[183]Para 4, sch 4 RPA 2000; reg 55 RP (E&W) Regs 12 2001.
[184]Para 8, sch 4, RPA 2000.
[185]S 56(2) and (3) RP (E&W) Regs 2001.
[186]S 56(3A) RP (E&W) Regs 2001.
[187]Para 6(3) and (3A), sch 4, RPA 2000; art 11(3) and (4) NAWRPO 2007
[188]Para 6, sch 4, RPA 2000; art 11(5) NAWRPO 2007.
[189]Para 4(1) and 5(1), sch 4, RPA 2000; reg 51 RP (E&W) Regs 12 2001.

2.72 An application to vote by post, whether for a particular election or a definite period or indefinitely, must arrive before 5pm on the eleventh day before polling day.[190]

2.73 In *Knight v Nicholls*,[191] a number of postal ballot papers were received late due to delay by the postal service. It was alleged in an election petition that this put the ERO in breach of his duty. The Court disagreed, holding that the ERO's duty was completed when he delivered the ballot papers to the postal service, correctly addressed to the voter.[192]

Refusal and appeal

2.74 Where the ERO refuses an application for postal or proxy vote, they must notify the applicant.[193] The applicant has fourteen days from receipt of the notice to notify the ERO that they wish to appeal and to specify the grounds for the same.[194] The ERO must forward that notice of appeal to the County Court together with a statement of the facts in the case, their decision and on any point raised by the appeal.[195]

Offences relating to applications for postal and proxy votes

2.75 It is an offence and a corrupt practice (for election petition purposes)[196] for a person to do any of the following acts if, by doing so, they intend to (a) deprive someone of an opportunity to vote, (b) gain a vote for themselves or someone else to which either are not entitled, or (c) gain money or property:

(i) Apply for a postal vote, proxy vote, or proxy postal vote[197] as some other person (whether that other person is living, dead, or fictitious);[198]

(ii) Make a false statement in, or in connection with, an application for a postal or proxy vote;[199] or

(iii) Induce the ERO or RO to send a postal ballot paper or any communication relating to a postal or proxy vote to an address not

[190] Reg 56(1) and (4) RP (E&W) Regs 2001.
[191] *Knight v Nicholls* [2004] EWCA Civ 68.
[192] *Knight v Nicholls* [2004] EWCA Civ 68, at 26, per Tuckey LJ.
[193] Reg 57(4) RP (E&W) Regs 2001.
[194] Reg 58(1) RP (E&W) Regs 2001.
[195] Reg 58(2) RP (E&W) Regs 2001.
[196] See Chapter 5.
[197] S 62A(4)(a) RPA 1983.
[198] S 62A(2)(d) RPA 1983; art 14(8)(a) NAWRPO 2007.
[199] S 62A(2)(b) RPA 1983; art 14(8)(b) NAWRPO 2007.

agreed to by the person entitled to the vote,[200] or cause it not to be delivered to the intended recipient.[201]

2.76 Thus the vote does not have to be cast to amount to corrupt practice.

2.77 It is likewise an offence to aid, abet, counsel or procure such an offence.[202]

2.78 In *Erlam v Rahman*,[203] the Election Court described three forms of this offence:

> "349 ...The first is to make an application for a postal vote ('ATV') on behalf of an existing person, to complete the details with one's own particulars and thereafter to use the postal voting documentation to cast the ballot. This is not only personation under s 60 but a corrupt practice in itself under s 62A.
>
> 350 The second is to obtain a copy of the voter's ATV and to use it to complete his personal voting statement ('PVS') which must accompany the postal ballot before submitting the PVS and the ballot paper to the returning officer.
>
> 351 The third is to persuade the voter to hand over a completed and signed PVS but a blank ballot paper, to complete the ballot and submit both to the returning officer."[204]

2.79 In *Ali v Bashir*,[205] the respondent was guilty by himself and his agents of offences relating to applications for postal and proxy votes, where discrepant signatures between voters' application for postal vote, application for registration, and postal vote statements, visible to the untrained eye and confirmed by expert handwriting witnesses, but missed by the RO's signature recognition computer.[206]

Lists

2.80 The ERO must maintain the following lists:

(i) The postal voters list, showing those whose applications to vote by post at a particular election have been granted, and those who are for the time being registered to vote by post;[207]

---

[200] S 62A(2)(c) RPA 1983; art 14(8)(c) NAWRPO 2007.
[201] S 62A(2)(d) RPA 1983; art 14(8)(d) NAWRPO 2007.
[202] S 62(5) RPA 1983; art 14(11) NAWRPO 2007.
[203] *Erlam v Rahman* [2015] EWHC 1215 (QB).
[204] *Erlam v Rahman* [2015] EWHC 1215 (QB) at 349-351.
[205] *Ali v Bashir* [2013] EWHC 2572 (QB).
[206] *Ali v Bashir* [2013] EWHC 2572 (QB), 152-156.
[207] Para 5(2) sch 4 RPA 2000; art 10(2) NAWRPO 2007.

(ii) The list of proxies, showing those whose applications to vote by proxy at the election have been granted, and those who are for the time being so registered to vote by post, together with the names and addresses of their proxies;[208] and

(iii) The personal identifiers record, containing the name, signature and dates of birth provided by successful applicants for proxy or postal voting.[209]

E. ALTERATION OF THE REGISTER

Application to amend

2.81 If a person who is entitled to register applies to amend the name and address on an existing entry, the ERO must make the alteration, albeit taking into account any objection by any other registered voter.[210]

Removal from register

2.82 A person's right to remain registered ceases (and the ERO must remove their entry) if the ERO determines that:

(i) They were not entitled to be registered in respect to the address at which they registered;

(ii) They no longer satisfy the requirements for registration; or

(iii) Someone else had applied for registration.[211]

2.83 The ERO must consider whether to make such a determination if:

(i) They become aware of information that causes them to suspect that one of these conditions is satisfied; or

(ii) They receive objection to a person's registration.[212] Such an objection may not be made about an anonymous entry and must be made by prescribed means.[213]

2.84 Entries cannot be removed from the registers on these grounds in the case of those in mental health hospitals or remanded in custody, or registered pursuant

[208] Para 5(3) sch 4 RPA 2000; art 10(3) NAWRPO 2007.
[209] Reg 61B RP (E&W) Regs 2001.
[210] S 10ZD RPA 1983.
[211] S 10ZE(1) and (2) RPA 1983.
[212] S 10ZE(5) RPA 1983.
[213] S 10ZE(6) and reg 27 RP (E&W) Regs 2001.

to declarations of local connection, service declarations or overseas' declarations.[214]

F. REGISTRATION APPEALS

2.85 Appeal lies to the County Court from the following ERO decisions:

(i) To refuse an application for registration;[215]

(ii) To refuse an application for registration following objection being made;[216]

(iii) Not to alter a register following an application for the same;[217]

(iv) To alter a register following an application in a case where an objection has been made;[218]

(v) That a person's entitlement to be registered has ceased, as a result of which their entitlement to remain registered terminates;[219]

(vi) Not to make a determination, following an objection, that a person's entitlement to be registered has ceased;[220]

(vii) To refuse an application for anonymous registration;[221] and

(viii) Disallowing a person's application to vote by proxy, by post, or by post as proxy, in any case where the application is not made for a particular election only.[222]

2.86 Appeal does not lie where the subject of the ERO decision has not first availed themselves of their right to make representations to the ERO on the matter.[223] The County Court's jurisdiction is likewise excluded if the appellant does not notify the ERO of the appeal within fourteen days of the decision under appeal.[224]

2.87 Where the appellant does give notice of their appeal in accordance with this statutory requirement, the ERO must, within seven days of receiving the notice, forward it by post to the County Court together with a statement of the material

[214] S 10ZE(7) RPA 1983.
[215] S 56(1)(a) RPA 1983.
[216] S 56(1)(aza) RPA 1983.
[217] S 56(1)(azb) RPA 1983.
[218] S 56(1)(azc) RPA 1983.
[219] S 56(1)(azd) RPA 1983.
[220] S 56(1)(aa) RPA 1983.
[221] S 56(1)(ab) RPA 1983.
[222] S 56(1)(b) RPA 1983; art 5(1) NAWRPO 2007.
[223] S 56(1) RPA 1983; reg 32(2) RP (E&W) Regs 2001.
[224] S 56(1) RPA 1983; reg 32(2) RP (E&W) Regs 2001.

facts which in the ERO's opinion have been established in the case, and the ERO's decision on the case and on any point which may be specified as a ground of appeal.[225] On appeal, the statement is admissible as evidence of the facts stated in them and the court can make any decision or draw any inference that could be made by the ERO.[226]

2.88 An appeal lies from the County Court to the Court of Appeal, but no appeal to the Supreme Court lies thereafter.[227]

2.89 An appeal pending when notice of an election is given does not prejudice the election,[228] unless, as a result of the decision on an appeal, an alteration in the register must be made and takes effect on or before the date of the poll.[229]

2.90 Notice of the decision of the County Court or Court of Appeal must be sent to the ERO, who must make such alterations in the register as necessary to give effect to the decision.[230]

Revised register: publication, supply and request

2.91 The ERO must publish a revised version of the registers each year, between the end of the annual canvass and 1st December, featuring any alterations that have been made.[231]

2.92 On publication of a revised version of the registers, each ERO must supply one, free, printed copy and one soft copy of any revised version of the register and list of overseas voters to the British Library.[232] Each ERO in England and Wales must also supply a copy on the same terms to the National Library of Wales[233] and the National Library of Scotland.[234]

2.93 Upon their request, the ERO must supply the following persons with a revised version of the register, a notice setting out an alteration, and a list of overseas voters:[235]

(i) Elected representatives (for electoral purposes or in connection with their office);[236]

---

[225] Reg 32(3) RP (E&W) Regs 2001.
[226] CPR PD52D.
[227] S 56(2) RPA 1983; art 5(2) NAWRPO 2007.
[228] S 56(3) RPA 1983.
[229] S 56(4A) RPA 1983.
[230] S 56(4) RPA 1983; art 5(4) NAWRPO 2007.
[231] S 13 RPA 1983.
[232] Reg 97 RP (E&W) Regs 2001.
[233] Reg 97A RP (E&W) Regs 2001.
[234] Reg 97B RP (E&W) Regs 2001.
[235] Reg 102 RP (E&W) Regs 2001.
[236] Reg 103 RP (E&W) Regs 2001.

(ii) Candidates (for the purpose of complying with the controls on donations);[237]

(iii) Persons within local constituency parties nominated by each registered political party's ("**RP**'s") registered nominating officer (for electoral purposes or the purposes of electoral registration);[238]

(iv) An RP other than a minor party (for electoral purposes and the purposes of complying with the controls on donations);[239]

(v) A recognised third party (campaigning organisations), other than an RP (for electoral purposes and the purposes of complying with the controls on donations);[240]

(vi) The Security Services (for indeterminate purpose), police forces and other agencies (prevention and detection of crime and the enforcement of the criminal law);[241]

(vii) A public library or local authority archives service (which may be made available for inspection but not so as to permit electronic search by name).[242]

2.94 The request must be made in writing, specify the documents requested, state whether a printed copy is requested rather than the default provision in data form, and state whether only current documents are sought or also any new documents when published and that the person requesting is entitled to receive.[243] Candidates can only request current documents.[244] The ERO must supply the requested part of the relevant documents.[245]

2.95 Recipients may not supply it to anyone else, disclose information on it, or use information on it other than for the purposes in brackets above.[246] It is an offence to do otherwise.[247]

---

[237]Regs 104 and 108 RP (E&W) Regs 2001.
[238]Reg 105 RP (E&W) Regs 2001.
[239]Reg 106(1); s 160(1) PPERA.
[240]Reg 106(1); s 85(5) PPERA.
[241]Ss 108A and 109 RP (E&W) Regs 2001.
[242]Reg 109A RP (E&W) Regs 2001.
[243]Reg 102(2) RP (E&W) Regs 2001.
[244]Reg 102(5) RP (E&W) Regs 2001.
[245]Reg 102(4) RP (E&W) Regs 2001.
[246]Reg 103(3)-109(3) RP (E&W) Regs 2001.
[247]Reg 115 RP (E&W) Regs 2001.

2.96 The ERO must supply a copy of the edited register to anyone pays the prescribed fee, which is, for soft copy, £20 plus £1.50 for every 1,000 entries, or, for hard copies, £10 plus £5 for every 1,000 entries.[248]

2.97 The ERO may not sell a copy of the full register or the list of overseas voters,[249] except to government departments, the Environment Agency, the Financial Conduct Authority, Prudential Regulation Authority, United Kingdom Security Vetting, the Security Services, or police forces or other security agencies (for the purpose of the prevention and detection of crime or vetting of employees pursuant to enactment or for the purpose of safeguarding national security).[250] If so, 'Z' is placed by the name of those whose entry is not include in the edited register.[251]

Alteration notices

2.98 Outside of this annual publication, the ERO must also issue notices specifying any change to the content of the registers.[252] The ERO must do so at prescribed intervals:

(i) On the 1st day of the month following the month in which any change to the registers is made, unless that is less than 14 days from the change, in which case the notice must be published on the 1st of the second month after the change;[253]

(ii) On either the 6th or 5th day before the date of the poll;[254]

(iii) On two 'interim publication dates': (i) the last day on which nomination papers may be delivered to the ERO for purposes of an election; and (ii) a day chosen by the ERO between the first interim publication date and before 'the appropriate publication date' (6th or 5th day before polling day)[255]. The change takes effect from the date of publication.[256] If that date is less than 5 days before polling day, the alteration does not have effect in that election,[257] unless:

a. The ERO receives notice of a County Court decision on a successful appeal against the ERO's decision not to register

---

[248] Reg 110 RP (E&W) Regs 2001.
[249] Reg 111 RP (E&W) Regs 2001.
[250] Reg 113 RP (E&W) Regs 2001.
[251] Reg 111(7) RP (E&W) Regs 2001.
[252] S 13A(1) and (2) RPA 1983.
[253] S 13A(2) RPA 1983.
[254] S 13B(3) and (5) RPA 1983.
[255] S 13AB(4)-(6) and 13B(5) RPA 1983.
[256] S 13AB(3) RPA 1983.
[257] S 13B(1) RPA 1983.

someone and it requires an alteration in the register,[258] and the ERO issues a notice specifying the appropriate alteration in the register, which takes effect from the beginning of the day on which the notice is issued;[259] or

b. Following representations that the register contains a clerical error,[260] the ERO determines that the register contains incorrect information and requires alteration,[261] and RO issues a notice specifying the appropriate alteration in the register, which takes effect from the beginning of the day on which the notice is issued.[262]

2.99 The ERO must also issue an alteration notice if, under the Recall of MPs Act 2015, a Speaker's notice is given in relation to a recall petition in respect of an MP, and a day is designated in relation to that petition.[263] If that date is less than five days before polling day, the alteration does not have effect in that election.[264]

G. ERRORS IN THE REGISTERS: VOTING UNAFFECTED

2.100 Where the registers (or any list, record, proxy paper, nomination paper, ballot paper, notice or other document) contain an inaccurate description of a person or place, the operation of the document is not affected if the description is nonetheless commonly understood.[265] This enables individuals with a right to vote to exercise that vote if they turn out to be mistakenly registered under a misnomer or inaccurate description.[266]

[258] S 13B(3A) and (3B) RPA 1983.
[259] S 13B(3A) and (3B) RPA 1983.
[260] S 13B(3E) RPA 1983.
[261] S 13B(3C) and (3D) RPA 1983.
[262] S 13B(3A) and (3B) RPA 1983.
[263] S 13BC(1) and (3) RPA 1983.
[264] S 13B(1) RPA 1983.
[265] S 50 RPA 1983; art 23 NAWRPO 2007.
[266] *R v John Thwaites* [1853] 1 El & Bl 704, p 602, per Lord Campbell CJ.

CHAPTER THREE

ELECTION CAMPAIGNS: AGENTS, EXPENSES AND OFFENCES

3.1 This chapter discusses the following six themes:

A. Candidature;

B. Elections agents;

C. Expenses and donations;

D. Candidates' rights;

E. Campaign offences;

F. Injunctions.

A. CANDIDATURE

Who may be a candidate?

3.2 Parliamentary elections ("**PE**"): To be able to be candidate, a person must not be: (a) an 'alien (neither a Commonwealth citizen,[1] a British-protected person, or a citizen of Ireland);[2] (b) younger than 18, i.e. not a child;[3] or (c) disqualified, by:

(i) Having been sentenced to more than one year's imprisonment,[4] found guilty of a corrupt or illegal practice on an election petition,[5] made subject to a bankruptcy restrictions order;[6] or

---

[1]S 4(6) RPA 1983 defines 'qualifying Commonwealth citizen' as Commonwealth citizen with leave to remain or who does not require it. S 37(1) British Nationality Act 1981 defines 'Commonwealth citizen' as a status enjoyed by British citizens, British Overseas Territory citizens, British Overseas citizens, British subjects, and citizens of independent Commonwealth countries listed in sch 3 British Nationality Act 1981.

[2]S 3 Act of Settlement 1700, as repealed in relation to British subjects and Irish citizens, by British Nationality Act 1948, sch 4; see Schofield's Election Law, 2-002; see Jowitt's Dictionary of English Law 5th Ed., 'Alien', 1.8.19.

[3]S 17(1) Electoral Administration Act 2006.

[4]S 1 RPA 1981.

[5] See Chapter 5.

[6]S 426A Insolvency Act 1986.

(ii) By being in an excluded category: peers,[7] judges (with exceptions), full-time members of the armed forces or police, members of a foreign parliament, member of certain bodies, or holder of certain offices.[8]

3.3 Local elections ("**LE**"): as for PE, save that:

(i) The person must be on the register of local government electors ("**LE register**") for the electoral area, or, for a minimum of twelve months prior to their nomination, have resided, occupied premises in, or had their principal place of work in the area;[9]

(ii) Citizens of EU countries will not be aliens until the legislation is amended and, thereafter, if they are citizens of countries with whom the UK has reached a bilateral reciprocal agreement on voting and candidacy will also not be aliens;[10]

(iii) The disqualifying criteria are: holding paid office or employment with the council (including teachers in maintained schools), having been convicted within the past five years of an offence for which they were sentenced to not less than three months' imprisonment without option of a fine.[11]

3.4 London Assembly elections ("**LAE**"): as for LE, save that the person may be on any LE register in Greater London, or resided or worked in any area in London.[12]

3.5 Welsh Assembly elections ("**WAE**"): as for PE, save that: (i) MPs cannot be Welsh Assembly candidates; (ii) the disqualifications list is slightly different.[13]

3.6 Police and crime commissioner elections ("**PCCE**"): To be a candidate, a person must be:

(i) 18 when nominated;[14]

(ii) England: on the LE register with an address in the police area on the date nominated and election day;[15]

(iii) Wales: on the date nominated and election day, either: (a) registered on the PE register at an address in the police area (not pursuant to an

---

[7] *In Re Parliamentary Election for Bristol South East* [1964] 2 QB 257, at pp 260-261.
[8] House of Commons Disqualification Act 1975.
[9] S 79 Local Government Act 1972.
[10] HL Deb, 18.6.19, cWS).
[11] S 80 Local Government Act 1972.
[12] S 20 Greater London Authority Act 1999.
[13] Sch 1 National Assembly for Wales (Disqualification) Order 2015.
[14] S 64(1)(a) Police Reform and Social Responsibility Act 2011.
[15] S 64(1)(b) Police Reform and Social Responsibility Act 2011.

overseas' elector's declaration); or (b) registered on the LE register at an address in the police area if an EU citizen or disqualified from voting in PE.[16]

Job share

3.7 Multiple candidates cannot stand as a single candidate on a job-share basis, and arts 8 and 14, and A3P1 ECHR do not require a court to interpret otherwise, even when a candidate is disabled or cares for disabled persons.[17]

When does someone become a 'candidate'?

3.8 A person becomes a candidate at a given election when: (a) that election has commenced (upon dissolution of Parliament (PE) or the Welsh Assembly (WAE) or the occurrence of the vacancy (PE or WAE), or the last day for publication of notice of the election (LE)); and (b) one of the following occurs:

(i) They declare themselves to be candidate;

(ii) They are declared by others as such;

(iii) They are nominated as such; or

(iv) A party list on which they feature is submitted (LAE London members).[18]

3.9 If the circumstances listed above occur before the election commences, then the person becomes candidate on the day the election commences.[19]

3.10 A person in respect to whom one of (i)-(iv) above has occurred may be termed, until the election commences, a 'prospective candidate'.

How does a candidate get on the ballot paper?

3.11 The law on the requirements for nomination is set out in Chapter 4, on the conduct of elections, but in summary: to be a candidate whom voters can vote for, a candidate has to be listed by the returning officer ("**RO**") on the statement of persons nominated. To be included on that list, the candidate, their proposer or their seconder must deliver the following to the RO, at a place fixed by the RO:

---

[16] S 64(1A)-(1C) Police Reform and Social Responsibility Act 2011.

[17] R. *(on the application of Cope) v Returning Officer for the Basingstoke Parliamentary Constituency* [2015] EWHC 3958 (Admin), 20-22.

[18] S 118A RPA 1983; s 84(2) NAWRPO 2007.

[19] S 118A RPA 1983.

(i) Nomination papers, in the form appended to the relevant rules, subscribed by two electors as proposer and seconder, and by eight (PE) or two (LE) other electors as assenting to the nomination;

(ii) Statement of consent to nomination;

(iii) Certificate issued by party nomination officers authorising use of a description;

(iv) Home address form (PE); and

(v) Deposit (not LE).

3.12 Delivery of nomination papers must be made between 10am and 4pm, no later than:

(i) PE: six days after the dissolution of Parliament (general elections),[20] or (by-elections) a date set by the RO, which may not be earlier than the third day after publication of the election notice and not later than later than the seventh day after that on which the writ is received;[21] or

(ii) LE, LAE, WAE and PCCE: the 19th day before the election.[22]

Withdrawal of candidature

3.13 Within the same window for delivery of nomination papers, and to the same place, a candidate may withdraw their candidacy by delivering notice of withdrawal of candidature, signed by them and attested by a witness.[23]

B. ELECTION AGENT

Appointment of election agent

3.14 An election agent is the person responsible for the management of a candidate's election campaign, particularly in terms of paying the candidate's election expenses and to make and submit the candidate's return as to election expenses.

3.15 Within the time for delivery of notices of withdrawals, each candidate must:

---

[20] R 1 sch 1 RPA 1983.

[21] R 1 sch 1 RPA 1983.

[22] R 1, schs 2 and 3, LEPAR 2006; r 7 GLAE Rules 2007; r 1 sch 5 NAWRPO 2007; r 1 sch 3 PCCEO 2012.

[23] R 13 sch 1 RPA 1983; r 13 of schs 2 and 3 LEPAR 2006; r 14(1) sch 1 GLAE Rules 2007; r 1 sch 5 NAWRPO 2007; r 1 sch 3 PCCEO 2012.

(i) Name one person as their election agent[24] which may be the candidate, naming themselves as election agent,[25] unless the candidate is a party list candidate;[26]

(ii) Provide written declaration as to the agent's name and address to the RO,[27] and signed by the agent or accompanied by signed written declaration of acceptance;[28]

(iii) The agent's address must be in the same or adjoining constituency, Welsh county borough or London borough, or electoral area;[29]

(iv) LAE and WAE: If they are a party list candidate: be named on a list submitted by that party's nominating officer.[30]

3.16 The RO must then give public notice of the agent's name and address.[31] This is the address for service of any claims, and the office to which all claims, notices, legal process and other documents may be sent.[32]

3.17 If no agent is appointed, then the candidate is deemed to have named themselves as election agent.[33]

3.18 The appointment may be revoked by the candidate.[34] If so, or the agent dies, another agent must be appointed and their name and address provided to the RO.[35]

3.19 It is an offence for a RO, officer or clerk, or their partner or clerk, to act as candidate's agent in the conduct or management of the election.[36]

Appointment of polling and counting agents

3.20 No later than the fifth day before polling day (excluding weekends or bank holidays), each candidate (or their election agent) may give notice in writing of their appointment of: (i) polling agents, to attend as observers at polling station

---

[24] S 67(3) RPA 1983; art 37 GLAER 2007; r 37(1) NAWRPO 2007; art 26(1)(a) PCCEO 2012.
[25] S 67(2) RPA 1983; r 37(2) NAWRPO 2007; art 26(2) PCCEO 2012.
[26] S 67(2A) RPA 1983; r 37(1) NAWRPO 2007.
[27] S 67(1) and (2) RPA 1983; art 37(1) NAWRPO 2007; art 26(1)(b) PCCEO 2012.
[28] S 67(5) RPA 1983.
[29] S 69(2) RPA 1983; art 39(2) NAWRPO 2007.
[30] S 67(2A) RPA 1983; art 37(3) NAWRPO 2007.
[31] S 67(6) RPA 1983; art 37(9) NAWRPO 2007; art 26(7) PCCEO 2012.
[32] S 69(3) RPA 1983; art 39(1) NAWRPO 2007.
[33] S 70 RPA 1983; art 37(5) NAWRPO 2007.
[34] S 67(3) RPA 1983; art 37(6) NAWRPO 2007.
[35] S 67(4) RPA 1983; art 37(7) NAWRPO 2007; art 26(5) PCCEO 2012.
[36] S 99(1) RPA 1983; art 71(1) NAWRPO 2007.

for the purpose to detect personation; and (ii) counting agents to attend at the counting of the votes.[37]

3.21 The RO may limit the number of counting agents so that each candidate has the same number, but that number can be less than the number of counting clerks divided by the number of candidates.[38]

3.22 LE and WAE: the same person may be appointed to both roles.[39]

3.23 LAE and PCCE: one of the counting agents may be authorised to request a recount.[40]

3.24 Not more than one polling agent may be admitted to a polling station per candidate. LE, LAE, and PCCE: the maximum number of polling agents for any candidate that are permitted to attend a particular polling station is four per polling station, or more if the RO so notifies, and if the number of appointed polling agents exceeds that cap, then lots are drawn.[41]

C. EXPENSES AND DONATIONS

3.25 This section of the chapter discusses the restrictions on candidates' election spending and on the donations they can receive, as well as their obligation to submit a return detailing that spending and the donations that they receive.

Expenses

Scope: meaning of 'election expenses'

3.26 'Election expense' was defined by the Court of Appeal in *R v Fiona Jones and R v Desmond Whicher*, adoption the trial judge's definition:[42]

> "An "election expense" is "spending during the election campaign or when it is reasonably imminent on something closely related to the machinery of the election, its processes, principally or primarily with the purpose and intention of promoting the candidate's election prospects".[43]

---

[37]R 30 sch 1 RPA 1983; r 31 sch 2 GLAER 2007; r 38 sch 5 NAWRPO 2007; r 31(1) sch 3 PCCEO 2012.

[38]R 30(2) sch 1 RPA 1983; r 27(4) sch 2 LEPAR 2006; r 30(6) sch 1 GLAER 2007; r 38(2) sch 5 NAWRPO 2007.

[39]R 27(2) sch 2 LEPAR 2006; para 30(2) sch 1 GLAER 2007.

[40]R 30(1)(b) and (3) sch 1 RPA 1983; r 27(1) sch 2 LEPAR 2006; r 30(1) sch 1 GLAER 2007.

[41]R 27(3) sch 2 LEPAR 2006; r 30(4) and (5) sch 1 GLAER 2007; r 31(4) sch 3 PCCEO 2012.

[42]R *v Fiona Jones and* R *v Desmond Whicher* [1999] 2 Cr App R 253.

[43]R *v Fiona Jones and* R *v Desmond Whicher* [1999] 2 Cr App R 253, p 256E-F, per Lord Bingham LCJ.

3.27 Where 'election expenses' means expenses incurred at any time in respect of any item on the following exhaustive list, when used to promote a candidate's election after the date when they become a candidate:[44]

(i) Advertising and attendant agency fees, design costs and other costs;[45]

(ii) Unsolicited material addressed to electors, plus any attendant fees;[46]

(iii) Transport and ancillary costs[47] (other than transport acquired by the candidate, or provided to them free of charge by someone else, principally for their personal use);[48]

(iv) Public meetings, plus attendant expenses;[49]

(v) The services of an election agent or other person engaged in connection with the candidate's election;[50]

(vi) Accommodation and administrative costs[51] (other than the candidate's sole or main residence).[52]

3.28 *R v Jones*,[53] the court held that the cost of compiling a *"data base recording which members of the public are thought to support a party's cause", "for use in an imminent general election, ... may well and perhaps (depending on the facts) normally would be an election expense."*[54]

3.29 The following fall outside the definition of 'election expenses':

(i) The payment of the deposit when delivering nomination papers;[55]

(ii) PE, LE and LAE: anything reasonably attributable to a candidate's disability;[56]

---

[44]S 90ZA(1)-(3) RPA 1983; art 63 NAWRPO 2007.
[45]Paras 1 sch 4A RPA 1983; para 1 sch 7 NAWRPO 2007.
[46]Paras 2 sch 4A RPA 1983; para 2 sch 7 NAWRPO 2007.
[47]Paras 3 sch 4A RPA 1983; para 3 sch 7 NAWRPO 2007.
[48]Paras 12 sch 4A RPA 1983; para 4 sch 7 NAWRPO 2007.
[49]Para 4 sch 4A RPA 1983; para 5 sch 7 NAWRPO 2007.
[50]Para 5 sch 4A RPA 1983; para 6 sch 7 NAWRPO 2007.
[51]Para 6 sch 4A RPA 1983; para 6 sch 7 NAWRPO 2007. This is the category into which the expenses in *R v Fiona Jones and R v Desmond Whicher*, unreported, 22.4.99, Court of Appeal (Criminal Division), case numbers 98/1801/S2 98/1802/S2 would have fallen: £350.00 shown for use during the election period of an office including telephones and computer equipment [transcript, pp 10-11].
[52]Paras 4 and 11 Sch 4A RPA 1983.
[53]R *v Fiona Jones and* R *v Desmond Whicher* [1999] 2 Cr App R 253.
[54]R *v Fiona Jones and* R *v Desmond Whicher* [1999] 2 Cr App R 253, p 263D-E.
[55]Para 7 sch 4A RPA 1983; para 7 sch 7 NAWRPO 2007.
[56]Para 7A sch 4A RPA 1983.

(iii) Publication of anything relating to the election in a newspaper or other periodical, or in a broadcast by the BBC or Sianel Pedwar Cymru, or in a programme included in any independent television service licensed by OFCOM;[57]

(iv) Facilities provided by local authority for meetings as candidate's election entitlement (see below);[58]

(v) The candidate's voluntary use of their own time;[59]

(vi) Accommodation that is the candidate's main residence;[60]

(vii) Transport by means originally acquired for personal use;[61]

(viii) Computer equipment originally acquired for personal use.[62]

3.30 Where property, goods or services (i) are provided to a candidate at greater than 10% discount on their commercial rate, (ii) used by the candidate, and (iii) would have constituted election expenses if paid for, then the extent of discount is treated as an election expense incurred by the candidate.[63] This is called 'notional expenditure'.

3.31 For notional expenditure to fall to be declared as a candidate's election expenses, rather than, say, their national party, property goods or facilities do not have to have been expressly authorised by the candidate or their agent, so long as they are used by them.[64] In *R v Mackinlay*,[65] the defendants were charged on indictment with knowingly making false declarations in relation to election expenses, or aiding and abetting or encouraging or assisting such offences. They relied on the fact that they had not expressly authorised the expenses and argued that concept of authorisation (*"ordinarily a necessary feature of constituency election expenses"* and employed *"in the equivalent contexts of party campaign expenses and third party controlled expenses"*)[66] was also applicable notional expenditure by candidates. The Supreme Court held it was not; there was no room for imputing an additional authorisation requirement.[67]

---

[57] Para 8 sch 4A RPA 1983; para 8 sch 7 NAWRPO 2007.
[58] Para 9 sch 4A RPA 1983; para 9 sch 7 NAWRPO 2007.
[59] Para 10 sch 4A RPA 1983; para 10 sch 7 NAWRPO 2007
[60] Para 11 sch 4A RPA 1983; para 11 sch 7 NAWRPO 2007
[61] Para 12 sch 4A RPA 1983; para 12 sch 7 NAWRPO 2007.
[62] Para 13 sch 4A RPA 1983; para 13 sch 7 NAWRPO 2007.
[63] S 90C RPA 1983.
[64] R *v Mackinlay* [2018] UKSC 42, 19 and 30.
[65] R *v Mackinlay* [2018] UKSC 42.
[66] S 90ZA(4) RPA 1983; *R v Mackinlay* [2018] UKSC 42, at 16.
[67] R *v Mackinlay* [2018] UKSC 42, at 19, per Lord Hughes.

3.32 The difficulties *R v Mackinlay*[68] may present election agents in distinguishing national (party) expenditure from their own is ameliorated by guidance issued by the Commission on notional expenditure.[69] Two examples therein indicate how the distinction can be made, for the scenario in which a candidate's party tells the candidate that it has made leaflets supporting the candidate and plans to distribute them in the candidate's area:

(i) If the candidate acknowledges the plan, thanks the party, and the party so distributes: this is deemed to be used by the candidate and amounts to expense incurred by the candidate;[70]

(ii) If the candidate tells the party that the candidate does not want the leaflets as the candidate has already produced their own and the party distributes the leaflets anyway, this is not deemed 'used' by the candidate and amounts to an expense incurred not by the candidate but by the party. It will fall subject to the regulation of donations to candidates,[71] set out below.

3.33 Another example given by the Commission's guidance is the position where a candidate's party sends them the itinerary for the party leader's campaign bus, showing that it is visiting the candidate's constituency. If the candidate does not attend, the candidate has not actively participated or accepted a donation, and it is therefore not candidate spending. If the candidate is invited to attend and accepts, this may be candidate spending, depending on what happens at the event: if the leader speaks on national issues and urges voters to vote for the party, this is spending on behalf of the party, not the candidate; but if the leader speaks on national issues but mentions the candidate at the end of the speech, *"a portion which is reasonable to reflect the candidate's use of the costs"* of the event is candidate spending.[72]

Payment of expenses must be through election agent

3.34 Any gift or loan of money or property to meet a candidate's election expenses must only be made to the candidate or their election agent.[73] It is an illegal practice to provide it to anyone else.[74]

---

68 *R v Mackinlay* [2018] UKSC 42.

69 Electoral Commission, 'Notional spending: How does it work for candidates and agents'. Cf. the Commission's guidance on apportionment, described by Lord Hughes as *"helpful"*: *R v Mackinlay* [2018] UKSC 42, at 28

70 Electoral Commission, 'Notional spending: How does it work for candidates and agents', p 3.

71 Electoral Commission, 'Notional spending: How does it work for candidates and agents', p 3.

72 Electoral Commission, 'Notional spending: How does it work for candidates and agents', p 4.

73 S 71A(3) RPA 1983; art 43 NAWRPO 2007.

74 S 71A(3) RPA 1983; art 43 NAWRPO 2007.

3.35 Any election expenses payment greater than £20 must be vouched for by an invoice stating the particulars and by a receipt.[75]

Expenses must be authorised by election agent

3.36 It is an offence and a corrupt practice for anyone other than the candidate, their election agent, or someone authorised by them in writing to promote the election of the candidate by incurring expenses by doing any of the following acts:

(i) Holding public meetings or organising any public display;[76]

(ii) Issuing advertisements, circulars, publications,[77] or any other means of presenting the candidate or their views, the extent or nature of promoter's backing; or disparaging another candidate.[78]

3.37 This offence does not apply to the following expenses:

(i) Expenses incurred by any person that are not incurred as part of a concerted plan between multiple people to procure the election of a candidate,[79] and do not exceed £700 (PE),[80] £500 (WAE: constituency election), £1,000 (WAE regional election),[81] or £50 plus 0.5p for every entry in the LE register (LE);[82]

(ii) Expenses incurred in travelling or in living away from home or similar personal expenses;[83]

(iii) Expenses incurred by an employee of the candidate or their agent, or someone otherwise engaged for payment does not have to send such a return;[84] or

(iv) Expenses incurred in connection with a candidate's party political television broadcast where the aim of the producers is to *"give the public information on political matters"*.[85]

3.38 To be authorised by the election agent (and to avoid committing the offence and an illegal practice), the person incurring the expense must, within 21 days

---

[75]S 73(2) RPA 1983; art 43(2) NAWRPO 2007.
[76]S 75(1)(a) RPA 1983; art 46 NAWRPO 2007.
[77]S 75(1)(b) RPA 1983; art 46 NAWRPO 2007.
[78]S 75(1)(c) RPA 1983; art 46 NAWRPO 2007.
[79]S 75(1)(1ZA) RPA 1983.
[80]S 75(1)(1ZZB)(a) and (1ZA)(a) RPA 1983.
[81]Art 46(3)(a) and (4) NAWRPO 2007.
[82]S 75(1)(1ZZB)(a) and (1ZA)(b) RPA 1983.
[83]S 75(1)(1ZZB)(b) RPA 1983; art 46(3)(b) S 75(1)(1ZZB)(a) and (1ZA)(a) RPA 1983.
[84]S 75(2) RPA 1983.
[85]*Grieve v Douglas-Home* [1965] S.C. 315 (Court of Session), p 332.

after the day on which the result of the election is declared,[86] deliver to the RO a return in the prescribed form[87]:

(i) Stating: (a) the amount of the expenses; (b) the election at which they were incurred; and (c) the candidate in whose support they were incurred;[88] and

(ii) Accompanied by: (a) a declaration verifying the return and giving details of the items for which the expenses were incurred;[89] (b) authorisation received from the election agent (as annex to the return).[90]

3.39 The RO must forward these documents to the ERO,[91] who must retain them in accordance with the procedure for retaining documents after the count.[92]

3.40 This offence is not concerned with expenses incurred before the candidate becomes the candidate, unless they are incurred in connection with anything which is then used or takes place after they become the candidate.[93]

3.41 It is also a corrupt practice to (a) aid, abet, counsel or procure any other person to incur expenses contrary to the above requirements;[94] or (b) knowingly makes the expense return declaration falsely.[95]

3.42 If the corrupt practice was by a company or unincorporated association, then the person who was its director, general manager, secretary or other similar officer at the time is guilty of this offence. They have a defence if they can prove that:

(i) The act or omission took place without their consent or connivance; and

(ii) They exercised all such diligence to prevent the commission of the offence as he ought to have exercised having regard to the nature of his functions in that capacity and to all the circumstances.[96]

3.43 Within six months of polling day, the RO or Electoral Commission may request a return of permitted expenditure in relation to a candidate from a person who

---

[86] S 75(4) RPA 1983; art 46(5) NAWRPO 2007.
[87] S 75(3) and reg 10(1) and Form C sch 3 RP (E&W) Regulations 2001; Forms CU sch 10 NAWRPO 2007.
[88] S 75(2)(b) RPA 1983.
[89] S 75(2)(b) RPA 1983; reg 10(1) and Form D sch 3 RP (E&W) Regs 2001; art 46(5)(b) and Forms CV sch 10 NAWRPO 2007.
[90] S 75(3)
[91] S 75(4B) RPA 1983; art 46(7) NAWRPO 2007.
[92] S 75(4C). That is: in accordance with r 57 of the Parliamentary Election Rules.
[93] S 75(8) RPA 1983; art 46(13) NAWRPO 2007.
[94] S 75(5)(a) RPA 1983; art 46(8)(a) NAWRPO 2007.
[95] S 75(5)(b) RPA 1983; art 46(8)(b) NAWRPO 2007.
[96] S 75(5) RPA 1983; art 46(12) NAWRPO 2007.

was not authorised by an agent to incur expenses (not WAE).[97] If so requested, such a person must provide the return within 21 days.[98]

3.44 That return must either: (i) set out all permitted expenses incurred in relation to a candidate; (ii) state that no such expenses were incurred; or (iii) state that the total of such expenses was £200 or less.

3.45 This return must be accompanied by a declaration (i) verifying the return, and (ii) detailing the matters for which the expenses were incurred. Failure to deliver the return or declaration renders you guilty of an illegal practice.[99] Knowingly making a false declaration constitutes a corrupt practice (for election petition purposes).[100]

Limit on election expenses

3.46 A candidate's election expenses must not exceed:

(i) PE county constituency: £8,700 plus 9p for every entry in the register of voters;[101]

(ii) PE borough constituency: £8,700 plus 6p for every entry in the register of voters;[102]

(iii) PE by-election: £100,000;[103]

(iv) LE: £740 plus 6p for every entry in the register of voters;[104]

(v) WAE county constituency: £8,700 plus 9p for every entry in the register of electors;[105]

(vi) WAE borough constituency: £8,700 plus 6p for every entry in the register of voters;[106]

(vii) WAE regional election: the aggregate maximum of each of borough and county constituencies in the region;[107]

---

[97] Ss 75ZA(1) and 75ZB(1)
[98] Ss 75ZA(1) and 75ZB(1)
[99] S 75ZB(3)
[100] S 75ZB(4)
[101] S 76(2) RPA 1983.
[102] S 76(2) RPA 1983.
[103] S 76(2) RPA 1983.
[104] S 76(2) RPA 1983.
[105] Art 47(3) NAWRPO 2007.
[106] Art 47(3) NAWRPO 2007.
[107] Art 47(3) NAWRPO 2007.

(viii) WAE constituency candidate at an election to fill a casual vacancy: £100,000.[108]

3.47 A candidate or agent who incurs expenses in excess of that amount, knowingly or where they ought reasonably to have known that there would be this excess, is guilty of an illegal practice.[109]

Pre-candidacy expense limits (PE)

3.48 PE: where Parliament dissolves more than 55 months after its first meeting, any election expenses incurred by a candidate or on their behalf in paying for something used before they formally become a candidate at the election is subject to a spending limit.[110] That limit is the sum of a certain percentage of £30,700 plus a sum for every entry in the register of electors: 9p for a candidate at an election in a county constituency and 6p for a candidate in a borough constituency.

3.49 That percentage increases according to when the dissolution takes place:

(i) 60% where the dissolution was during its 56th month of a Parliament;

(ii) 70% where the dissolution was during its 57th month;

(iii) 80% where the dissolution was during its 58th month;

(iv) 90% where the dissolution was during its 59th month;

(v) 100% where the dissolution was during or after the 60th month of the Parliament.[111]

3.50 A candidate who incurs, or authorised the incurring of, election expenses in excess of the permitted amount is guilty of an illegal practice (for election petition purposes).[112]

Time for sending in and paying claims

3.51 Unless a claim against a candidate or his election agent in respect of election expenses is sent to the election agent within 21 days of the day the election result is declared, it is barred and must not be paid.[113]

---

108 Art 47(3) NAWRPO 2007.
109 S 76(1B) RPA 1983; art 47(2) NAWRPO 2007.
110 S 76ZA(1) RPA 1983.
111 S 76ZA(3) RPA 1983.
112 S 76ZA(5) RPA 1983.
113 S 78(1) RPA 1983; art 49(1) NAWRPO 2007.

3.52 Those expenses claims that are made in time must be paid within 28 days after that day (i.e. within 49 days of the result being declared).[114]

3.53 The candidate or their agent may however apply to the High Court or county court for permission to pay a late claim for election expenses.[115]

3.54 Application for relief from the consequences of breach of may be made to the High Court or an Election Court, with notice to the DPP, on grounds that:

(i) There had been an act or omission constituting illegal practice, payment, employment or hiring, for contravening the RPA 1983;[116]

(ii) The act or omission arose from inadvertence, accidental miscalculation, or some other similarly reasonable cause, and not from any want of good faith;[117]

(iii) Sufficient notice of the application has been given in the constituency or electoral area for which the election was held;[118] and

(iv) It is just that the person to whom the application relates should not be subject to any of the consequences of the act or omission.[119]

3.55 Ignorance of the law may be 'inadvertence' within the meaning of these provisions.[120] Lack of care or the degree of it is not relevant to it.[121] In *Finch v Richardson*, [122] the candidate directed the driver provided by his employer to deliver election materials to voters during the driver's work hours and without reimbursing his employer the driver's wages. He and his agent failed to include it in the election return as a service provided for free.[123] Included, the total expenditure exceeded the limit. This was an illegal practice that could have invalidated the candidate's election.[124] On the basis that ignorance of the law could constitute 'inadvertence', and findings that (i) the *"overwhelming probability"* was that, had the claimant known the law, he *"would have arranged for their distribution by other means, either personally or through others who were neither paid by them nor being paid by others"*;[125] and (ii) that the claimants had no interest or need to spending more than was permitted,[126] the Divisional

[114] S 78(1) and (2) RPA 1983; art 49(2) NAWRPO 2007.
[115] S 78(4) RPA 1983; art 49(5) NAWRPO 2007.
[116] S 167(2)(a) RPA 1983; art 119(3)(a) NAWRPO 2007.
[117] S 167(2)(b) RPA 1983; art 119(3)(b) NAWRPO 2007.
[118] S 167(2)(c) RPA 1983; art 119(3)(c) NAWRPO 2007.
[119] S 167(2) RPA 1983; art 119(3) NAWRPO 2007.
[120] *Finch v Richardson* [2008] EWHC 3067 (QB) (DC), per Tugendhat J at 46.
[121] *Finch v Richardson* [2008] EWHC 3067 (QB) (DC).
[122] *Finch v Richardson* [2008] EWHC 3067 (QB) (DC), per Tugendhat J at 17-19.
[123] *Finch v Richardson* [2008] EWHC 3067 (QB) (DC), per Tugendhat J at 17-19.
[124] *Finch v Richardson* [2008] EWHC 3067 (QB) (DC), per Tugendhat J at 23.
[125] *Finch v Richardson* [2008] EWHC 3067 (QB) (DC), per Tugendhat J at 49.
[126] *Finch v Richardson* [2008] EWHC 3067 (QB) (DC), per Tugendhat J at 49.

Court granted them relief of the consequences of having exceeded the election expense limit and from the errors and false statements in the return and declarations.[127]

Disputed claims

3.56 If the agent disputes a claim sent within the 21 days, or does not pay it within the 28, then the claim is deemed a 'disputed claim', and its claimant my bring an "*action for a disputed claim*" in "*any competent court*".[128]

Donations to meet candidates' expenses

Scope: meaning of 'donations'

3.57 'Donations' comprises any gift, sponsorship (help to meet expenses), direct payment of election expenses, loans other than on commercial terms, provision of any property, services or facilities otherwise than on commercial terms, or overpayment for property or services.[129]

3.58 The following do not constitute donations:

(i) Expenses incurred in connection with a candidate's party political television broadcast where the aim of the producers is to "*give the public information on political matters*";[130]

(ii) Facilities provided pursuant the candidate's election-time statutory right to the same (see below);[131]

(iii) An individual's free and voluntary services, provided in their own time;[132]

(iv) Interest accruing from any impermissible donation before it is returned or given to the Commission for entering into the Consolidated Fund;[133]

(v) Donations not greater than £50.[134]

---

[127] *Finch v Richardson* [2008] EWHC 3067 (QB) (DC), per Tugendhat J at 9.
[128] S 79 RPA 1983; art 50 NAWRPO 2007.
[129] Sch 2A RPA 1983; sch 6 NAWRPO 2007.
[130] *Grieve v Douglas-Home* [1965] S.C. 315 (Court of Session), p 332.
[131] Para 4(1)(a) sch 2A RPA 1983; para 4(1)(a) sch 6 NAWRPO 2007.
[132] Para 4(1)(b) sch 2A RPA 1983; para 4(1)(b) sch 6 NAWRPO 2007.
[133] Para 4(1)(c) sch 2A RPA 1983; para 4(1)(c) sch 6 NAWRPO 2007.
[134] Para 4(2) sch 2A RPA 1983; para 4(2) sch 6 NAWRPO 2007.

Donor controls

3.59 A donor commits an offence if they to do any of the following:[135]

(i) Provide their donation to anyone other than the candidate or agent;[136]

(ii) If the donation is money: fail to provide the candidate or their agent with details of the amount;[137]

(iii) If the donation is of something other than money: fail to provide details as to the nature of the donation and its value;[138] or

(iv) If the donation is provided by someone ("**the principal donor**") on behalf of others or on behalf of the principal donor and the others: fail to provide the amount or value[139] and, unless the principal donor is to be treated as the donor, provide certain information about the donor:[140]

Candidate and election agent controls

3.60 A candidate or their election agent commit an offence (that for election petition purposes constitutes an illegal practice) if they accept a donation from an impermissible donor:[141] i.e. (a) an individual not on a UK electoral register, (b) an organisation not registered in the UK, or (c) if an unincorporated association, not carrying or activities in the UK and with its main office here).[142]

3.61 The candidate will be deemed to have accepted a donation if they fail, within 30 days, to (a) repay it to the donor, (b) if the donor is unidentifiable, return it to the person or financial institution that transmitted it, or (c) if neither of these are identifiable, send it to the Commission.[143]

3.62 This offence is subject to a defence of having taken all reasonable steps to verify (or ascertain) whether the donor was permissible, and concluding that they were.[144]

3.63 The candidate must transfer any donations received to their election agent, along with any information provided by a donor acting as principal donor or agent, and any information that the agent will need to comply with their duties

---

135 Para 6(6) sch 2A RPA 1983.

136 S 71A RPA 1983; arts 41(1) and 43(1) NAWRPO 2007.
137 Para 6(7) and 11(a) sch 2A RPA 1983.
138 Paras 2(1)(a), (b), (d) and (e) and 5(1)(a) and (2)-(4) sch 2A.
139 Para 11 of sch 2A.
140 Para 11 of sch 2A RPA 1983, and para 2 of sch 6 PPERA 2000.
141 Para 6 sch 2A RPA 1983; para 6(1) sch 6 NAWRPO 2007.
142 S 54(2) PPERA 2000.
143 Para 7 sch 2A RPA 1983; para 7 sch 6 NAWRPO 2007; and s 56(5) PPERA 2000.
144 Para 7(1) sch 2A RPA 1983 and s 56(3A) PPERA 2000.

in relation to donations to their candidate.[145] If the candidate receives and deals with an impermissible donation before they have appointed an agent, they must do so as soon as reasonably practicable after so appointing them.[146]

General offences

3.64 It is an offence to knowingly:

(i) Enter into, or do any act in furtherance of, an arrangement designed or likely to facilitate donations to a candidate by an impermissible donor, whether by concealment or disguise or otherwise (evasion);[147] or

(ii) Give a candidate or their election agent any false information, or withhold any material information, relating to the amount or source of a donation, with the intent to deceive.[148]

Return and declarations as to election expenses and donations

Statement of expenses

3.65 Within 35 (PE, LE or WAE) or 70 (LAE and PCCE) days after the day on which the result of the election is declared, each election agent must deliver to the RO a return containing a statement of all:

(i) Election expenses incurred by or on behalf of the candidate; and

(ii) Payments made by the election agent, together with receipts.[149]

3.66 The form of return and declaration is prescribed by statute.[150]

3.67 The election agent must make a declaration as to the completeness and accuracy of the return, in the appropriate form.[151] The candidate must deliver the declaration either with the return delivered by the agent or within seven days thereafter.[152] If the candidate is acting as their own agent, they need not make

---

145 Para 8(2) sch 2A RPA 1983; para 8 sch 6 NAWRPO 2007.

146 Para 8(6)-(8) sch 2A RPA 1983.

147 Para 9 sch 2A RPA 1983; para 9 sch 6 NAWRPO 2007.

148 Para 9 sch 2A RPA 1983.

149 S 81(1) and (1A) RPA 1983; art 52(1) NAWRPO 2007; art 40(1) PCCEO 2012.

150 Sch 3 RPA 1983; art 52(8) and Form CW sch 10 NAWRPO 2007; art 40(5) PCCEO 2012.

151 S 82(1) RPA 1983; arts 53(1) and 54(1) and Form CX or CY sch 10 NAWRPO 2007; ; art 41(1) PCCEO 2012; https://www.electoralcommission.org.uk/sites/default/files/pdf_file/Declaration-agent-local-government-elections-GB-version-Final.pdf

152 S 82(2) RPA 1983; art 53(2) NAWRPO 2007; art 41(2) PCCEO 2012.

this agent's declaration.[153] If a candidate or their election agent knowingly makes the declaration falsely, they are guilty of a corrupt practice.[154]

3.68 Once they receive the return and declarations, the RO (PE, LE or WAE) or proper officer (LE) must:

(i) Make a copy available for inspection for two years, in their office *"or some other convenient place"* of their choice, and, if requested, on payment of the specified fee, supply anyone with a copy of the return or declaration and any accompanying documents; [155]

(ii) Within ten days of the deadline for delivery to them of the return and declarations, publish, in at least two local newspapers, notice of the time and place at which they can be inspected, and notify the agents of the same.[156] WAE: this can be two newspapers circulating in the Assembly constituency or three newspapers circulating in the Assembly electoral region;[157]

(iii) PE, WAE and PCCE: as soon as reasonably practicable, send a copy of it to the Commission.[158]

3.69 A candidate or agent who fails to deliver either the return or declarations is guilty of an illegal practice[159] and the candidate must not sit or vote in the House of Commons, council, or Assembly, or is disqualified from being a police and crime commissioner, until either:

(i) The return and declarations have been delivered; or

(ii) They obtain an authorised excuse for the failure from the High Court, an Election Court, or the County Court.[160]

3.70 The candidate must forfeit £100 (PE and WAE) or £50 (LE) for every day that they sit or vote despite this prohibition, and civil proceedings may be commenced within a year of the date of this penalty being incurred.[161]

3.71 If a candidate in a London mayoral election fails to deliver the return and declarations as to election expenses in time, the candidate is disqualified from being elected in that election.[162]

---

[153] S 82(5) RPA 1983; art 53(4) NAWRPO 2007; art 41(5) PCCEO 2012.
[154] S 82(6) RPA 1983; art 53(5) NAWRPO 2007; art 41(6) PCCEO 2012.
[155] S 89 RPA 1983; art 62(1) NAWRPO 2007; art 49(1) PCCEO 2012.
[156] S 88 RPA 1983; art 61(1)(a) NAWRPO 2007; art 48(1)(a) PCCEO 2012.
[157] Art 61(1)(a) NAWRPO 2007.
[158] S 87A(2) RPA 1983; art 60 NAWRPO 2007; art 47 PCCEO 2012.
[159] S 84 RPA 1983; art 56 NAWRPO 2007; art 43 PCCEO 2012.
[160] S 85 and 86 RPA 1983; art 57(1) NAWRPO 2007; art 44(1) PCCEO 2012.
[161] S 85(1) and (2) RPA 1983; art 57(2) NAWRPO 2007.
[162] S 85A RPA 1983.

Authorised excuses for failures as to return and declarations

3.72 If a candidate or their agent fails to deliver the expenses return and declaration on time, or have made an error or false statement therein, they may apply to the High Court, election court or election court for relief from the consequences of the act or omission.[163]

3.73 The grounds for so applying are that the failure, error or false statement: (a) did not arise for lack of good faith on the applicant's part; and (b) did arise from:

(i) Inadvertence or similar;

(ii) The applicant's illness;

(iii) The absence, death, illness or misconduct of a current (if it is the candidate is applying for relief) or prior election agent or sub-agent, or of any clerk or officer of such agent, without the *"sanction or connivance"* of the candidate, who took all reasonable steps to prevent the agent's act or omission.[164]

False declaration as to expenses offence

3.74 A candidate or election agent who knowingly makes a false declaration as to election expenses is guilty of a corrupt practice.[165]

3.75 In *R v Fiona Jones and R v Desmond Whicher*,[166] Lord Bingham LCJ held: *"Before any defendant may be convicted of an offence under section 82(6) of the Act, the tribunal of fact must be satisfied[:]*

> (1) that the defendant made a declaration as to election expenses as required by the section;
>
> (2) that such declaration was false, in that expenses which should have been included were omitted or expenses which were included were understated, or both;
>
> (3) that the defendant knew such declaration to be false, either because the defendant knew that expenses which should have been included were omitted or because the defendant knew that expenses which were included were understated, or both."[167]

---

[163] S 86(1) and (2) RPA 1983; art 58(1) NAWRPO 2007; art 45(1) PCCEO 2012.

[164] S 86(3) and (5) RPA 1983; art 58(4) NAWRPO 2007; art 45(4) PCCEO 2012. If the election agent makes the application, they cannot rely on the absence or misconduct of a prior agent: s 86(3)(c) RPA 1983.

[165] S 82(6) RPA 1983.

[166] R *v Fiona Jones and* R *v Desmond Whicher* [1999] 2 Cr App R 253 (CA).

[167] R *v Fiona Jones and* R *v Desmond Whicher* [1999] 2 Cr App R 253 (CA), p 258E-F.

3.76 As to the second, Lord Bingham LCJ held:

> "There is no simple and decisive test to determine whether an expense is or is not an election expense within the meaning of the Act. Some expenses obviously are, some obviously not. But there may be some expenses about which reasonable people, applying themselves to the question in all good faith, could reach different conclusions, either as to whether an expense should be included at all or, if it appears that some part of a larger sum should be included, in what smaller sum. In this intermediate area, questions of judgment may arise. But no crime can be committed unless it is clearly shown that an election expense which should have been included has been either omitted or understated. (We can for practical purposes ignore cases in which expenses have been wrongly included or overstated)."[168]

3.77 On the third, Lord Bingham held:

> "The third requirement is crucial, because it defines the dishonest knowledge which constitutes the mens rea of the statutory crime and which must be established before a defendant is convicted. It is not a crime to declare an honest belief in a declaration of election expenses in which some expenses which should have been included have been omitted or some expenses have been understated by showing an expense smaller than should have been shown, unless the person making the declaration knows that it is false in one or other respect or both. **Honest belief in the truth of the declaration, and thus in the completeness and accuracy of the figures disclosed, is a complete defence. But it is, of course, for the prosecution to prove lack of honest belief and not for the defendant to prove his honesty**. The nub of the offence is the declaration of an honest belief in the accuracy of a disclosure which is known to be incomplete or inaccurate."[169] (emphasis added).

3.78 In *Sharma v DPP*,[170] the Divisional Court allowed an appeal by a LE candidate convicted of making a false declaration as to his election expenses. The conviction had been entered because his expenses return was non-compliant and he had signed it. The appeal was allowed because

(i) There had been a *"critical finding"* at first instance that the candidate was *"a man of honesty and integrity who completely trusted his agent as he*

[168] R *v Fiona Jones and* R *v Desmond Whicher* [1999] 2 Cr App R 253 (CA), p 258G-259A.
[169] R *v Fiona Jones and* R *v Desmond Whicher* [1999] 2 Cr App R 253 (CA), p 259B-C.
[170] *Sharma v DPP* [2005] EWHC 902 (QB) (DC)

had trusted him on previous occasions, apparently with justification",[171] but this time *"was let down by him"*;[172] and

(ii) The appellant had examined his agent's return and honestly believed that it was correct;[173]

(iii) Parliament could but had not passed legislation requiring *"a candidate to perform the role of an auditor...and to be on the look-out to see if his agent is not only deceiving the returning officer, but also deceiving him, the candidate"*.[174]

Statement of relevant donations

3.79 In the return, a candidate's election agent must include a statement of relevant donations,[175] recording:

(i) In relation to permissible donations: (a) the amount (if money), nature and value (if not money) of the donation, (b) the date accepted, and (c) name and address of the donor (a particular address, depending on the donor);[176]

(ii) In relation to impermissible donations returned: (a) the name and address of the donor; (b) the amount (if money) or nature and value (if not money), (c) date received, and (d) date repaid;[177]

(iii) In relation to impermissible donations whose donor is unascertainable: (a) the manner in which the donation was made; (b) the amount (if money) or nature and value (if not money), the date received; and (c) date when it was either returned to the person or financial institution that conveyed it, or none then sent to the Commission.[178]

---

[171] *Sharma v DPP* [2005] EWHC 902 (QB) (DC) at 16.
[172] *Sharma v DPP* [2005] EWHC 902 (QB) (DC) at 16.
[173] *Sharma v DPP* [2005] EWHC 902 (QB) (DC) at 17.
[174] *Sharma v DPP* [2005] EWHC 902 (QB) (DC) at 17.
[175] Para 10 sch 2A RPA 1983; para 10 sch 6 NAWRPO 2007; para 10 sch 5 PCCEO 2012.
[176] Para 11 sch 2A RPA 1983; para 2 sch 6 PPERA 2000; para 11 sch 6 NAWRPO 2007; para 11 sch 5 PCCEO 2012.
[177] Para 12(2) sch 2A PPERA 2000; para 12(2) sch 6 NAWRPO 2007; para 10 sch 5 PCCEO 2012; para 12(2) sch 5 PCCEO 2012.
[178] Para 12(3)(c) sch 2A PPERA 2000; para 12(3) sch 6 NAWRPO 2007; para 12(3) sch 5 PCCEO 2012.

D. CANDIDATE'S RIGHTS

Right to send one free election address post

3.80 PE and WAE: a candidate has the right to send, free of postal charge, one unaddressed election communication, weighing less than 60 grammes, to:

(i) Every address in the constituency or every voter in the constituency; and

(ii) Each person entered in the list of proxies for the election.[179]

3.81 As long as they pay security to Royal Mail, until the RO publishes the statement of persons nominated, any person declaring themselves to be a candidate may exercise this right.[180]

Right to free use of school rooms for meetings

3.82 Between (i) the receipt of the writ (PE) or the last day on which notice of the election may be published (WAE, LE, LAE) and (ii) the day before polling day, a candidate is entitled to the free use of a suitable room, hall, gallery or gymnasium in a maintained school in the constituency or electoral area, for the purpose of holding public meetings in support of their candidature.[181]

3.83 Local authorities must prepare and maintain a list of such rooms.[182] Arrangements for such use are to be made with the local authority who maintains the school.[183]

3.84 Such a room is only available between reasonable times and on reasonable notice.[184]

3.85 The candidate must pay the expense incurred in preparing, warming, lighting and cleaning the room, restoring the room to its usual condition after the meeting, and any damage done.[185]

Right to impartial broadcasting

3.86 Election broadcasts may only be made pursuant to arrangements for reception and re-transmission of the same made with the BBC, Sianel Pedwar Cymru, or the holder of an Ofcom-issued licence.[186] It is an offence and an illegal practice

---

179 S 91 RPA 1983; art 65 NAWRPO 2007.

180 S 91(3) RPA 1983.

181 Ss 95(1)-(3) and 96(1)-(3) RPA 1983; arts 69 and 147 NAWRPO 2007; art 56(1) PCCEO 2012.

182 Para 2 of sch 5 RPA 1983; sch 8 NAWRPO 2007; art 57(2) PCCEO 2012.

183 Para 1 of sch 5 RPA 1983.

184 S 95(1), (4) and (5) RPA 1983; art 69(5) NAWRPO 2007.

185 Ss 95(4) and 96(4) RPA 1983; art 69(4) NAWRPO 2007; art 56(4) PCCEO 2012.

186 S 92(1) RPA 1983.

for anyone else to do so.[187] The effect is to prohibit election broadcasts from outside the UK.

3.87 Television and radio services (other than restricted radio services) must ensure their programmes (a) exclude the views or opinions of the person providing the service, (b) preserve due impartiality on the part of the person providing the service (across a series of programmes), and (c) prevent undue prominence being given to the views and opinions of particular persons or bodies (across all programmes) in relation to:

(i) Matters of political or industrial controversy; and

(ii) Matters relating to current public policy.[188]

3.88 The BBC, Sianel Pedwar Cymru, and OFCOM's Standards Code particularises the rules to be observed in the application of this impartiality law.[189]

3.89 Operation under an Ofcom licence and obligation to comply with its broadcast codes does not mean a commercial broadcaster like ITV is exercising a public function.[190] For this reason, in *R (Liberal Democrats) v ITV Broadcasting Ltd*,[191] ITV's decision to exclude the Liberal Democrats and the SNP from a leader's debate in the lead up to the 2019 GE was held unamenable to judicial review.[192] In any case, that decision was also held not to breach the above impartiality obligations, because the Ofcom code gives flexibility in the format of debates and permits impartiality to be achieved over a period, by a series of linked programmes such as ITV planned.[193]

E. CAMPAIGN OFFENCES

3.90 A large number of election offences arise from misconduct by candidates during the election campaign. For election petition purposes, the first three are corrupt practices and the rest illegal practices.

---

[187] S 92(2) RPA 1983; art 66 NAWRPO 2007.

[188] S 320(1)-(4) Communications Act 2003.

[189] S 93(1) RPA 1983; art 67 NAWRPO 2007; s 320(5) Communications Act 2003; https://www.ofcom.org.uk/tv-radio-and-on-demand/broadcast-codes/broadcast-code/section-six-elections-referendums; Ofcom Guidance Notes, Section Six: Elections and Referendums (22.3.17).

[190] *R (Liberal Democrats) v ITV Broadcasting Ltd* [2019] EWHC 3282 (Admin), Davis LJ and Warby J at 93.

[191] *R (Liberal Democrats) v ITV Broadcasting Ltd* [2019] EWHC 3282 (Admin).

[192] *R (Liberal Democrats) v ITV Broadcasting Ltd* [2019] EWHC 3282 (Admin), Davis LJ and Warby J at 94.

[193] *R (Liberal Democrats) v ITV Broadcasting Ltd* [2019] EWHC 3282 (Admin), Davis LJ and Warby J at 110-111.

Bribery[194]

3.91 A person is guilty of the corrupt practice of bribery if they:

(i) Give money to a voter or procure them a position or job (a) with the aim of inducing them or others to vote or refrain from voting,[195] or (b) on account of their having voted or refrained from voting;[196]

(ii) Give money to anyone or procure anyone a position or job with the (a) aim of inducing them to endeavour to procure votes or the return of a candidate, or (b) result that they procure or engage, promise or endeavour to procure such votes or return;[197] or

(iii) Receive, agree or contract for either of the above.[198]

3.92 This includes:

(i) Gifts or procurement made: (a) directly or indirectly,[199] including payment by the candidate to X to induce Y;[200] (b) in person or through others,[201] or (c) to the voter or to someone on their behalf;[202]

(ii) Grants,[203] e.g. ostensibly made on behalf of a local authority, but channelled by the person accused of the offence;[204]

(iii) Overpayment for services;[205]

(iv) Loans or agreements to lend;[206]

(v) Payments to a voluntary organisation;[207]

(vi) Payments to the media;[208]

(vii) Promises to procure office or employment;[209]

---

[194] S 113 RPA 1983; art 79 NAWRPO 2007; art 67 PCCEO 2012.
[195] S 113(2)(a) RPA 1983; art 79(2)(a) NAWRPO 2007.
[196] S 113(2)(b) RPA 1983; art 79(2)(b) NAWRPO 2007.
[197] S 113(2)(c) RPA 1983; art 79(2)(c) NAWRPO 2007.
[198] S 113(5) and (6) RPA 1983; art 79(6) NAWRPO 2007.
[199] S 113(2) RPA 1983.
[200] R *(Rahman) v Election Court* [2016] EWHC 1280 (Admin) (DC) at 26 (Lloyd Jones LJ).
[201] S 113(2) RPA 1983.
[202] S 113(2)(a) RPA 1983.
[203] R *(Rahman) v Election Court* [2016] EWHC 1280 (Admin) (DC) at 24 (Lloyd Jones LJ).
[204] R *(Rahman) v Election Court* [2016] EWHC 1280 (Admin) (DC) at 28 (Lloyd Jones LJ).
[205] R *(Rahman) v Election Court* [2016] EWHC 1280 (Admin) (DC) at 32 (Lloyd Jones LJ).
[206] S 113(2)(i) RPA 1983.
[207] R *(Rahman) v Election Court* [2016] EWHC 1280 (Admin) (DC) at 24 (Lloyd Jones LJ).
[208] *Erlam v Rahman* [2015] EWHC 1215 (QB) at 507.
[209] S 113(2)(ii) RPA 1983.

(viii) Paying money with the intent that it be used for election bribery;[210]

(ix) Paying money with the knowledge it is to discharge or repay money spent on election bribery;[211] and

(x) Gifts and procurement where bribery is not the sole purpose or even the dominant purpose.[212]

3.93 It does not include:

(i) Money spent on legal expenses incurred in good faith during an election;[213]

(ii) Having been induced to vote through a payment to a third party (e.g. a voluntary organisation that then holds a lunch club for them) by a person later found guilty of bribery,[214] without agreeing to vote accordingly;[215] or

(iii) 'Pork-barrel politics', involving abuse of position to channel grant money to organisations in order to secure votes. Unlike the offence of 'bribery', 'pork-barrel politics' *"is not in the hands of a single individual or directed to the election of an individual candidate"*.[216] In *Erlam v Rahman*, Mr Rahman's conduct was *"the wrong side of the line"* because he was *"the sole controller of the grant funds and he manipulated them for his own personal electoral benefit"*.[217]

3.94 In *Erlam v Rahman*,[218] the Election Court found the respondent and his agents guilty of s 113(2) bribery in making grants and payments to the media. Key findings that led to this conclusion were:

(i) Instances of grants being paid to those who were ineligible or who had not applied for them, including for lunch clubs at which attendees were told that the respondent mayor had made it possible;[219]

(ii) Findings that a substantial number of grants were made not in accordance with the advice of the council were sufficient to make out

---

[210] S 113(3) RPA 1983.
[211] S 113(3) RPA 1983.
[212] *R (Rahman) v Election Court* [2016] EWHC 1280 (Admin) (DC) at 27 (Lloyd Jones LJ).
[213] S 113(4) RPA 1983.
[214] *R (Rahman) v Election Court* [2016] EWHC 1280 (Admin) (DC) at 29 (Lloyd Jones LJ).
[215] *R (Rahman) v Election Court* [2016] EWHC 1280 (Admin) (DC) at 29 (Lloyd Jones LJ).
[216] *Erlam v Rahman* [2015] EWHC 1215 (QB) at 498; inferably endorsed by Lloyd Jones LJ in *R (Rahman) v Election Court* [2016] EWHC 1280 (Admin) (DC) at 27.
[217] *Erlam v Rahman* [2015] EWHC 1215 (QB) at 498, per Commissioner Richard Mawrey QC.
[218] *Erlam v Rahman* [2015] EWHC 1215 (QB).
[219] *Erlam v Rahman* [2015] EWHC 1215 (QB) at 492.

the offence, notwithstanding the Commissioner's statement that the number of grants was greater than this;[220] and

(iii) Arranging for the chief political correspondent of a TV channel to be employed by the council at taxpayers' expense, to publicise the candidate and to ensure favourable coverage continued at that channel and in the media generally, with £20,000 of payments not represented by time sheets and no evidence to show that that they carried out any work on behalf of the council.[221]

Treating[222]

3.95 A person is guilty of the corrupt practice of 'treating' if they:

(i) In person or through another;[223]

(ii) Before, during or after an election;[224]

(iii) Directly or indirectly;[225]

(iv) Provide food, drink, entertainment or other provision, or contribute to the expense of doing so;[226]

(v) For the purpose of corruptly influencing someone to vote or refrain from voting[227] or on account of them having done so.[228]

3.96 A voter or proxy who accepts the same is also guilty of treating.

3.97 There is a remoteness issue. In *Erlam and Rahman*,[229] the commissioner held: *"The more distant the episode relied on as treating from the election itself, the more difficult it is to establish that an electoral offence has been committed"*.[230] Accordingly, in *Erlam v Rahman*,[231] the court found the respondent not guilty of treating where a political dinner was held for the sole purpose of promoting him and his campaign, and the guests did not pay for their meal, but (i) it was held four months before the election, (ii) there was no evidence that the guests

---

220 *Erlam v Rahman* [2015] EWHC 1215 (QB) at 499-500; R *(Rahman) v Election Court* [2016] EWHC 1280 (Admin) (DC) at 21 (Lloyd Jones LJ).
221 R *(Rahman) v Election Court* [2016] EWHC 1280 (Admin) (DC) at 32 (Lloyd Jones LJ).
222 S 114 RPA 1983; art 80 NAWRPO 2007; art 68 PCCEO 2012.
223 S 114(2) RPA 1983.
224 S 114(2) RPA 1983.
225 S 114(2) RPA 1983.
226 S 114(2) RPA 1983.
227 S 114(2)(a) RPA 1983.
228 S 114(2)(a) RPA 1983.
229 *Erlam v Rahman* [2015] EWHC 1215 (QB).
230 *Erlam v Rahman* [2015] EWHC 1215 (QB) at 523.
231 *Erlam v Rahman* [2015] EWHC 1215 (QB).

were persuaded to vote for the respondent, (iii) there was no evidence of any fundraising.[232]

Undue influence[233]

3.98 Undue influence may take two forms.

3.99 The first way in which a person is guilty of the corrupt practice of 'undue influence' if they:

(i) Directly or indirectly;

(ii) Either (a) make use of force, (b) inflict any temporal or spiritual injury, loss or damage, or (c) threaten either; and

(iii) Do so either (a) with the aim of inducing or compelling someone to vote or refrain from voting, or (b) on account of them having done so.

3.100 The second is if they:

(i) By abduction, duress or any fraudulent device or contrivance;

(ii) Impede the free exercise of the franchise of an elector or proxy of an electors or induce a voter or proxy to vote or to refrain from voting.

3.101 As with treating, the candidate must be personally guilty and it is insufficient that the undue influence was committed by someone else by or with their knowledge or consent.[234] This may be academic if the candidate is guilty by their agents.[235] As to the four-fold test for avoiding a finding of guilt by agency, see below in relation to s 158.[236]

Force, violence, restraint, or duress

3.102 Where the form of undue influence alleged is 'intimidation', to satisfy s 115(2):

(i) There must be a *"high degree of physical intimidation"*;[237]

(ii) It is not necessary for the person complaining of intimidation to prove an *"actual assault or the physical barring of electors from polling stations"*, [238] only that *"the level of force or violence [was] such as induce a voter to change his mind as to his vote or to refrain from voting altogether"*;[239]

---

[232] *Erlam v Rahman* [2015] EWHC 1215 (QB) at 523.
[233] S 115 RPA 1983; art 81 NAWRPO 2007; art 69 PCCEO 2012.
[234] S 158(2)(a) RPA.
[235] S 158(3) RPA.
[236] S 158(3) RPA.
[237] *Erlam v Rahman* [2015] EWHC 1215 (QB) at 168.
[238] *Erlam v Rahman* [2015] EWHC 1215 (QB) at 168.
[239] *Erlam v Rahman* [2015] EWHC 1215 (QB) at 168.

(iii) So long as the intimidation reaches this high level, *"[i]t is not essential to prove that any individual voter did change his vote because s 115(2)(b) makes an intention to induce the voter so to act an offence"*.[240]

3.103 Where it is intimidation at polling stations, rather than look at individual polling stations, *"when assessing whether there has been undue influence contrary to s 115 of the 1983 Act, the court ought to stand back and look at the bigger picture"*.[241]

3.104 In *Erlam v Rahman*,[242] where a voter was spat at,[243] and 20-30 activists *"beset"* a polling station shouting that the rival candidates were not good Muslims,[244] bringing one voter to tears,[245] the commissioner found sufficient threat of force and duress at polling stations to state that the common law offence of intimidation would have been made out,[246] and that it had the requisite intent to induce voters to vote a certain way,[247] but nonetheless found that it was insufficient force to establish the *"serious level of violence"* required to make out the 'undue influence' offence,[248] bearing in mind the criminal standard of proof.[249] The commissioner added that it *"is quite possible that a differently constituted court might feel that this approach is unduly cautious"*.[250]

Spiritual injury

3.105 In *Erlam v Rahman*, Richard Mawrey QC derived the following principles from the 19th century caselaw on this form of the undue influence offence:

(i) *"[W]while clergy of all religions are fully entitled, as are all citizens, to hold and to express political views and to argue for or against candidates at elections, there is a line which should not be crossed between the free expression of political views and the use of the power and influence of religious office to convince the faithful that it is their religious duty to vote for or against a particular candidate"*;[251]

(ii) *"It does not matter whether the religious duty is expressed as a positive duty – 'your allegiance to the faith demands that you vote for X' – or a negative*

---

[240] *Erlam v Rahman* [2015] EWHC 1215 (QB) at 168.
[241] *Erlam v Rahman* [2015] EWHC 1215 (QB) at 584.
[242] *Erlam v Rahman* [2015] EWHC 1215 (QB).
[243] *Erlam v Rahman* [2015] EWHC 1215 (QB) at 601.
[244] *Erlam v Rahman* [2015] EWHC 1215 (QB) at 605.
[245] *Erlam v Rahman* [2015] EWHC 1215 (QB) at 603.
[246] *Erlam v Rahman* [2015] EWHC 1215 (QB) at 615.
[247] *Erlam v Rahman* [2015] EWHC 1215 (QB) at 618.
[248] *Erlam v Rahman* [2015] EWHC 1215 (QB) at 619.
[249] *Erlam v Rahman* [2015] EWHC 1215 (QB) at 620.
[250] *Erlam v Rahman* [2015] EWHC 1215 (QB) at 619.
[251] *Erlam v Rahman* [2015] EWHC 1215 (QB) 158.

duty – 'if you vote for Y you will be damned in this world and the next'. The mischief at which s 115 is directed is the misuse of religion for political purposes";[252]

(iii) *"[A] distinction must be made between a sophisticated, highly educated and politically literate community and a community which is traditional, respectful of authority and, possibly, not fully integrated with the other communities living in the same area. As with undue influence in the civil law sphere, it is the character of the person sought to be influenced that is key to whether influence has been applied";*[253]

(iv) Clerics merely writing to the press to issue *"a general ecclesiastical bleat about how politics has gone to the dogs"*[254] does not amount to undue spiritual influence, but *"a specially targeted letter aimed at one particular body of the faithful, telling them their religious duty is to vote for candidate A and not for candidate B"* may do so.[255]

3.106 S 115 undue spiritual influence potentially engages arts 9 and 10 and A3P1 ECHR.[256] It has been held that this balance is already captured by the pre-ECHR undue spiritual influence caselaw.[257]

3.107 In *Erlam v Rahman*, the Election Court found undue spiritual influence contrary to s 115(2) where:

(i) A letter, signed by a high proportion of Imams and other religious leaders and scholars in the borough, was printed in a local newspaper, solely in Bengali, and widely reported in the other press and broadcast media and on social media,[258] designed to persuade Muslim voters that it was their religious duty to vote for the respondent;[259]

(ii) It was not accepted that the document was composed entirely by the clerics and without the respondent's knowledge;[260]

(iii) The influence was likely to have affected the result of the election:

> "If those responsible for the Imams' letter had not thought that it would have a significant influence on the votes of the Bengali-speaking devout Muslim voters of Tower Hamlets, they would

---

[252] *Erlam v Rahman* [2015] EWHC 1215 (QB) 158.
[253] *Erlam v Rahman* [2015] EWHC 1215 (QB) at 159.
[254] *Erlam v Rahman* [2015] EWHC 1215 (QB) at 554.
[255] *Erlam v Rahman* [2015] EWHC 1215 (QB) at 554.
[256] *Erlam v Rahman* [2015] EWHC 1215 (QB) at 160.
[257] *Erlam v Rahman* [2015] EWHC 1215 (QB) at 161.
[258] *Erlam v Rahman [2015] EWHC 1215 (QB)*at 555.
[259] *Erlam v Rahman [2015] EWHC 1215 (QB)*at 552 and 564.
[260] *Erlam v Rahman [2015] EWHC 1215 (QB)*at 559.

not have gone to the considerable trouble of organising the letter and obtaining 101 signatures to it. One cannot put a document of that kind into the public domain and then say 'I didn't think it would have any effect.' If that were the case, why do it?";[261]

(iv) The respondent could not rely on the fact that knowledge and consent are insufficient to fix guilt in the case of undue influence[262] because the Election Court found him party to the undue spiritual influence in his own right,[263] as he and the senior cleric who led the list of signatures on the letter were found to be *"working hand-in-glove"*.[264]

3.108 The respondent sought permission to claim judicial review on grounds that that the Commissioner had not identified any threat to inflict spiritual injury or loss by the religious leaders.[265] The court granted permission on this ground,[266] but the grant of permission had not been resisted on this ground[267] and the court's permission decision seems more concerned with the wide importance of the point than the individual merits.[268] The substantive hearing did not take place because the court fee was not paid,[269] was then reopened following application to the Administrative Court,[270] but did not go to substantive hearing. Therefore, the question of how s 115 should operate in modern society in respect of spiritual injury awaits determination by the Divisional or appellate courts.

3.109 In *Rehman v Khan*,[271] Timothy Straker QC, sitting as a commissioner, dismissed a petition relying on a Facebook post depicting the respondent candidate seated with a religious leader and next to the words *"All Pir Sahibin Darbars in Birmingham have ordered mureeds to vote Labour"* as:

(i) There was no evidence that their words were published by the religious leader, the respondent, nor on the respondent's behalf, nor shared by the respondent;[272]

---

261 *Erlam v Rahman* [2015] EWHC 1215 (QB) at 562.
262 S 158(2)(a) RPA.
263 *Erlam v Rahman* [2015] EWHC 1215 (QB) at 569.
264 *Erlam v Rahman* [2015] EWHC 1215 (QB) at 544.
265 R *(Rahman) v Local Government Election Court* [2015] EWHC 4186 (Admin) (DC) at 35.
266 R *(Rahman) v Local Government Election Court* [2015] EWHC 4186 (Admin) (DC) at 39.
267 R *(Rahman) v Local Government Election Court* [2015] EWHC 4186 (Admin) (DC) at 35.
268 R *(Rahman) v Local Government Election Court* [2015] EWHC 4186 (Admin) (DC) at 36-38.
269 R *(Rahman) v Local Government Election Court* [2017] EWHC 1413 (Admin) (DC) (Lloyd Jones LJ and Supperstone J) at 83.
270 R *(Rahman) v Local Government Election Court* [2017] EWHC 1413 (Admin) (DC) (Lloyd Jones LJ and Supperstone J) at 10. The decision to reopen was by Ouseley J on 24.7.17.
271 *Rehman v Khan* [2015] EWHC 4168 (Admin), at 44-48.
272 *Rehman v Khan* [2015] EWHC 4168 (Admin), at 40 and 49.

(ii) An order to vote in a particular way did not amount to a threat of spiritual injury: the electors were not all one of a kind and it could not be accepted that a large part of them would fear damnation, as alleged, moreover spiritual injury implied 'in life'.[273]

'Fraudulent device'

3.110 In *R v Rowe ex p Mainwaring*,[274] a mock leaflet containing statements of policy that the impersonated party's spokesmen had in fact made was agreed to be a fraudulent device because it *"lied about its own genesis"*.[275] In *Rowe*, key to that finding was the fact that requirement that the material be endorsed with the name and address of the agent of the party publishing it was complied with, but in minuscule print.[276]

3.111 Nonetheless, in the absence of any witnesses found to have been impeded, the Court of Appeal held it was not permissible to find impediment through drawing inferences that the fraudulent device must have impeded the exercise of the franchise by an uncalled and uncross-examined witness.[277] If one voter is found to have been impeded, however, such inferences, by commissioner or High Court on review, would not be so prohibited.

3.112 In *Banwait v Bettany*,[278] the Election Court held, obiter, that a leaflet headed 'Labour News', printed in Labour Party colours, with a Labour Party rose on it that had merely been *"tinkered around with"*, and miniscule print on the back referring to UKIP was a fraudulent device indistinguishable from *Rowe*.[279] The offence was not made out for lack of evidence of circulation with the intent to unduly influence. There must be evidence of dissemination of the fraudulent device.[280]

False statement about candidates[281]

3.113 A person is guilty of an illegal practice if they make a statement that:

(i) Relates to a candidate (including the maker of the statement);

(ii) Is made before or during an election;

---

[273] *Rehman v Khan* [2015] EWHC 4168 (Admin), at 44-48.
[274] R *v Rowe ex p Mainwaring* [1992] 1 WLR 1059 (CA).
[275] R *v Rowe ex p Mainwaring* [1992] 1 WLR 1059 (CA), 1062H, per Farquharson LJ.
[276] R *v Rowe Ex p Mainwaring* [1992] 1 WLR 1059 (CA), 1061H.
[277] R *v Rowe Ex p Mainwaring* [1992] 1 WLR 1059, 1067G-H; 1070D-E.
[278] *Banwait v Bettany* [2018] EWHC 3263 (QB).
[279] *Banwait v Bettany* [2018] EWHC 3263 (QB) at 89-90.
[280] *Banwait v Bettany* [2018] EWHC 3263 (QB) at 85.
[281] S 106 RPA 1983; art 73 NAWRPO 2007; art 61 PCCEO 2012.

(iii) Is a statement of fact;

(iv) Relates to a person's personal character or conduct and not their politics (whether complimentary or disparaging);

(v) Is false; and

(vi) Is made for the purpose of affecting the return of any candidate at the election.[282]

Candidate

3.114 For purposes of this illegal practice, a person becomes a 'candidate' as soon as they declare themselves as such or are formally selected as a party's candidate.[283] This is earlier than the general rule on when a person becomes a candidate.[284] The candidate can be the maker of the statement.[285]

Meaning

3.115 The Election Court will start by determining the meaning of the statement. It will determine the meaning in the following manner:

> "[I]n ascertaining the meaning of the election addresses it is necessary to consider what the words used would mean to the ordinary and reasonable reader of them in the constituency. Such a reader is neither naïve nor unduly suspicious. He would not analyse the words like a lawyer and so the court should be wary of conducting an over elaborate analysis of the words used or of taking an over literal approach; see *Skuse v Granada Television* (1996) EMLR 278 at 285-287 (per Sir Thomas Bingham MR). The natural and ordinary meaning may be inferred by an ordinary reader using his ordinary personal general knowledge and experience of worldly affairs. The meaning should be the true meaning in the context of the publication; see *The North Louth* case per Gibson J. at pages 158-160."[286]

3.116 Analogy with non-electoral, defamation law interpretive principles may be made,[287] but the statement can be complimentary (if about the speaker) and not just disparaging as to another candidate.[288]

---

[282]*Woolas v Woolas* [2010] EWHC 2702 (QB) at 59 and 63.
[283]*Erlam v Rahman* [2015] EWHC 1215 (QB) at 106.
[284]*Erlam v Rahman* [2015] EWHC 1215 (QB) at 106.
[285]*Morrison v Carmichael* [2015] ECIH 71, at 16 and 20. The respondent candidate lied about awareness of a leak.
[286]*Watkins v Woolas* [2010] EWHC 2702 (QB), 61.
[287]*Watkins v Woolas* [2010] EWHC 2702 (QB), 74.
[288]*Morrison v Carmichael* [2015] ECIH 71, at 24.

3.117 In *Watkins v Woolas*,[289] a PE petition challenging the election of a candidate whom the petitioner alleged had published several false statements of fact in relation to the petitioner' personal character or conduct during the general election campaign (that the petitioner was willing to condone threats of violence[290] and had reneged on his promise to live in the constituency).[291] Meaning was derived from an adjoining picture, a legend below a picture, an adjoining editorial, and juxtaposition with that adjoining article.[292]

Statement of fact

3.118 In determining whether a statement is a statement of fact or opinion, it is relevant to consider whether and the extent to which a statement is value-laden,[293] and whether a value-laden judgment becomes a statement of fact in the context used.[294]

3.119 Rhetorical questions can be statements of fact in that they imply answers,[295] just as *"it is rumoured that"* can also be a statement of fact.[296]

3.120 A comment such as 'it is remarkable that the X has not rejected the endorsement of him by an extremist group' (as in *Watkins v Woolas*)[297] is a statement of fact (namely that the candidate had not rejected the endorsement of him by an extremist group or condemned their actions).[298]

3.121 Calling someone a racist is a statement of fact,[299] as is calling someone homophobic,[300] or a liar.[301]

Directly relates to personal conduct or character

3.122 The rationale for the illegal practice only encompassing statements relating to personal conduct or character and not political position was explained by Thomas LJ in *R (Woolas) v The Parliamentary Election Court*:[302]

---

[289] *Watkins v Woolas* [2010] EWHC 2702 (QB).
[290] R *(Woolas) v Parliamentary Election Court* [2010] EWHC 3169 (Admin), 120.
[291] R *(Woolas) v Parliamentary Election Court* [2010] EWHC 3169 (Admin) (DC), 117.
[292] *Watkins v Woolas* [2010] EWHC 2702 (QB), 67.
[293] *Watkins v Woolas* [2010] EWHC 2702 (QB), 74, applying *British Chiropractic Association v Singh* [2010] EWCA Civ 350 at 22 and 27.
[294] *Watkins v Woolas* [2010] EWHC 2702 (QB), 76.
[295] *Watkins v Woolas* [2010] EWHC 2702 (QB), 92.
[296] *Watkins v Woolas* [2010] EWHC 2702 (QB), 91.
[297] *Watkins v Woolas* [2010] EWHC 2702 (QB).
[298] *Watkins v Woolas* [2010] EWHC 2702 (QB), 102.
[299] *Erlam v Rahman* [2015] EWHC 1215 (QB) at 381.
[300] *Morrison v Carmichael* [2015] ECIH 71, at 17.
[301] *Banwait v Bettany* [2018] EWHC 3263 (QB) at 62.
[302] R *(Woolas) v The Parliamentary Election Court* [2010] EWHC 3169 (Admin) (DC).

> "It was as self-evident in 1895 as it is today, given the practical experience of politics in a democracy, that unfounded allegations will be made about the political position of candidates in an election. The statutory language makes it clear that Parliament plainly did not intend the 1895 Act to apply to such statements; it trusted the good sense of the electorate to discount them. However, statements as to the personal character of a candidate were seen to be quite different. The good sense of the electorate would be unable to discern whether such statements, which might be highly damaging, were untrue; a remedy under the ordinary law in the middle of an election would be difficult to obtain. Thus the distinction was drawn in the 1895 Act which is re-enacted in section 106 of the 1983 Act".[303]

3.123 As to what directly relates to personal character, this is likely to include:

(i) Statements relating to a candidate's family, religion, sexual conduct, business or finances;[304]

(ii) A statement that is ostensibly about a candidate's political position but that nonetheless directly relates to their personal character, personal honesty, or criminality e.g. by accusing the candidate of corruption, even if that corruption in office;[305]

(iii) A statement that a candidate was willing to condone threats of violence is a statement about his personal character;[306]

(iv) Calling someone a 'racist';[307]

(v) A press release implying that a rival candidate has been guilty of a hate crime and that this has been endorsed by the EHRC *"clearly meets the test of being a statement about the candidate's personal character and conduct"*;[308]

(vi) A statement by a candidate that they had never been convicted of something of which they had, or a statement that they would never leak an internal confidential memorandum which they had.[309]

---

303 R *(Woolas) v The Parliamentary Election Court* [2010] EWHC 3169 (Admin) (DC) at 110.
304 R *(Woolas) v Parliamentary Election Court* [2010] EWHC 3169 (Admin) (DC), 112.
305 R *(Woolas) v Parliamentary Election Court* [2010] EWHC 3169 (Admin) (DC), 114.
306 R *(Woolas) v Parliamentary Election Court* [2010] EWHC 3169 (Admin), 120.
307 *Erlam v Rahman* [2015] EWHC 1215 (QB) at 381. Richard Mawrey QC sitting as Commissioner added *"In the multi-racial, multi-cultural society that is 21st century Britain there can be few more damaging statements to make about anyone."*
308 *Erlam v Rahman* [2015] EWHC 1215 (QB), at 430.
309 *Morrison v Carmichael* [2015] ECIH 71, at 57.

3.124 The following are more likely to relate to political rather that personal character:

(i) Statements relating to a candidate's political position only impliedly impugn their personal character;[310]

(ii) A statement about a candidate's political position, e.g. implying that he is a hypocrite or untrustworthy because of the political position he is taking;[311]

(iii) A statement that a candidate has reneged on his promise to live in the constituency;[312]

(iv) Calling someone a liar;[313]

(v) A candidate's false statement implying non-involvement with a leak is not a false statement in relation to their personal character or conduct.[314] The court must decide whether the statement is as to personal or political character or conduct; the statement cannot be both.[315]

3.125 To satisfy s 106, *"the false statement of fact must be directly related to the personal character of conduct of the candidate."*[316]

Belief defence

3.126 If the respondent relies on the defence of having *"reasonable grounds for believing, and did believe, the statement to be true"*,[317] then they must discharge an evidential burden of adducing evidence of the same.

3.127 Because the defence demands *"reasonable belief"*, subjective, actual belief is insufficient if not reasonably held.

3.128 The petitioner need not prove that the false statements were dishonestly made; it is sufficient that there were negligently or carelessly made, however honestly so.[318]

3.129 In *Watkins v Woolas*,[319] the respondent submitted that *"it was sufficient that the respondent had reasonable grounds for believing in the truth of the meaning he*

---

310 R *(Woolas) v Parliamentary Election Court* [2010] EWHC 3169 (Admin) (DC), 112.

311 R *(Woolas) v Parliamentary Election Court* [2010] EWHC 3169 (Admin) (DC) at 113.

312 R *(Woolas) v Parliamentary Election Court* [2010] EWHC 3169 (Admin) (DC) at 117.

313 *Woolas* (Thomas LJ) at 117; *Banwait v Bettany* [2018] EWHC 3263 (QB) at 65.

314 *Morrison v Carmichael* [2016] SC 598, at 59.

315 R *(Woolas) v Parliamentary Election Court* [2010] EWHC 3169 (Admin) at 116, disapproving *North Division of the County of Louth* [1911] 6 OM & H 103 on this point.

316 *Fairbairn v Scottish National Party* (1979) SC 393 per Lord Ross.

317 S 106(1) RPA 1983.

318 R *(Woolas) v Parliamentary Election Court* [2010] EWHC 3169 (Admin) at 84 and 96.

319 *Watkins v Woolas* [2010] EWHC 2702 (QB).

understood the article to have, even though that was not the meaning which the ordinary and reasonable reader understood the article to have".[320] The Election Court held that it was unnecessary for it to decide whether this principle was correct in relation to s 106 because on its view the statements were not ambiguous.[321] The court nonetheless held, obiter, that: *"This is an important submission with regard to the extent of the defence of reasonable belief afforded by section 106"*.[322] Accordingly, in a case where the meaning is found to be more ambiguous than in *Woolas*, this *Bonnick* consideration may need to be revisited.

3.130 It is insufficient that there should be mere *"grounds for believing"* that a respondent did not hold the professed belief; the court must be *"sure"* that they did not.[323] Nonetheless, even if the court cannot be sure that a respondent was aware of evidence that would have shown them that their belief lacked reasonable grounds, nonetheless the same evidence may make the court sure that they had no reasonable grounds to hold that belief

3.131 In *Watkins v Woolas*,[324] the Election Court considered the respondent's diary and email correspondence with members of his election team, revealing their pessimism as to their chance of success and choices to pursue strategies that explained some of the statements. The court took this correspondence into account as explanation as to why the respondent made statements *"the truth of which he had no reasonable grounds to believe"*.[325]

3.132 Where the respondent is not cross-examined on their belief, it may be difficult for the petitioner to discharge their legal burden of proving lack of reasonable grounds.[326]

3.133 Where no enquiries have been made to establish the veracity of the belief and simple enquiries would do so, the court may take this into account in finding lack of reasonable belief.[327]

3.134 In *Erlam v Rahman*,[328] the known falsity or dishonesty element was supplied where the respondent's agent relied on a letter and comments that they knew had been retracted.[329]

---

[320] *Watkins v Woolas* [2010] EWHC 2702 (QB), 189, drawing analogy with defamation case *Bonnick v Morris* [2003] 1 AC 300.
[321] *Watkins v Woolas* [2010] EWHC 2702 (QB) at 190.
[322] *Watkins v Woolas* [2010] EWHC 2702 (QB) at 190.
[323] *Watkins v Woolas* [2010] EWHC 2702 (QB) at 194.
[324] *Watkins v Woolas* [2010] EWHC 2702 (QB).
[325] *Watkins v Woolas* [2010] EWHC 2702 (QB), 199.
[326] *Watkins v Woolas*, 204.
[327] *Watkins v Woolas* [2010] EWHC 2702 (QB), 206.
[328] *Erlam v Rahman* [2015] EWHC 1215 (QB).
[329] *Erlam v Rahman* [2015] EWHC 1215 (QB) at 439-440, 443 and 450.

Burden of proof

3.135 The burden of proof is on the petitioner.[330] If the respondent relies on the defence of having *"reasonable grounds for believing, and did believe, the statement to be true"*,[331] then the respondent must discharge an evidential burden of adducing evidence of the same.

Standard of proof

3.136 The standard of proof is the criminal standard ('beyond reasonable doubt') even though petitions are civil proceedings.[332] Further, a petition alleging illegal practice contrary to s 106 is likely to engage art 10 ECHR (freedom of expression),[333] such that the court in *Watkins v Woolas*[334] accepted that the engagement of art 10 meant that *"the court should only find an illegal practice contrary to section 106 in clear cases"*.[335] On the other hand, s 106 protects a pressing social need, for art 10(2) purposes, in that it *"is directed at protecting the right of the electorate to express its choice at an election, which right is protected by [A3P1]"*.[336] This ensures that the threshold for establishing s 106, and for justifying interference with any freedom of expression, is not so high as to be unattainable.

Who may be guilty

3.137 It is an offence for anyone to make a false statement about a candidate, not just candidates and their agents.[337]

Liability for agents

3.138 'Agent' has a broader meaning than in non-electoral law, extending beyond the candidate's official 'election agent to canvassers, committees and supporters, for whose actions the candidate is taken to be responsible though he may not have appointed them as agents or know what they are doing.[338]

3.139 A candidate is only liable for a statement by such an agent if (i) it can be shown that the candidate or their election agent authorised or consented to the false

---

[330] *Watkins v Woolas* [2010] EWHC 2702 (QB) (Teare and Griffith Williams JJ), 58.
[331] S 106(1) RPA 1983.
[332] *Woolas*, 48.
[333] *Woolas*, 41.
[334] *Watkins v Woolas* [2010] EWHC 2702 (QB).
[335] *Woolas*, 47.
[336] *Woolas*, 46.
[337] S 106(1); R *(Woolas) v The Parliamentary Election Court* [2010] EWHC 3169 (Admin).
[338] *Simmons v Khan* [2008] EWHC B4 (QB) at 58, citing *Westbury Case* (1869) 20 LT 16 and *Tewkesbury Case, Collings v Price* (1880) 44 LT 192 for canvassers, *Stalybridge Case, Ogden Woolley* and *Buckley v Sidebottom* (1869) 20 LT 75 for committees, and *Great Yarmouth Borough Case, White v Fell* (1906) 5 O'M&H 176 for supporters".

statement constituting the illegal practice or paid for its circulation; or (ii) an Election Court finds and reports that their election was *"procured or materially assisted"* by the false statement.[339]

Interim injunction

3.140 There is a right to apply to the High Court for an injunction restraining repetition of the false statement or similar statement.[340] Either an interim or permanent injunction can be sought. If the former, only prima facie proof of the falsity of the statement is needed.[341] Nonetheless, the court must have *"particular regard"* to the importance of the ECHR right to freedom of expression.[342]

Art 10 ECHR

3.141 If the court finds the elements of this illegal practice made out, it is unlikely to be forestalled in finding the respondent guilty by its duty to act compatibly with art 10 ECHR by not disproportionately interfering with the respondent's freedom of expression. In *R (Woolas) v Parliamentary Election Court*,[343] where the respondent sought JR of the Election Court's decision on art 10 grounds, Thomas LJ held:

> "125 Nor in our judgment for the reasons we have expressed would the conclusion we have reached in any way infringe the balance that article 10 of the Convention requires. The statements made were not of a trivial nature; they were a serious personal attack on a candidate by saying he condoned violence by extremists and refused to condemn those who advocated violence."[344]

Details to appear on election publications[345]

3.142 Any material that can reasonably be regarded as intended to promote or procure the election of a candidate, irrespective of any other purposes it may have or whether it mentions a candidate,[346] must not be published unless it features the following:

---

[339] S 106(2) RPA 1983.
[340] S 106(3) RPA 1983; art 73(4) NAWRPO 2007; art 61(3) PCCEO 2012.
[341] S 106(3) RPA 1983.
[342] S 12(1) and (4) Human Rights Act 1998.
[343] R *(Woolas) v Parliamentary Election Court* [2010] EWHC 3169 (Admin).
[344] R *(Woolas) v Parliamentary Election Court* [2010] EWHC 3169 (Admin), 125.
[345] S 110 RPA 1983; art 76 NAWRPO 2007; art 64 PCCEO 2012.
[346] S 109(14)

(i) The name and address of the promoter of the material (person causing the material to be published);[347]

(ii) The name and address of any person on whose behalf the material is being published (who is not the promoter); and

(iii) If printed, the name and address of the printer of the document.[348]

3.143 These 'identifiers' must be situated in a particular place:

(i) Single-sided printed document: on the face of the document;[349]

(ii) Multi-sided printed document: on the first or the last page of the document;[350]

(iii) Advert contained in a newspaper or periodical: (a) the name and address of the printer of the newspaper or periodical must appear on the first or last page; and (b) the name and address of the promoter of the material and any person on whose behalf it is being published must be included in the advert itself.[351]

3.144 There is provision for any other material to published in accordance with regulations.[352] This is where regulation of online election publications is likely to appear, if DCMS select committee and Commission recommendation is accepted and implemented by the Government.

3.145 If material is published in breach of these requirements, its promoter, publisher and printer are guilty of an offence[353] and the candidate or their election agent are guilty of an illegal practice.[354]

3.146 Each has a defence if they can prove that (i) the breach arose from circumstances beyond their control; and (ii) they took all reasonable steps, and exercised all due diligence, to ensure that the breach would not arise.[355]

Prohibition of paid canvassers[356]

3.147 If a person is engaged or employed for payment as a canvasser, to promote or procure the success of a candidate, then both the canvasser and the person

---

[347]S 110(13) RPA 1983.
[348]S 110(3) and (7)
[349]S 110(4)
[350]S 110(5) RPA 1983.
[351]S 110(6) RPA 1983.
[352]S 110(7) and (8) RPA 1983.
[353]S 110(9) RPA 1983.
[354]S 110(12) RPA 1983.
[355]S 110(11) RPA 1983.
[356]S 111 RPA 1983; art 77 NAWRPO 2007; art 65 PCCEO 2012.

engaging or employing them are guilty of illegal employment. This includes payment before, during or after an election. It also includes the promise of payment.[357]

3.148 'Canvasser' means: *"A person who solicits and persuades voters to vote for a candidate"*.[358]

3.149 In *Erlam v Rahman*,[359] the Election Court found this offence committed on the following facts:

(i) Three witnesses claimed to have spoken to individuals who admitted they were paid to canvass by the respondent's party or his agent, the party's treasurer;

(ii) The alleged payer was a party treasurer who kept no books or accounts;

(iii) The alleged paid canvassers were seen in that treasurer's ward; and

(iv) The agent was found not be a truthful witness.[360]

3.150 This conclusion was reached despite the following also being present:

(i) The paid canvassers were not identified;

(ii) The alleged payer (the respondent candidate's agent) denied the allegation;

(iii) Three of the witnesses were partisan to the petitioner; and

(iv) The evidence was not particularly strong.[361]

3.151 The Divisional Court then rejected as unarguable a challenge to this decision brought on grounds of insufficient evidence to satisfy the criminal standard.[362]

Other campaign offences

3.152 The following also constitute offences and illegal practices or payments:

(i) Corruptly inducing or procuring another person to withdraw from being a candidate, in consideration of payment or promise of payment, with the inducement causing them to so withdraw;[363]

---

[357] S 111 RPA 1983.
[358] Stroud's Judicial Dictionary 9th Ed., citing *Plymouth, Drake Division Case* (1929) 70 M&H 101.
[359] *Erlam v Rahman* [2015] EWHC 1215 (QB).
[360] *Erlam v Rahman* [2015] EWHC 1215 (QB), at 453-455.
[361] *Erlam v Rahman* [2015] EWHC 1215 (QB), at 456.
[362] R *(Rahman) v Election Court* [2016] EWHC 1280 (Admin) (DC) at 17-18, par Lloyd-Jones LJ.
[363] S 107 RPA 1983; art 74 NAWRPO 2007; art 62 PCCEO 2012.

(ii) Knowingly paying a voter or their proxy (unless they are an advertising agent in the ordinary course of their business)[364] either (a) to exhibit any address, bill or notice for the purpose of promoting or procuring the election of a candidate, or (b) for the use of any house, land, building or premises for such exhibition;[365]

(iii) Destroy, defacing or removing without lawful authority any notice published or made available by the ERO in connection with their duties;[366]

(iv) Promoting a candidate's election by issuing a document so closely resembling an official poll card as to be calculated to deceive;[367]

(v) Seeking to disrupt a lawful meeting held during the election period by acting disorderly or inciting others to do so;[368]

(vi) A member of a police force seeking to persuade someone voting in a constituency or electoral area within the area policed by that force to vote or not vote;[369] and

(vii) Knowingly providing money for: (a) any payment that constitutes an electoral offence; (b) any expense incurred in excess of the maximum amount allowed; or (c) replacing any money expended in any such payment or expenses.[370]

Application for relief

3.153 If a person does something that constitutes an illegal practice, payment, employment or hiring, then they may apply to a High Court master,[371] the County Court if it concerns the time for sending in and paying expense claims,[372] or to an Election Court during a petition[373] for an order that they be given an authorised excuse and not subject to any of the consequences that would otherwise result.[374]

---

[364]S 109(1)(a) and (b) RPA 1983; art 75(1) NAWRPO 2007.
[365]S 110(1) and (2) RPA 1983; art 75 NAWRPO 2007; art 63 PCCEO 2012.
[366]Reg 11 RP (E&W) Regs 2001; art 146 NAWRPO 2007; art 89 PCCEO 2012.
[367]S 94(1) RPA 1983; art 68 NAWRPO 2007; art 55 PCCEO 2012.
[368]S 97(1) RPA 1983; art 70 NAWRPO 2007; art 58 PCCEO 2012.
[369]S 100(1) RPA 1983; art 72 NAWRPO 2007.
[370]S 112 RPA 1983; art 78 NAWRPO 2007; art 66 PCCEO 2012.
[371]A provision requiring the application to be heard by one of the judges on the rota for the hearing of parliamentary election petitions and not by a master [s 167(4) RPA 1983] was repealed on 16.2.2001 by para 1 sch 22 PPERA 2000.
[372]S 167(1) RPA 1983.
[373]S 167(1) RPA 1983.
[374]S 167(2) RPA 1983.

3.154 To obtain such an order, the applicant must satisfy the court that:

(i) It arose from their *"inadvertence or from accidental miscalculation or some other reasonable cause of a like nature"*;

(ii) Not from lack of good faith on their part;

(iii) They have given sufficient notice of the application in the constituency or electoral area for which the election was held (to the relevant RO and parties' national election agents or nominating officers has been held sufficient)[375] and to the DPP; and

(iv) It would be just that they should not be subject to any of the consequences of the act or omission.[376]

3.155 Although the provision states that the court may determine that either the application *"or any other person should not be subject to any of the consequences"*, it should be interpreted more narrowly, as meaning *"no such person shall be subject to any of the consequences"* (emphasis added).[377] This avoids the problem of the applicant being denied relief because someone else's act or omission was not mere accident but involved bad faith.[378]

3.156 An equivalent power in analogous context was exercised to grant relief to the applicant election agent for inadvertent failure to include the requisite details in election material.[379]

F. INJUNCTIONS

3.157 Whilst the specific provision for restraining false statements about candidates is not replicated in other corrupt or illegal practices, the court has jurisdiction to grant them in other cases.

3.158 In *Jessie Patterson v David Steven Merrick v Michael Hammond*,[380] the Court of Appeal (May and Woolf LJJ) dismissed an appeal against an application to discharge an injunction against restraining the appellant from describing

---

[375] *Mabbutt (on his own behalf and on behalf of the Conservative Party)* [2014] EWHC 2244 (QB) at 12, per Nicol J.

[376] S 167(2) RPA 1983.

[377] *Mabbutt (on his own behalf and on behalf of the Conservative Party)* [2014] EWHC 2244 (QB) at 12, per Nicol J interpreting identical provision in reg 108 European Parliamentary Election Regulations 2004.

[378] *Mabbutt (on his own behalf and on behalf of the Conservative Party)* [2014] EWHC 2244 (QB) Nicol J at 12.

[379] *Mabbutt (on his own behalf and on behalf of the Conservative Party)* [2014] EWHC 2244 (QB) Nicol and Popplewell JJ.

[380] *Jessie Patterson v David Steven Merrick v Michael Hammond* [1988] WL 1608805, 2.11.88, unreported, May and Woolf LJJ.

himself as *"the Official Byron Ward Conservative"* candidate in a Nottingham City Council by-election. May LJ held:

> "Clearly the description which this appellant applied to himself in relation to his nomination was capable of confusion with the description applied to herself by the plaintiff and we have no doubt that it was for that reason that the learned judge made the original injunction in October."[381]

3.159 In *Spencer v Huggett*,[382] Longmore J held that the court had jurisdiction to entertain a candidate's application for interim injunction restraining another candidate from breach and threatened repeated breach of s 115(2)(b) (undue influence: fraudulent device or contrivance) through false description in nomination papers submitted to the RO. Longmore J referred to the speech of Lord Fraser in *Gouriet v Union of Post Office Workers*[383] that:

> "The general rule is that a private person is only entitled to sue in respect of interference with a public right if either there is also interference with a private right of his or the interference with the public right will inflict special damage on him."[384]

3.160 Applying that principle, he held:

> "Here the plaintiffs are candidates in the pending General Election. In my view, there is a right recognised at common law, and, I believe, confirmed by arts 8A to 8C of the Treaty of European Union, which is conferred on all persons to stand at a Parliamentary Election. That is a right to stand at an election not tainted by what the 1983 Act calls 'corrupt practice'. The rights, of course, in one sense are public rights, that an election should be conducted properly and without taint, but in my view an individual candidate has a special right to that effect.
>
> Even if that is wrong, and it is correct to regard the rights conferred by s.115(2)(b) as purely and only public rights, the plaintiffs may be able to show that they suffer damage peculiar to themselves from the interference, or the threatened interference, with the public right which may be proved to be intended by the defendants."

---

[381] *Jessie Patterson v David Steven Merrick v Michael Hammond* [1988] WL 1608805, 2.11.88, unreported, May and Woolf LJJ.
[382] *Spencer v Huggett* [1997] 94(30) L.S.G. 30, Times, June 12, 1997, [1997] CLY 2185.
[383] *Gouriet v Union of Post Office Workers* [1978] AC 435, [1977] 3 All ER 70.
[384] *Gouriet v Union of Post Office Workers* [1978] AC 435, [1977] 3 All ER 70, at page 518E.

3.161 He cautioned nonetheless: *"it is obviously a jurisdiction which has to be exercised with extreme delicacy, but I do hold that for the purposes of this interlocutory application there is a strong prima facie case that it does exist"*.[385]

3.162 Where jurisdiction is established, the principles by which the application is tested are those in *American Cyanamid Co v Ethicon Ltd*,[386] namely: (i) a serious question to be tried; and then (ii) where the balance of convenience lies.

---

[385] *Spencer v Huggett* [1997] 94(30) L.S.G. 30, Times, June 12, 1997, [1997] CLY 2185.
[386] *American Cyanamid Co v Ethicon Ltd* [1975] AC 396, [1975] 1 All ER 504.

CHAPTER FOUR

RETURNING OFFICERS AND THEIR CONDUCT OF ELECTIONS

4.1 This chapter covers the statutory schemes governing the conduct of parliamentary elections ("**PE**"), local elections ("**LE**"), Welsh Assembly elections ("**WAE**"), the London Assembly elections ("**LAE**"), and police and crime commissioner elections ("**PCCE**"). It divides this subject into the following sections:

A. The returning officer ("**RO**");

B. When an election is to be held;

C. The initial stages;

D. Nominations;

E. RO preparations for the poll;

F. Polling day;

G. The count;

H. After the count;

I. Judicial review of RO decision before the result.

A. THE RO

Who must appoint an RO

4.2 In England, every non-metropolitan county council must appoint an RO for county council elections, and every district council must appoint an RO for both district council elections and elections to parish councils within that district.[1]

4.3 In Wales, every county council or county borough council must appoint (i) an RO for county or county borough elections; and (ii) another RO for county or county borough community elections.[2]

[1] S 35(1) Representation of the People Act 1983 ("RPA 1983").

[2] S 35(1A) RPA 1983.

Who is to be the RO

4.4 The office of RO is a distinct office from the one that causes a person to become the acting RO,[3] e.g. the Chief Executive of the local authority.

4.5 PE or LE in England: the RO must be:

(i) In a county constituency[4] that is coterminous with or wholly contained in a county: the sheriff of the county;[5]

(ii) In a borough constituency that is coterminous with or wholly contained in a district: the chairman of the district council;[6]

(iii) In any other constituency wholly outside Greater London: the RO is such sheriff or chairman of a district council as may be designated in an order by the Secretary of State;[7]

(iv) In a constituency that is coterminous with or wholly contained in a London borough: the mayor of the borough[8] (or 'chairman' if the London borough is one with executive arrangements that involve a mayor and cabinet executive);[9] in this case, the RO's duties are performed by the registration officer as 'acting RO';[10]

(v) In a constituency wholly or partly in Greater London which is situated partly in one London borough and partly in a district or any other London borough: the mayor or the chairman of such London borough or the chairman of such district council as designated in an order by the Secretary of State.[11]

4.6 WAE: the RO must be:

(i) In a county constituency coterminous with or wholly contained in a preserved county: the sheriff of the county;[12]

(ii) In a borough constituency coterminous with or wholly contained in a county or county borough: the chairman of the county or county

---

[3]S 27(1) RPA 1983.
[4]Parliamentary constituencies are designated 'county constituency' or 'borough constituency' by para 1 sch 1 Parliamentary Constituencies (England) Order 2007.
[5]S 24(1)(a) RPA 1983.
[6]S 24(1)(b) RPA 1983.
[7]S 24(1)(b) RPA 1983.
[8]S 24(1)(d) RPA 1983.
[9]S 24(1)(dd) RPA 1983.
[10]S 28(1)(a) RPA 1983.
[11]S 24(1)(e) RPA 1983.
[12]S 24(1)(aa) RPA 1983

borough council[13] (in this case the RO's duties are performed by the registration officer as 'acting RO');[14]

(iii) In any other constituency in Wales: such sheriff or chairman of a county or county borough council as may be designated in an order by the Secretary of State.[15]

4.7 LAE: the RO must be:

(i) Elections of party list members ('London members') of the London Assembly: the 'Greater London RO', namely: the proper officer of the Greater London Authority;[16]

(ii) Election of a constituency member of the London Assembly: the 'constituency RO', namely: the LE RO for each borough.[17]

4.8 PCCE: the RO must be:

(i) In respect to position of 'local RO', exercising functions in relation to that PCCE voting area:[18] the same person as the LE RO;[19]

(ii) In respect to the 'police area RO': the RO for the corresponding PE constituency.[20]

General duties of the RO

4.9 PE and WAE: In addition to their duty to conduct the election in accordance with the relevant election rules, the RO is under a general duty *"to do all such acts and things as may be necessary for effectually conducting the election in the manner provided by those"* rules.[21] In *Sanders v Chichester*,[22] Dyson J interpreted the purpose of this general duty as being:

> "[T]o empower the [RO] to do things which are not expressly provided for by the Rules or elsewhere in the statute if they are necessary for

---

[13]S 24(1)(bb) RPA 1983.
[14]S 28(1)(b) RPA 1983.
[15]S 24(1)(cc) RPA 1983
[16]S 35(2C) RPA 1983. Below, all references to 'RO' refer to 'GLRO' in the context of London member election or 'CRO' in the constituency member election context.
[17]S 35(2A) RPA 1983 and art 2(b) Greater London Authority (Assembly Constituencies and Returning Officers) Order 1999.
[18]Reg 2A of the Police and Crime Commissioner Elections (Functions of Returning Officers) Regulations 2012.
[19]Art 2(1) Police and Crime Commissioner Elections Order 2012 ("**PCCEO 2012**").
[20]Art 2 and sch 1 Police and Crime Commissioner Elections (Designation of Police Area Returning Officers) Order 2020.
[21]S 23(2) RPA 1983; art 17(2) NAWRPO 2007.
[22] *Sanders v Chichester* [1995] 92(3) LSG 37, [1995] 139 SJLB 15.

effectually conducting the election in the manner provided for by the Rules. It is directed to matters of detail which are not covered by the Rules or to be found elsewhere in the statute."[23]

4.10 The court was clear that the general duty was *"not, however, intended to detract"* from the *"the principal rule for the conduct of elections, which is that they are to be conducted in accordance with the Rules."*[24] Accordingly, the court rejected an argument that the general duty empowered the RO to carry out investigations into the facts underlying those stated on a nomination paper.[25]

4.11 LE and LAE: There is no equivalent general duty; simply they must be conducted in accordance with the relevant election rules.[26]

Human rights duty

4.12 ROs exercise a public function and so should be classed as a public authority for purposes of the Human Rights Act 1998.[27] Public authorities are under a duty to act compatibly with the ECHR.[28] That duty does not apply to acts where the RO, due to primary legislation, could not act differently (e.g. the PE rules, scheduled to the RPA 1983).[29] Acts required by secondary legislation (all the other election rules) do not have the same exemption, unless *"they cannot be read or given effect acting so as to give effect in a way which is compatible with the Convention rights"*.[30] The tightly circumscribed discretion within election rules, and the absence of a general duty other than at PE, therefore largely disapplies this human rights duty from ROs.

4.13 This does not mean that there is no scope for raising the duty on other public authorities where the rules themselves give rise to a disproportionate interference with a right protected by the ECHR: whether before the courts, which are public authorities[31] and under an duty to interpret all legislation compatibly with the ECHR *"so far as it is possible to do so"*,[32] or by way of judicial review of the legislation itself.[33]

---

[23] *Sanders v Chichester* [1995] 92(3) LSG 37, [1995] 139 SJLB 15, p 30 (transcript), per Dyson J.
[24] *Sanders v Chichester* [1995] 92(3) LSG 37, [1995] 139 SJLB 15, p 30 (transcript), per Dyson J.
[25] *Sanders v Chichester* [1995] 92(3) LSG 37, [1995] 139 SJLB 15, p 31 (transcript), per Dyson J.
[26] S 36(1) RPA 1983.
[27] S 6(3)(b) HRA 1998.
[28] S 6(1) HRA 1998.
[29] S 6(2)(a) HRA 1998.
[30] S 6(2)(b) HRA 1998.
[31] S 6(3)(a) HRA 1998.
[32] S 3(1) HRA 1998.
[33] E.g. *R (Robertson) v Wakefield MDC* [2001] EWHC 915 (Admin), at 42, per Maurice Kay J. See Chapter 6.

RO power to correct procedural errors in elections

4.14 The RO may take such steps as they think appropriate, save recount the votes after declaring the result, to remedy any act or omission of (i) theirs, (ii) a person providing them with goods or services, (iii) an ERO, (iv) a presiding officer ("**PO**") appointed by the RO to a polling station, or (v) the deputy of each.[34] The power may be exercised, if (a) the act or omission arises in connection with any of the functions or those of a relevant person in relation to the election, and (b) that act or omission is *"not in accordance with the rules or any other requirements applicable to the election"*.[35]

Breach of official duty

4.15 No civil liability attaches to RO's breach of official duty,[36] but it is an offence for the RO, along with the ERO and POs, to breach their official duties.[37] This offence is subject to a 'reasonable cause' defence and a defence available where, before the conviction takes place or any penalty is imposed, the RO exercises their power to remedy the act or omission in full by taking such steps as they think appropriate.[38]

B. WHEN AN ELECTION IS TO BE HELD

The normal day for elections and the exceptions

4.16 Elections must be held on first Thursday in May,[39] every five years (PE and WAE)[40] or four years (LE, LAE, PCCE, or parish council elections),[41] unless:

(i) PE: the House of Commons passes one of two motions: (a) a motion, by two-thirds majority, *"That there shall be an early parliamentary general election"*; or (b) a motion, by simple majority, that *"That this House has no confidence in Her Majesty's Government"* and, within fourteen days, does not pass another motion that *"That this House has confidence in Her Majesty's Government"*.[42] In either case, the day for the election becomes

---

[34]S 46(4) Electoral Administration Act 2006; art 21 NAWRPO 2007.
[35]S 46(1) Electoral Administration Act 2006; art 21 NAWRPO 2007.
[36]S 63(2) RPA 1983; art 32(2) NAWRPO 2007. This excludes the hitherto-recognised possibility of RO liability in damages at common law for denying a voter a vote: *Ashby v White* [1703] 92 ER 126, p 136-138, per Holt CJ (obiter and dissenting, but upheld by HL at pp 138-139).
[37]S 63(3) RPA 1983; art 32(1) NAWRPO 2007.
[38]S 63(4) and (5); art 32(4) NAWRPO 2007.
[39]S 1 Fixed-term Parliaments Act 2011; s 3(1) Government of Wales Act 2006; s 50(3) Police Reform and Social Responsibility Act 2011.
[40]S 1(3) Fixed-term Parliaments Act 2011; s 3(1) Government of Wales Act 2006.
[41]Ss 7 and 16(3) Local Government Act 1972; s 50(3) Police Reform and Social Responsibility Act 2011.
[42]S 2 Fixed-term Parliaments Act 2011.

that proclaimed by the monarch on recommendation by the Prime Minister;[43]

(ii) WAE: A polling day not more than one month before or after the 1st Thursday in May is proclaimed by the Queen upon proposal by the Presiding Officer of an alternative,[44] or an extraordinary general election is held because the Welsh Assembly resolves by two-thirds majority that it should dissolve or the time for nominating a First Minister expires;[45]

(iii) LE, LAE and PCCE: The Secretary of State or (PCCE) Minister for the Cabinet Office fixes an alternative date by 1st February in the year before the election.[46]

By-elections

4.17 By-elections must be held where a seat becomes vacant (PE and WAE) or a casual vacancy occurs (LE, LAE constituency member,[47] and PCCE),[48] through:

(i) Death;

(ii) Disqualification;

(iii) Non-acceptance of office;

(iv) Resignation;

(v) An election being declared void on an election petition;

(vi) PE: recall petition triggered by (a) conviction leading to imprisonment; (b) House of Commons suspension for at least ten days; or (c) conviction for false or misleading information for allowances claims,[49] and then signed by at least 10% of registered PE voters;[50] or

(vii) The previous incumbent ceasing to be a member of a local authority by reason of failure to attend meetings and subsequent declaration that their office is vacated by the High Court or local authority.[51]

---

[43]S 2(6) and (7) Fixed-term Parliaments Act 2011.
[44]S 4 Government of Wales Act 2006.
[45]S 5(1)-(3) Government of Wales Act 2006.
[46]Ss 37 and 37(ZA) RPA 1983; s 50(4) Police Reform and Social Responsibility Act 2011.
[47]Vacancies amongst London members (i.e. party list members) are filled from the party list: s 11 Greater London Authority Act 1999.
[48] S 51 Police Reform and Social Responsibility Act 2011.
[49]S 1 Recall of MPs Act 2015; Erskine May, 12th edition, part 1, ch 2, para 2.9.
[50]S 14(3) Recall of MPs Act 2015
[51]S 10 Government of Wales Act 2006; s 87 Local Government Act 1972.

4.17 As to timing of by-elections:

(i) PE: as soon as practicable after the Speaker's warrant for a writ for a by-election in the constituency where the vacancy occurred, the Clerk of Crown will issues the writ to the RO for that constituency; for the by-election to the RO for the constituency where the vacancy occurred;[52]

(ii) WAE: by-elections are held on a date fixed by the Assembly's Presiding Officer within three months of the occurrence of the vacancy;[53]

(iii) LE, LAE constituency member, and PCCE: by-elections following casual vacancies must be held within 35 days.[54]

Parish polls

4.18 Parish polls (polls of LE voters entitled to attend parish meetings, concerning questions arising at such a meeting)[55] must be held where:

(i) Such a poll is demanded before the conclusion of the parish meeting;

(ii) The poll concerns any question arising at the meeting, subject to regulations (which as yet have not been made)[56] and subject to the topic being a parish affair;[57] and

(iii) Either the person presiding at the meeting consents to the poll, or it is demanded by at least ten or one-third (whichever is fewer) of the LE voters present.[58]

4.19 Where these conditions are satisfied, parish polls proceed according to the rules governing parish council elections.[59]

---

[52]R 1 sch 1 RPA 1983. Erskine May, 12th edition, part 1, ch 2, para 2.12.
[53]S 10(4) and (5) Government of Wales Act 2006.
[54]S 89(1) Local Government Act 1972; s 10(5) Greater London Authority Act 1999; s 51(4) Police Reform and Social Responsibility Act 2011.
[55]Para 18(5) sch 12 Local Government Act 1972.
[56]Para 18(7) sch 12 Local Government Act 1972.
[57]*R (Letchworth Garden Heritage Foundation) v Returning Officer for the District of North Hertfordshire* [2009] EWHC 841 (Admin), at 17, per Irwin J.
[58] Para 18(4) sch 12 Local Government Act 1972.
[59] Sch 1 Parish and Community Meetings (Polls) Rules 1987.

C. INITIAL STAGES

Dissolution and the writ (PE)

4.20 Parliament must dissolve on the 25th day before the election.[60] As soon as practicable thereafter, the Clerk of Crown must issue the writ for a PE to ROs.[61]

4.21 With by-elections, the Clerk of Crown issues the writ as soon as practicable after the Speaker's warrant for the writ. The warrant is issued on the motion of chief whip of the party whose MP vacated their seat if agreed by MPs.[62]

Notice of election

4.22 The RO must publish the notice of election by the following deadlines:

(i) PE: by 4pm, 2 days after receipt of the writ;[63]

(ii) LE, WAE and PCCE: by the 25th day before the election;[64]

(iii) LAE: by the 30th day before the election.[65]

4.23 The notice of election must state:[66]

(i) The place and times at which nomination papers are to be delivered;

(ii) That forms of nomination paper may be obtained at that place and those times;

(iii) The date of the poll in the event of a contest;

(iv) How to pay the deposit (not LE); and

(v) The deadline by which postal and proxy vote applications much reach the ERO.

4.24 In *Howes v Turner*,[67] where the notice stating the last day for delivery of nomination papers erroneously stated that day to be a Saturday, the election was declared void and a new election ordered. That was because the notice was so

---

[60] S 3 Fixed-term Parliaments Act 2011.
[61] R 1 sch 1 RPA 1983.
[62] R 1 sch 1 RPA 1983. Erskine May, 12th edition, part 1, ch 2, para 2.12.
[63] R 1 sch 1 RPA 1983.
[64] R 1 schs 2 and 3 Local Elections (Principal Areas) (England and Wales) Rules 2006 ("**LEPAR 2006**"); r 1 sch 5 National Assembly for Wales (Representation of the People) Order 2007 ("**NAWRPO 2007**"); r 1 sch 3 PCCEO 2012.
[65] Para 3 sch 1 and 2 Greater London Authority Election Rules 2007 ("**GLAER 2007**").
[66] R 5 sch 1 RPA 1983; r 3 sch 2 and 3 LEPAR; r 3 sch 2 and 3 GLAER 2007; r 3 sch 5 NAWRPO 2007; r 4 sch 3 PCCEO 2012.
[67] *Howes v Turner* [1876] 1 CPD 670.

defective as to be calculated to mislead the candidates and prevent a fair election. Indeed, one had been misled and delivered their papers on the Saturday.[68]

Polling cards

4.25 As soon as practicable after publishing notice of an election, the RO must send an official poll card, in the prescribed form,[69] to voters (to their qualifying address) and to their proxies (to the address shown in the list of proxies.[70]

Issue and receipt of postal ballot papers

4.26 As soon as practicable,[71] the RO must issue the prescribed ballot paper, postal voting statement ("**PVS**"), and envelope for return to those registered by vote by post.[72]

4.27 The RO must also provide and information on how to obtain directions and guidance in other forms (braille, non-English, graphical, audible).[73] There may be no charge for this provision.[74]

4.28 When a postal ballot is returned, the RO must immediately place the covering envelope unopened in a postal voters' ballot box[75] and mark the postal voters list or proxy postal voters list, as appropriate.[76]

4.29 Everyone attending proceedings for issue of receipt of postal ballot papers must maintain the secrecy of voting and it is an offence to do any of the following:

(i) Communicate, before the poll is closed, information as to the official mark, unless for lawful purpose;

(ii) Communicate at any time any information as to the number or other unique identifying mark on the back of a ballot paper sent to someone, unless for lawful purpose;

---

[68] *Howes v Turner* [1876] 1 CPD 670, p 680.
[69] R 28(3) sch 1 RPA 1983; r 25(4) sch 2 and 3 LEPAR; r 26(3) schs 1 and 2 GLAER 2007.
[70] R 28(1) sch 1 RPA 1983; r 25(2) sch 2 and 3 LEPAR; r 26(2) schs 1 and r 27(2) sch 2 GLAER; r 38 sch 5 NAWRPO 2007; r 28 sch 3 PCCEO 2012.
[71] Reg 71 RP (E&W) Regs 2001.
[72] R 24 sch 1 RPA 1983; para 22(1) sch 2 LEPAR 2006; para 23(1) sch 1 GLAER 2007; r 25(1) sch 3 PCCEO 2012.
[73] R 24(2) sch 1 RPA 1983; para 22(2) sch 2 LEPAR 2006; para 23(4) sch 1 GLAER 2007; r 33(4) sch 5 NAWRPO 2007; r 25(2) sch 3 PCCEO 2012.
[74] R 24(4) sch 1 RPA 1983; para 22(4) sch 2 LEPAR 2006.
[75] Reg 82 RP (E&W) Regs 2001.
[76] Para 31A, sch 1 RPA 1983; para 29 sch 2 LEPAR 2006; para 32 sch 1 GLAER 2007; r 40(1) sch 5 NAWRPO 2007; r 33(1) sch 3 PCCEO 2012.

(iii) Attempt to ascertain the number or other unique identifying mark on the back of any completed ballot paper receive, unless for lawful purpose;

(iv) Attempt to ascertain how any vote is given on a particular ballot paper or communicate such information.[77]

D. NOMINATIONS

4.30 To stand nominated, the candidate, their proposer or seconder must deliver the following to the RO, at a place fixed by the RO:

(i) Nomination papers;[78]

(ii) Statements of consent to nomination;[79]

(iii) Certificates issued by party nomination officers authorising use of a description (if applicable);[80] and

(iv) The appropriate deposit (not LE).[81]

4.31 Delivery must be made between 10am and 4pm by the following deadlines:

(i) PE: six days after the dissolution of Parliament (general election); or a date set by the RO, which may not be earlier than the third day after publication of the election notice and not later than later than the seventh day after that on which the writ is received (by-election);

(ii) LE, LAE by-elections, WAE and PCCE: 4pm on the 19th day before the election;[82]

(iii) LAE (London member elections): 4pm on the 24th day before the day of election.[83]

4.32 If a candidate delivers their nomination papers late and goes on to win the election, the election has not been conducted in accordance with the law of elections and is therefore not valid.[84]

---

[77]S 66(4) RPA 1983; art 35(4) NAWRPO 2007.
[78]R 6(1) sch 1 RPA 1983; r 4 schs 2 and 3 LEPAR; r 6 schs 1 and 2 GLAER 2007.
[79]R 8 sch 1 RPA 1983; r 7 schs 2 and 3 LEPAR 2006; r 7 sch 1 and r 9 sch 2 GLAER 2007.
[80]R 6 sch 1 RPA 1983; para 5, schs 2 and 3 LEPAR 2006; r 6(5) sch 1 and 2 GLAER 2007.
[81]R 9 sch 1 RPA 1983; r 8(1) sch 1 and r 10(1) sch 2 GLAER 2007.
[82]R 1 schs 2 and 3, LEPAR 2006; r 7 GLAER 2007; r 1 sch 5 NAWRPO 2007; r 1 sch 3 PCCEO 2012.
[83]R 3 schs 1 and 2 GLAER 2007.
[84]*Cutting v Windsor* [1924] 22 LGR 345

Nomination paper

4.33 The nomination paper must:

(i) Be in the appropriate form, as appended or scheduled to the relevant rules;[85]

(ii) State the candidate's full names (surname first);[86]

(iii) Be subscribed as follows:

- PE and LE: subscribed by two persons registered to vote in that constituency or area, as proposer and seconder, with the electoral number of each, excluding anonymous voters,[87] plus eight further voters assenting to the nomination;[88]
- LAE: no subscription needed (though London Mayoral candidates require 330);[89]
- WAE: subscribed by one person, who may be the candidate;[90]
- PCCE: subscribed by two voters registered to vote in that police area, as proposer and seconder, and by 98 other voters assenting to the nomination;[91] and

(iv) Be accompanied by the 'home address form', which must state full name and home address, or may state that the candidate requires the home address not to be made public and instead just state the constituency where their home address is situated.[92]

4.34 The nomination paper may:

---

[85]R 6(1) sch 1 RPA 1983; r 4(1) schs 1 and 2 LEPAR 2006; r 6(1) sch 1 and rr 6(1) and 7(1) sch 2 GLAER 2007; r 4(1) sch 5 NAWRPO 2007; r 5(1) sch 3 PCCEO 2012.
[86]R 6(2)(a) sch 1 RPA 1983; para 4(2)(a), sch 2 LEPAR 2006; r 6(2)(a) sch 1 and rr 6(2)(a) and 7(2)(c) sch 2 GLAER 2007; r 4(2)(a) sch 5 NAWRPO 2007; r 5(2)(a) sch 3 PCCEO 2012.
[87]R 7(6) and (7) sch 1 RPA 1983; r 6(8) schs 2 and 3 LEPAR 2006.
[88]R 7 sch 1 RPA 1983; r 6(7) and (8) sch 2 LEPAR 2006.
[89]R 7(1) sch 3 GLAER 2007.
[90]R 4, 6(4) and 7(6) sch 5 NAWRPO 2007.
[91]R 7(1) and (5) sch 3 PCCEO 2012.
[92]R 6(4) and (5) sch 1 RPA 1983; r 4(5) and (6), sch 2 LEPAR 2006 (in England); r 6(9A) GLAER 2007. Nb Welsh LE nomination papers do not require accompanying a home address form: r 4 sch 2 LEPAR 2007.

(i) State the commonly used surname or forename in addition to the other name, if the candidate commonly uses a different forename or surname;[93]

(ii) State a description that is either (a) the word 'Independent', or (b) the name of a party that registered with the Commission ("**RP**") no later than two days before the last day for delivery of nomination papers),[94] authorised by a certificate issued by or on behalf of the party's registered nominating officer and received by the RO before the deadline for delivery of nomination papers.[95]

4.35 If requested, the RO must supply any elector with a form of nomination paper at the place and during the time for delivery of nomination papers, and (PE and LE) at their request, prepare a nomination paper for signature.[96]

Candidate names

4.36 Full names and home address are mandatory and represent *"fundamental"* identifiers of a candidate.[97]

4.37 In *Mather v Brown*,[98] a misdescription consisting of stating one of the first names of a candidate by the initial letter only was held to be such a misnomer as to render the nomination paper void.[99]

4.38 In *Harford v Linskey*,[100] the Divisional Court held that formal defect was not the only ground on which the RO could reject nomination papers. Wright J held (before the RPA 1918 extended the franchise to women over 30):

> "If the nomination paper is; on the face of it, a mere abuse of the right of nomination or an obvious unreality, as, for instance, if it purported to nominate a woman or a deceased sovereign, there can be no doubt that it ought to be rejected, and no petition could be maintained in respect of its rejection".[101]

---

[93] R 6(2A) sch 1 RPA 1983; para 4(3) schs 2 and 3 LEPAR 2006, r 6(3) schs 1 and 2 GLAER 2007; rr 4(3) and 6(3) sch 5 NAWRPO 2007.
[94] R 6A(3)(a) sch 1 RPA 1983.
[95] R 6(3) sch 1 RPA 1983; paras 4(2)(c) and (4) and 5, sch 2 LEPAR 2006; rr 6(4)-(6) and 7(2)-(3) sch 1 GLAER 2007; r 5(2) sch 5 NAWRPO 2007; rr 5(4), and 6(1) sch 3 PCCEO 2012.
[96] R 7(4), sch 1 RPA 1983; para 6(4) of sch 2 LEPAR 2006; rr 4(6), 6(5), 7(7) sch 5 NAWRPO 2007; r 7(4)(b) sch 3 PCCEO 2012.
[97] *Sanders v Chichester* [1995] 92(3) LSG 37; [1995] 139 SJLB 15.
[98] *Mather v Brown* [1876] 1 CPD 596.
[99] *Mather v Brown* [1876] 1 CPD 596, p 601.
[100] *Harford v Linskey* [1899] 1 QB 852 (DC).
[101] *Harford v Linskey* [1899] 1 QB 852 (DC), p 862

4.39 In *R v Bennet ex p Margaret Thatcher*,[102] the applicant had changed his name by deed poll to Margaret Thatcher (and his address to *"Downing Street Mansions at 83, Northfield House"*).[103] The RO rejected his nomination paper as an abuse of the right of nomination and an obvious unreality (as well as defective for lack of attested consent to nomination). His judicial review was refused and his appeal dismissed by the Court of Appeal because of the inherent intent to mislead voters and alternatively because judicial relief should be refused for abuse of court process.[104] Stephenson LJ (with whom Eveleigh and May LJJ agreed) held:

> "If it was the object and the possible effect of this adoption of this well-known name, even without the "Hilda", it seems to me that it was intended to be an abuse of the electoral procedure, and, whether or not the returning officer has … the power to reject as he did for the abuse of the right of nomination, it seems to me that this court has the power and the duty to refuse this relief as an abuse of its process. It does not seem to me to be right that the court should lend its aid to the appellant in seeking to confuse the electorate in this constituency in the way in which he has done."[105]

4.40 This case was the example considered by the court in *Sanders v Chichester*[106] when stating *"The law has always treated sham documents and transactions as nullities"*.[107]

Candidate address

4.41 Whether a candidate is resident in the place they claim as residence is a question of fact and degree, with no bright dividing line.[108]

4.42 Even if the object of the residence is to obtain a vote, that does not detract from the right of the candidate to use it as their address if it is their actual residence.[109]

---

[102] *R v Returning Officer for the Parliamentary Constituency of Barnet and Finchley ex parte Bennett v Thatcher* (CA), unreported, 3.6.83, [1983] Lexis Citation 2175, [1983] CA Bound Transcript 237).
[103] *R v Returning Officer for the Parliamentary Constituency of Barnet and Finchley ex parte Bennett v Thatcher* (CA), unreported, 3.6.83, [1983] Lexis Citation 2175, [1983] CA Bound Transcript 237), p 2.
[104] *R v Returning Officer for the Parliamentary Constituency of Barnet and Finchley ex parte Bennett v Thatcher* (CA), unreported, 3.6.83, [1983] Lexis Citation 2175, [1983] CA Bound Transcript 237), pp 4-5 per Stephenson LJ.
[105] *R v Returning Officer for the Parliamentary Constituency of Barnet and Finchley ex parte Bennett v Thatcher* (CA), unreported, 3.6.83, [1983] Lexis Citation 2175, [1983] CA Bound Transcript 237), pp 4-5 per Stephenson LJ.
[106] *Sanders v Chichester* [1995] 92(3) LSG 37, [1995] 139 SJLB 15.
[107] *Sanders v Chichester* [1995] 92(3) LSG 37, [1995] 139 SJLB 15, transcript p 40, per Dyson and Forbes JJ.
[108] *R v Mayor of Exeter* [1868-69] LR 4 QB 110, p 113.
[109] *Whithorn v Thomas* 7 MAN & G 1; cited in *R v Mayor of Exeter* (1868-69) LR 4 QB 110, p 112.

4.43 Merely paying rent or entering into a contract to stay at an address is insufficient to constitute 'residence'.[110]

4.44 Sleeping once or twice in a place is insufficient to make out residence,[111] nor a dozen times across seven months, and 15-20 times across the whole year.[112] Which property the putative resident's partner resides in is indicative of the former's residence.[113]

4.45 A candidate's place of business cannot suffice as their place of residence, even if in the same ward and even if the candidate is better known by their business address.[114]

4.46 In *R v Deighton*,[115] an inaccurate though not fraudulent description of place of residence was sufficient for Lord Denman CJ to give judgment for the Crown in its *quo warranto* action against the successful candidate.[116] Similarly, in *R v Coward (Thomas)*,[117] the court held that a description of a candidate's address that was *"positively wrong"* ('Gonville Place' when it had actually been 'Newmarket Road') could not be saved on the statutory grounds that provided that mere inaccuracy in description of place would not vitiate the election.[118] Patteson J held: *"what we have here is not an inaccuracy in describing the place: there is an accurate description of a place; but it is the wrong place. Now the only thing cured is an inaccurate description of the right place"*.[119]

4.47 By contrast, where a street whose name had recently been changed from to *"W.Street"* (Winton Street) from *"H.Street"* (High Street) but remained commonly known as the latter, and in his nomination paper a candidate's seconder used the latter, the court held that the address was sufficiently described.[120]

4.48 Notwithstanding the strictness of the rule, where the RO decides a candidate is validly nominated not knowing they had used a false address, they have not acted unlawfully for failing to investigate or discover the falsity. In *R v Election Court, ex p Sheppard*,[121] the Divisional Court refused an application for judicial review of an Election Court's decision that the applicant was not duly elected.

---

110 *Whithorn v Thomas* [1844] 7 MAN & G 8 (*'the Tewkesbury case'*), p 4.
111 R *v Mayor of Exeter* (1868-69) LR 4 QB 110, p 113.
112 *Whithorn v Thomas* [1844] 7 MAN & G 8, p 4.
113 *Whithorn v Thomas* [1844] 7 MAN & G 8, p 4.
114 R *v Hammond* [1852] 17 QB 772, p 1477.
115 R *v Deighton* (1844) 5 QB 896.
116 R *v Deighton* (1844) 5 QB 896, p 1488.
117 R *v Coward (Thomas)* [1851] 16 QB 819.
118 R *v Coward (Thomas)* [1851] 16 QB 819, p 1100.
119 R *v Coward (Thomas)* [1851] 16 QB 819, p 1100.
120 *Soper v Mayor of Basingstoke* [1877] 2 CPD 440, p 443, per Denman J.
121 R *v Election Court, ex p Sheppard* [1974] 3 WLR 517 (DC).

The applicant's nomination paper gave a false address as his home address yet the RO had decided he was validly nominated and later declared him duly elected. The Divisional Court accepted that an RO is only required to check whether a nomination papers is valid on its face (in the sense of checking with the prescribed particulars are present); not whether the content of those particulars is correct,[122] as the RO *"cannot possibly be expected to know where every candidate lives and where everybody who has supported the candidature is to be found"*.[123] Yet the Court held this principle did not save an election where the nomination was defective, Lord Widgery CJ concluding: *"In my judgment if the nomination is defective, the election is defective"*.[124]

4.49 Not only is the RO not obliged to look behind the particulars on the face of the paper, but if they do proactively investigate their accuracy and reject that nomination paper, then the election may be declared void.[125] In *Greenway-Stanley v Paterson*,[126] O'Connor J held:

> "It seems to me that the returning officer's duty is confined to seeing that the nomination papers are in due form. Obviously that must include, if he so wishes, a check against the electoral roll because, for example, the subscribers have to give their electoral roll numbers, and it would be perfectly proper for the returning officer to look at the electoral roll and if he finds a discrepancy to take action on it, and if it is not put right the paper on the face of it is invalid and it can be so declared; but it does not entitle him to embark on an enquiry as to the validity of the candidate's particulars which, on their face, are unobjectionable."[127]

4.50 The same principle of non-investigation applied to nomination papers descriptions (i.e. that the candidate was a given party's representative).[128] This is less material now that descriptions must be authorised by certificate issued by RP nominating officer, but the principle is burnished by Parliament hereby finding this solution rather than expand the RO's investigative duty at nomination stage.

4.51 The requirement for candidates to provide their full address even where they have received death threats has been held not irrational, nor contrary to art 2

[122] R *v Election Court, ex p Sheppard* [1974] 3 WLR 517 (DC), p 1324E-F.
[123] R *v Election Court, ex p Sheppard* [1974] 3 WLR 517 (DC), p 1324E-F, per Lord Widgery CJ
[124] R *v Election Court, ex p Sheppard* [1974] 3 WLR 517 (DC), p 1325D
[125] *Greenway-Stanley v Paterson* [1977] 2 All E.R. 663, 670.
[126] *Greenway-Stanley v Paterson* [1977] 2 All E.R. 663.
[127] *Greenway-Stanley v Paterson* [1977] 2 All ER 663, at p 670B-C.
[128] *Sanders v Chichester* [1995] 92(3) LSG 37; [1995] 139 SJLB 15, p 26 (of transcript).

ECHR (the right to life),[129] where the threats were a year old and did not satisfy the *"real and immediate risk"* test for whether the art 2 operational duty was engaged.[130]

Descriptions

4.52 Nomination papers may not include descriptions likely to lead voters to associate the candidate with an RP, unless the description is authorised by that RP's nominating officer and sent to the RO before the deadline for nomination papers.[131] This rule followed *Sanders v Chichester*,[132] in which the court (Dyson and Forbes JJ) held that a nomination paper describing the candidate as a member of *"Literal Democrats"* were nonetheless as required by law and the RO was not in breach of the RO's duty to (a) examine all nomination papers delivered to them and (b) decide whether the candidates named had been validly and lawfully nominated.[133] Dyson J held that *"it might be thought obvious that the description "Literal Democrat" was calculated to confuse the voters and mislead supporters of [the Liberal Democrat candidate] Mr Sanders into thinking that [the Literal Democrat candidate] Mr Huggett was Mr Sanders"*.[134]

4.53 In *R (De Beer) v Balabanoff*,[135] where the description was authorised by the election agent but not the RP's registered nominating officer or someone acting on their behalf, the RO rejected the candidates' nomination papers featuring the description. The candidates' claim for judicial review of that decision was refused. Relying on *Sanders v Chichester*,[136] Scott Baker J held:

> "In my judgment when considering the question whether a description in a nomination paper is authorised by a certificate, the returning officer is not entitled to look beyond the nomination paper and the certificate. Only within the four corners of those documents does his judgment fall to be exercised."[137]

---

[129] R *(Jarvis) v Secretary of State for Housing, Communities and Local Government and another* [2018] EWHC 1259 (Admin) (Choudhury J) at 16.

[130] R *(Jarvis) v Secretary of State for Housing, Communities and Local Government and another* [2018] EWHC 1259 (Admin) (Choudhury J) at 26.

[131] R 6A(1) sch 1 RPA 1983; R 5(1) schs 2 and 3 LEPAR; r 6(5) sch 1 GLAER 2007; r 5(1) and (3) NAWRPO 2007.

[132] *Sanders v Chichester* [1995] 92(3) LSG 37; [1995] 139 SJLB 15; para 2 sch 2 Registration of Political Parties Act 1998 (24.3.99).

[133] *Sanders v Chichester* [1995] 92(3) LSG 37; [1995] 139 SJLB 15, p 48 (of transcript).

[134] *Sanders v Chichester* [1995] 92(3) LSG 37; [1995] 139 SJLB 15, p 49 (of transcript).

[135] R *(De Beer) v Balabanoff* [2002] EWHC 670 (Admin).

[136] *Sanders v Chichester* [1995] 92(3) LSG 37; [1995] 139 SJLB 15, Dyson and Forbes JJ.

[137] R *(De Beer) v Balabanoff* [2002] EWHC 670 (Admin), at 34.

4.54 In *Jessie Patterson v David Steven Merrick v Michael Hammond*,[138] the Court of Appeal (May and Woolf LJJ) dismissed an appeal against an application to discharge an injunction against restraining the appellant from describing himself as *"the Official Byron Ward Conservative"* candidate in a Nottingham City Council by-election. The plaintiff was a further candidate, who was and whose description was *"the Official Conservative Party candidate"*. The Court held:

> "Clearly the description which this appellant applied to himself in relation to his nomination was capable of confusion with the description applied to herself by the plaintiff and we have no doubt that it was for that reason that the learned judge made the original injunction in October."

Subscribers

4.55 In relation to subscribers' names, the authorities are kind to candidates. In *Bowden v Besley*,[139] a nomination paper at a ward election was subscribed with the initials rather than the full name of three of those assenting to a candidate's nomination, the court held the nomination paper to be duly subscribed, as the subscribers' electoral number was as in the register and there was nothing in the legislation requiring nominators to give their full name.[140]

4.56 In *Harding v Cornwell*,[141] where a nomination paper at a ward election was subscribed with the correct name entered in reverse (*"Davenport, Henry D, Evereux"*), the nomination paper was held valid.

4.57 Similarly, in *Melton Mowbray (Egerton Ward) Urban DC Election*,[142] where a nomination paper was held by the respondent RO to be invalid because the person subscribing it had written a different formulation of their name to that on the electoral register (*"E.Marment'* rather than *"Marment, Nellie"*), the Divisional Court held the RO was wrong to so hold, because the relevant rules provided that a person subscribing a nomination paper as assenting should use their usual signature.[143]

---

[138] *Jessie Patterson v David Steven Merrick v Michael Hammond* [1988] WL 1608805, unreported, 2.11.1988, May and Woolf LLJ.

[139] *Bowden v Besley* (1888) 21 QBD. 309.

[140] *Bowden v Besley* (1888) 21 QBD. 309, p 312.

[141] *Harding v Cornwell* (1889) 60 LT 959.

[142] *Melton Mowbray (Egerton Ward) Urban DC Election, Re* [1969] 1 QB 192, [1968] 3 WLR 886 (DC)

[143] *Melton Mowbray (Egerton Ward) Urban DC Election, Re* [1969] 1 QB 192, [1968] 3 WLR 886 (DC), p 891.

4.58 There is less scope for inaccuracy with electoral numbers. In *Gothard v Clark*,[144] where the incorrect register number was mistakenly written in a nomination paper, objections were made and allowed by the RO, the court held that the RO was right to object, even though no one had been or could be misled, and the mistake could not be remedied under the statutory saving provisions. Grove J held:

> "There may be a clerical error, such as by making the figure 9 with too short a tail so as to look like the cypher 0. It may be, although I do not give judgment on it, that the mayor is to treat that reasonably. There may be a clerical error which is obviously a mere clerical error ex facie. Or suppose the name Jones were written "Jone," the letter " s " being omitted. The mayor might perhaps be justified in treating that as the subject of correction. But here we have a real change of number. It is not "704" but "695"; not a figure is right, and there is no possibility of this being a mere clerical error."[145]

4.59 There is equally limited lee-way in relation the requirement that proposer and seconder be from the constituency or area. These were the facts of *Parkinson v Lewis*,[146] where the election of candidates whose proposer and seconders were not registered in the ward was held void.[147] Further, because the defect was the subscribers' and not the RO's error, the election could be saved under the statutory provision for saving immaterial RO errors.[148]

Consent to nomination

4.60 To stand nominated, a candidate must deliver their consent to nomination within the month (PCCE: 31 days) ending with the deadline for delivery of nomination papers, attested by one witness, and the attested consent is delivered at the place and within the time for the delivery of nomination papers.[149] If they are abroad, they may send their consent by email (PE).[150]

4.61 A template consent to nomination form is appended to the respective election rules, to ensure the prescribed information is provided.

4.62 In *Talbot v Gordon and Thornley*,[151] the candidates gave the wrong declaration of eligibility to stand (that they had resided in the area for the twelve months

---

[144] *Gothard v Clark* (1880) 5 CPD 253.
[145] *Gothard v Clark* [1880] 5 CPD 253, p 260.
[146] *Parkinson v Lewis* [2016] EWHC 725 (QB).
[147] *Parkinson v Lewis* [2016] EWHC 725 (QB), at 18 and 115.
[148] *Parkinson v Lewis* [2016] EWHC 725 (QB), at 100. I.e. s 48 RPA 1983.
[149] R 8 sch 1 RPA 1983; r 7(a) of sch 2 LEPAR 2006; r 7 sch 1 and r 9 sch 2 GLAER 2007; r 9 sch 5 NAWRPO 2007; r 8 sch 3 PCCEO 2012.
[150] R 8(2) sch 1 RPA 1983.
[151] *Talbot v Gordon and Thornley* [1989] CLY 1390.

preceding the relevant day rather than that they were local government electors in the area). On a petition questioning their election, the commissioner held that the errors were not trivial, the election was void, and a fresh election was ordered.

Deposit

4.63 At the place for delivery of nomination papers, the candidate must deposit £500 (PE and WAE),[152] £1,000 (LAE constituency member election),[153] or £5,000 (LAE London member election and PCCE)[154] with the RO. This is recoverable if more than a 20th of the vote is polled, but otherwise forfeited.[155]

Right to inspect and object (PE, WAE and PCCE)

4.64 The following persons are entitled to attend nomination proceedings in which to inspect and object to the validity of any nomination paper (PE and WAE) and associated home address form (PE and PCCE):[156]

(i) A person standing nominated as a candidate (having delivered their own nomination paper, candidate's consent, home address form, and deposit);[157]

(ii) Their election agent (or someone named by the candidate if they are their own agent);[158] or

(iii) Their proposer or seconder (PE and PCCE)[159] or their party's registered nominating officer (WAE);[160] and

(iv) A representative of the Commission, an accredited observer, and one other person chosen by the candidate are the only people who may also attend, but do not have the right to object and inspect.[161]

4.65 They may exercise this right on the last day for delivery of nomination papers, between 10am and 5pm.[162] The only objections that may be made from 12-

---

[152]R 9 sch 1 RPA 1983; r 10 sch 5 NAWRPO 2007.

[153]R 8 sch 1 GLAE 2007.

[154]R 10 sch 2 GLAE 2007; r 9(1) sch 3 PCCEO 2012.

[155]R 53(4) sch 1 RPA 1983; r 55(5) sch 1 GLAER 2007; r 65(6) sch 5 NAWRPO 2007; r 63(5) sch 3 PCCEO 2012.

[156]R 11(3) sch 1 RPA 1983; r 10(5) sch 3 PCCEO 2012.

[157]R 11(1)(a) sch 1 RPA 1983; r 12(1)(a) and (2)(a) sch 5 NAWRPO 2007; r 10(2)(a) sch 3 PCCEO 2012.

[158]R 11(1)(b) sch 1 RPA 1983; r 12(1)(b) and (2)(b) sch 5 NAWRPO 2007; r 10(2)(b) sch 3 PCCEO 2012.

[159]R 11(1)(b) sch 1 RPA 1983; r 10(2)(b) sch 3 PCCEO 2012.

[160]R 12(1)(c) and (2)(c) sch 5 NAWRPO 2007.

[161]R 11(1) sch 1 RPA 1983; r 12 sch 5 NAWRPO 2007; r 10(2)(c) sch 3 PCCEO 2012.

[162]R 1, sch 1 RPA 1983; r 1 sch 5 NAWRPO 2007; r 1 sch 3 PCCEO 2012.

5pm, however, are to nomination papers delivered within the previous 24 hours.[163] Objection made on grounds that the nominated person is disqualified may be made on the day after the last day for delivery of nomination papers.[164]

4.66 If nomination proceedings are on a day interrupted by riot or open violence, they are abandoned for that day. If the nomination proceedings are held on the last day for delivery of nomination papers, then the nomination proceedings continue on the next day, with that day then treated as the last day.[165]

Right to inspect (LE and LAE)

4.67 LE and LAE: after the latest time for delivery of nomination papers and before the date of the poll, during ordinary office hours on any working day, any person may inspect and take copies of, or extracts from, nomination papers and consents to nomination.[166] Home address forms may only be inspected (not copied) and only by candidates standing nominated, their election agent, or if they have no agent then someone they nominate.[167]

RO decisions on validity of nomination papers

4.68 If a candidate delivers on time and to the correct address their nomination paper, consent to nomination, and (PE or PCCE) the home address form and deposit, they are deemed to stand nominated, unless:

(i) The RO decides that the nomination paper is invalid or that the home address form is non-compliant;

(ii) PCCE: the nomination paper is not accompanied by a compliant home address form;

(iii) Proof is given to the RO's satisfaction of the candidate' death; or

(iv) The candidate withdraws.[168]

Invalidity

4.69 The RO must make their decision on whether a candidate has been validly nominated as soon as practicable after each nomination paper and home address form have been delivered. PE and WAE: that decision must be made within 24

[163]R 1 sch 1 RPA 1983; r 1 sch 5 NAWRPO 2007; r 1 sch 3 PCCEO 2012.
[164]Rr 1 and 15(2), sch 1 RPA 1983; rr 1 and 19 sch 5 NAWRPO 2007.
[165]R 16 sch 1 RPA 1983; r 20 sch 5 NAWRPO 2007.
[166]R 11 schs 2 and 3 LEPAR 2006; para 12, sch 1 GLAER 2007.
[167]Rr 11(4) and 11A sch 2 LEPAR 2006; r 12A sch 1 GLAER 2007.
[168]R 12(1) sch 1 RPA 1983; r 11(1) sch 2 and r 10(1) sch 3 GLAER 2007; r 11(1) sch 3 PCCEO 2012.

hours,[169] along with decision on any objection to a nomination paper at nomination proceedings.[170] LE and LAE: only invalidity decisions based on use of an unauthorised RP description are subject to this longstop deadline.[171]

4.70 They must send notice of the decision to each candidate.[172]

4.71 The RO may decide a nomination paper is invalid on the following grounds:

(i) The candidate's or one of their subscribers' particulars are not as required by law;[173]

(ii) The paper is not properly subscribed;[174] and

(iii) The candidate is disqualified by the RPA 1981; or

(iv) The papers includes a description of the candidate likely to lead electors to associate them with one or multiple registered political parties but without (a) each party being a qualifying party in that constituency or (b) authorisation for that description existing in a certificate issued by the party's registered nominating officer and received by the RO by the deadline for delivering nomination papers).[175]

4.72 It is the responsibility of the candidates to make sure the nomination form is properly completed.[176] That error does not transfer to the RO.[177] As the above cases show, there is no obligation on the RO to help candidates to complete their forms correctly, only to apply the rules, with limited discretion.[178]

4.73 If the RO decides the nomination paper is invalid, the RO must endorse and sign on the nomination paper his decision, along with his reasons.[179]

Correction of minor errors

4.74 Until the RO publishes the statement of persons nominated,[180] the RO may correct the following minor errors in a nomination paper or home address form:

---

[169] R 12(3) sch 1 RPA 1983; rr 13(3) and 14(3) NAWRPO 2007.
[170] R 12(3) sch 1 RPA 1983; r 13(3) NAWRPO 2007.
[171] R 8(3) schs 2 and 3 LEPAR 2006; r 9(3) and (4) sch 1 GLAER 2007.
[172] R 8(6) schs 2 and 3 LEPAR 2006.
[173] R 12(2)(a) sch 1 RPA 1983; r 8(2)(a) sch 2 LEPAR 2006.
[174] R 12(2)(b) sch 1 RPA 1983; r 8(2)(b) sch 2 LEPAR 2006.
[175] R 12(3A) sch 1 RPA 1983; r 13(4) sch 5 NAWRPO 2007.
[176] *Begum v RO for Tower Hamlets* [2006] EWCA civ 733 at 39.
[177] *Begum v RO for Tower Hamlets* [2006] EWCA civ 733 at 39.
[178] *R (De Beer) v Balabanoff* [2002] EWHC 670 (Admin), at 33; *R (Wilson) v Dover DC* [2016] EWHC 2556 (Admin), at 36.
[179] R 12(4) sch 1 RPA 1983; r 8(5) schs 2 and 3 LEPAR 2006; and r 9(5) sch 1 and r 10(5) sch 2 GLAER 2007.
[180] R 14A sch 1 RPA 1983; r 10 sch 2 LEPAR 2006; r 11 sch 1 GLAER 2007; r 18 sch 5 NAWRPO 2007; r 12(1) sch 3 PCCEO 2012.

(i) Errors as to a person's electoral number;[181]

(ii) Obvious errors of spelling in relation to the details of a candidate;[182]

(iii) PE, LAE, and PCCE: errors as to the information in the home address form.[183]

4.75 The RO must have regard to guidance issued by the Electoral Commission for the purposes of this rule.[184] Its guidance states:

> "**Errors in elector numbers**
>
> 3.134 Where an elector number has been entered incorrectly, you may amend it if you are satisfied that an error has been made. However, where the elector number has been omitted altogether, this does not amount to an error, and the nomination form should be rejected on the basis that the number has not been supplied and so the particulars are not as required.
>
> **Errors of spelling in details of candidates**
>
> 3.135 Dealing with the 'obvious' errors of spelling may be more difficult, as what is obvious to one person may not be so to another. Care should be taken in exercising this power.
>
> **Errors in a home address**
>
> 3.136 Where a home address is not absolutely correct there may not be a need to make a correction. By law, errors in a home address do not affect the full operation."[185]

Challenge to decision on nomination validity

4.76 An RO decision that a nomination paper is valid cannot be challenged in any legal proceedings.[186] An RO decision that a nomination paper is invalid or to correct a minor error can be challenged after an election by way of election

---

[181]R 14A(2)(a) sch 1 RPA 1983; r 10(2)(a) sch 2 LEPAR 2006; r 11(2)(a), sch 1 GLAER 2007; r 12(2)(a) sch 3 PCCEO 2012.

[182]Para 14A(2)(b) sch 1 RPA 1983; para 10(2)(b) sch 2 LEPAR 2006; para 11(2)(b), sch 1 GLAER 2007; r 18(2) sch 5 NAWRPO 2007; r 12(2)(b) sch 3 PCCEO 2012.

[183]R 14A(2)(c) sch 1 RPA 1983; para 11(2)(c), sch 1 GLAER 2007; r 12(2)(c) sch 3 PCCEO 2012.

[184]R 14A(4) sch 1 RPA 1983; r 10(4) schs 2 and 3 LEPAR 2006; para 11(2)(c), sch 1 GLAER 2007; r 18(4) sch 5 NAWRPO 2007.

[185]Electoral Commission, 'Part C - Administering the poll: UK Parliamentary elections in Great Britain: guidance for (Acting) Returning Officers', November 2018.

[186]R 13(5) and (6) and 14A sch 1 RPA 1983; r 8(8) sch 2 and 3 LEPAR 2007; r 9(7) sch 1 and r 11(10) sch 2 GLAER 2007; r 14(10) sch 5 NAWRPO 2007; r 11(7) sch 3 PCCEO 2012.

petition[187] and before an election by JR.[188] The ambit for doing so is limited by how mandatory the election rules are that ROs operate within.[189] However, if they do not operate within those rules, greater scope for JR may lie.

4.77 Notwithstanding the immunity given to RO decisions that a nomination paper is valid, the broader question of whether a candidate was validly nominated can be challenged by JR, e.g. if they had been legally incapable of standing for election at the relevant time.

Withdrawal of candidate

4.78 Within the same window for delivery of nomination papers (see above), and to the same place, a candidate may withdraw their candidacy by delivering notice of withdrawal, signed by them and attested by a witness.[190]

Death of candidate

4.79 LE, LAE, PCCE: if the election is contested and before the result of the election is declared the RO receives evidence that satisfies them that a candidate has died, the RO must: (i) countermand notice of the poll or (if polling has begun) direct that the poll be abandoned (PCCE: notify the appropriate officer for the police area that the poll is countermanded);[191] and (ii) order an election to fill the vacancy on a day appointed by him but within 35 days.[192] No fresh nomination is necessary and no other nominations are permitted, except for the RP for whom the deceased stood, who must deliver their new nomination by the seventh working day after the day on which the writ is taken to be received.

4.80 PE and WAE: the above procedure is followed if the candidate was standing for a RP, and the new polling day must be fixed for 21-27 working days after the date on which the writ is deemed received.[193] The exception is if the deceased had been an independent candidate, in which case:

(i) If the deceased independent candidate proceeds to win a majority of votes, then the RO must: (a) declare that the majority of votes has been

---

[187]Rr 13(5) and (6) and 14A(3) sch 1 RPA 1983; r 8(8) sch 2 and 3 LEPAR 2007; r 11(3) sch 1 and r 13(3) sch GLAER 2007; rr 14(10) and 18(3) sch 5 NAWRPO 2007; rr 11(8) and 12(3) sch 3 PCCEO 2012.

[188]R *(Wilson) v Dover DC* [2016] EWHC 2556 (Admin), at 31-32, per Cranston J. A challenge to a PCCE nomination decision, relying on procedural fairness and legitimate expectation.

[189]R *(Wilson) v Dover DC* [2016] EWHC 2556 (Admin), at 31-32, per Cranston J. A challenge to a PCCE nomination decision, relying on procedural fairness and legitimate expectation.

[190]R 13 sch 1 RPA 1983; r 13 of sch 2 LEPAR 2006; para 14(1), sch 1 GLAER 2007; r 15 sch 5 NAWRPO 2007; r 15 sch 3 PCCEO 2012.

[191]Art 79 PCCEO 2012.

[192]R 55 sch 2 LEPAR 2006; r 60 sch 1 and 2 GLAER 2007; s 39(1) RPA 1983; s 51 Police Reform and Social Responsibility Act 2011.

[193]S 39(5)(b) RPA 1983.

given to the deceased candidate but that no member is returned;[194] (b) give public notice of the total number of votes given for each candidate together with the number of rejected ballot papers under each head shown in the statement of rejected ballot papers;[195] (c) commence election proceedings afresh,[196] in which no fresh nomination is necessary in the case of a person shown in the statement of persons nominated and no other nomination may be made (thereby preventing a substitute independent candidate, arguably contrary to A3P1);[197]

(ii) If they do not win a majority, the rules apply as if they had not died;[198]

(iii) If only two candidates had stood nominated, the RO must treat the election as uncontested, either countermanding the notice of the poll (if polling has not begun), or (if it has) declare that polling is abandoned;[199]

(iv) If there is a tie, the votes for the deceased candidate are ignored.[200]

Statement of persons nominated and notice of poll

4.81 The RO must give public notice of a statement showing:[201]

(i) The persons who stand nominated, in alphabetical order;

(ii) Those have been but no longer stand nominated, with reasons why;

(iii) Their names (or commonly used name if used in the nomination paper, unless likely to mislead of confuse voters, or is obscene or offensive);

(iv) Their addresses or, if their home address form contained a statement made and signed by the candidate that he requires the home address not to be made public, a statement of the constituency within which they live;

(v) Their descriptions, if any;

(vi) The names of those subscribing their nomination and home address forms;

---

[194]R 61(2) and 63(2)

[195]R 61(2) and 63(2)

[196]R 61(4)-(9) and 63(4)-(9) RPA 1983.

[197]R 61(6) RPA 1983. There may be a substitute willing to step into the place of the deceased independence who may have won a massive majority for, say, saving a hospital, but no new candidates are permitted, unlike when a RP candidate dies.

[198]R 60 sch 1 RPA 1983; r 70 sch 5 NAWRPO 2007.

[199]R 60(1) and (4)

[200]R 62

[201]R 14 sch 1 RPA 1983; r 9 schs 2 and 3 LEPAR 2006; 10 sch 1 and r 12 sch 2 GLAER 2007; r 16 sch 5 NAWRPO 2007; r 13 sch 3 PCCEO 2012.

(vii) PE and WAE: if more than one person stands nominated: a notice of the poll, stating the day on which and hours during which the poll will be taken,[202] and the location of each polling station and who may vote there.[203] This may be published separately from the statement of persons nominated, but if so a copy must be given to each candidate's election agents.[204]

4.82 The RO must publish the statement by the following times:

(i) PE: at the close of time for objecting (unless objections are made to nomination papers, in which case: within 24 hours of the deadline for objecting);[205]

(ii) LE, WAE, and PCCE: by 4pm on the 18th day before polling day;[206]

(iii) LAE: Not later than 4pm on the 22nd day before polling day.[207]

4.83 PE, WAE and PCCE: the RO must send a copy of the statement to the Commission.[208]

4.84 PE and WAE: If it appears to the RO that any of the persons nominated might be disqualified, the RO must instead prepare a 'draft statement of persons nominated', omitting the names of persons subscribing the papers, and containing a notice stating that anyone who wishes to object to the nomination of any candidate on grounds that they are disqualified from nomination under RPA 1981 may do so between 10am-4pm on a certain day (which must be the day after the last day for delivery of papers) at the place specified in the notice.[209]

Nomination offences

Tampering with nomination papers

4.85 It is an offence to fraudulently deface or destroy any nomination paper (as it is with ballot papers).[210]

---

[202] R 23(2) sch 1 RPA 1983; r 32 sch 5 NAWRPO 2007.
[203] R 23(2), sch 1 RPA 1983.
[204] R 23(2) sch 1 RPA 1983; para 21(3) sch 2 LEPAR 2006.
[205] R 1 sch 1 RPA 1983;
[206] R 1 schs 2 and 3 LEPAR 2006; r 1 sch 5 NAWRPO 2007; r 1 sch 3 PCCEO 2012.
[207] R 3, sch 1, GLAER 2007.
[208] R 14(5) sch 1 RPA 1983; rr 16(8) and 17(14) sch 5 NAWRPO 2007; r 13(13)(b) sch 3 PCCEO 2012.
[209] R 15 sch 1 RPA 1983; r 19 sch 5 NAWRPO 2007.
[210] S 65(1)(a) sch 1 RPA 1983; art 33(1)(a) NAWRPO 2007; art 20(1)(a) PCCEO 2012.

False statements in nomination papers etc

4.86 Including any of the below in document given to the RO is a corrupt practice, as is permitting it to be so included:

(i) Anything that purports to be the signature of a voter proposing, seconding or assenting to, the nomination a candidate, in the knowledge it was not written by that voter or was not but not for the purported purpose;[211]

(ii) A statement of a candidate's name or home address that they know to be false in any way;[212]

(iii) PE, WAE and PCCE: a home address form they know to be false in any way;[213]

(iv) PE, WAE and PCCE: a certificate authorising a candidate's use of a description, if the person providing it knows that the candidate is standing at an election in another constituency in which an election is being held on the same day,[214] or (WAE) for another RP at that election.[215]

4.87 It is an offence for a candidate to provide an RO with a statement as to their qualification and consent to be elected that contains a statement that they know to be false in relation to their:

(i) Date of birth;[216]

(ii) Qualification for being elected at that election;[217]

(iii) Not being a candidate in any other constituency election being held on the same day;[218]

(iv) Not being a party list candidate when standing as an individual candidate (WAE);[219] or

---

[211] S 65A(1)(b) RPA 1983; art 34(1)(b) NAWRPO 2007; art 21(1)(c) PCCEO 2012. See *R v Alingham (Tammy)* [2015] EWCA Crim 1358 for an example of this.
[212] S 65A(1)(a) RPA 1983; art 34(1)(a) NAWRPO 2007; art 21(1)(a) PCCEO 2012.
[213] S 65A(1)(aa) RPA 1983; art 21(1)(b) PCCEO 2012.
[214] S 65A(1)(c) RPA 1983; art 34(1)(b) NAWRPO 2007; art 21(1)(d) PCCEO 2012.
[215] Art 34(1)(d) NAWRPO 2007.
[216] S 65A(1A)(a) RPA 1983; art 34(2)-(4)(a) NAWRPO 2007; art 21(2)(a) PCCEO 2012.
[217] S 65A(1A)(b) RPA 1983; art 34(2)-(4)(b) NAWRPO 2007; art 21(2)(b) PCCEO 2012. See *R v Fadaka* [2015] EWCA Crim 1017 for an instance of this offence.
[218] S 65A(1A)(c) RPA 1983; art 34(2)(c) NAWRPO 2007; art 21(2)(c) PCCEO 2012.
[219] Art 34(3)(c) NAWRPO 2007.

(v) Not being on another party's list (WAE).[220]

Fraudulent certificate authorising description

4.88 Only a RP's nominating officer may issue a certificate authorising a description that nominated candidates may then use. If someone fraudulently purports to issue such a certificate on behalf of a nominating officer, they commit an offence and are guilty of a corrupt practice.[221]

Election by default or contested election

4.89 If the statement shows just one person standing nominated, then, as soon as practicable after the latest time for the delivery of notices of withdrawals of candidature, the RO must:

(i) Declare them to be elected and enter their name into the statement of persons nominated;

(ii) Give public notice of their name;[222]

(iii) Return the winner's name to the Clerk of the Crown (PE),[223] or send the notice to the proper officer[224] of the council for which the election was held (LE),[225] or the minister and local RO (PCCE).[226]

4.90 If the statement shows more than one person standing nominated, the election proceeds to a poll, with votes given by ballot, and the winner being the candidate given most votes.[227]

E. RO PREPARATIONS FOR THE POLL

Notice of poll

4.91 LE, LAE and PCCE: the RO must publish notice of the poll no later than the sixth day before the election,[228] stating the date and hours fixed for the poll, number of councillors to be elected (LE), names and other particulars of the candidates, and names of persons subscribing their nomination paper.[229] LAE:

---

220 Art 34(4)(c) NAWRPO 2007.
221 R 6A(2) sch 1 RPA 1983; r 5(7) sch 5 NAWRPO 2007; r 6(5) sch 3 PCCEO 2012.
222 R 54(4) sch 1 GLAER 2007; r 62(2) sch 3 PCCEO 2012.
223 R 50(2)
224 S 270(3) Local Government Act 1972. A statutory role performed by an officer appointed to that role, especially in relation to governance issues.
225 Para 50(2) sch 2 LEPAR 2006; para 15(2) sch 1 GLAER 2007.
226 R 62(4) sch 3 PCCEO 2012.
227 R 17 sch 1 RPA 1983; para 14(1) sch 2 LEPAR 2006; para 15(1) sch 1 GLAER 2007; r 18 sch 3 PCCEO 2012.
228 R 1 sch 2 LEPAR 2006; r 1 sch 1 GLAER 2007; r 1 sch 3 PCCEO 2012.
229 R 21 sch 2 LEPAR 2006; r 22 sch 1 GLAER 2007; r 24(3) sch 3 PCCEO 2012.

at ordinary election, the notice must also state *"Greater London Authority Election"*.[230] As soon as practicable after publishing the notice, it must be sent to each candidate's election agent.[231]

Ballot papers

4.92 Ballot papers must: [232]

(i) Be in the prescribed form appended to the relevant rules;

(ii) Be printed in accordance with directions;

(iii) Contain the names and other particulars of the candidates as shown in the statement of persons nominated,[233] in the same order (alphabetical);

(iv) Be capable of being folded up (not LAE – because of the automatic counting machines);[234]

(v) Have a number and other unique identifying mark printed on the back;

(vi) Contain an appropriate security marking ("**the official mark**"), which must be kept secret.[235] The same official mark cannot be used in the same constituency more frequently than every seven (PE and WAE) or five (LE, LAE and PCCE) years;[236] and

(vii) Be in different colours where different elections are held on the same day.[237]

4.93 Ballot papers may:

(i) Contain a party's emblem, if requested by the candidate and the candidate is authorised to use it;[238] and

---

[230]R 22 sch 1 GLAER 2007.

[231]R 21(3) schs 2 and 3 LEPAR 2006; r 22 sch 1 and r 23(2) sch 2 GLAER 2007; r 24(4) sch 3 PCCEO 2012.

[232]R 19(2) sch 1, and Appendix of Forms, RPA 1983; r 16(2) sch 2 and 3 LEPAR 2007; r 17(1), sch 1, and Forms Schedule, GLAER 2007; rr 24(3) and 25(3) sch 5 NAWRPO 2007; r 19 sch 3 PCCEO 2012.

[233]R 19(2)(a) sch 1 RPA 1983; para 16(2)(a) sch 2 LEPAR 2006; para 17(3)(b) sch 1, and Forms Schedule, GLAER 2007.

[234]R 19(2)(b) sch 1 RPA 1983; para 16(2)(b) sch 2 LEPAR 2006; rr 24(3)(b) and 25(3)(c) sch 5 NAWRPO 2007.

[235]R 20 sch 1 RPA 1983; para 18 sch 2 LEPAR 2006; para 19 sch 1 GLAER 2007; r 21 sch 3 PCCEO 2012.

[236]R 20 sch 1 RPA 1983; para 18 sch 2 LEPAR 2006; r 29 sch 5 NAWRPO 2007; r 21(3) sch 3 PCCEO 2012.

[237]R 16(d) sch 3 LEPAR 2006; r 17(8) sch 1 GLAER 2007; r 28 sch 5 NAWRPO 2007.

[238]R 19(2A), sch 1, RPA 1983; para 16(3) sch 2 LEPAR 2006; para 17(4) sch 1, and Forms Schedule, GLAER 2007.

(ii) LAE: be marked *"do not fold"*.[239]

Corresponding number list

4.94 The RO must prepare a list of the numbers and other unique identifying marks of all the ballot papers that they will issue or provide on polling day.[240]

Presiding officers ("POs")

4.95 The RO must appoint and pay a PO for each polling station, plus such clerks as necessary to assist them.[241] The RO may themselves act as a PO.[242] Neither PO nor their clerks may be someone employed by a candidate *"in or about the election"* (all but PCCE)[243] or *"in the election"* (PCCE).[244]

Polling stations and equipment

4.96 The RO must provide sufficient polling stations and sufficient screening compartments therein.[245] There may be more than one polling station in the same room.[246]

4.97 The RO must equip each PO with:[247]

(i) Such number of ballot boxes (constructed so that ballot papers can be put in it, but not withdrawn without being unlocked) and ballot papers as the RO considers necessary. At a combined poll, if the RO thinks fit, the same ballot box may be used for both (as the papers will be different colours);

(ii) Materials to enable voters to mark the ballot papers;

---

[239]Para 17(3)(d) sch 1, and Forms Schedule, GLAER 2007. For electronic counting purposes.
[240]R 19A sch 1 RPA 1983; para 17 sch 2 LEPAR 2006; para 18 sch 1 GLAER 2007; r 27 sch 5 NAWRPO 2007.
[241]R 26 sch 1 RPA 1983; para 24(1) sch 2 LEPAR 2006; para 25(1) sch 1 and r 26(1) sch 2 GLAER 2007; r 35 sch 5 NAWRPO 2007; r 27(1) sch 3 PCCEO 2012.
[242]R 26(2) sch 1 RPA 1983; para 24(2) sch 2 LEPAR 2006; r 25(2) sch 1 and r 26(2) sch 2 GLAER 2007; r 35(3) sch 5 NAWRPO 2007.
[243]R 26 sch 1 RPA 1983; para 24(1) sch 2 LEPAR 2006; r 25(1) sch 1 and r 26(1) sch 2 GLAER 2007; r 35(1) sch 5 NAWRPO 2007.
[244]R 27(2) sch 3 PCCEO 2012.
[245]R 25 sch 1 RPA 1983; para 23(1) sch 2 LEPAR 2006; para 24 sch 1 GLAER 2007; r 34 sch 5 NAWRPO 2007; r 26(1) sch 3 PCCEO 2012.
[246]R 25(2) sch 1 RPA 1983l para 23(2) sch 2 LEPAR 2006; para 24(2) sch 1 GLAER 2007; r 34 sch 5 NAWRPO 2007; r 26(2) sch 3 PCCEO 2012.
[247]R 29 sch 1 RPA 1983; r 26 schs 2 and 3 LEPAR 2006; r 28 sch 1 GLAER 2007; r 37 sch 6 NAWRPO 2007; r 29(3) sch 3 PCCEO 2012.

(iii) Copies of the register of electors or the part containing the electors allotted to the station, plus the notices of late alteration to the register and the parts of the 'special lists' of postal and proxy postal voters;

(iv) The part of the corresponding numbers list containing the numbers (only) corresponding to the ballot papers provided to that PO;

(v) A notice giving guidance in voting, in large print, to be exhibited inside and outside every polling station;

(vi) A notice in prescribed form, telling voters (a) how many votes to cast and whether by X or order of preference, (b) to make no other mark on the ballot paper, and (c) in combined polls, specifying which colour ballot paper is for which election;[248]

(vii) At least one large version of the ballot paper, which the PO or their clerks must display inside the polling station to assist partially-sighted voters;

(viii) A tactile voting device ("**TVD**") with candidates' names and parties in Braille, as well as indicating where crosses can be marked, to enable blind or partially-sighted voters to vote without any need for assistance from the PO or any companion.

4.98 In *R (Andrews) v Minister for the Cabinet Office*,[249] Swift J found:

> "[T]here is no way using the TVD alone, that a blind person can know the name of the candidate, or the name of the party the candidate represents. The TVD will only permit a blind person to vote without assistance, if she memorised the order of candidates on the ballot paper either before she went to the polling station or while she was there."[250]

4.99 He therefore held that the candidates and/or the names of their RPs should also be present in Braille and/or raised lettering in corresponding position, on the left-hand side of the device.[251] This was because being given merely sufficient assistance to mark the paper, without sufficient assistance to be able to be sure to have marked in the box desired, did not fulfil the purposive meaning that should be given to the words 'to vote'."[252]

---

[248] R 26(1), sch 3 LEPAR 2006.

[249] R *(Andrews) v Minister for the Cabinet Office* [2019] EWHC 1126 (Admin).

[250] R *(Andrews) v Minister for the Cabinet Office* [2019] EWHC 1126 (Admin) at 9.

[251] R *(Andrews) v Minister for the Cabinet Office* [2019] EWHC 1126 (Admin) at 30-31.

[252] R *(Andrews) v Minister for the Cabinet Office* [2019] EWHC 1126 (Admin) at 20. At para 19 departing from permission decisions of Hickinbottom J and Blake J in R *(Kolendowicz) v Proper Officer of the Greater London Authority* CO/1672/2016.

Notice of secrecy requirements

4.100 The RO must give a copy in writing of the provision in the relevant legislation for that election that requires every RO, PO, clerk, candidate, election agent, polling agent, or Commission observer to maintain the secrecy of voting, and which makes it an offence for them to disclose before polls close the name or electoral number of who has or has not voted, or as to the official mark.[253]

4.101 Attempt to interfere with a voter when voting, including by asking them in the polling station whom they are about to vote for or have voted for, or by disclosing the same information subsequently, or inducing them to display whom they have voted for.[254]

F. POLLING DAY

Hours

4.102 Polling must take place between 7am-10pm.[255] However, if, at the close of the poll, a voter is in the polling station, or in a queue outside the polling station, they remain entitled to apply for a ballot paper.[256]

4.103 In *Gill v Reed and Holmes (the Hackney Case)*,[257] where it was proved that, in one district of the borough, the two polling stations were closed for the whole polling day, and four other stations in the borough were closed for part of the day, Grove J held the election was invalid not just under the then legislation but at common law.[258]

Riot or open violence

4.104 If proceedings at any polling station are interrupted or obstructed by riot or open violence, the PO must adjourn the proceedings till the following day and must *"forthwith"* give notice to the RO.[259]

---

[253] S 66(1), (3) and (6) RPA 1983; r 28 schs 2 and 3 LEPAR 2006; r 31 sch 1 and r 32 sch 2 GLAER 2007; art 35 and r 39 sch 5 NAWRPO 2007; art 22 and r 32 sch 3 PCCEO 2007.

[254] S 66(1), (3) and (6) RPA 1983; r 28 schs 2 and 3 LEPAR 2006; r 31 sch 1 and r 32 sch 2 GLAER 2007; art 35 and r 39 sch 5 NAWRPO 2007; art 22 and r 32 sch 3 PCCEO 2007.

[255] R 1 sch 1 RPA 1983; r 1 sch 2 LEPAR 2006; r 3 sch 1 GLAER 2007; r 1 sch 5 NAWRPO 2007; r 1 sch 3 PCCEO 2012.

[256] R 37(7) sch 1 RPA 1983; para 35(6), sch 2 LEPAR 2006; para 38(8) sch 1 GLAER 2007; r 46(8) sch 5 NAWRPO 2007; r 39(8) sch 3 PCCEO 2012.

[257] *Hackney Case, Gill v Reed and Holmes* (1874) 39 JP 151, 2 O'M & H 77, 31 LT 69.

[258] *Hackney Case, Gill v Reed and Holmes* (1874) 39 JP 151, 2 O'M & H 77, 31 LT 69.

[259] R 42 of sch 1 RPA 1983; r 42 of sch 2 LEPAR 2006; r 45(1) sch 1 GLAER 2007; r 20 sch 5 NAWRPO 2007; r 46 sch 3 PCCEO 2012. The Law Commission has recommended abandonment of this rule: Law Commission and Scottish Law Commission, 'Electoral Law: a joint final report', HC145 SG/2020/35, Law Com No 389, Scot Law Com No 256 ("the Law Commission Report"), para 8.93.

Prohibition of disclosure of vote

4.105 A person may not be required to disclose for whom they voted, even in legal proceedings.[260] Voting compartments that do not wholly enclose the voter, but nonetheless afford them, if ordinarily careful, reasonable facilities for marking their papers in secret, are sufficient to screen from observation.[261]

Venue

4.106 For the purpose of taking the poll, the RO may use, free of charge, a room in a maintained school or other room maintained out of public funds.[262]

Sealing of ballot boxes

4.107 Immediately before the commencement of the poll, the PO must show the ballot boxes to those present in the polling station, so that they may see that they are empty.[263] The PO must then lock the ballot boxes and place their seal on them (so that opening one would break its seal), then place them in their view for receipt of ballot papers.[264]

Permitted attendees

4.108 The PO must exclude all but the below from the polling station:[265]

(i) Voters;

(ii) Children accompanying voters;

(iii) The candidates, their election agents and no more than one of their appointed polling agents[266] at the same time;

(iv) Clerks appointed by the RO;

(v) Representatives of the Commission and accredited observers;

(vi) The constables on duty (who must vote only at their allotted polling station); and

---

[260] R 21 sch 1 RPA 1983; r 19 sch 2 LEPAR 2006; r 20 sch 1 GLAER 2007; r 30 sch 5 NAWRPO 2007; r 22 sch 3 PCCEO 2012.

[261] *Nicolson v Wick Magistrates* 1922 S.C. 374, p 384.

[262] R 34 sch 1 RPA 1983; r 20 sch 2 LEPAR 2006; r 21 sch 1 GLAER 2007; r 31 sch 5 NAWRPO 2007; r 23 sch 3 PCCEO 2012.

[263] R 34 sch 1 RPA 1983; r 32, sch 2 LEPAR 2006; r 35(a) sch 1 GLAER 2007; r 43(a) sch 5 NAWRPO 2007; r 36 sch 3 PCCEO 2012.

[264] R 34 sch 1 RPA 1983; r 32, sch 2 LEPAR 2006; r 35 sch 1 GLAER 2007; r 43(b)-(d) sch 5 NAWRPO 2007.

[265] R 32(1) sch 1 RPA 1983; para 30(1) sch 2 LEPAR 2006; r 33(1) sch 1 GLAER 2007; r 41(1) sch 5 NAWRPO 2007; r 34 sch 3 PCCEO 2012.

[266] See chapter 3 for candidates' appointment of polling and counting agents.

(vii) Companions of voters with disabilities.

4.109 Further, the PO must regulate the total number of attendees.[267]

Keeping order

4.110 It is the PO's duty to keep order at polling stations, but they cannot order the arrest, exclusion or removal of any person from the polling station.[268] They may however order that a person who (i) engages in misconduct in a polling station, or (ii) fails to obey the PO's lawful orders be immediately removed from the polling station by *"a constable in or near that station"* or any other person authorised in writing by the RO to perform that function.[269] As to voter intimidation at polling stations, see Chapter 3.

PO's permitted questions

4.111 One of PO's core duties is to give (*"deliver"*) a ballot paper bearing the official mark to those asking (*"applying"*) for their ballot papers,[270] but before so delivering they or their clerks may ask the voter the prescribed questions in the following table.[271] The PO must accept the answer unless it is unsatisfactory, in which case they must not be given a ballot paper.[272] That discretion to ask these questions becomes a duty if (i) a candidate's election or polling agent requests that the question be asked; and (ii) it is one of the questions marked '[R]' in the below table.[273] Other than the below questions, no other inquiry may be made of the person applying for a ballot paper as to their right to vote.[274]

	Person applying for ballot paper		Questions
1	Person applying to vote in person.	(a)	PE: *"Are you the person registered in the register of parliamentary electors for this election as follows (read out the whole entry from the register)? [R]"*

---

[267]R 30 sch 2 LEPAR 2006; r 33(2) sch 1 GLAER 2007

[268]R 26(3) sch 1 RPA 1983; r 24(3) sch 2 LEPAR 2006; r 25(2) sch 1 GLAER 2007; r 35(4) sch 5 NAWRPO 2007.

[269]R 33 sch 1 RPA 1983; r 31(2) sch 2 LEPAR 2007; r 34(2) sch 1 and r 35(2) sch 2 GLAER 2007; r 42(2) sch 5 NAWRPO 2007; r 35 sch 3 PCCEO 2012.

[270]*Pickering v James* (1872-73) LR 8 CP 489, p 489.

[271]R 26(1) sch 1 RPA 1983; *R v Spalding* (1842) Car. & M. 568, p 638.

[272]R 35 sch 1 RPA 1983; r 33(3), sch 2 LEPAR 2006; r 37(3) sch 1 GLAER 2007; r 37(3) sch 3 PCCEO 2012.

[273]R 35 sch 1 RPA 1983; r 33 sch 2 LEPAR 2006; r 36 sch 1 GLAER 2007; r 44 sch 1 NAWRPO 2007; r 37(1)(b) sch 3 PCCEO 2012.

[274]R 35(4) sch 1 RPA 1983; r 33(4) schs 2 and 3 LEPAR 2006; r 36(4) sch 1 and 37(4) sch 2 GLAER 2007; r 44(7) sch 1 NAWRPO 2007; r 37(4) sch 3 PCCEO 2012.

			LE, LAE and WAE: *"Are you the person registered in the register of local government electors for this election as follows? read the whole entry from the register [R]"* PCCE: *"Are you the person registered in the register of electors as follows (read out the whole entry from the register)? [R]"*
		(b)	PE and WAE: *"Have you already voted, here or elsewhere, at this election, otherwise than as proxy for some other person? [R]"* LE: *"Have you already voted here or elsewhere at this election for *(this county) *(this district) *(this London borough) *(this county borough), *delete whichever is inapplicable (adding, in the case of an election for several electoral areas, in this or any other electoral area) otherwise than as proxy for some other person? [R]"* LAE (constituency member election): *"Have you already voted, here or elsewhere at this election for a constituency member, otherwise than as proxy for some other person? [R]"* LAE: (London member election): *"Have you already voted, here or elsewhere in Greater London at this election for London members, otherwise than as proxy for some other person?[R]"* PCCE: *"Have you already voted in this election of a police and crime commissioner, here or elsewhere, otherwise than as a proxy for some other person? [R]"*
		(c)	Election held in Northern Ireland: *"What is your date of birth?"*
		(d)	WAE where person applying is a voter entitled to two votes, and PO has asked one or more of the questions at row 1(a) and 1(b): *"Have you already cast a constituency vote and an electoral region vote at this election, here or elsewhere, otherwise than as a proxy for some person? [R] "*
2	Person applying as proxy.	(a)	*"Are you the person whose name appears as A.B. in the list of proxies for this election as entitled to vote as proxy on behalf of C.D.? [R]"* PCCE: *"Are you the person whose name appears as A B in the list of proxies for this election of a police A person applying as proxy and crime commissioner as the person entitled to vote as proxy on behalf of C D? [R]"*

		(b)	PE, WAE and LAE: *"Have you already voted here or elsewhere at this election, as proxy on behalf of C.D.? [R]"* LE: *"Have you already voted here or elsewhere at this election for *(this county) *(this district) *(this London borough) *(this county borough), *delete whichever is inapplicable (adding in the case of an election for several electoral areas, in this or any other electoral area) as proxy on behalf of C.D.? [R]"* LAE (constituency member): *"Have you already voted here or elsewhere at this election for a constituency member, as proxy on behalf of C.D.?[R]"* LAE (London member): *"Have you already voted here or elsewhere in Greater London at this election for London members, as proxy on behalf of C.D.?[R]"* PCCE: *"Have you already voted in this election of a police and crime commissioner, here or elsewhere, as the person entitled to vote as proxy on behalf of C D? [R]"*
		(c)	*"Are you the spouse, civil partner, parent, grandparent, brother/sister, child or grandchild of C.D.?" [R]"*
		(d)	WAE, where person is applying to vote as proxy for a voter entitled to cast two votes, and PO has asked one or more of the questions at row 2(a) and 2(b): *"Have you already cast a constituency vote and an electoral region vote, at this election here or elsewhere, on behalf of C.D.?"[R]"*
3	Person applying to vote as proxy for voter with an anonymous entry (instead of the questions at entry 2 above).	(a)	*"Are you the person entitled to vote as proxy on behalf of the elector whose number on the register of electors is (read out the number from the register)?" [R]"*
		(b)	*"Have you already voted here or elsewhere as proxy on behalf of the elector whose number on the register of electors is (read out the number from the register)? [R]"* PCCE: *"Have you already voted in this election of a police and crime commissioner, here or elsewhere, as proxy on behalf of the elector whose number on the register of electors is (read out the number from the register)? [R]"*

		(c)	*"Are you the spouse, civil partner, parent, grandparent, brother/sister, child or grandchild of the person whose number on the register of electors is (read out the number from the register)? [R]"*
		(d)	WAE, where person is applying as proxy for a voter with an anonymous entry and with entitlement to two votes, and the PO has asked one or more of the questions at row 3(a) and 3(b): *""Have you already cast a constituency vote and an electoral region vote, here or elsewhere, at this election, on behalf of the elector whose number on the register of electors is (read out the number from the register)? [R]"*
4	Person applying as proxy if the question at entry 2(c) or 3(c) is not answered in the affirmative.		• PE, WAE and LAE: *"Have you at this election already voted in this constituency on behalf of two persons of whom you are not the spouse, civil partner, parent, grandparent, brother/sister, child or grandchild?"* [R] • LE: *"Have you already voted at this election for *(this county) *(this district) *(this London borough) *(this county A person applying as proxy if the question at entry 2(c) or 3(c) is not answered in the affirmative borough), *delete whichever is inapplicable (adding, in the case of an election for several electoral areas, in this or any other electoral area) on behalf of two persons of whom you are not the spouse, civil partner, parent, grandparent, brother, sister, child or grandchild? [R]"* • LAE (constituency member): *"Have you already voted here or elsewhere at this election for a constituency member, on behalf of two persons of whom you are not the spouse, civil partner, parent, grandparent, brother, sister, child or grandchild?[R]"* • LAE (London member): *"Have you already voted here or elsewhere in Greater London at this election for London members, on behalf of two persons of whom you are not the spouse, civil partner, parent, grandparent, brother, sister, child or grandchild?[R]"* • WAE: *""Have you at this election already voted in this constituency on behalf of two persons of whom you are not the spouse, civil partner, parent, grandparent, brother/ sister, child or grandchild?"[R]"* • PCCE: *"Have you already voted in this election of a police and crime commissioner, here or elsewhere, on behalf of two persons of whom you are not the spouse, civil partner, parent, grandparent, brother/ sister child or*

		grandchild? [R]"
5 Person applying to vote in person yet with entry in the postal voters list.	(a)	*"Did you apply to vote by post?"*
	(b)	*"Why have you not voted by post?"*
6 Person applying to vote as proxy yet named in the proxy postal voters list.	(a)	*"Did you apply to vote by post as proxy?"*
	(b)	*"Why have you not voted by post as proxy?"*

Challenge of voter: personation, misnomer and misdescription

4.112 The fact that a candidate or their election or polling agent declares that they have reasonable cause to believe that a voter has committed a personation offence, or even if the voter is arrested on grounds that he is suspected of committing or of being about to commit that offence, does not mean the accused or suspect cannot vote.[275]

4.113 If a voter has been entered into the register under a different name to that the name on the birth certificate and different also to the name by which they are generally known, it does not amount to personation for them to give that registered name when applying to the PO for a ballot paper.[276] This enables individuals with a right to vote, but who turn out to be mistakenly registered under a misnomer or inaccurate description, to nonetheless vote.[277]

Pilot identification document schemes

4.114 The Secretary of State and Minister for the Cabinet Office have the power to approve schemes proposed by local authorities for different provision as to *"(a) when, where and how voting at the elections is to take place; (b) how the votes cast at the elections are to be counted; (c) the sending by candidates of election communications free of charge for postage"*.[278] The *"statutory purpose"* behind this

[275]R 36 sch 1 RPA 1983; para 34 sch 2 LEPAR 2006; para 37 sch 1 GLAER 2007; r 45(a) sch 5 NAWRPO 2007; r 38 sch 3 PCCEO 2012.
[276]*R v Fox* (1887) 16 Cox CC 166; *R v John Thwaites* (1853) 1 El. & Bl. 704, p 603.
[277]S 50 RPA 1983; *R v John Thwaites* (1853) 1 El. & Bl. 704, p 601.
[278]S 10(2) RPA 2000.

power is *"improving the voting process"*[279] and considering whether a piloted scheme inhibits some voters from voting, including whether there is greater impact on disadvantaged groups.[280]

4.115 Pursuant to this power, on 26.2.19, 27.2.19 and 4.3.19, the Minister approved pilot schemes inserting into the LE rules a provision stating *"a ballot paper must not be delivered to a voter unless that voter has produced a specified document to the presiding officer or a clerk"*.[281] This decision was held to fall within the meaning of *"how voting at the elections is to take place"* and within the scope of the sort of schemes that could be implemented.[282]

4.116 Following a pilot scheme, the Commission must prepare a report on the scheme for the Secretary of State or Minister and the relevant local authority,[283] assessing the scheme's success in facilitating voting, the counting of votes, encouraging voting, and enabling voters to make informed decisions,[284] including statement as to whether they consider turnout would have been higher without the scheme and whether there was increase in electoral malpractice.[285] The local authority must publish the report within three months.[286] If, in light of the Commission's report, the Secretary of State or Minister consider it *"desirable"* for provision similar to the scheme to be rolled out generally and permanently, in other elections, they may do so by statutory instrument approved by both Houses of Parliament, if the Commission recommends the same.[287] This Commission recommendation precondition and the legislative approval needed has been held sufficient safeguard to mean that the power to generalise the pilot schemes by secondary legislation does not breach the principle of legality.[288]

---

[279] R *(Coughlan) v Minister for the Cabinet Office* [2020] EWCA Civ 723, at 77.

[280] R *(Coughlan) v Minister for the Cabinet Office* [2020] EWCA Civ 723, at 80.

[281] Sch 1 Braintree District Council (Identification in Polling Stations) Pilot Order 2019, Broxtowe Borough Council (Identification in Polling Stations) Pilot Order 2019, Craven District Council (Identification in Polling Stations) Pilot Order 2019; Derby City Council (Identification in Polling Stations) Pilot Order 2019, Mid-Sussex District Council (Identification in Polling Stations) Pilot Order 2019, North Kesteven District Council (Identification in Polling Stations) Pilot Order 2019, North-West Leicestershire District Council (Identification in Polling Stations) Pilot Order 2019, Pendle Borough Council (Identification in Polling Stations) Pilot Order 2019; Watford Borough Council (Identification in Polling Stations) Pilot Order 2019, and Woking Borough Council (Identification in Polling Stations) Pilot Order 2019.

[282] R *(Coughlan) v Minister for the Cabinet Office* [2020] EWCA Civ 723, at 81. The challenge did not raise equalities law. Pre-pilot equalities considerations were published by the Cabinet Office (5.3.19), post-pilot evaluation in July 2019.

[283] S 10(6) and (9) RPA 2000.

[284] S 10(7) RPA 2000.

[285] S 10(8)(a) RPA 2000.

[286] S 10(10) RPA 2000.

[287] S 11 RPA 2000.

[288] R *(Coughlan) v Minister for the Cabinet Office* [2020] EWCA Civ 723, at 81.

Voting procedure

4.117 Unless unable satisfactorily to answer one of the PO's statutory questions, the voter who asks for a ballot paper must be provided with one.[289]

4.118 Immediately before being given the ballot paper, the PO or their clerks must:[290]

(i) Call out the number and (unless they have an anonymous entry, in which case he must show the PO his official poll card)[291] the name of the voter as stated in the copy of the register or any notice of alteration;

(ii) Mark the voter number on the corresponding number list, beside the number of the ballot paper to be issued to them;[292]

(iii) Place a mark next to the voter's number in the register or any notice of alteration, to record that the ballot paper has been received, making sure not to note the ballot paper number;[293] and

(iv) Place a mark against the proxy's name in the list of proxies, in the case of someone voting as a proxy.

4.119 The PO also must keep a list of persons given a ballot paper pursuant to a notice of late alteration to the register.[294]

4.120 The voter must then go to one of the compartments in the polling station, secretly mark their paper, fold it up so as to conceal their vote (unless LAE), show the back of the paper to the PO so as to disclose the number and other unique identifying mark, put the folded up ballot paper into the ballot box in the PO's presence, then leave without *"undue delay"*.[295] If the voter instead tries to leave the polling station with the ballot paper, the PO must stop them.[296]

---

[289]R 37 sch 1 RPA 1983; r 35 sch 2 LEPAR 2006; r 38(1) sch 1 GLAER 2007; r 46 sch 5 NAWRPO 2007.

[290]R 37(1)(a) and (3), sch 1 RPA 1983; r 35(1)(a) and (3), sch 2 LEPAR 2006; r 38(1)(a) sch 1 GLAER 2007; r 46(1) sch 5 NAWRPO 2007.

[291]R 37(2) sch 1 RPA 1983; r 35(2), sch 2 LEPAR 2006; r 38(2) sch 1 GLAER 2007; r 46(2) sch 5 NAWRPO 2007.

[292]See *Fermanagh and South Tyrone* [2010] NIQB 113, at para 30, for an example of error in this procedure giving rise to missing votes and the election being challenge on petition.

[293]Para 37(1)(c) and (3), sch 1 RPA 1983; para 35(1)(c) and (3), sch 2 LEPAR 2006; para 38(1)(c) sch 1 GLAER 2007. In a combined poll, the same copy of the register or alteration notice may be used for each election.

[294]R 41A sch 1 RPA 1983; r 41 sch 2 LEPAR 2006; r 44 sch 1 and r 45 sch 2 GLAER 2007; r 51 sch 5 NAWRPO 2007.

[295]R 37(5) and (6) RPA 1983; r 35(4) and (5), sch 2 LEPAR 2006; r 38(4) and (5) sch 1 GLAER 2007; r 46(4) sch 5 NAWRPO 2007; r 39(4) and (5) sch 3 PCCEO 2012.

[296]*Pickering v James* (1872-73) LR 8 CP 489, p 508.

Voting and disability

4.121 If a voter cannot comply with these requirements due to blindness, other disability, or inability to read, they can notify the PO of this fact and the PO must mark the ballot paper in the manner the voter wishes.[297] The PO must then write the voter's name and electoral register number on the 'list of votes marked by the PO', along with the reason for why the PO marked it.[298] In the case of a proxy voter, the number written must be the voter's number not the proxy's.[299]

4.122 A voter who is unable to vote without assistance from a companion due to blindness, other disability, or inability to read may apply to the PO for permission to vote with the assistance of a companion.[300] Upon such application, the PO must grant the request if they are satisfied that the voter is so disabled or unable to read and by the voter and companion providing the following declarations:

(i) Voter: a declaration, oral or in writing, as to whether they are so incapacitated by their blindness, other disability, or inability to read, as to be unable to vote without assistance;[301]

(ii) Companion: a declaration in the prescribed form,[302] which states that: (a) they have been requested to assist the elector above to record their vote at the election; (b) they are a qualified person (i.e. whether by being a person who is entitled to vote as a voter at the election, or by being the father, mother, brother, sister, spouse, civil partner, son or daughter of the voter, and in either case are over 18 years old); and (c) have not previously assisted more than one voter with disabilities to vote at the election.[303]

---

[297]R 38(1), sch 1 RPA 1983; para 36(1), sch 2 LEPAR 2006; r 39(1) sch 1 GLAER 2007; r 47(1) sch 5 NAWRPO 2007; r 40(1) sch 3 PCCEO 2012.

[298]R 38(2) and (3), sch 1 RPA 1983; r 36(2) and (3) sch 2 LEPAR 2006; r 39(2) sch 1 GLAER 2007; r 47(2) sch 5 NAWRPO 2007; r 40(2) sch 3 PCCEO 2012.

[299]R 38(2) and (3), sch 1 RPA 1983; r 36(2) and (3) sch 2 LEPAR 2006; r 39(2) sch 1 GLAER 2007; r 47(3) sch 5 NAWRPO 2007; r 40(2) sch 3 PCCEO 2012.

[300]R 39(1) and (3), sch 1 RPA 1983; r 37(1) sch 2 LEPAR 2006; r 40(1) sch 1 GLAER 2007; r 48 sch 5 NAWRPO 2007; r 41(1) sch 3 PCCEO 2012.

[301]R 39(1), sch 1 RPA 1983; para 37(1), sch 2 LEPAR 2006; r 40(1) sch 1 GLAER 2007; r 48(2) sch 5 NAWRPO 2007; r 41(2)(a) sch 3 PCCEO 2012.

[302]R 39(5)(a) sch 1 and Appendix (available from Commission's website) RPA 1983; r 37(6)(a) sch 2, r 37(7)(a) sch 3, and Appendix (available from Commission's website) LEPAR 2006; r 40(6)(a) sch 1, r 41(6)(a) sch 2, and Form 19 sch 10 GLAER 2007; r 48(7)(a) sch 5 and Form CQ sch 10 NAWRPO 2007; r 41(4) and Form 18 sch 3 PCCEO 2012.

[303]R 39(2), sch 1 RPA 1983; r 37(2), sch 2 LEPAR 2006; r 40(2) sch 1 GLAER 2007; r 48(2)(b) and (7) sch 5 and Form CQ sch 10 NAWRPO 2007; r 42(2)(b) sch 3 PCCEO 2012.

4.123 If satisfied by these declarations, the PO must grant the application[304] then enter the name and electoral roll number on a 'list of voters with disabilities assisted by companions'.[305]

Tendered ballot papers

4.124 A person the electoral roll must vote using a 'tendered ballot paper' if they ask for a ballot paper and it turns out that: (i) another person has already voted in person as them;[306] or (ii) they are on the postal voters list without having applied to vote by post at the election.[307]

4.125 A person on the list of proxies (and not entitled to vote by post as proxy) must vote using a tendered ballot paper if, upon asking for a ballot paper, it turns out that: (i) another person has already voted in person as the voter or proxy;[308] or (ii) they are themselves also named on that list, and they claim that they did not so apply.[309]

4.126 A person on the postal voters list who claims not to have received their postal vote must use a tendered ballot paper if the deadline for applying for a postal ballot paper has expired.[310]

4.127 To be given the tendered ballot paper, the person finding themselves in one of the above situations must first satisfactorily answer the permitted statutory questions (see 'permitted questions' above).[311]

4.128 A tendered ballot paper must be a different colour to other ballot papers and must be given to the PO rather than put in the ballot box.[312] The PO must then:

---

[304]R 39(2) sch 1 RPA 1983; para 37(2) sch 2 LEPAR 2006; r 40(2) sch 1 GLAER 2007; r 48(2) sch 5 NAWRPO 2007; r 42(2) sch 3 PCCEO 2012.

[305]R 39(4) sch 1 RPA 1983; para 37(4) sch 2 LEPAR 2006; r 40(4) sch 1 GLAER 2007; r 48(4) sch 5 NAWRPO 2007.

[306]R 40(1) sch 1 RPA 1983; r 38(1)(a) sch 2 LEPAR 2006; r 41(1)(a) sch 1 GLAER 2007; r 49(1)(a) sch 5 NAWRPO 2007; r 42(2) sch 3 PCCEO 2012.

[307]R 40(1ZA) and (1ZC) sch 1 RPA 1983; r 38(2) sch 2 LEPAR 2006; r 41(2) sch 1 GLAER 2007; r 49(1)(c) sch 5 NAWRPO 2007; r 42(4) sch 3 PCCEO 2012.

[308]R 40(1); r 38(1)(b) sch 2 LEPAR 2006; r 41(1)(b) sch 1 GLAER 2007; r 49(1)(b) sch 5 NAWRPO 2007; r 42(3) sch 3 PCCEO 2012.

[309]R 40(1ZB) and (1ZC); r 38(3) sch 2 LEPAR 2006; r 41(3) sch 1 GLAER 2007; r 49(1)(d) sch 5 NAWRPO 2007; r 42(5) sch 3 PCCEO 2012.

[310]R 40(1ZD) sch 1 RPA 1983; r 38(5) schs 2 and 3 LEPAR 2006; r 41(5) sch 1 and r 42(5) sch 2 GLAER 2007; r 42(6) sch 3 PCCEO 2012.

[311]R 35 sch 1 RPA 1983; para 33 sch 2 LEPAR 2006; r 41(1) sch 1 GLAER 2007; r 49(1) sch 5 NAWRPO 2007; r 42(1) sch 3 PCCEO 2012.

[312]R 40(2) sch 1 RPA 1983; r 39(1) sch 2 LEPAR 2006; r 42(1) sch 1 GLAER 2007; r 49(7)(a) sch 5 NAWRPO 2007; r 43(1) sch 3 PCCEO 2012.

(i) Endorse the tendered ballot paper with the name of the voter and their electoral roll number;[313]

(ii) Set it aside in a separate pack;[314]

(iii) Enter the name of the voter or proxy voter and the voter's electoral roll number on a 'tendered votes list' (unless they have an anonymous entry in the register).[315]

Spoilt ballot papers

4.129 If a voter accidently does something to their ballot paper that mean it cannot conveniently be used as a ballot paper, if they can satisfy the PO that it was accidental, the PO must give them a second ballot paper to replace the spoilt ballot paper, and the spoilt ballot paper must be immediately cancelled.[316]

Remedy for PO refusal to provide ballot paper

4.130 If a PO refuses to provide a ballot paper, the refusal is amenable to review on electoral petition.[317] A petition may be brought by the person refused a ballot, because, as well as candidates and voters, persons with a right to vote also have standing to bring a petition.[318] In an LE petition, they would have to be joined by three or more other voters or persons with a right to vote.[319]

Receipt of postal votes

4.131 If not returned by post in the prescribed manner, a postal ballot paper or PVS may be returned to a polling station by hand, and placed in a postal voters' ballot box (if within an envelope) or postal ballot box (if not).[320] The PO must then deliver it to the RO in the same manner and at the same time as the other ballot papers sealed and delivered to the RO.[321]

---

[313]R 40(2) sch 1 RPA 1983; r 39(1)(b) sch 2 LEPAR 2006; r 42(1)(b) sch 1 GLAER 2007; r 49(7)(b) sch 5 NAWRPO 2007; r 43(3) sch 3 PCCEO 2012.

[314]R 40(2) sch 1 RPA 1983; r 39(1)(b) sch 2 LEPAR 2006; r 42(1)(b) sch 1 GLAER 2007; r 49(7)(b) sch 5 NAWRPO 2007; r 43(4) sch 3 PCCEO 2012.

[315]Para 40(3) sch 1 RPA 1983; para 39(2), sch 2 LEPAR 2006; para 42(2) sch 1 GLAER 2007; r 49(8) sch 5 NAWRPO 2007; r 43(5) sch 3 PCCEO 2012.

[316]Para 41 sch 1 RPA 1983; para 40, sch 2 LEPAR 2006; para 43 sch 1 GLAER 2007; r 50 sch 5 NAWRPO 2007; r 44 sch 3 PCCEO 2012.

[317]R 40A sch 1 RPA 1983; r 48 sch 2 and 3 LEPAR 2006; r 51 sch 1 and r 52 sch 2 GLAER 2007; r 59 sch 5 NAWRPO 2007.

[318] Ss 121(1A) and 128(1) RPA 1983; art 87(1)(a) and (b) and (2) NAWRPO 2007. Ss 121(1) and 128(1) RPA 1983. See Chapter 5.

[319] S 128(1) RPA 1983. See Chapter 5.

[320]Reg 81 RP (E&W) Regs 2001.

[321]R 45(1B) sch 1 RPA 1983; reg 79 RP (E&W) Regs 2001; r 49(2)(a) and (2A) sch 3 PCCEO 2012.

Correction of errors on day of poll

4.132 The PO must keep a list of voters given a ballot paper pursuant to an alteration notice.[322] In a combined poll, the same list may be used for each election.[323]

Procedure on close of poll

4.133 As soon as practicable after the close of the poll, the PO must, in the presence of any polling agents appointed by the candidates, make up the following separate packets, sealed with the PO's seal and, if they wish, that of the polling agents:[324]

(i) Each ballot box in use at the station, with the key attached;

(ii) The unused and spoilt ballot papers;

(iii) The tendered ballot papers;

(iv) The marked copies of the register of electors, list of proxies, and list of persons to whom ballot papers are provided pursuant to an alteration notice;

(v) The completed corresponding number lists, including the parts which were marked beside the number of the ballot paper issued;

(vi) The certificates as to employment on duty on the day of the poll;

(vii) The lists of tendered votes, voters with disabilities assisted by companions, and votes marked by the PO, plus a statement of the number of voters whose votes marked by the PO under the heads *"disability"* and *"unable to read"* and the declarations made by the companions of voters with disabilities.

4.134 The PO must make a ballot paper account to accompany the packets, stating the number of ballot papers entrusted to the PO, under the heads of: (i) ballot papers issued and not otherwise accounted for, (ii) unused, (iii) spoilt, and (iv) tendered ballot papers.[325] The accuracy of the ballot paper account depends on the meticulousness of the PO and their clerks' marking of the corresponding number list when delivering ballot papers.[326]

---

[322] R 41 sch 3 LEPAR 2006; r 44(1) sch 1 GLAER 2007; r 51 sch 5 NAWRPO 2007; r 45 sch 3 PCCEO 2012.

[323] R 41, sch 3, LEPAR 2006; para 44(2) sch 1 GLAER 2007.

[324] R 43(1) sch 1 RPA 1983; r 43(1), sch 2 LEPAR 2006; r 46(1) sch 1 GLAER 2007; r 53 sch 5 NAWRPO 2007; r 47(1) sch 3 PCCEO 2012.

[325] R 43(3) sch 1 RPA 1983; r 43(3) sch 2 LEPAR 2006; r 46(4) sch 1 GLAER 2007; r 53(4) sch 5 NAWRPO 2007; r 47(6) sch 3 PCCEO 2012.

[326] *Fermanagh and South Tyrone* [2010] NIQB 113, at 31, per Morgan LCJ.

4.135 The PO must then deliver the packets to the RO.[327] If not in person, the arrangements for delivery must be approved by the RO.[328]

Voting offences

Personation

4.136 A person shall be deemed to be guilty of the corrupt practice of personation if they:

(i) Vote in person as some other person, whether as voter or proxy, and whether that other person is living, dead or fictitious;[329]

(ii) Vote as a proxy when they knows or have reasonable grounds for supposing that their appointment as proxy is no longer in force.[330]

4.137 To commit the offence, the vote does not have to have been counted. A person is deemed to have 'voted' when a person applies for a ballot paper to vote in person or marks and returns a postal ballot paper.[331]

4.138 It is likewise an offence to assist or encourage the commission of the offence of personation.[332]

4.139 A form that personation may take is the phenomenon of 'ghost voters', described by the Election Court as follows:

> "Ghost voters are registered which are, as said above, either fictitious names or persons who exist but who do not reside at the address concerned. The latter category comprises those who have no connection at all with the property at which they are registered and those who have a connection with the property but are not resident there in the sense that the law requires."[333]

4.140 The petitioner only has to prove that there was at least one bogus vote: *"if arranged by the candidate or someone who is in law his agent, [it] will unseat the candidate, however large his majority"*.[334]

---

[327]Para 43(1) sch 1 RPA 1983; para 43(1), sch 2 LEPAR 2006; r 46(1) sch 1 and r 47(1) sch 2 GLAER 200; r 53(3) sch 5 NAWRPO 2007; r 47(4) sch 3 PCCEO 2012.

[328]Para 43(1) sch 1 RPA 1983; para 43(1), sch 2 LEPAR 2006; r 53(3) sch 5 NAWRPO 2007; r 47(5) sch 3 PCCEO 2012.

[329]S 60(2)(a) RPA 1983; art 30(2)(a) NAWRPO 2007; art 17(2)(a) PCCEO 2012.

[330]S 60(2)(b) RPA 1983; art 30(2)(b) NAWRPO 2007; art 17(2)(b) PCCEO 2012.

[331]S 60(3) RPA 1983; art 30(3) NAWRPO 2007; art 17(3) PCCEO 2012.

[332]S 60(1) RPA 1983; art 30(1) NAWRPO 2007.

[333]*Erlam v Rahman and Williams [2015] EWHC 1215 (QB)*, Commissioner Richard Mawrey QC, at 310.

[334]*Erlam v Rahman and Williams* [2015] EWHC 1215 (QB) at 312.

4.141 Relevant evidence may include:

(i) Statistics (e.g. whether the number of late registrations greatly exceeds the number in comparator wards or polling districts; whether these registrations obtained postal votes; whether the overall electorate suddenly increases; whether the evidence supports an explanation for a sudden increase in the voting population in the ward);[335]

(ii) Examining who actually lives at the addresses used for the late registrations;[336]

(iii) Expert handwriting evidence,[337] to identify instances of signatures not matching corresponding electoral documents.[338]

4.142 In *Afzal v Jahan*,[339] the Election Court found that local elections in two wards in Birmingham should be declared void because of corrupt and illegal practices relating to postal voting in which the six elected councillors had been involved, with the effect that the councillors should be removed from office. The commissioner's finding in relation to one of the councillors was quashed by the Court of Appeal,[340] but the Court of Appeal was not concerned with the rest of his findings, namely: fourteen different types of fraud proven beyond reasonable doubt. The Court of Appeal called the following *"particularly egregious"* examples therein:

> "1. An elector who was in prison at the time of the election, neither asked for nor received a postal vote. Nevertheless his postal vote for the Labour Candidates was returned to the Election Office.
>
> 2. Two electors, a married couple, were persuaded to sign a form to register for postal votes. They did not receive the voting pack and were told that they could not vote when they turned up at the polling station on polling day. Their postal votes for Labour Party candidates were nevertheless submitted to the Election Office.
>
> 3. Evidence from a rival candidate in the election indicated that he saw one of those who were elected as councillors collect a black bag from a postman, which he assumed contained postal votes. In another incident,

---

[335] *Simmons v Khan* [2008] EWHC B4 (QB) at 236-246.

[336] *Simmons v Khan* [2008] EWHC B4 (QB) at 250-298. At 291, Commissioner Richard Mawrey QC found that one street *"proved richer in ghosts than the Tower of London. No fewer than 38 ghost voters are listed in the schedule as occupying (or possibly haunting) numbers 4, 6, 19, 31, 37, 38, 41, 43, 50 and 66"*.

[337] *Simmons v Khan* [2008] EWHC B4 (QB) at 229 and 308-323.

[338] *Simmons v Khan* [2008] EWHC B4 (QB) at 323.

[339] *Afzal v Jahan*, 4.4.15, Richard Mawrey QC sitting as a Commissioner]

[340] R *(Afzal) v Election Court* [2005] EWCA Civ 647.

a postman was seen handing postal votes to the same elected councillor outside a house belonging to his brother."[341]

4.143 In *Erlam v Rahman*,[342] the Election Court found personation by agents of the respondent proven to the requisite standard where there was evidence of the agents having registered twice in the ward in which they were voting. The court decided one of two things happened: both votes were cast by one person (an offence under s 61(2): 'false voting'), or the second vote was cast by a second person but with the first person's connivance (which was personation under s 60).[343] Personation thus dovetails with s 61(1) false voting. The Court held *"[a]nyone who votes in the name of* ***another person*** *who is falsely registered commits personation. Anyone who has falsely registered* ***himself*** *and then votes commits an offence under s 61(1) of the 1983 Act"* (emphasis added).[344] This means that, where there are two votes cast in one voter's name, alternative offences can be investigated by the Election Court.[345]

4.144 A third illustration of personation is provided by *Ali v Bashir*,[346] where personation was found where votes were cast in the names of properly registered voters who were away during the election.[347]

Voting despite legal incapacity or more than once

4.145 A person is guilty of this illegal practice if they:

(i) Vote despite knowing they were under a legal incapacity to do so at that election;[348]

(ii) Vote as proxy for someone subject to a legal incapacity to vote;[349]

(iii) Apply for a proxy vote, knowing they or the proxy are subject to a legal incapacity to vote.

4.146 It is also an offence for a person to vote more than once, by any of the following means:

---

341 R *(Afzal) v Election Court* [2005] EWCA Civ 647, at 8.
342 *Erlam v Rahman* [2015] EWHC 1215 (QB).
343 *Erlam v Rahman* [2015] EWHC 1215 (QB), at 341.
344 *Erlam v Rahman* [2015] EWHC 1215 (QB), at 336.
345 *Erlam v Rahman* [2015] EWHC 1215 (QB), at 339.
346 *Ali v Bashir* [2013] EWHC 2572 (QB).
347 *Ali v Bashir* [2013] EWHC 2572 (QB), at 216, 225.
348 S 61(1)(a) RPA 1983; art 31(2)(a) NAWRPO 2007; art 18(1)(a) PCCEO 2012. Not including things done before polling day by someone not yet 18 but who will be on election day.
349 S 61(1) RPA 1983; art 31(2)(c) NAWRPO 2007; art 18(1)(b) PCCEO 2012.

(i) Voting more than once (unless one of these votes was as proxy), whether in the same constituency or area[350] or different constituencies or areas;[351]

(ii) Voting as proxy for the same voter more than once, whether in the same constituency or area, or different ones;[352]

(iii) Voting in person at an election at which they have a postal vote;[353]

(iv) Voting in person when they have a proxy in force in another constituency or area;[354]

(v) Voting in person as proxy for a voter who has proxy postal vote;[355]

(vi) Voting in person as proxy for a voter they know has already voted in person at the election;[356]

(vii) Vote as proxy for more than two persons of whom they are not the spouse or civil partner, parent, grandparent, brother, sister, child or grandchild;[357]

(viii) Applying for a person to be appointed as their proxy without applying for the cancellation of another proxy appointment still in force;[358]

4.147 As with personation, there is an inchoate version of the offence, made out by knowingly assisting or encouraging someone else to do something that would constitute one of the above offences.[359]

4.148 Unless the candidate knowingly assists or encourages the offence, if their agent commits one of the above voting offences, the candidate is not liable nor their election avoided.[360]

4.149 A person is deemed to have 'voted' for purposes of the above offences if they have:

(i) Applied for a ballot paper in a polling station for the purpose of voting in person; or

---

[350] S 61(2)(a)(i) RPA 1983; art 31(4)(a)(i) NAWRPO 2007; art 18(1)(c) PCCEO 2012.
[351] S 61(2)(a)(ii) RPA 1983; art 31(4)(a)(ii) NAWRPO 2007.
[352] S 61(3)(a) RPA 1983; art 31(5)(a)(i) and (ii) NAWRPO 2007; art 18(3)(a) PCCEO 2012.
[353] S 61(2)(b) RPA 1983; art 31(4)(b) NAWRPO 2007; art 18(2)(b) PCCEO 2012.
[354] S 61(2)(c) RPA 1983; art 31(4)(a)(iii) NAWRPO 2007; art 18(2)(c) PCCEO 2012.
[355] S 61(3)(b) RPA 1983; art 31(5)(b) NAWRPO 2007; art 18(3)(b) PCCEO 2012.
[356] S 61(3)(c) RPA 1983; art 31(5)(c) NAWRPO 2007; art 18(3)(c) PCCEO 2012.
[357] S 61(4) RPA 1983; art 31(6) NAWRPO 2007; art 18(4) PCCEO 2012.
[358] S 61(2)(d) RPA 1983; art 31(4)(d) NAWRPO 2007.
[359] S 61(5) RPA 1983; art 31(7) NAWRPO 2007; art 18(5) PCCEO 2012.
[360] S 61(7)(b) RPA 1983; art 31(9)(b) NAWRPO 2007.

(ii) Marked and returned a ballot paper issued for voting by post.[361]

4.150 This offence was found in *Erlam v Rahman*.[362] Two votes by the same voter either indicated the voter committing the s 61 'other voting offence' or s 60 personation by a fraudster.[363] It was also said by the commissioner that s 61 offence was made out where a person votes following false registration,[364] which would suggest voting despite incapacity (not actually being resident at the registered address).

Tampering with ballot papers

4.151 It is an offence and an illegal practice to fraudulently:

(i) Deface or destroy a ballot paper, or the official mark on any ballot paper, or any postal voting statement or declaration of identity or official envelope used in connection with voting by post;[365]

(ii) Put any paper into a ballot box other than the ballot paper that you are authorised by law to put in;[366]

(iii) Take a ballot paper out of the polling station;[367] or

(iv) Attempt to do any of the above.[368]

4.152 It is also an offence to, without due authority:

(i) Supply a ballot paper to someone;[369]

(ii) Interfere with a ballot box or packet of ballot papers being used for the purposes of an election; [370] or

(iii) Attempt to do any of the above.[371]

4.153 In *Ali v Bashir*,[372] the respondent was found guilty of this offence where various forms of misconduct concerned with tampering with ballot papers were found

---

361 S 61(6) RPA 1983; art 31(1) NAWRPO 2007; art 18(6) PCCEO 2012.
362 *Erlam v Rahman* [2015] EWHC 1215 (QB).
363 *Erlam v Rahman* [2015] EWHC 1215 (QB) at 339.
364 *Erlam v Rahman* [2015] EWHC 1215 (QB) at 336.
365 S 65(1)(b) RPA 1983; art 33(1)(b) NAWRPO 2007; art 20(1)(b) PCCEO 2012.
366 S 65(1)(d) RPA 1983; art 33(1)(d) NAWRPO 2007; art 20(1)(d) PCCEO 2012.
367 S 65(1)(e) RPA 1983; art 33(1)(e) NAWRPO 2007; art 20(1)(e) PCCEO 2012.
368 S 65(1)(g) RPA 1983; art 33(1)(g) NAWRPO 2007; art 20(1)(g) PCCEO 2012.
369 S 65(1)(c) RPA 1983; art 33(1)(c) NAWRPO 2007; art 20(1)(c) PCCEO 2012.
370 S 65(1)(f) RPA 1983; art 33(1)(f) NAWRPO 2007; art 20(1)(f) PCCEO 2012.
371 S 65(1)(g) RPA 1983; art 33(1)(g) NAWRPO 2007; art 20(1)(g) PCCEO 2012.
372 *Ali v Bashir* [2013] EWHC 2572 (QB).

in connection with manifest 'roll-stuffing', *"the deliberate entry in the register of ineligible persons for the purpose of using their votes fraudulently"*.[373]

Breach of secrecy requirements

4.154 As set out above, it is an offence for the RO, PO, PO's clerks, candidate, election agent, polling agent, Commission representative or appointed observer attending a polling station to breach their duty to maintain and aid in maintaining the secrecy of voting.[374]

4.155 The offence also captures conduct whereby a person:[375]

(i) Interferes with a voter when voting;

(ii) Obtains information as to who a voter is about to vote or has voted;

(iii) Communicates that information to someone else, or information as to the number or other unique identifying mark on the back of that voter's ballot paper;

(iv) Induces a voter to display his ballot paper after he has marked it;[376]

(v) When assisting a blind voter (PE) or voter with disabilities (WAE), to reveal whom the voter intends to vote for, has voted for, or the number or other unique identifying mark on the back of their ballot paper.[377]

4.156 The exception applying to the above proscribed acts is if the purpose for doing the act is authorised by law.[378]

Prohibition on publication of exit polls

4.157 Before the poll is closed, it is an offence to publish to the public at large or a section of it, in whatever form and means:

(i) Any statement as to how voters have voted where that statement is (or might reasonably be taken to be) based on information given by voters after they have voted; or

(ii) Any forecast or estimate as to the result of the election which is (or might reasonably be taken to be) based on information so given.[379]

---

[373] *Ali v Bashir* [2013] EWHC 2572 (QB), at 83.
[374] S 66(1) and (6) RPA 1983; art 35(1) NAWRPO 2007; art 22(1) PCCEO 2012.
[375] S 66(3) RPA 1983; art 35(3) NAWRPO 2007; art 22(5) PCCEO 2012.
[376] S 61(3) RPA 1983.
[377] S 66(5) RPA 1983; art 35(5) NAWRPO 2007.
[378] S 66(1) and (4)
[379] S 66A RPA 1983; art 36 NAWRPO 2007; art 23 PCCEO 2012.

4.158 This could apply to statements as to how postal voters have voted.

G. THE COUNT

Time of the count and notice

4.159 The RO must make arrangements for votes to be counted *"as soon as practicable after the close of the poll"* and, in the case of a PE, must take reasonable steps to begin counting within four hours of the close of the poll.[380] The RO must give candidates' counting agents written notice of when and where the RO will begin counting, that they may be present.[381]

Attendance at verification and counting of votes

4.160 The only people who may attend the count are:[382]

(i) The RO and his clerks, plus: the RO's technical assistants and the GLRO (LAE), and the regional RO (WAE regional elections);[383]

(ii) The candidates, their election agents and counting agents, plus one other person chosen by each candidate; and

(iii) Representatives of the Commission and appointed observers; may be present at the counting of the votes.

4.161 The RO may allow others to attend, but only if the RO (i) is satisfied that *"the efficient counting of the votes will not be impeded"*; and (ii) has either: consulted the election agents or thought it impracticable to do so.[384]

Breach of secrecy requirement offence

4.162 Everyone attending the count must maintain the secrecy of voting and it is an offence to:

(i) Attempt to ascertain the number or other unique identifying mark on the back of any ballot paper; or

---

[380]R 44(6) and 45(3A) sch 1 RPA 1983; r 44(4) sch 2 LEPAR 2006; r 47(4) sch 1 GLAER 2007; r 54(1)(a) sch 5 NAWRPO 2007; r 48(1) sch 3 PCCEO 2012.

[381]R 44(1) sch 1 RPA 1983; r 44(1) sch 2 LEPAR 2006; r 54(1)(a) sch 5 NAWRPO 2007; r 48(2) sch 3 PCCEO 2012.

[382]R 44(2) sch 1 RPA 1983; r 44(2), sch 2 LEPAR 2006; r 47 sch 1 and 2 GLAER 2007; r 54(1)(b) sch 5 NAWRPO 2007; rr 48(3) and (4), and 51(4) sch 3 PCCEO 2012.

[383]R 47(2) sch 1 GLAER 2007; r 54(5)(f) sch 5 NAWRPO 2007.

[384]R 44(3) sch 1 RPA 1983; r 44(3), sch 2 LEPAR 2006; r 47(3) sch 1 GLAER 2007; r 54(6) sch 5 NAWRPO 2007; r 51(3)(b) and (5) sch 3 PCCEO 2012.

(ii) Communicate any information obtained at the counting of votes as to how any vote is given on any ballot paper.[385]

Counting agent facilities

4.163 The RO must give the candidates' counting agents facilities for overseeing the count and information about the proceedings,[386] in particular they must be allowed to satisfy themselves that ballot papers are correctly sorted according to the candidate for whom the vote is given.[387]

4.164 Nonetheless, the RO need only afford such facilities up to the point that it can be done *"consistently with the orderly conduct of the proceedings and the discharge of his duties"*,[388] including the RO's duty to take reasonable steps to begin counting the votes given on the ballot papers as soon as practicable and (PE) within four hours of the close of the poll.[389]

Electronic counting

4.165 LAE: the GLRO may provide the RO with an electronic counting system for the purpose of (a) counting the number of ballot papers and votes cast on them, and (b) verifying the ballot paper accounts.[390] References below to 'count' refer, in the context of LAE, to 'causing the electronic counting system to count'.

Verification of ballot paper accounts

4.166 First, in the presence of the candidates' counting agents, the RO must open each ballot box, including each postal voters' ballot box,[391] and record the number of ballots[392] or covering envelopes[393] inside. When doing so, the RO must keep the ballot papers face-up and prevent anyone from seeing the numbers or other unique identifying marks printed on the back of the papers.[394]

---

[385] S 66(2) RPA 1983; art 35(2) NAWRPO 2007.
[386] R 44(4) sch 1 RPA 1983; r 47(4) sch 1 GLAER 2007; r 54(7) sch 5 NAWRPO 2007; rr 51(6) and 52(6) sch 3 PCCEO 2012.
[387] R 44(5) sch 1 RPA 1983; r 51(7) sch 3 PCCEO 2012.
[388] R 44(4) sch 1 RPA 1983; r 47(4) sch 1 GLAER 2007; r 54(7) sch 5 NAWRPO 2007; rr 51(6) and 52(6) sch 3 PCCEO 2012.
[389] R 44(6) and 45(3A) sch 1 RPA 1983; r 44(4), sch 2 LEPAR 2006; r 47(4) sch 1 GLAER 2007.
[390] R 48(1) sch 1 GLAER 2007.
[391] Reg 83 RP (E&W) Regs 2001
[392] R 45(1)(a) sch 1 RPA 1983; r 45(1)(a), sch 2 LEPAR 2006; r 49(1) sch 1 GLAER 2007; r 55(1)(a) sch 5 NAWRPO 2007; r 49(1) sch 3 PCCEO 2012.
[393] Reg 84 RP (E&W) Regs 2001.
[394] R 45(4) sch 1 RPA 1983; r 45(6) sch 2 LEPAR 2006; r 49(7) sch 1 GLAER 2007; r 55(11) sch 5 NAWRPO 2007; r 49(3) sch 3 PCCEO 2012.

4.167 Secondly, in the presence of the candidates' election agents,[395] the RO must verify each ballot paper account provided by each PO, by comparing it with:[396]

(i) The number of ballot papers the RO has recorded;

(ii) The unused and spoilt ballot papers (opening and resealing the packets containing the unused and spoilt ballot papers);

(iii) The tendered votes list and tendered postal votes list (opening and resealing the packets containing the tendered votes list and tendered postal votes list).

4.168 The RO must then draw up a statement as to the result of the verification, which any counting agent may copy.[397] PCCE: the RO must then inform the police area RO of the contents of the statement.[398]

4.169 Thirdly, the RO must count and record the number of duly returned postal ballot papers.[399] A postal ballot paper is 'duly returned' if: [400]

(i) Both it and the PVS are returned by hand or post to the RO or by hand to a polling station in the constituency before the close of the poll;

(ii) The PVS is signed and states the date of birth of the voter or proxy;

(iii) The RO satisfies themselves that the PVS is duly completed, by comparing the date of birth and signature on the PVS with those contained in the personal identifier record relating to the person to whom the postal ballot was addressed;

(iv) PE in Northern Ireland: it is accompanied by the declaration of identity duly signed and authenticated, stating the voter's date of birth, and the RO is satisfied that the date stated corresponds with the date supplied as the date of the elector's birth pursuant.[401]

4.170 PCCE: If the verification takes place at a different location to that at which the count will take place, after completing the above three steps, the RO must (i) make the ballot papers and postal ballot papers up into packets, seal them in

---

[395]R 45(1)(b) sch 1 RPA 1983; r 51(1)(b) sch 5 NAWRPO 2007.
[396]R 45(5) of sch 1 RPA 1983; r 45(7) sch 2 LEPAR 2006; r 49(6) sch 1 GLAER 2007; r 55(12) sch 5 NAWRPO 2007; r 49(5)(a) sch 3 PCCEO 2012.
[397]R 45(5) sch 1 RPA 1983; r 45(7) sch 2 LEPAR 2006; r 49(6) sch 1 GLAER 2007; r 55(12) sch 5 NAWRPO 2007; r 49(5)(b) and (6) sch 3 PCCEO 2012.
[398]R 49(6) sch 5 PCCEO 2012.
[399]R 45(1) sch 1 RPA 1983; r 45(1)(c) sch 2 LEPAR 2006; r 49(1)(b) sch 1 GLAER 2007; r 55(1)(c) sch 5 NAWRPO 2007; r 49(1)(c) sch 3 PCCEO 2012.
[400]R 45(1B)(a) sch 1 RPA 1983; r 45(3)(a) and (4) of sch 2 LEPAR 2006; r 49(2)(a) and (3) sch 1 GLAER 2007; r 55(6) sch 5 NAWRPO 2007; r 49(2) sch 3 PCCEO 2012.
[401]R 45(2)

containers, and endorse on them the voting area and police area to which that the ballots contained relate; (ii) deliver them or cause them to be delivered to the place where the counting will take place.[402] When the containers are then opened for counting, the counting agents must be present.[403]

Counting of votes given

4.171 The RO must first mix the ballot and postal ballot papers with the ballot papers from at least one other ballot box.[404] The exception to the mixing rule is LAE, where the RO must not mix the contents of any ballot box with the contents of any other ballot box during the conduct of any count or re-count.[405]

4.172 The RO must then count the number of votes given for each candidate and record the number counted.[406] PCCE: the RO must count the number of first preferences given to each candidate, unless the election is contested by only two candidates, in which the RO must count the votes given to each candidate.[407]

4.173 During the count, the RO must:

(i) Keep the ballot papers face-up and prevent anyone from seeing the numbers or other unique identifying marks printed on the back of the papers;[408]

(ii) Not count any tendered ballot paper or any tendered postal ballot paper;[409]

(iii) So far as practicable, proceed continuously with the counting of votes, allowing only time for refreshment (though see below on the overnight break).[410]

4.174 In a combined poll, the RO must separate the ballot papers for each election and make them up into packets, sealed up in separate containers, endorsing on each a description of the area to which the ballot papers relate, then deliver those

---

402 R 50 sch 3 PCCEO 2012.
403 R 52(1) sch 3 PCCEO 2012
404 R 45(1A) sch 1 RPA 1983; r 45(2) sch 2 LEPAR 2006; r 55(18) sch 5 NAWRPO 2007; r 52(2) sch 3 PCCEO 2012.
405 R 49(1)(c) sch 1 GLAER 2007
406 R 45(1)(c) sch 1 RPA 1983; r 45(1)(a) sch 2 and r 45(4) sch 3 LEPAR 2006; r 49(1)(b) sch 1 GLAER 2007; r 55(5) sch 5 NAWRPO 2007.
407 R 52(3) sch 3 PCCEO 2012.
408 R 45(4) of sch 1 RPA 1983; para 45(6) of sch 2 LEPAR 2006; r 49(7) sch 1 GLAER 2007; r 55(11) sch 5 NAWRPO 2007; r 52(5) sch 3 PCCEO 2012.
409 R 45(3) of sch 1 RPA 1983; r 45(5) of sch 2 LEPAR 2006; r 52(1) sch 5 PCCEO 2012; r 52(4) sch 3 PCCEO 2012.
410 R 45(6) sch 1 RPA 1983; r 45(8) sch 2 and r 45(12) sch 3 LEPAR 2006; r 49(8) sch 1 and r 50(8) sch 3 GLAER 2007; r 55(13) sch 5 NAWRPO 2007; r 52(6) sch 5 PCCEO 2012.

containers to the RO for the other election, along with the ballot paper accounts and statement of verification.[411]

Overnight break in counting

4.175 If the RO and the agents agree (and GLRO if LAE), the RO may break between 7pm and 9am the next morning (LAE: 5pm-10am).[412]

4.176 If the overnight break is taken, the RO must *"take proper precautions for the security of the papers and documents"*,[413] including placing the ballot papers and other election documents under their seal and that of any of the counting agents who want to affix their seals too.[414]

4.177 The overnight storage of ballot boxes at the count venue does not raise a rebuttable presumption that interference and tampering with the boxes and ballot papers has occurred, rather the contrary (the presumption that administrative acts are properly performed).[415] That is then confirmed if, in the exceptional situation in which counting pauses overnight, the count centre is vacated, closed, chained and sealed, and found to be in the same state as when it had been closed and sealed when re-opened in the morning.[416]

Rejecting ballot papers

4.178 A ballot paper will be void, not counted, and marked *"rejected"* by the RO if:

(i) It does not bear the official mark; [417]

(ii) Votes (or first preferences: PCCE) are given for more than one candidate (unless it is an election in which the voter is entitled to vote for more than one candidate); [418]

---

[411]R 45(1)(d)-(f), sch 3, LEPAR 2006; r 49(1) sch 5 GLAER 2007; r 20 sch 4 NAWPRO 2007.

[412]R 45(6) of sch 1 RPA 1983; r 45(8) of sch 2 LEPAR 2006; r 49(8) sch 1 GLAER 2007; r 55(13) sch 5 NAWRPO 2007; r 52(6) sch 5 PCCEO 2012.

[413]R 45(7)(b) of sch 1 RPA 1983; r 45(9)(b) of sch 2 LEPAR 2006.

[414]R 45(7)(a) of sch 1 RPA 1983; r 45(9)(a) of sch 2 LEPAR 2006; r 49(10) sch 1 GLAER 2007; r 55(13) sch 5 NAWRPO 2007; r 52(7) sch 5 PCCEO 2012.

[415]*Williams v Patrick* [2014] EWHC 4120 (QB), at 45.

[416]*Williams v Patrick* [2014] EWHC 4120 (QB), at 46.

[417]R 47(1) of sch 1 RPA 1983; r 47(1) of sch 2 LEPAR 2006; r 50(1) sch 1 GLAER 2007; r 58(1)(a) sch 5 NAWRPO 2007; r 53(1)(a) sch 3 PCCEO 2012; *Gunn v Sharpe* [1974] QB 808 (98/189 ballots papers not stamped with official mark due to error).

[418]R 47(1) of sch 1 RPA 1983; r 47(1) sch 2 LEPAR 2006; r 50(1) sch 1 GLAER 2007; r 55(1)(b) sch 5 NAWRPO 2007; r 53(1)(b) sch 3 PCCEO 2012.

(iii) It bears writing or a mark by which the voter can be identified (except the printed number and other unique identifying mark on the back);[419] or

(iv) It is unmarked or void for uncertainty.[420]

4.179 A ballot paper marked in the wrong place, not by a cross, or by more than one mark, will **not** be deemed to be void, so long as:[421]

(i) Intention to vote for one of the candidates clearly appears (PCCE: at least one);[422]

(ii) The paper does not identify the voter; and

(iii) It is not shown that voter can be identified by it.

4.180 Applying these rules or the principle on which they are founded, the following have been held valid:

(i) Ballot papers on which a perforating machine has made less than the required number of perforations;[423]

(ii) Ballot papers on which the voter wrote the name of the preferred candidate (their handwriting did not sufficiently identify the voter);[424]

(iii) A ballot paper on which the voter had placed their mark outside the ruled compartments on the paper, as the mark was nonetheless opposite the name of a candidate and leaving no doubt for whom the voter intended to vote;[425]

(iv) A ballot paper on which the voter had put a cross immediately above the vacant space left for their mark, but with the ends of the cross at least extending *"very slightly"* into the space opposite the name of the first candidate upon the paper;[426]

---

[419] R 47(1) of sch 1 RPA 1983; para 47(1) of sch 2 LEPAR 2006; para 50(1) sch 1 GLAER 2007; r 55(1)(c) sch 5 NAWRPO 2007; r 53(1)(c) sch 3 PCCEO 2012.

[420] R 47(1) of sch 1 RPA 1983; r 47(1) sch 2 LEPAR 2006; r 50(1) sch 1 GLAER 2007; r 55(1)(d) sch 5 NAWRPO 2007; r 53(1)(d) and (e) sch 3 PCCEO 2012.

[421] R 47(2) sch 1 RPA 1983; r 47(3) sch 2 LEPAR 2006; r 50(2) sch 1 GLAER 2007; r 55(2) sch 5 NAWRPO 2007; ; r 53(2)-(4) sch 3 PCCEO 2012.

[422] R 53(3)-(5) sch 3 PCCEO 2012.

[423] *Kingston upon Hull Municipal Election Petition, Re* [1948] 2 All ER 503.

[424] *Ruffle v Rogers* [1982] 3 WLR 143, p 146B-H.

[425] *Pontardawe Rural DC Election Petition* [1907] 2 KB 313; *Cooper v Ogden, Re Oldham Case* [1908] 6 LGR 373, 72 JP 115, 52 Sol Jo 192, 24 TLR 242.

[426] *Cooper v Ogden, Re Oldham Case* [1908] 6 LGR 373, 72 JP 115, 52 Sol Jo 192, 24 TLR 242.

(v) A ballot paper on which the voter had crossed out the names of all but one candidate (in an election in which only one candidate was to be elected);[427]

(vi) A ballot paper on which the cross had been recorded in the part of the paper in which the candidate's name appeared, but with a small portion of one line extending into the part containing the other candidate's name;[428]

(vii) A ballot paper was marked in the proper space, but by a pencil of which the lead had broken off, leaving only an impression;[429]

(viii) Ballot papers featuring pencil marks over the cross against the name of one of the candidates;[430]

(ix) Ballot papers on which the official mark stamp does not show clear and distinct impression of every part of the stamp, as long as the stamp was applied there with the intention of making the required mark;[431]

4.181 The following have been held invalid:

(i) A ballot paper on which the cross deleted the names of A and C, but the centre of which was over A's name;[432]

(ii) A ballot paper marked with 1, 2, and 3, instead of with a cross;[433]

(iii) A ballot paper on which the voter had marked their initials.[434]

4.182 The Commission has produced a booklet to assist ROs in adjudicating doubtful ballot papers at PE, containing examples of 'allowed' and 'rejected' ballot papers, based on the above legislation and case law.[435]

4.183 LE with votes for more than one candidate: if only one of multiple votes is void for uncertainty, the RO must mark it *"rejected in part"*.[436]

4.184 LAE:

---

[427] *Levers v Morris* [1972] 1 QB 221 (DC), p 230E.
[428] *Fryer v Harris*, Times, July 30, 1955, [1955] CLY 921.
[429] *Cooper v Ogden, Re Oldham Case* [1908] 6 LGR 373, 72 JP 115, 52 Sol Jo 192, 24 TLR 242.
[430] *Kingston upon Hull Municipal Election Petition, Re* [1948] 2 All ER 503.
[431] *Gloucester (County) Cirencester Division Case, Lawson v Chester Master* (1893) 4 O'M. & H. 194, [1893] 1 WLUK 13; *Kingston upon Hull Municipal Election Petition, Re* [1948] 2 All E.R. 503
[432] *Cornwell v Marshall* [1977] 75 LGR 676, [1977] CLY 908 (DC).
[433] *Cornwell v Marshall* [1977] 75 LGR 676, [1977] CLY 908 (DC).
[434] *Kingston upon Hull Municipal Election Petition, Re* [1948] 2 All ER 503.
[435] Electoral Commission, 'Dealing with doubtful ballot papers in GB', 2017, https://www.electoralcommission.org.uk/sites/default/files/pdf_file/UKPE-doubtfuls-booklet.pdf
[436] R 47(2) of sch 2 LEPAR 2006.

(i) Where the electronic counting system identifies a ballot paper that has been marked, but which appears to be void, an image of the ballot paper must be examined by a clerk appointed by the RO, shown on a screen so as to be visible to those attending the count.[437] If the clerk considers the vote void, the CRO must examine it in the same way, and thereafter give their decision on validity.[438]

(ii) No count attendee can require the clerk or RO to examine a ballot paper or to provide a paper copy for the attendee to inspect.[439]

4.185 If a counting agent objects to a rejection, the RO will also endorse the paper with *"rejection objected to"*,[440] except in LAE, where this endorsement will only be made where manual rather than electronic counting is used.[441]

4.186 The RO must draw up a statement showing the number of ballot papers rejected under each head (want of official mark, voting for more than one candidate (or more than one first preference: PCCE), mark identifying voter, unmarked or void for uncertainty).[442]

Re-counts

4.187 When the counting is completed, candidates, election agents, and (PCCE) counting agents present must have a reasonable opportunity to request that the RO have the votes re-counted.[443] A second recount may be requested, e.g. if the first produces the inverse result to the original count.[444] If in their opinion the request is unreasonable, the RO may refuse the request.[445]

4.188 LAE: where an electronic counting system is used, the recount may be done manually or electronically.[446]

4.189 PCCE: if they have reason to doubt the accuracy of the count, the police area RO may direct that the RO to conduct a re-count.[447] If so, the RO must do so

---

437 R 50(3) and (6) sch 1 GLAER 2007.
438 R 50(4), (5) and (6) sch 1 GLAER 2007.
439 R 50(8) sch 1 GLAER 2007.
440 R 47(3) sch 1 RPA 1983; r 47(4) sch 2 and 3 LEPAR 2006; r 58(4) sch 5 NAWRPO 2007; r 53(6) sch 3 PCCEO 2012.
441 Substitution for r 50 sch 1 and r 51 sch 2, sch 4 GLAER 2007.
442 R 47(4) sch 1 RPA 1983; r 47(5) sch 2 LEPAR 2006; r 50(11) sch 1 GLAER 2007; r 61(1)(b) sch 5 NAWRPO 2007; r 53(7) sch 3 PCCEO 2012.
443 R 46(1) sch 1 RPA 1983; r 46 sch 2 LEPAR 2006; r 51(1) and (2) sch 1 GLAER 2007; rr 56(2) and 57(1) sch 5 NAWRPO 2007; r 54 sch 3 PCCEO 2012.
444 R 46(1) sch 1 RPA 1983; r 46 sch 2 LEPAR 2006; r 56(1) sch 5 NAWRPO 2007; *Petition of Rowe* [2001] All ER (D) 329 (Dec) (DC).
445 R 46(2) sch 1 RPA 1983; r 46 sch 2 LEPAR 2006; r 56(2) sch 5 NAWRPO 2007; r 54(2) sch 3 PCCEO 2012.
446 R 48(5) sch 1 GLAER 2007.
447 R 55 sch 3 PCCEO 2012.

as soon as practicable and if not immediately then at a time notified to the counting agents.[448]

RO reconsideration

4.190 Until they declare the result of the election, an RO is entitled to reconsider which ballot papers should be rejected if they conclude that a previously rejected ballot paper was in fact valid.[449]

Petition questioning RO decision that ballot paper invalid

4.191 The decision of the RO in respect of a ballot paper is subject to review on an election petition.[450]

4.192 The Election Court approaches a question of the validity of a ballot, e.g. where the voter has marked the paper but not in accordance with the instructions, as a question of fact, not law.[451] Where a cross extends over more than one box, it is a matter of impression whether the ballot paper is a vote for a particular candidate or not.[452]

Supplementary vote system (PCCE)

4.193 Because PCCEs use the supplementary vote system, if the police area RO determines that none of the candidates has received more than half of all the first preference votes given in the police area, then the two candidates who received the greatest number of first preference votes remain in the contest, the other candidates are eliminated, and the police area RO must direct that each RO should count second preference votes given for each candidate.

4.194 As soon as practicable after the conclusion of the count (including any re-count), the RO must:[453]

(i) Draw up a statement showing: (a) the total number of ballot papers used; (b) the total number of rejected ballot papers; (c) the total number of votes given for each candidate (PCCE contested by three or more candidates: the total number of first preference votes given, and the number of first preference votes given for each candidate;

(ii) PCCE: inform the police area RO of the contents of the statement and, once authorised by them, inform the candidates and election agents

---

448 R 55(3) sch 3 PCCEO 2012.

449 *Fermanagh and South Tyrone* [2010] NIQB 113, at 43, per Morgan LCJ.

450 R 48 sch 1 RPA 1983; r 48 sch 2 LEPAR 2006; r 51 sch 1 GLAER 2007; r 59 sch 5 NAWRPO 2007; r 56 sch 3 PCCEO 2012.

451 *Cornwell v Marshall* [1977] 75 LGR 676, [1977] CLY 908 (DC).

452 *Petition of Rowe* [2001] All ER (D) 329 (Dec) (DC)

453 R 57 sch 3 PCCEO 2012.

present of the contents of the statement showing the total votes and the statement of votes rejected;

(iii) Give public notice of the content of those statements.

4.195 With this information, the police area RO must:

(i) If three or more candidates: ascertain whether a candidate has an overall majority of first preference and is to be returned;[454]

(ii) If two candidates: ascertain the total number of votes given for each candidate;

(iii) Inform the election agents present as to these figures and afford them a reasonable opportunity to satisfy themselves of the accuracy of the calculation.[455] The agents may request that the figures be recalculated, but the police area RO may refuse if in their opinion the request is unreasonable;[456]

(iv) If a candidate has an overall majority of first preferences or (where two candidates only) votes, proceed to the declaration (see below: 'declaration of result');

(v) If no candidate has an overall majority of first preferences, proceed to the second calculation.

4.196 The second calculation proceeds as follows: the RO must:

(i) Notify the counting agents of those candidates not eliminated of the time and place at which the count of second preference votes will take place;

(ii) Count the number of second preference votes given in the voting area for each of the remaining candidates, applying the rules on ballot paper validity;

(iii) Draw up a statement of the number of second preference votes given to each remaining candidate;

(iv) Inform the police area RO of the content of this statement;

(v) Once authorised by the police area RO, inform the candidates and their agents of the same, and give public notice of the same.

4.197 The statement from the ROs in hand, the police area RO must add second preferences to first preference votes.[457] They must provide the number of second

---

[454] Para 3 sch 9 Police Reform and Social Responsibility Act 2011.
[455] R 59(1) and (2) sch 3 PCCEO 2012.
[456] R 59(3) sch 3 PCCEO 2012.
[457] Para 4(6) sch 9 Police Reform and Social Responsibility Act 2011; r 61 sch 3 PCCEO 2012.

preferences given to each candidate in the election area and their calculation ascertain the total number of first and second preferences to the election agents present, who must be afforded a reasonable opportunity to satisfy themselves as to the accuracy of the calculation.[458] A recalculation may be requested of the police area RO, who may decline if deeming it unreasonable.[459]

4.198 The person to be returned as police and crime commissioner for the police area is the candidate with the total number of preference votes.[460]

Equality of votes (a tie)

4.199 After the count (and any re-count), if there is a tie, the RO must straightaway decide between the tied candidates by lot, tossing a coin or pulling a name out of a hat. The candidate on whom the lot falls is treated as if they had received an additional vote.[461] WAE: this rule only applies in constituency elections, not regional.[462] PCCE: this process is only used where there is only two candidates.[463]

Declaration of result

4.200 Once the result is ascertained, the RO must as soon as possible declare to be elected:[464]

(i) PE, WAE, and PCCE with two candidates: the candidate with the majority of votes;[465]

(ii) PCCE with three or more candidates: the candidate with the overall majority of first preference votes;[466]

(iii) LE: the candidates to whom more votes have been given (up to the number of councillors to be elected).

---

[458]R 61(2) and (4) sch 3 PCCEO 2012.
[459]R 61(3) sch 3 PCCEO 2012.
[460]Para 4(7) sch 9 Police Reform and Social Responsibility Act 2011; r 60 sch 3 PCCEO 2012.
[461]R 49 sch 1 RPA 1983; r 49 sch 2 LEPAR 2006; r 53 sch 1 GLAER 2007; r 60 sch 5 NAWRPO 2007; r 59(7) sch 3 PCCEO 2012.
[462]R 60 sch 5 NAWRPO 2007.
[463]Para 4(8) sch 9 Police Reform and Social Responsibility Act 2011 and r 59(7) sch 3 PCCEO 2012.
[464]R 51 sch 1 RPA 1983; r 50 sch 2 LEPAR 2006; r 62 sch 5 NAWRPO 2007.
[465]S 57(2) Police Reform and Social Responsibility Act 2011; rr 59(6) and 62(1)(a) sch 3 PCCEO 2012.
[466]Para 4(8) sch 9 Police Reform and Social Responsibility Act 2011; r 59(5)(a) and 62(1)(b) sch 3 PCCEO 2012.

Steps following declaration of result

4.201 Once the result is declared, the RO (PCCE: police area RO) must:[467]

(i) Give public notice of the name of the elected candidate(s) and their authorised description, the total number of votes (or first preferences: PCCE) for each candidate, the total number of rejected ballot papers under each head shown in the statement of rejected ballot papers, and (PCCE) the total number, if any, of second preferences counted and ballot papers rejected during the second count;

(ii) Give notice of the winner's name to the Clerk of the Crown (PE), proper officer of the council (LE), GLRO and proper officer of the Greater London Authority (LAE), Clerk to the Assembly (WAE), or the Secretary of State or Minister for the Cabinet Office and the RO (PCCE);

(iii) PE: return the writ, by endorsing it with the winning candidate's name, title and address, endorse a certificate in the prescribed form,[468] then deliver the writ to the postmaster of principal post office for the area or an official designated for that purpose by a universal postal service provider. They must send the endorsed writ by the next post, free of charge, to the Clerk of the Crown with the words *"Election Writ and Return"* endorsed on the envelope.

H. AFTER THE COUNT

Return of deposit

4.202 Not LE: the RO must return the candidates' deposit no later than the first working day after the result is declared.[469] If a candidate is found not to have polled more than one-twentieth of the total votes, their deposit is forfeited.[470]

Notice of delayed counting (PE)

4.203 If the counting did not begin within the guideline four hours,[471] the RO must, within 30 days of polling day, send the Commission a statement stating the time at which the counting began, describe the steps taken to begin counting the

---

[467] R 51 sch 1 RPA 1983; r 50 sch 2 LEPAR 2006; r 62 sch 5 NAWRPO 2007; r 62(2) sch 3 PCCEO 2012.

[468] Appendix to sch 1 RPA 1983.

[469] R 53; r 55(1) and (2) sch 1 GLAER 2007; r 65(2) NAWRPO 2007; r 63 sch 3 PCCEO 2012.

[470] R 53(4) sch 1 RPA 1983; r 55(5) sch 1 GLAER 2007; r 63(5) sch 3 PCCEO 2012.

[471] R 45(3A) sch 1 RPA 1983.

vote, explain why the counting of the votes given on the ballot papers did not start within the guidelines four hours.[472]

Disposal of documents by the RO

4.204 After the count, the RO must, seal up in separate packets the counted and rejected ballot papers (including those rejected in part).[473]

4.205 LAE: seal up in separate packet an electronic record of votes counted using the electronic counting system, which record must then be removed from that system.[474]

4.206 The RO must then forward the following to the ERO for the electoral area, or the area in which the constituency is situated (or the area with greater number of registered voters if the constituency spans more than one),[475] each endorsed with description of its contents, date of the election, and name of the constituency or area for which the election was held:[476]

(i) The packets of ballot papers;

(ii) The ballot paper accounts;

(iii) The statements of rejected ballot papers;

(iv) The statements of the result of the verification of the ballot paper accounts;

(v) The tendered votes lists;

(vi) The lists of voters with disabilities assisted by companions;

(vii) The lists of votes marked by the PO and the related statements;

(viii) The lists of voters to whom ballot papers are delivered pursuant to notices of late alteration to the register;

(ix) The declarations made by the companions of voters with disabilities;

(x) The packets of the completed corresponding number lists;

(xi) The packets of certificates as to employment on duty on the day of the poll;

---

[472] R 53(ZA) sch 1 RPA 1983.

[473] R 54(1) sch 1 RPA 1983; r 51(1) sch 2 LEPAR 2006; r 66 sch 5 NAWRPO 2007; r 68 sch 5 NAWRPO 2007; r 65(1) sch 5 NAWRPO 2007.

[474] R 56(2) and (3) sch 1 GLAER 2007.

[475] R 55(1A) sch 1 RPA 1983; para 52(2) of sch 2 LEPAR 2006.

[476] R 55(1) sch 1 RPA 1983; r 52(1) of sch 2 LEPAR 2006; r 57(1) sch 1 GLAER 2007; r 67 sch 5 NAWRPO 2007; r 66 sch 3 PCCEO 2012.

(xii) The packets containing marked copies of (a) registers (including any marked copy register alteration notices, (b) lists of proxies of the postal voters list, (c) lists of proxies and (d) the proxy postal voters list.

4.207 The RO must destroy each candidate's home address form either:

(i) On the first working day 21 days (PE and PCCE) or 35 days (LAE) after the officer has returned the name of the member elected;[477] or

(ii) If a petition is brought, within 21 days of (PE) or as soon as practicable after (LAE) the conclusion of proceedings on the petition or on appeal from such proceedings.[478]

Order for production of documents

4.208 No person may inspect any rejected or counted ballot papers in the possession of an ERO or to open any sealed packets of the completed corresponding number lists or certificates, except by court order.[479]

4.209 The House of Commons (PE), or, if satisfied by evidence on oath that it is necessary for an election petition or the prosecution for an offence in relation to ballot papers, the High Court (PE and WAE), county court (PE, LE, WAE, LAE, and PCCE),[480] or Election Court (solely for petition purposes) may make an order for the:[481]

(i) Inspection or production of any rejected ballot papers in the custody of the RO; or

(ii) Opening of a sealed packet of the completed corresponding number lists or of certificates as to employment on duty on the day of the poll or the inspection of any counted ballot papers in his custody.

4.210 Appeal lies to the High Court from any order of the County Court for any such inspection, production or opening order.[482]

4.211 Where uncounted ballot papers are discovered after the result is declared, the County Court has jurisdiction to make an order for inspection, production or opening prior to the presentation of a contemplated election petition, and an

[477]R 53A(a); r 59A(1) sch 1 GLAER 2007; r 68 sch 5 NAWRPO 2007; r 64 sch 3 PCCEO 2012.
[478]R 53A(a) sch 1 RPA 1983; r 53 schs 2 and 3 LEPAR 2007; r 59A(1) sch 1 GLAER 2007; r 68 sch 5 NAWRPO 2007; r 64 sch 3 PCCEO 2012.
[479]R 56(8) of sch 1 RPA 1983; r 53(1) of sch 2 LEPAR 2006; r 68(1) sch 1 GLAER 2007.
[480]R 53(1) of sch 2 LEPAR 2006; r 58(1) sch 1 GLAER 2007.
[481]Rr 55 and 56(1) of sch 1 RPA 1983; r 53(2) of sch 2 LEPAR 2006; r 58(2) sch 1 GLAER 2007; rr 67(2) and 68(1) and (2) sch 5 NAWRPO 2007; r 67(1) and (2) sch 3 PCCEO 2012.
[482]R 53(4) of sch 2 LEPAR 2006; r 58(4) sch 1 GLAER 2007; r 67(5) sch 3 PCCEO 2012.

RO has standing to make such an application.[483] Given the purpose is to discover whether that petition is needed, if the uncounted votes do not outnumber the winning margin and election petition would then be unlikely to follow such application, such application is likely to be granted. Interested parties should be given notice so they may attend the hearing of the application.[484]

Retention of documents by the ERO

4.212 The ERO must retain for one year all documents forwarded to him under the Rules by an RO, and then destroy them, unless otherwise directed by order of the House of Commons or the High Court, Crown Court, or magistrates' court (PE) or County Court, Crown Court, Magistrates' Court or Election Court (LE, LAE, PCCE).[485]

4.213 All these retained documents must be open to public inspection, except ballot papers, the completed corresponding number lists, and certificates as to employment on duty on the day of the poll.[486]

I. JUDICIAL REVIEW OF RO DECISION BEFORE THE RESULT

4.214 Decisions of ROs are amenable to judicial review, but the courts are slow to intervene. In *R (De Beer) v Balabanoff*, Scott Baker J held:

> "In my judgment, although judicial review does lie, this is an area in which the courts should be extremely slow to interfere with the decision of a returning officer. No doubt where a returning officer has plainly acted unlawfully relief will lie. But ordinarily returning officers should be left to conduct the election process as provided by Parliament."

4.215 In *De Beer*,[487] a challenge to an RO decision to reject the nomination papers featuring an improperly authorised description, Scott Baker J held:

> "It is, in my judgment, important to keep in mind the role of the returning officer in the election process. He is in a sense the referee. He is there to see fair play and to ensure that the rules are complied with. As a matter of policy, it seems to me, the fewer occasions on which he is called upon to exercise questions of judgment and thereby lay himself

---

[483] *Gough v Local Sunday Newspapers (North) Ltd (No.2)* [2003] EWCA Civ 297, at 50-51 (concerning the predecessor to r 53: r 47 of the 1986 Rules).

[484] *Gough v Local Sunday Newspapers (North) Ltd (No.2)* [2003] EWCA Civ 297, at 50.

[485] R 57(1) of sch 1 RPA 1983; r 54 of sch 2 LEPAR 2006; r 59 sch 1 GLAER 2007; r 68(1) sch 3 PCCEO 2012.

[486] R 57(2) of sch 1 RPA 1983; r 54 of sch 2 LEPAR 2006; r 69 sch 5 NAWRPO 2007; r 68(2) and (3) sch 3 PCCEO 2012.

[487] R *(De Beer) v Balabanoff* [2002] EWHC 670 (Admin).

open to criticism by one or more of the candidates the better. This is particularly pertinent if the exercise of judgment were to go outside issues that can readily be resolved by looking at a document or documents, and which involves weighing up facts or surrounding circumstances."[488]

4.216 As to why this should be such an area where the courts should be extremely slow to interfere, it may in part be attributed to *De Beer* concerning a RO's decision to reject nomination papers, the only RO function on which the election rules state that the RO's decision is *"final"* and *"shall not be questioned"*: *"The returning officer's decision that a nomination paper is valid shall be final and shall not be questioned in any proceeding whatsoever."*[489]

4.217 That Scott Baker J's decision held that this provision does not oust the court's jurisdiction is therefore significant. In relation to a power that the draftsman have not described in terms redolent of judicial immunity, a smaller margin of appreciation would be appropriate.

[488] R *(De Beer) v Balabanoff* [2002] EWHC 670 (Admin), at 28.
[489] R 12(5) sch 1 RPA 1983; r 13(6) sch 5 NAWRPO 2007.

CHAPTER FIVE

ELECTION PETITIONS: PRINCIPLES AND PROCEDURE

5.1 Election petitions are a statutory remedy, governed by largely self-contained statutory schemes.

5.2 This chapter discusses them across the following themes:

A. The jurisdiction;

B. Undue election: grounds of challenge;

C. No return;

D. Undue return;

E. Petition procedure;

F. Aftermath;

G. Appeal to the Court of Appeal;

H. Judicial review of Election Court.

A. THE JURISDICTION

Exclusive jurisdiction

5.3 Petitions are the exclusive means provided to the courts by Parliament for challenging election results.[1] Prior to this legislative provision, election petitions were tried by election committees within Parliament, with obvious risk of bias amongst nominees, so leading to the transfer of the functions to the courts.[2]

5.4 The exclusivity is such that a Returning Office ("**RO**") cannot correct their own declaration as to who was returned. In *Pritchard v Bangor Corp*,[3] the RO had corrected his decision as to who was duly elected, having overnight considered the objection of the unsuccessful candidate. The House of Lords held he had

[1]Ss 120 and 127 Representation of the People Act 1983 ("**RPA 1983**"); art 86 National Assembly for Wales (Representation of the People) Order 2007 ("**NAWRPO 2007**").

[2] Parliamentary Elections Act 1868.

[3]*Pritchard v Bangor Corp* (1888) 13 App. Cas. 241.

no jurisdiction to do so: the proper method for determining the objection was by election petition.

5.5 The House of Commons retains the power to receive election petitions that do not question the return of the sitting MP.[4]

5.6 In *R (Wilson) v Prime Minister*,[5] the Court of Appeal doubted but left open the question of whether, *"absent power granted by Parliament, the court has a residual common law power to interfere in an election"*.[6] In practice, there would be clear basis for refusing judicial review on grounds of adequate alternative remedy. Judicial review of any Election Court following a petition, however, does lie and is discussed later in this chapter, in section H.

What may be challenged

5.7 Election petitions may complain of: (i) undue election (the process leading to the return of the winning candidate), (ii) undue return (the RO has returned the wrong name), or (iii) no return (the RO has omitted or declined to return the name of the member elected).[7]

What conclusions may be reached

5.8 At the conclusion of the trial, the Election Court must determine:

(i) Whether the person whose election is complained of was duly elected; if not

(ii) Whether any other person was duly elected; or

(iii) Whether the election is void.[8]

Petitioner

5.9 A petition may be presented by:

(i) A person (Parliamentary elections ("**PE**") and Welsh Assembly elections ("**WAE**")) or four or more persons (local elections ("**LE**"), London Assembly elections ("**LAE**") and police and crime commissioner elections ("**PCCE**")) who voted at the election or had a right to vote, with the exception of anonymous voters;[9]

---

[4]Erskine May, part 1, ch 2, para 2.23.
[5]R *(Wilson and others) v Prime Minister* [2019] EWCA Civ 304.
[6]R *(Wilson and others) v Prime Minister* [2019] EWCA Civ 304, at 35-36, per Hickinbottom LJ.
[7]Ss 120 and 127 RPA 1983.
[8]Ss 144(1) and 145(1) RPA 1983; *Edgell v Glover* [2003] EWHC 2566 (QB) (DC), 18
[9]Ss 121(1A) and 128(1) RPA 1983; art 87(1)(a) and (b) and (2) NAWRPO 2007; para 1 sch 9 PCCEO 2012.

(ii) A person claiming to have been a candidate at the election;[10]

(iii) A person claiming to have had a right of election or to be returned in an election region vacancy (WAE).[11]

5.10 If a petition is brought by someone who was ineligible for election, the petition is defective and may not be amendable.[12]

Respondents

5.11 The successful candidate must be named as respondent, as it is their election being questioned and they have a right to be heard.[13] The RO must also be named, if the petition questions their conduct of the election.[14]

Election Court

5.12 A PE and WAE petition must be tried by two High Court judges on the rota for the trial of petitions.[15] A judge not on the rota for the trial of petitions has no jurisdiction to determine *ex parte* applications to amend petitions.[16] An LE petition consists of one commissioner, appointed by the judges on the PE petition rota.[17] Both constitutions are referred to as 'the Election Court'.[18]

5.13 In trying petitions, an Election Court has the same powers and authority as a High Court judge.[19]

Nature of jurisdiction

5.14 There is difference in view as to whether election petitions are public law proceedings[20] or private legal process.[21] It is clear that they are partly inquisitorial and partly adversarial. In *Erlam v Rahman*,[22] Commissioner Richard Mawrey QC gave this overview:

> "39 … An Election Court is, in some ways, a unique tribunal. Election petitions are presented and pursued in a very similar manner to claims made in the civil courts and, procedurally, the basic rules

---

[10]Ss 121(1) and 128(1) RPA 1983; para 1 sch 9 PCCEO 2012.
[11]Art 87(1)(c) and (d) NAWRPO 2007.
[12]*Hobson v Fishburn* [1991] 155 LG Rev 56. For the rules on amendment, see below.
[13]Ss 121(2) and 8(2) RPA 1983; *Absalom v Gillett* [1995] 1 WLR 128.
[14]Ss 121(2) and 8(2) RPA 1983; *Absalom v Gillett* [1995] 1 WLR 128.
[15]S 123(1) RPA 1983; art 89 NAWRPO 2007.
[16]*Shaw v Reckitt* [1893] 2 QB 59 (CA).
[17]S 130(1) and (3) RPA 1983.
[18]Ss 123(1) and 130(1) RPA 1983.
[19]S 123(2) and 130(5) RPA 1983; art 89(2) NAWRPO 2007.
[20]*Scarth v Amin* [2008] EWHC 2886 (QB), at 28.
[21] Law Commission, Research Paper: Legal Challenge to Elections, para 1.14.
[22]*Erlam v Rahman and Williams* [2015] EWHC 1215 (QB) at 39.

to be applied are those of the Civil Procedure Rules ('CPR'). Accordingly election proceedings have an adversarial character. Nevertheless, election petitions differ in a number of ways from civil actions.

40 An election judge occupies an intermediate position between that of a civil court judge, whose function is (in general) to determine the issues as between the parties to the action being tried, and a coroner, whose function is an inquisitorial function to determine the cause of death and surrounding circumstances. …

41 An Election Court possesses elements of both systems. The election judge must hear and determine the issues between the Petitioner and the Respondent: to that extent he is a civil court judge. He must also enquire more widely into possible electoral malpractice both in the electoral area in question and in the wider electoral area. In the present case the questioned election, as it happens, encompasses the entirety of the electoral area (the Borough of Tower Hamlets) but where the petition concerns only one or two wards within a larger electoral area, the election judge is charged under s 145(3) of the 1983 Act with the duty to state 'whether any corrupt practices have, or whether there is reason to believe that any corrupt practices have, extensively prevailed at the election in the area of the authority for which the election was held or in any electoral area of that authority's area'. …

42 The practical consequence of the combined adversarial and inquisitorial nature of an Election Court is that an election judge must necessarily be more interventionist than would normally be the case. In criminal cases, judicial intervention during evidence is usually kept to a minimum and, in civil cases, though the level of intervention is often higher (particularly if the case involves technicalities which require explanation), it is still not an important part of the process. In election cases, however, the inquisitorial function, though falling well short of the control of proceedings exercised by a coroner, does mean that judges ask a lot more questions than would be the norm in civil cases.

43 In the present case, as in many Petitions, the resources available to the protagonists were limited. … The focus of the parties being, quite properly, the pleaded issues, it was left to the court to examine the wider picture."[23]

---

[23] *Erlam v Rahman and Williams* [2015] EWHC 1215 (QB) at 39.

5.15 The inquisitorial element means that (i) a petition does not necessarily become otiose when a new election is pending: it retains jurisdiction to investigate, for instance, alleged corruption; (ii) the Election Court can examine anyone in court, irrespective of whether they are called by a party;[24] (iii) on a no return petition, the Election Court can substitute its decision as the number of votes for that of the RO and declare a different candidate duly returned.[25]

Art 6 ECHR

5.16 An Election Court decision that a respondent is guilty of electoral offences does not amount to an imputation of criminal liability.[26] Therefore, the presumption of innocence in art 6(2) ECHR is not violated by such decisions[27] and a commissioner need not stay proceedings until the respondent's guilt or innocence is determined by a criminal court.[28] The exception may be situation where a respondent shows that, at the time of the decision, there are parallel criminal proceedings in which they are a suspect.[29]

5.17 Although proceedings before the Election Court are not criminal proceedings for art 6 ECHR purposes, where a respondent is alleged to have committed electoral offences the criminal standard of proof applies.[30]

Art 3 to Protocol 1 ECHR ("A3P1")

5.18 The scope and content of A3P1 is discussed in the next chapter, but a summary is provided here because of its relevance to the petition jurisdiction.

5.19 A3P1 provides:

> "The High Contracting Parties undertake to hold free elections at reasonable intervals by secret ballot, under conditions which will ensure the free expression of the opinion of the people in the choice of the legislature."

5.20 The courts must act compatibly with the ECHR, including therefore A3P1, and legislation such as the Election Petition Rules 1960 must be read so far as possible so that it is compatible with A3P1.

5.21 In *Scarth v Amin*,[31] Tugendhat J held:

---

[24] S 140(4) RPA 1983.

[25] Ss 144(1) and 145(1) RPA 1983.

[26] R *(Rahman) v Local Government Election Court* [2017] EWHC 1413 (Admin) (DC) at 74-75.

[27] R *(Rahman) v Local Government Election Court* [2017] EWHC 1413 (Admin) (DC) at 74-75.

[28] R *(Rahman) v Local Government Election Court* [2017] EWHC 1413 (Admin) (DC) at 74-75.

[29] R *(Rahman) v Local Government Election Court* [2017] EWHC 1413 (Admin) (DC) at 48.

[30] R *(Afzal) v Election Court* [2005] EWHC 721 (Admin) at 9-10, undisturbed by the subsequent Court of Appeal decision in R *(Afzal) v Election Court* [2005] EWCA Civ 647 at 31.

[31] *Scarth v Amin* [2008] EWHC 2886 (QB).

> "16 All legislation must be interpreted in the light of the objective which the legislature must be taken to have been pursuing. There are competing public interests at stake. On the one hand, the rules requiring timely and proper presentation of a petition are strict, because it is in the public interest that there should be early clarity as to who has been elected. …
>
> 17 On the other hand, there is a countervailing public interest that there should be free elections under conditions which will ensure the free expression of the opinion of the people: see article 3 of the First Protocol to the European Convention for the Protection of Human Rights and Fundamental Freedoms and Part II of Schedule I to the Human Rights Act 1998. This principle has long been recognised in English law, and goes back before article 8 of the Bill of Rights 1689 (1 Will & Mary, sess 2, c 2), (That election of Members of Parliament ought to be free). For there to be free elections there must be a procedure for determining what opinion the people have expressed in cases where an election is questioned, and for elections to be declared void in appropriate cases. It would be wrong in principle to adopt an interpretation of the 1960 Rules which placed conditions upon the presentation of valid petitions which were more restrictive than necessary to achieve the certainty that is required, and which obstructed the determination of what opinion the people had expressed."

Scope

5.22 An election that takes place without a poll, for instance because certain candidates are held by the RO not to have been validly nominated, may still be challenged by petition.[32]

5.23 PE: an Election Court retains jurisdiction to try a petition even if the respondent candidate vacates their seat or Parliament is prorogued.[33]

B. UNDUE ELECTION: GROUNDS OF CHALLENGE

5.24 Petitions questioning the election may be brought on the following grounds:[34]

(i) Breach of the relevant election rules, rendering the election not substantially in accordance with the law and affecting the result;

(ii) Miscount;

---

[32] *Absalom v Gillett* [1995] 1 WLR 128, 134E-F.
[33] S 139(3) RPA 1983.
[34] S 127 RPA 1983

(iii) The election was avoided by corrupt practice or illegal practices (on the part of a candidate or those to be treated as their agents);

(iv) The person elected was disqualified at the time of the election;

(v) General corruption so extensively prevailing as to be presumed to effect the result;[35] or

(vi) The person elected employed a corrupt agent.[36]

Ground 1: Breach of rules rendering election not substantially in accordance with the law and affecting the result)

5.25 An election must be declared invalid or void[37] if:

(i) There has been an act or omission by the RO or any other person (including the ERO) in breach of their official duty in connection with the election;[38]

(ii) The election was not conducted *"substantially in accordance with the law as to elections"*;[39] and

(iii) The act or omission affected the result.[40]

5.26 As to breach, there are two discrete exclusions to the scope of what breaches may be challenged:

(i) Candidates cannot rely on these saving provisions if the error is their own,[41] e.g., make errors in the nomination papers;[42] and

(ii) Petitioners cannot challenge RO decisions that nomination papers are valid, only that they are invalid or that the nomination itself involved

---

35S 164 RPA 1983

36S 165 RPA 1983

37 Used interchangeably: s 23 and 48 used 'invalid'; the courts have used 'void': e.g. *Gunn and others v Sharpe* [1974] 2 All ER (QBD), p 812D.

38Ss 23(3) and 48(1) RPA 1983; *Morgan v Simpson* [1975] QB 151 (CA) at 12; *Williams v Patrick* [2014] EWHC 4120 (QB) at 61; *Baxter v Fear* [2015] EWHC 3136 (OB) at 36. These rules are set out in relevant conduct of election chapter.

39Ss 23(3) and 48(1) RPA 1983; *Morgan v Simpson* [1975] QB 151 (CA); *Edgell v Glover* [2003] EWHC 2566 (QB) by Newman J at 23, followed in *Considine v Didrichsen* [2004] EWHC 2711 (QB) at 23.

40Ss 23(3) and 48(1); *Morgan v Simpson* [1975] QB 151 (CA); *Edgell v Glover* [2003] EWHC 2566 (QB) by Newman J at 23 [followed in *Considine v Didrichsen* [2004] EWHC 2711 (QB) at 23. 'Result' means the success of one candidate over the others, not the number of votes recorded for a candidate: *East Clare Case* 4 O'M&H 162, at 164; *Williams v Patrick* [2014] EWHC 4120 (QB) at 60.

41*Parkinson v Lewis* [2016] EWHC 725 (QB) at 108.

42*Parkinson v Lewis* [2016] EWHC 725 (QB) at 108.

an error of law (e.g. unbeknownst to the RO the candidate was disqualified).[43]

5.27 As to *"substantially in accordance"*, there is no burden of proof in determining this question;[44] *"it is for the court to make up its mind on the evidence as a whole"*.[45] Further, the Election Court is not assisted by doing so according to a standard of proof, though it does require *"a preponderance of evidence"* to declare an election void.[46] The court may draw inferences in connection with the character of the errors which it is established have been made.[47]

5.28 This three-limb test creates three classes of case.[48]

Class 1: Not substantially in accordance with the law (irrespective of whether affected result): *<u>election invalid</u>*

5.29 *Gill v Reed (Hackney Election Petition case).*[49] Two out of 19 polling stations were closed all day, the RO failed to provide ballot boxes at one of the voting place, and 5,000 voters were unable to vote. The election was held void.

5.30 *Haverfordwest Election Petition, Davies v Lord Kensington.*[50] The sheriff (in the position of the modern RO) refused to put the petitioner down as a candidate because the petitioner refused to pay a deposit as security for the payment of his share of the expenses of preparing for the election (before a requirement to pay a deposit was incorporated into the election rules).[51] The court held the sheriff was not entitled to request this prepayment as it was prepayment of expenses for which the sheriff was primarily responsible. As his refusal to put the petitioner in nomination was without justification, the court held the election void.

5.31 *Howes v Turner.*[52] The court declared the election void where the notice stating the last day for delivery of nomination papers erroneously stated that the last day was a Saturday and failed to leave seven days before the election. Two candidates delivered their papers on that Saturday. The court (Brett J) held:

---

[43] R 12(5) and (6) sch 1 RPA 1983; *Sanders v Chichester* [1994] 11 WLUK 163, transcript, pp 44 and 48, per Dyson J.
[44] *Kensington North Parliamentary Election, Re* [1960] 1 WLR 762, 766. This concerned the predecessor provision, s 16(3) RPA 1949.
[45] *Kensington North Parliamentary Election, Re* [1960] 1 WLR 762, 766.
[46] *Edgell v Glover* [2003] EWHC 2566 (QB), 29.
[47] *Edgell v Glover* [2003] All ER (D) 44 (Nov), 35.
[48] *Morgan v Simpson* [1975] QB 151 (CA), p 164E-G.
[49] *Hackney Election Petition case* [1874] 2 O'M&H 77.
[50] *In Re Haverfordwest Election Petition, Davies v Lord Kensington* [1873-74] LR 9 CP 720.
[51] *In Re Haverfordwest Election Petition, Davies v Lord Kensington* [1873-74] LR 9 CP 725.
[52] *Howes v Turner* [1876] 1 CPD 670.

"I do not think that a mere defect in the notice which misleads no one can have the effect of rendering the election altogether void. But it is another thing to say that no defect in the notice will avoid the election. In my opinion, if the defect be so great that the electors or a great number of them are misled, and so the result of the election is contrary to the real views of the constituency, the Court may declare the election to be void: there has in truth been no election at all. Here, it is clearly proved that one of the candidates was misled by the error in the notice,—an error which even a skilful person might very well have committed. It is impossible to say which of the candidates would have been elected if that mistake had not occurred. It seems to me, therefore, that such a defect as has had that result is fatal, and on that ground I think we ought to hold this notice to be so bad as to have rendered the whole election void, and under the circumstances to have disqualified the successful candidate from being elected."[53]

5.32 *R v Election Court, ex p Sheppard.*[54] The High Court dismissed an application to quash an Election Court decision that the applicant was not duly elected because his nomination form gave the wrong address.[55] The Court suggested this was because he was not duly nominated (*"a candidate is not duly nominated, can he be duly elected?"*),[56] i.e. irrespective whether the RO made any error.

5.33 *Gunn v Sharpe.*[57] The RO erroneously rejected 102 ballot papers for not bearing the official stamp. 98 of the 102 came from one polling station and representing more than half the papers issued at that station, and two of the three petitioning candidates would have been elected had the rejected ballots been counted. The Divisional Court declared void the election of the two respondents found not to have a majority. Applying the *Hackney Election Petition case,*[58] the Divisional Court reasoned: *"where a very large proportion of voters are prevented from voting through no fault of their own, there is not an election in a real sense. The election, to a large extent, never took place at all".*[59] The third respondent still had a majority after the discounted votes were counted back in, so the Court held his election unaffected by the avoidance of the election of the other two.

---

[53] *Howes v Turner* [1876] 1 CPD 670, pp 679-680.

[54] R *v Election Cour, Ex p Sheppard* [1974] 3 WLR 517 (DC).

[55] R *v Election Cour, Ex p Sheppard* [1974] 3 WLR 517 (DC), p 1325C-E, per Lord Widgery CJ.

[56] R *v Election Cour, Ex p Sheppard* [1974] 3 WLR 517 (DC), p 1325D, per May J and Lord Widgery CJ.

[57] *Gunn and others v Sharpe* [1974] 2 All ER (QBD) (DC).

[58] *Hackney Election Petition case* [1874] 2 O'M&H 77.

[59] *Gunn and others v Sharpe* [1974] 2 All ER (QBD) (DC), p 812F.

Class 2: Substantially in accordance with the law but error affected the result: election invalid

5.34 *Morgan v Simpson.*[60] 44 ballot papers across 18 polling stations were rejected the RO at the count because the presiding officers had failed to stamp them with the official mark. Had the unstamped papers been counted in, the unsuccessful candidate would have had a majority of seven votes. Although the election had been conducted substantially in accordance with the law, omitting the unstamped ballot papers affected the result. Lord Denning MR held: *"Any breach of the local elections rules which affects the result of an election is by itself enough to compel the tribunal to declare the election void"*.[61]

5.35 *Considine v Didrichsen.*[62] Printers' error led to ballot packs for one ward being sent to the wrong ward. The winning majority was only seven. There were 779 voters in the roads affected by the error. An unknown number of voters received ballot papers intended for a different ward. 17 voters made statements saying they did not receive ballot papers for their ward. Another 68 voters initially did not receive the correct ballot papers then applied for and received them. An unknown number of voters did not apply for replacement papers because they thought they did not need to. Jack J concluded: *"the breach may well have affected the result and, therefore, that it does not appear that it did not affect it. Section 48(1)(b) is not satisfied"*.[63] The RO unsuccessfully argued that voter apathy in failing to (i) spot the error before sending off their votes or (ii) respond to publicity following discovery of the error was the operative cause of votes not being cast. The Election Court held that voters could not be blamed for not checking their papers first, even if a conscientious voter would, nor for interpreting the unclear publicity as stating that new ballot papers would be sent out without need for action on their part.[64]

5.36 *Baxter v Fear.*[65] Batches of ballot papers were mislabelled and sent to the neighbouring wards. The RO took extensive steps to cure the error, including sending door a knocking team to invite the affected voters to return to vote a second time. 56 returned. 115 electors were affected by the error *"to the extent that they were effectively disenfranchised"*.[66] It was nonetheless agreed that the election was conducted substantially in accordance with the law as to elections. The Election Court held:

---

[60] *Morgan v Simpson* [1975] QB 151 (CA).
[61] *Morgan v Simpson* [1975] QB 151 (CA), p 168D, per Lord Denning MR.
[62] *Considine v Didrichsen* [2004] EWHC 2711 (QB).
[63] *Considine v Didrichsen* [2004] EWHC 2711 (QB) at 24.
[64] *Considine v Didrichsen* [2004] EWHC 2711 (QB) at 25.
[65] [2015] EWHC 3136 (QB).
[66] *Baxter v Fear* [2015] EWHC 3136 (QB) at 12.

"[T]he role of the court is not to attempt to reach any conclusion as to the hypothetical result, absent the relevant acts and omissions having taken place. This would be terra incognita, namely the very territory which in terms of principle and policy must be regarded as constitutionally sacred. By enacting section 48 of the 1983 Act, Parliament cannot be treated as somehow empowering the judicial arm of Government to peer into the voting booth, whether by drawing informed, probabilistic inferences or otherwise."[67]

5.37 As to the 56 returning voters issued with a second ballot paper in breach of the rules, they were cast on invalid ballot papers but nonetheless fell to be taken into account until an issue was raised as to their validity by the RO at the count or if necessary upon election petition. *"LEPAR contains no mechanism for correcting errors once the ballot paper has been folded and placed into the ballot box"*,[68] and *"no room for discretionary decision-making by ROs"*.[69]

Class 3: Substantially in accordance with the law and error not affecting the result: election not invalid

5.38 *James Deans and Another v David Stevenson and Others (Magistrates and Councillors of Haddington).*[70] A presiding officer ("**PO**") marked voters' electoral number on about one-third of the total ballot-papers issued. It was not proven that any one was deterred from voting by this loss of secrecy. Even when excluding these ballot papers, the same candidates were successful, albeit in different order.[71] The court held this invalidated the marked papers but not the election as they did not affect its result.[72]

5.39 *The Islington case.*[73] A PO issued fourteen ballot papers after polls closed. The court held that the election was conducted substantially in accordance with the law and late issue of ballots did not affect the result.

5.40 *Re Kensington North Parliamentary Election.*[74] The court found that there had been breaches of the Parliamentary Elections Rules in that (i) three to four voters had no marks placed against their electoral numbers to show their ballot papers had been received by them; (ii) the count had been attended by persons who

---

[67] *Baxter v Fear* [2015] EWHC 3136 (QB) at 27.
[68] *Baxter v Fear* [2015] EWHC 3136 (QB) at 44.
[69] *Baxter v Fear* [2015] EWHC 3136 (QB) at 46.
[70] *James Deans and Another v David Stevenson and Others (Magistrates and Councillors of Haddington)* [1882] 9 R 1077.
[71] *James Deans and Another v David Stevenson and Others (Magistrates and Councillors of Haddington)* [1882] 9 R 1077, p 1080.
[72] *James Deans and Another v David Stevenson and Others (Magistrates and Councillors of Haddington)* [1882] 9 R 1077, p 1091.
[73] *In re Islington West Division; Medhurst v Lough* [1901] 17 TLR 210.
[74] *Kensington North Parliamentary Election, Re* [1960] 1 WLR 762.

were not amongst those specified as so entitle and by persons who had not taken the declaration of secrecy. Notwithstanding the breaches, the court held the conduct of the election substantially in accordance with the law[75] and not to have affected its result. Streatfield J held:

> "Obviously the reason for the rules concerning the persons who are authorised to attend is in order to safeguard the count, so as to make quite sure that only reliable people are there who can be trusted not to walk off with packets of voting papers and so on, but there is not a shred of evidence to suggest—and the petitioner does not contend—that there was anything wrong with the count."[76]

5.41 *Levers v Morris.*[77] Failure by an RO to hold a re-count upon request did not vitiate the result.

5.42 *James v Davies.*[78] A discrepancy in the statutory notices published, where one said that only one candidate could be voted for and the other said that two could be, did not prevent an election being held to have been conducted substantially in accordance with the law and was held to have had no real likelihood of affecting the result.

5.43 *Fitch v Stephenson.*[79] Due to oversight, just 4,930 ballot papers were counted out of the 9,099 issued. This did not render the election invalid where, following a subsequent count, not in the presence of the candidates, it was agreed the uncounted votes would have had no effect on the outcome of the election.

5.44 *Re Parliamentary Election for Fermanagh and South Tyrone.*[80] Omission to provide scrutiny facilities at the count did not affect the result, in light of extensive opportunities to examine doubtful votes and make representations at the recount.[81]

Ground 2: Miscount[82]

5.45 A petitioner may question whether the winner was duly elected by alleging that the RO discounted votes that should have been counted in or counted in votes

---

[75] *Kensington North Parliamentary Election, Re* [1960] 1 WLR 762, Streatfield and Slade JJ, p 769.
[76] *Kensington North Parliamentary Election, Re* [1960] 1 WLR 762, Streatfield and Slade JJ, p 769.
[77] *Levers v Morris* [1971] 3 All ER (QBD).
[78] *James v Davies* [1978] 76 LGR 189 [1978] CLY 878 (DC).
[79] *Fitch v Stephenson* [2008] EWHC 501 (QB) (DC).
[80] *Fermanagh and South Tyrone* [2010] NIQB 113.
[81] *Fermanagh and South Tyrone* [2010] NIQB 113, at 44, per Morgan LCJ.
[82] This ground is also considered by commentators to come under undue election: Halsbury's Laws of England, Elections and Referendums, vol 38A, para 762, fn 3.

that should have been discounted.[83] This requires an application for a scrutiny of the votes recorded as having been cast,[84] where the petitioner can argue that votes counted by the RO should not have been and vice-versa.[85]

5.46 Votes discounted by the RO at the count may be added on grounds of having been:

(i) Improperly accepted or rejected at the count (see the 'Rejecting ballot papers' in Chapter 4);[86] or

(ii) Overlooked at the count.[87]

5.47 Votes not rejected by the RO may struck out on the following grounds:

(i) Voter not of voting age;[88]

(ii) Voter not a Commonwealth citizen, a citizen of the Republic of Ireland, or a British citizen registered as a parliamentary elector in pursuance of an overseas elector's declaration;[89]

(iii) Voter was subject to a legal incapacity to vote;[90]

(iv) Votes given to a disqualified candidate at an election, so long as there are clear facts enabling inference that the voter had notice of the facts creating the candidate's disqualification.[91]

5.48 Votes by the following are also to be struck off from the number of votes cast if found by the Election Court:

(i) Voters bribed, treated or unduly influenced by a candidate proved to have been guilty of bribery, treating or undue influence;[92]

(ii) Votes by persons found guilty of corrupt or illegal practice, payment, employment or hiring at the election;[93]

---

[83] See e.g. *Gunn and others v Sharpe* [1974] 2 All ER (QBD) (DC).

[84] A process described below, under 'Petition Procedure'.

[85] See e.g. *Cornwell v Marshall* [1977] 75 LGR 676 [1977] CLY 908 and *Re Parliamentary Election for Fermanagh and South Tyrone* [2010] NIQB 113, Morgan LCJ.

[86] Halsbury's Laws of England, vol 38A, para 846, citing *Re South Newington, Kingston-upon-Hull, Municipal Election Petition, Lewis v Shepperdson* [1948] 2 All ER 503

[87] Halsbury's Laws of England, vol 38A, para 839, citing *Barnet local election*, Times (2 July 1974).

[88] S 49(5)(a) RPA 1983; art 26(3)(a) NAWRPO 2007.

[89] S 49(5)(b) RPA 1983; art 26(3)(b) NAWRPO 2007.

[90] S 49(5)(c) RPA 1983; art 26(3)(c) NAWRPO 2007.

[91] Halsbury's Laws of England, vol 38A, para 845, citing *Re Bristol South East, Parliamentary Election* [1964] 2 QB 257, [1961] 3 All ER 354, DC.

[92] S 166(1) RPA 1983

[93] S 166(2) RPA 1983

(iii) Votes of persons found guilty of personation and of persons impersonated (the tendered vote stands instead).[94]

Ground 3: Candidate's corrupt or illegal practices

5.49 If the successful candidate is reported by an Election Court to be personally guilty or guilty by their agents of any corrupt or illegal practice, or illegal payments, employments and hirings, then their election must be declared void.[95] This does not mean the whole election is declared void: another person may be declared elected in place of the person whose election is declared void.[96]

5.50 The main differences between illegal and corrupt practice are the longer disqualification period for candidates reported guilty of the latter (three and five years, respectively),[97] and that if a prosecution follows, the penalties differ:

(i) Corrupt practice: two years' imprisonment and/or a fine if convicted on indictment for personation or postal or proxy vote fraud, one year's imprisonment and/or a fine for conviction on indictment of any other corrupt practice, and six months and/or a fine on summary conviction;[98]

(ii) Illegal practice or payment, triable summarily only: an unlimited fine. On a prosecution it is sufficient for the prosecution to allege that the person charged was found guilty of an illegal practice.[99]

5.51 The burden of proof in respect of the charges of corrupt or illegal practices rests on the petitioner.[100] The standard of proof for each allegation of corrupt practice is 'beyond reasonable doubt',[101] i.e. the court must be sure the respondent is guilty of the alleged corrupt or illegal practice.[102]

Corrupt practices

5.52 'Corrupt practice' is not defined in RPA 1983. Rather, a number of individual electoral offences are declared to be 'corrupt practices'. The following is a list of those corrupt practices:

(i) False registration for postal or proxy vote;[103]

---

[94] Halsbury's Laws of England, vol 38A, para 844, citing *Finsbury, Central Division Case* (1892) 4 O'M&H 171 at 175 and *Gloucester Borough Case, Guise v Wait* (1873) 2 O'M&H 59 at 64.
[95] S 159(1) RPA 1983; art 109 NAWRPO 2007.
[96] S 135(1) RPA 1983.
[97] S 160(5) RPA 1983.
[98] S 168 RPA 1983; art 120 NAWRPO 2007.
[99] Ss 169 and 175 RPA 1983; arts 121 and 127 NAWRPO 2007.
[100] *Simmons v Khan* [2008] EWHC B4 (QB) at 61.
[101] *Mainwaring*, per Farquharson LJ at 1068D.
[102] *Woolas*, 48.
[103] S 62A 1983; art 14 NAWRPO 2007; art 18 PCCEO 2012.

(ii) False statements in nomination papers etc;[104]

(iii) Fraudulent authorisation of candidate description certificate;[105]

(iv) Bribery;[106]

(v) Treating;[107]

(vi) Undue influence;[108]

(vii) Personation;[109]

(viii) Publication of exit polls;[110]

(ix) Expenses not authorised by election agent;[111]

(x) False declaration as to election expenses.[112]

Illegal practices

5.53 As with 'corrupt practices', there is no statutory definition of 'illegal practices'. Not all offences in the RPA 1983 are expressly designated 'illegal practices' (capable of avoiding an election), but the Election Courts have treated them as such.[113]

5.54 The following is a list of the illegal practices, on which grounds a candidate's election may be voided, with reference to where in the book the elements of each are particularised:

(i) Voting, etc, despite legal incapacity,[114] thought this does not void an election if it was committed without the candidate's knowledge;[115]

(ii) Breach of controls of donations to candidates, including providing donations other than to the candidate or their agent;[116]

---

[104]S 65A RPA 1983; art 34 NAWRPO 2007; art 21 PCCEO 2012.
[105]R 6A(2) sch 1 RPA 1983; art 34(1)(c) NAWRPO 2007; art 21(1)(d) PCCEO 2012.
[106]S 113 RPA 1983; art 79 NAWRPO 2007; art 67 PCCEO 2012.
[107]S 114 RPA 1983; art 80 NAWRPO 2007; art 68 PCCEO 2012.
[108]S 115 RPA 1983; art 81 NAWRPO 2007; art 69 PCCEO 2012.
[109]S 60 RPA 1983; art 30 NAWRPO 2007; art 17 PCCEO 2012.
[110]S 66A RPA 1983; art 36 NAWRPO 2007; art 23 PCCEO 2012.
[111]S 75 RPA 1983; art 43 NAWRPO 2007; art 34 PCCEO 2012.
[112]Ss 75ZB(4) and 82 RPA 1983; art 53(5) NAWRPO 2007; art 34(9)(b) PCCEO 2012.
[113]*Simmons v Khan* [2008] EWHC B4 (QB) at 29-30.
[114]S 61 RPA 1983; art 31(2) NAWRPO 2007; art 18(1) PCCEO 2012.
[115]S 189 RPA 1983.
[116]S 71A and sch 2A RPA 1983; art 41 and sch 6 NAWRPO 2007; art 30 and sch 5 PCCEO 2012.

(iii) Payment of candidate expenses other than through election agent;[117]

(iv) Failure to deliver expenses return;[118]

(v) Exceeding limit on election expenses;[119]

(vi) Late payment of election expenses;[120]

(vii) Unauthorised broadcast;[121]

(viii) Imitation poll cards;[122]

(ix) Disturbing an election meeting;[123]

(x) False statement about a candidate, including their withdrawal;[124]

(xi) Payments for exhibition of election notices;[125]

(xii) Election publications not displaying prescribed details;[126]

(xiii) Employment of paid canvassers;[127]

(xiv) Providing money for illegal purposes;[128]

(xv) Evading controls on donations to candidates;[129]

(xvi) Providing false information on registration;[130]

(xvii) PE: exceeding pre-candidacy expenses;[131]

(xviii) Failure to deliver return and declarations as to election expenses;[132]

(xix) Canvassing by police officers;[133]

---

[117]S 73 RPA 1983; art 43 NAWRPO 2007; art 31 PCCEO 2012.
[118]S 84 RPA 1983; art 56 NAWRPO 2007; art 43 PCCEO 2012.
[119]S 76 RPA 1983; art 47 NAWRPO 2007; art 35 PCCEO 2012.
[120]S 78 RPA 1983; art 49 NAWRPO 2007; art 37 PCCEO 2012.
[121]Ss 92-93 RPA 1983; art 64 NAWRPO 2007; art 53 PCCEO 2012.
[122]S 94 RPA 1983; art 68 NAWRPO 2007; art 55 PCCEO 2012.
[123]S 97 RPA 1983; art 70 NAWRPO 2007; art 58 PCCEO 2012.
[124]S 106 RPA 1983; art 73 NAWRPO 2007; art 61 PCCEO 2012.
[125]S 109 RPA 1983; art 75 NAWRPO 2007; art 63 PCCEO 2012.
[126]S 110 RPA 1983; art 76 NAWRPO 2007; art 64 PCCEO 2012.
[127]S 111 RPA 1983; art 77 NAWRPO 2007; art 65 PCCEO 2012.
[128]S 112 RPA 1983; art 78 NAWRPO 2007; art 66 PCCEO 2012.
[129]Para 9 sch 2A RPA 1983; para 9 sch 6 NAWRPO 2007; para 9 sch 5 PCCEO 2012.
[130]S 13D RPA 1983.
[131]S 76ZA RPA 1983.
[132]S 84 RPA 1983; art 56 NAWRPO 2007; art 43 PCCEO 2012.
[133]S 100 RPA 1983; art 72 NAWRPO 2007; art 60 PCCEO 2012.

(xx) Corrupt withdrawal from candidature;[134]

(xxi) Breach of official duty;[135]

(xxii) Tampering with nomination papers, ballot papers etc;[136]

(xxiii) Breach of secrecy requirements;[137]

(xxiv) Offences as to local connection or service declarations;[138]

(xxv) RO, their clerk, or their partners acting as candidate's election agent.[139]

5.55 There is a right to apply to the Election Court for judicial relief in respect to illegal practices, payments, employment or hiring.[140] PCCE: relief may only granted in relation to failures as to return and declarations.[141] Relief will be granted if the act or omission (i) arose from inadvertence or accident rather than lack of good faith or recklessness; (ii) notice of the relief application has been given in the relevant constituency or area, and to the Director of Public Prosecutions ("**DPP**") (who otherwise may wish to prosecute; and (iii) the court deems it just that they should not be subject to any of the consequences of the act or omission.[142]

Ground 4: Incapable of being elected: successful candidate was disqualified

5.56 A petition may be brought on grounds that the successful candidate was incapable of standing for elective office, due to having already been reported by an Election Court personally guilty of a corrupt or illegal practice, and still within their five years (for corrupt practices) or three years (for illegal practices) disqualification period.[143]

5.57 If the election was after the date on which the candidate became disqualified and the petition is upheld, the votes for the disqualified candidate are 'thrown away' rather than remaining with the RP whom the disqualified candidate represented.[144] The questionable logic may be that voters should have known.

---

[134]S 107 RPA 1983; art 74 NAWRPO 2007; art 62 PCCEO 2012.
[135]S 63 RPA 1983; art 32 NAWRPO 2007; art 19 PCCEO 2012.
[136]S 65 RPA 1983; art 33 NAWRPO 2007; art 20 PCCEO 2012.
[137]S 66 RPA 1983; art 35 NAWRPO 2007; art 22 PCCEO 2012.
[138]S 62 RPA 1983; art 78 NAWRPO 2007; art 66 PCCEO 2012.
[139]S 99 RPA 1983; art 71 NAWRPO 2007; art 59 PCCEO 2012.
[140]S 167(1) RPA 1983; art 119 NAWRPO 2007; art 66 PCCEO 2012.
[141]Art 45(3) PCCEO 2012.
[142]S 167(2) PRA 1983; art 119(3) NAWRPO 2007; art 45(4) PCCEO 2012.
[143]S 160(5) RPA 1983; *Erlam v Rahman and Williams* [2015] EWHC 1215 (QB) at 31.
[144]*Beresford-Hope v Sandhurst* [1889] 23 QBD 79, p 95, per Lord Coleridge LCJ; *Re Bristol South-East Parliamentary Election* [1961] 3 WLR 577, p 609. The Law Commission has recommended abolition of the 'thrown away' rule: Law Com No 389, 13.10.

This raises A3P1 issue, similar to the death of an independent candidate who secures a majority of votes.

5.58 Such a petition does not require a scrutiny; the candidate who secured the second highest number of votes wins.

Ground 5: General corruption

5.59 If on a petition it is proven that corrupt or illegal practices, or illegal payments, employments or hirings, committed to promote the successful candidate or procure their election, *"so extensively prevailed that they may be reasonably supposed to have affected the result"*, then their election is void and they are disqualified from being elected to fill the vacancy.[145]

5.60 The burden of proof in respect of the allegation of general corruption is on the petitioner.[146]

5.61 There are thus two elements to prove:

(i) That there has been general corruption designed to secure the election of the candidate;

(ii) That this may reasonably be supposed to have affected the result.[147]

5.62 The criminal standard of proof applies to the former (that there has been general corruption designed to secure the election of the candidate), despite the fact that general corruption does not involve the making of findings of corrupt or illegal practices against any named individual.[148] The civil standard of proof applies to the latter (whether it may reasonably be supposed to have affected the result).[149]

5.63 Like petitions alleging personal guilt of corrupt or illegal practice, if established, the candidate's election is avoided.[150] Unlike petitions concerning an individual candidate's alleged corrupt or illegal practices:

(i) The petitioner does not have to prove that the corrupt or illegal practices were committed by the candidate or his agents - only that the practices were directed to securing the successful candidate's election;[151] and

---

[145]S 164(1) RPA 1983; art 116 NAWRPO 2007; sch 9 PCCEO 2012.
[146]*Simmons v Khan* [2008] EWHC B4 (QB) at 61.
[147]*Simmons v Khan* [2008] EWHC B4 (QB) at 63.
[148]*Simmons v Khan* [2008] EWHC B4 (QB) at 65 and 66.
[149]*Simmons v Khan* [2008] EWHC B4 (QB) at 67 and 68; *Erlam v Rahman and Williams* [2015] EWHC 1215 (QB) at 49.
[150]S 164(1) RPA 1983; art 116(1)(a) NAWRPO 2007.
[151]*Simmons v Khan* [2008] EWHC B4 (QB) at 55.

(ii) If proven and the election voided, the candidate is not reported guilty of corrupt practice, personally or by his agents.[152]

'Agent'

5.64 In this context, 'agent' has a broader meaning than in non-electoral law, extending beyond the candidate's appointed election agent to canvassers, committees and supporters, for whose actions the candidate is taken to be responsible though he may not have appointed them as agents or know what they are doing.[153]

"Extensively prevailed"

5.65 In *Erlam v Rahman*,[154] the 'extensively prevailed' test was held satisfied by those of the corrupt and illegal practices found proven and to have operated *"borough-wide"*: *"the making of false statements about [the rival candidate] (which were repeated and embellished across the Borough and beyond), the bribery of the Bangladeshi electorate by the distribution of grants and the use of undue spiritual influence"*.[155] The unlawful payment of canvassers was not held to a breadth that satisfied this test.[156]

"Reasonably supposed to have affected the result"

5.66 In practice, it is difficult to see how this causation element will not be found satisfied if the corrupt or illegal practices have been found to have extensively prevailed. If a respondent is also found personally guilty or by their agents, it will be particularly difficult for them to persuade the court that their efforts did not affect the result.[157]

5.67 In *Simmons v Khan*,[158] where the Election Court held that the evidence on the first element ('extensively prevailed') was *"such as to make inevitable a decision that the general corruption involved in the Central Ward must reasonably be supposed to have affected the result"*,[159] the Election Court commented that, in the 21st century, the requirement, once corruption bent on procuring the

---

[152] *Simmons v Khan* [2008] EWHC B4 (QB) at 55(c); *Erlam v Rahman and Williams* [2015] EWHC 1215 (QB) at 57.
[153] *Simmons v Khan* [2008] EWHC B4 (QB) at 58, citing *Westbury Case* (1869) 20 LT 16 and *Tewkesbury Case, Collings v Price* (1880) 44 LT 192 for canvassers, *Stalybridge Case, Ogden Woolley* and *Buckley v Sidebottom* (1869) 20 LT 75 for committees, and *Great Yarmouth Borough Case, White v Fell* (1906) 5 O'M&H 176 for supporters".
[154] *Erlam v Rahman* [2015] EWHC 1215 (QB).
[155] *Erlam v Rahman* [2015] EWHC 1215 (QB) at 629.
[156] *Erlam v Rahman* [2015] EWHC 1215 (QB) at 628.
[157] *Simmons v Khan* [2008] EWHC B4 (QB), at 331.
[158] *Simmons v Khan* [2008] EWHC B4 (QB).
[159] *Simmons v Khan* [2008] EWHC B4 (QB), at 333.

successful candidate has been found to have extensively prevailed, for the petitioner to then establish an additional element of causation was *"obsolete"* and in need of *"wholesale revision"* by Parliament.[160]

5.68 The only circumstance where satisfaction of the causation limb of the test would not follow from satisfaction of the first is likely to be where the general corruption had not been directed to the successful candidate's election but one of the losers.[161]

Ground 6: Employing a corrupt agent

5.69 If a candidate or their election agent engages, or knows and consents to the engagement,[162] of a canvasser or an agent for the conduct or management of the election someone they have reasonable grounds for believing to be subject to an incapacity to vote due to having been convicted or reported of any corrupt or illegal practice, then the candidate is incapable of being elected to fill any of the vacancies for which the election is held.[163] The wasted vote does not pass to another candidate, but the candidate with the next highest number of votes may be declared duly elected.

C. NO RETURN

5.70 In an election culminating with the RO returning to the Clerk of the Crown (PE) of the Clerk of the Assembly (WAE) the name of the candidate whom the RO has declared elected,[164] if the RO declines or omits to return that name, a petitioner may question the election on grounds of 'no return'.[165] Special provision is made for such a petition, enabling the High Court to simply make an order compelling a return to be made, rather than holding a petition trial.[166]

D. UNDUE RETURN

5.71 PE and WAE may be questioned on grounds of 'undue return'.[167] 'Undue return', like 'undue election', is not defined by the respective statutes, but 'return' refers to the RO's function in returning to the Clerk of the Crown (PE) or Clerk to the Assembly (WAE) the name of the candidate whom the RO has

---

[160] *Simmons v Khan* [2008] EWHC B4 (QB) at 37-38.
[161] *Simmons v Khan* [2008] EWHC B4 (QB) p 13 fn 5.
[162] *North Norfolk case* (1869) 1 O'M&H 236; *Norwich case* (1871) 2 O'M&H 38.
[163] S 165(1) RPA 1983; art 117(1) NAWRPO 2007.
[164] LE and LAE: the winner's name is not 'returned' but notified to the proper officer (LE) or Greater London RO (LAE).
[165] S 120(2) RPA 1983.
[166] S 120(2) RPA 1983; art 86(1) NAWRPO 2007.
[167] S 120(1) RPA 1983; art 86(1) NAWRPO 2007.

declared elected once the result of the poll has been ascertained.[168] 'Undue return' thus refers to the RO's returning the wrong name to the respective Clerk.

5.72 This may either be due to simple error (the candidate who is declared elected was duly elected but the RO returned the wrong name) or because the candidate whose name is returned was unduly elected on one of the above five grounds. Thus, a petitioner may petition for a declaration of undue return as well as for a declaration of undue election. If they are petitioning for a declaration that someone other than the person elected should be declared elected, [169] as opposed to fresh elections, they will have to seek a declaration of undue return to undo this step.

E. PETITION PROCEDURE

Time limit for presentation of petition

5.73 A petition must be presented within 21 days of (a) the day the return is made (PE and WAE); or (b) the day on which the election was held (LE, LAE and PCCE).[170]

5.74 If the petition concerns a payment made pursuant to a corrupt practice, or that was an illegal payment, and made after the return, the petitioner has 28 days from the date of that payment.[171] A petition alleging the corrupt practice of expenses not having been authorised by an election agent is subject to the illegal practice time limit.[172]

5.75 PE and WAE petitions alleging illegal practice in relation to a candidate's expenses return must be presented within 31 days after the deadline for delivering returns to the RO[173] or, if occurring later than this, then 21 days from the date on which:

(i) The RO receives both the return and declarations as to election expenses by that member and their agent, the later if on different days;

---

[168]R 50 sch 1 RPA 1983; r 62 sch 5 NAWRPO 2007

[169]Ss 144(1) and 145(1) RPA 1983; *Edgell v Glover* [2003] EWHC 2566 (QB) (DC) at 18

[170]Ss 122(1) and 129(1) RPA 1983; art 88(1) NAWRPO 2007; para 1 sch 9 PCCEO 2012. The gov.uk website gives this guidance: *"On the last day you're allowed to apply, you can apply any time before midnight. Put your petition in the letterbox opposite room E113 if the office is closed. Call the Royal Courts of Justice if you need to get access to the letterbox. Royal Courts of Justice. Phone: 0207 947 6000".* This guidance should be approached with caution: *Croke v Secretary of State for Communities and Local Government* [2019] EWCA Civ 54, at 17 and 19. If the petition is to be filed on the last day for doing so, the petitioner would be astute to do so within court office hours.

[171]S 122(2) and 129(2) and (3) RPA 1983; art 88(2) NAWRPO 2007.

[172]Ss 122(6)(b) and 129(7)(b) RPA 1983; art 88(6)(b) NAWRPO 2007.

[173]S 122(3) and (4) RPA 1983; art 88(3) and (4) NAWRPO 2007.

(ii) An allowance is made of an excuse for failing to make the return and declarations.[174]

5.76 LE petitions alleging that election expenses have been allowed pursuant to an illegal practice must be presented within fourteen days of the date on which:

(i) The proper officer for of the council for which the election is held receives the return and declarations as to election expenses by the respondent candidate and their election agent, the later if on different days; or

(ii) An allowance is made of an excuse for failing to make the return and declarations.[175]

5.77 A petition brought on grounds of general corruption[176] is deemed to be an allegation of corrupt practice, notwithstanding that the offences are or include illegal practices.[177]

Computation of time

5.78 Weekends, Christmas Eve, Christmas Day, Good Friday are excluded when calculating time limits.[178] Bank holidays, or day appointed for public thanksgiving or mourning are also excluded, so long as they were appointed before dissolution of Parliament (PE).[179]

Amending petition

5.79 A petition can be amended with leave of the High Court until the expiry of the time for filing it.[180]

5.80 A petition alleging illegal practice presented in time may be amended, on application to the High Court, up to 31 days from the candidates' deadline for delivering expenses returns to the RO.[181]

---

[174]S 122(3) and (4) RPA 1983.
[175]S 129(5) RPA 1983.
[176]S 164 RPA 1983; art 116 NAWRPO 2007.
[177]Ss 122(7) and 129(8) RPA 1983; art 88(7) NAWRPO 2007
[178]S 119 RPA 1983.
[179]R 2(2A) sch 1 RPA 1983.
[180]S 122(5) and 129(6) RPA 1983; art 88(5) NAWRPO 2007.
[181]S 122(5) RPA 1983.

How to start proceedings

The petition form

5.81 The petition must be in the prescribed form[182] and state the following prescribed matters:

(i) In which capacities the petition is brought,[183] i.e. (a) person(s) who voted at the election or had a right to vote;[184] (b) person claiming to have been a candidate at the election;[185]or (c) (WAE) person claiming to have had a right of election or to be returned in an election region vacancy;[186]

(ii) The date and result of the election, plus, for PE petitions, the date on which the return was made to the Clerk of the Crown of the member declared to have been elected;[187]

(iii) For a petition relying on the special time limits in relation to expenses or illegal payments: the date from which the time for the presentation of the petition is to be calculated;[188]

(iv) *"The grounds on which relief is sought, setting out with sufficient particularity the facts relied on but not the evidence by which they are to be proved"*;[189]

(v) A prayer setting out particulars of the relief claimed.[190]

5.82 The requirement that the petition should state the result of the election does not mean that the petition has to include the number of votes given for each candidate.[191]

5.83 A template petition is appended to the Election Petition Rules[192] and available for download on the Gov.uk website.[193]

---

[182]S 121(3) RPA 1983 and sch 1 Election Petition Rules 1960.
[183]R 4(1)(a) Election Petition Rules 1960.
[184]Ss 121(1A) and 128(1) RPA 1983; art 87(1)(a) and (b) and (2) NAWRPO 2007; para 1 sch 9 PCCEO 2012.
[185]Ss 121(1) and 128(1) RPA 1983; para 1 sch 9 PCCEO 2012.
[186]Art 87(1)(c) and (d) NAWRPO 2007.
[187]R 4(1)(b) Election Petition Rules 1960.
[188]R 4(1)(c) Election Petition Rules 1960.
[189]R 4(1)(d) Election Petition Rules 1960.
[190]R 4(1) Election Petition Rules 1960.
[191]*Scarth v Amin* [2008] EWHC 2886 (QB) (DC), [2009] PTSR 827.
[192]Sch 1 Election Petition Rules 1960.
[193]https://www.gov.uk/government/publications/election-petition-template.

Where to present the petition

5.84 The petition must be filed with and three copies left at the Election Petitions Office, Room E113, Royal Courts of Justice, Strand, London WC2A 2LL.[194]

5.85 The QBD master at that time performing the duties of prescribed officer must send a copy to the RO of the constituency to which the petition relates, for publication.[195]

Security for costs

5.86 When presenting the petition, or within three days thereafter, the petitioner must give security for costs that may be payable to the witnesses they summon or to the respondent.[196]

5.87 The petitioner must do so by applying to a master to fix the amount of such security for costs,[197] using form N244, enclosing a £100 application fee, cheque or postal order payable to 'HM Courts and Tribunals Service', and delivering both to Election Petitions Office, Room E113, Royal Courts of Justice, Strand, London WC2A 2LL.

5.88 The security is such amount as the High Court directs on application by the petitioner, capped at £5,000 for PE and WAE petitions, and £2,500 for LE petitions.[198] In LE, the £2,500 cap is also the normal order.[199] Nonetheless, where a LE petitioner was in receipt of Jobseeker's Allowance and payments thereunder reduced to £15 owing to sanction, and in his application adduced a food bank certificate, the amount of security has been set by a master at £10.[200]

5.89 Security is given either by making a deposit or by up to four sureties entering into a recognisance, or a mixture of both.[201]

5.90 The master will direct the date by which security for costs is to be paid into court,[202] but the operative date remains three days from presentation of the petition, even if the date directed by master falls after that deadline.[203]

---

[194] Queen Bench Guide 2018, 27.5.
[195] S 121(4) RPA 1983.
[196] S 136(1) RPA 1983; art 92(1) NAWRPO 2007.
[197] R 5(1) Election Petition Rules 1960.
[198] S 136(2) RPA 1983.
[199] *Scarth v Amin* [2008] EWHC 2886 (QB) at 42.
[200] *Waghorn v Fry and Secretary of State for Work and Pensions* [2015] EWHC 744 (QB) at 9.
[201] S 136(2) RPA 1983; art 92(2) NAWRPO 2007.
[202] S 136(3) RPA 1983; art 92(3) NAWRPO 2007.
[203] *Waghorn v Fry and Secretary of State for Work and Pensions* [2015] EWHC 744 (QB) at 9.

5.91 If the petitioner fails to give security, the petition may not proceed and is a nullity.[204]

5.92 Even where the master's directions for payment of the security reach the petitioner after expiry of the three-day time limit from presentation of the petition, it has been held that a master does not have the power or discretion to extend the time by which the security for costs was ordered to be paid.[205] That decision was based upon reasoning that primary legislation cannot be read down under s 3 Human Rights Act 1998.[206] This appears to be incorrect and the court did not consider authority on s 3's application to statutory time limits.[207]

5.93 Until the application of s 3 HRA 1998 is revisited, the petitioner must either pay the maximum amount (and hope subsequently for a refund) or guess the amount at which the master will fix the security.[208]

Service of notice of presentation of petition and amount of security

5.94 Within five days after giving the security, the petitioner must serve on the respondent(s) and the DPP a notice of:

(i) The presentation of the petition;

(ii) The amount and nature of the security; and

(iii) A copy of the petition.[209]

5.95 These time limits cannot be extended or varied.[210] The requirement to serve the respondent is mandatory.[211] Failure to do so in time renders the petition incompetent and susceptible to strike out.[212]

5.96 Service must be effected in the manner in which a claim form is served under the CPR;[213] namely the methods listed by CPR 6.3:

(i) Personal service (for which, if on an individual, it is not enough to leave the document somewhere to be forwarded to that individual)[214];

---

204 S 136(8) RPA 1983; art 92(7) NAWRPO 2007.
205 *Stoddart and Hume v Gartland & Little* [2014] EWHC 2817 at 9-10 and 27-28.
206 *Stoddart and Hume v Gartland & Little* [2014] EWHC 2817 at 26; followed in *Waghorn v Fry* [2015] EWHC 744 (QB), at 35.
207 E.g. *Pomiechowski v Poland* [2012] UKSC 20; R *(Adesina) v Nursing and Midwifery Council* [2013] EWCA Civ 818.
208 *Waghorn v Fry* [2015] EWHC 744 (QB), at 34.
209 S 136(3) RPA 1983; r 5(1) Election Petition Rules 1960; art 92(3) and sch 9 NAWRPO 2007.
210 *Ahmed v Kennedy* [2003] 71 WLR 120 (CA), at 31-32.
211 *Absalom v Gillett* [1995] 1 WLR 128 (DC), p 183
212 *Ali v Haques* [2006] 10 WLUK 304 at 34.
213 R 6(2) Election Petition Rules 1960. *Ali v Haques* [2006] 10 WLUK 304 at 25.
214 *Ali v Haques* [2006] 10 WLUK 304 at 29.

(ii) First class post, document exchange or other service which provides for delivery on the next business day;

(iii) Leaving it at a place specified in CPR 6.7 (respondent's solicitor's business address, if they or respondent give it as address for service), CPR 6.8 (respondent's residential or business address, if respondent gives it as address for service), CPR 6.9 (respondent's usual or last known address, if respondent does not give address for service);

(iv) Fax or other means of electronic communication; or

(v) Any method authorised by the court under CPR 6.15 (following application in advance).[215]

5.97 In serving the successful candidate, if the petitioner does not want to effect personal service and respondent does not give their address for service, *"usual or last known residence"* does not include the town hall, as the respondent does not reside there.[216]

5.98 By contrast, in serving the RO, service of a copy of the petition at their place of business **is** effective service.[217]

5.99 If relying on authorised alternative method, this must comply with the requirements that the application must be made within the 21-day time limit for presentation of a petition, and be served within the five-day time limit for service of notice of presentation of the petition and of the amount of security.[218] Further, absent good reason, the court will not grant retrospective authorisation of alternative service, only prospective.[219] The difficulty of achieving personal service on an MP who may be Westminster not in the constituency has been held to not be a good reason where no attempts to identify the residential address for postal service and no other attempts made to bring a petition to the MP's attention had been made.[220]

5.100 A certificate of service must be filed as soon as practicable after service.[221]

---

[215] *Ali v Haques* [2006] 10 WLUK 304 at 32.

[216] *Ali v Haques* [2006] 10 WLUK 304 at 29.

[217] *Scarth v Amin* [2008] EWHC 2886 (QB) (DC), at 39, not following *Fitch v Stephenson* [2008] EWHC 501 (QB). In *Scarth*, the petitioner handed the petition to an official at the reception desk of the council's electoral services unit. This was held to be good service: *Scarth*, at 8(5)(c).

[218] *Ali v Haques* [2006] 10 WLUK 304 at 32; *Scarth v Amin* [2008] EWHC 2886 (QB).

[219] *Ireland v Dorries* [2015] EWHC 2781 (QB) (DC). No attempt had been made to bring the petition to respondent's attention by other means or to discover their residential address.

[220] *Ireland v Dorries* [2015] EWHC 2781 (QB) (DC), at 30-35.

[221] R 6(2) Election Petition Rules 1960.

5.101 Failure to name the successful candidate as respondent and to serve them with the petition, will found an application for strike out.[222]

5.102 Failure to notify the respondent to a petition of the nature and amount of security deposited amounts to non-compliant notice.[223]

5.103 A petitioner may apply for an extension of time to serve notice of security for costs.[224]

Respondent objection to recognisance

5.104 Following service notice of presentation of the petition and amount of security, the respondent has fourteen days to serve on the petitioner any written objection to any recognisance on the grounds that any surety:

(i) Is insufficient;

(ii) Is dead;

(iii) Cannot be found or ascertained;

(iv) For want of sufficient description in the recognisance; or

(v) Has not duly acknowledged the recognisance despite being named by the petitioner.[225]

5.105 Within 14 days, the respondent must also issue and serve on the petitioner an application notice to determine the validity of the objection.[226]

5.106 The respondent's application must be heard by a master,[227] who may either dismiss the application or allow it.

5.107 If allowed, the High Court master must determine what sum would make the security sufficient.[228] To remove the objection, the petitioner must then deposit that sum within five days of the master's decision,[229] or the petition may proceed no further.[230]

---

[222] *Absalom v Gillett* [1995] 1 WLR 128 (DC), p 138E-F.
[223] *Ahmed v Kennedy* [2003] 71 WLR 120 (CA), *Ullah v Pagel* [2002] EWCA Civ 1793.
[224] *Miller v Bull and others* [2009] EWHC 260 (QB), per Tugendhat J at 37-39 and 92.
[225] S 136(4) RPA 1983; r 5(1) Election Petition Rules 1960; art 92(4) and sch 9 NAWRPO 2007.
[226] R 5(1) Election Petition Rules 1960.
[227] R 5(2) Election Petition Rules 1960.
[228] S 136(7) RPA 1983.
[229] R 7 Election Petition Rules 1960.
[230] S 136(8) RPA 1983; r 7(7)

Petition at issue

5.108 A petition becomes 'at issue' from the expiry of time for objections, or disallowance or removal of any objections.[231]

Preparation for trial

Listing for trial

5.109 Within 28 days of issuing the petition, the petitioner must apply by form N244 to a High Court master[232] for a time and place to be fixed for its trial.[233] If the petitioner fails to do so, within a further 28 days, any respondent may do so in their stead. [234] If neither so apply, the master must fix the time and place.[235]

5.110 Once that date is fixed, not less than fourteen days (PE and WAE) or seven days (LE, LAE and PCCE) beforehand, the master must display notice of the time and place of the trial in a conspicuous place in the election petitions office and post notice to the parties;[236] namely:

(i) The petitioner;

(ii) The respondent;

(iii) The DPP; and

(iv) The RO (who must publish forthwith in their constituency).[237]

Order for production

5.111 Either the High Court or the County Court may order:

(i) The inspection or production of any rejected or counted ballot papers in the custody of the relevant RO;

(ii) The opening of a sealed packet of the completed corresponding number lists or of certificates as to employment on duty on the day of the poll.[238]

5.112 An Election Court may order:

(i) The opening of a sealed packet of the completed corresponding number lists or of certifications; or

[231] S 137 RPA 1983; art 92(7) NAWRPO 2007.

[232] The master performing the duties of prescribed officer must refer the matter to a rota judge.

[233] R 9(1) Election Petition Rules 1960.

[234] R 9(1) Election Petition Rules 1960.

[235] R 9(2) and (5) Election Petition Rules 1960.

[236] S 139(1) RPA 1983; and art 95(1) NAWRPO 2007.

[237] R 9(3)

[238] R 56(1) sch 1 RPA 1983

(ii) The inspection of any counted ballot papers in the relevant RO's custody.[239]

List of unlawful votes

5.113 Where the petitioner claims they had a majority of lawful votes, every party must, not less than seven days before the day fixed for the trial, file and serve a list of the votes they claim were wrongly admitted or rejected, stating in respect of each such vote the grounds for that claim.

5.114 If a party does not list a particular vote, unless the Election Court then grants permission, they cannot at trial give evidence or argument against its admission or rejection.[240]

Respondent's grounds

5.115 In a petition complaining of undue election and claiming the seat or office for another for someone else (e.g. the petitioner), a respondent may give evidence at trial to prove that that other person was not duly elected.[241] To do so, not less than **seven days** before trial, they must file and serve (on the petitioner and DPP) a list of their objections to the election of that person.[242]

Scrutiny

5.116 If a petitioner claims that the elected candidate did not have a majority of lawfully cast votes, they may apply for a 'scrutiny' to ascertain, by striking off votes or adding votes, which candidate did have the majority of lawful votes.[243] The scrutiny is a preliminary procedure (the process of which is outlined in Petition procedure section below), and an adversarial one: each party advocating for a particular decision on each ballot. Afterwards, the petitioner may ask for a judicial recount. The Election Court commissioner (LE, LAE and PCCE) or master (PE and WAE) will then take into account the determinations on the votes in issue and perform a judicial recount to identify the amended result.[244] If it is a tie, neither respondent nor anyone else can be declared duly elected and

---

[239]R 56(2)

[240]R 10(4)(a)

[241]S 139(5) RPA 1983.

[242]R 10(2)

[243]Halsbury's Laws of England, vol 38A, para 839; *Taunton Case, Williams and Mellor v Cox* (1869) 21 LT 169 at 173, 1 O'M&H 181 at 186; *York County West Riding, South-ern Division Case* (1869) 1 O'M&H 213 at 215; *Petition of Rowe* [2001] All ER (D) 329 (Dec) (DC).

[244]See, e.g., *Gunn and others v Sharpe* [1974] 2 All ER (QBD) (DC), p 814B-E, and *Petition of Rowe* [2001] All ER (D) 329 (Dec) (DC).

the result of the election is void.[245]If the other candidate has a majority, they are declared duly elected.[246]

5.117 A scrutiny may also be held to establish the matrix of facts relevant to a petition that alleges, say, ballot paper tampering, postal vote fraud, or personation.[247] Using the number and other unique identifying mark printed on the back of the ballot papers, the court can trace each vote the corresponding numbers list and postal voters list, which should show which voters were allocated which ballots and whom they voted for (or whom their impersonator voted for).

5.118 In *R (Afzal) v Election Court*,[248] Lord Phillips MR described the process in these terms:

> "Most election petitions undergo a "Scrutiny" prior to the substantive petition being heard. An officer of the court (usually the Senior Master) examines the original election documents with a view to finding the factual framework surrounding the petition. The parties to the petition and their lawyers are entitled to attend the Scrutiny and to make representations. The Scrutiny rarely lasts for more than a few hours."[249]

5.119 A respondent whose election is proved to be void may still continue the scrutiny to show that the person for whom the seat is claimed has not obtained a majority of lawful votes, even though they do not stand to win.[250]

Tied vote

5.120 If it appears that the candidates have the same number of votes, then the provision in the respective election rules as to procedure in the event of ties must in so far as it be effective for the purposes of the petition (decision by lot).[251]

Special case stated

5.121 A party to a petition may apply by application notice (form N244) to the Divisional Court[252] for it to direct that the case raised by the petition be stated as a special case to be heard by the Divisional Court.[253] The Divisional Court may so direct if it appear that the case raised by the petition can be conveniently

---

245 See, e.g., *Petition of Rowe* [2001] All ER (D) 329 (Dec) (DC).
246 See e.g. *Cornwell v Marshall* [1977] 75 LGR 676 [1977] CLY 908
247 See e.g. *Ali v Bashir* [2013] EWHC 2572 (QB), at 6.
248 R *(Afzal) v Election Court* [2005] EWCA Civ 647.
249 R *(Afzal) v Election Court* [2005] EWCA Civ 647, 12.
250 Halsbury's Laws of England, vol 38A, para 848, citing *Norwich Case* (1869) 19 LT 615 at 620–621.
251 S 139(6) RPA 1983; r 49 sch 1 RPA 1983; art 95(7)(b) NAWRPO 2007.
252 R 11
253 S 146(4) RPA 1983.

so stated.[254] An Election Court may postpone the certification of its determination until the question has been determined by the Divisional Court. Where the parties agree, the hearing of the special case stated can be treated as the hearing of the petition.[255]

5.122 In *Considine v Didrichsen*,[256] Jack J described the mechanism in these terms:

> "The special case procedure is attractive because it avoids the additional costs which a trial would involve. It requires the parties to agree the facts. That may require some compromise, some give and take. It means that some factual assertions have to be abandoned because other parties will not accept them. The parties in this case sought to a degree to have the best of both situations, by appending to the case material such as statements, which was in dispute. We understand that this is not uncommon. The result was that we read this material only to be told that it was not agreed and that we should not take it into account. That complicated our task. A further result was that on occasion counsel sought to rely on points derived from the appended disputed material favourable to their case, even while objecting to others doing likewise. The only material which should be appended to a special case should be material which the parties are agreed that the court should take full account of for whatever it may be worth."[257]

Protective costs orders

5.123 A petitioner may apply for a protective costs order, directing that there be no order as to costs against either party, no order as to costs if they lose, or capping their maximum costs liability to the respondents at a particular figure.[258]

5.124 In *Erlam v Rahman*,[259] the principles governing PCOs were agreed between the parties as being those restated by Lord Phillips MR in *R (Corner House Research) v Secretary of State for Trade and Industry*:[260]

> "74. We would therefore restate the governing principles in these terms:

[254]S 146(1) RPA 1983; art 102 NAWRPO 2007.
[255]*Gunn and others v Sharpe* [1974] 2 All ER (QBD) (DC), p 811F-G.
[256]*Considine v Didrichsen* [2004] EWHC 2711 (QB).
[257]*Considine v Didrichsen* [2004] EWHC 2711 (QB) at 26.
[258]*Erlam v Rahman* [2014] EWHC 2766 (QB) (DC) at 49.
[259]*Erlam v Rahman* [2014] EWHC 2766 (QB) (DC) at 48.
[260]*Erlam v Rahman* [2014] EWHC 2766 (QB) (DC), 43-44.

1. A protective costs order may be made at any stage of the proceedings, on such conditions as the court thinks fit, provided that the court is satisfied that:

   i) The issues raised are of general public importance;

   ii) The public interest requires that those issues should be resolved;

   iii) The applicant has no private interest in the outcome of the case;

   iv) Having regard to the financial resources of the applicant and the respondent(s) and to the amount of costs that are likely to be involved it is fair and just to make the order;

   v) If the order is not made the applicant will probably discontinue the proceedings and will be acting reasonably in so doing.

2. If those acting for the applicant are doing so pro bono this will be likely to enhance the merits of the application for a PCO.

3. It is for the court, in its discretion, to decide whether it is fair and just to make the order in the light of the considerations set out above.

75. A PCO can take a number of different forms and the choice of the form of the order is an important aspect of the discretion exercised by the judge. In the present judgment we have noted:

   i) A case where the claimant's lawyers were acting pro bono, and the effect of the PCO was to prescribe in advance that there would be **no order as to costs** in the substantive proceedings whatever the outcome (R (Refugee Legal Centre) v Secretary of State for the Home Department [2004] EWCA Civ 1296);

   ii) A case where the claimants were expecting to have their reasonable costs reimbursed in full if they won, but sought an **order capping (at £25,000)** their maximum liability for costs if they lost (Campaign for Nuclear Disarmament) v Prime Minister [2002] EWHC 2712 (Admin));

   iii) A case similar to (ii) except that the claimants sought an order to the effect that there would be **no order as to costs if they lost** (R v Lord Chancellor, Ex p Child Poverty Action Group [1999] 1 WLR 347);

iv) The present case where the claimants are bringing the proceedings with the benefit of a CFA, which is otherwise identical to (iii)." [261] (emphasis added).

5.125 In *Erlam v Rahman*,[262] the petitioners' application for a PCO was dismissed for lack of evidence as to their means.[263] The Divisional Court stated, *obiter*:

> "49 In so far as it is necessary to have regard to the merits of the substantive application, it appears to us that Mr Straker **may well be correct in his submission that the protective costs regime is inapt for an election petition**. Elections and election petitions are specially provided for with their own particular legislative regime, which includes provision as to costs. By section 154 of the 1983 Act all costs of or incidental to the presentation of an election petition and the proceedings consequent on it, except as provided for by the Act, shall be defrayed by the parties to the petition in such proportions as the Election Court or High Court may determine. We understand that a PCO has never been made in an election case. There are, in our view, good reasons why this is so, **but it is not necessary for us to decide the point and we do not do so**".[264] (emphasis added).

5.126 The Law Commission has recommended that the power to make PCOs should *"if necessary"* be given statutory footing.[265]

Dismissal (strike out)

5.127 A respondent can apply to the Election Court or a Divisional Court to stay or dismiss a petition before the day fixed for the trial.[266]

5.128 They must do so by lodging an application notice, setting out grounds for so applying, at the election petitions officer, and serving it on the petitioner, any other respondent, the RO (if not also a respondent) and the DPP.[267]

5.129 They must do so no later than seven days before a date appointed for such application by the court.[268]

---

261 R *(Corner House Research) v Secretary of State for Trade and Industry* [2005] 1 WLR 2600, 74-75, per Lord Phillips MR.
262 *Erlam v Rahman* [2014] EWHC 2766 (QB) (DC) at 48.
263 *Erlam v Rahman* [2014] EWHC 2766 (QB) (DC) at 48.
264 *Erlam v Rahman* [2014] EWHC 2766 (QB) (DC) at 49.
265 Law Commission and Scottish Law Commission, 'Electoral Law: a joint final report', HC145 SG/2020/35, Law Com No 389, Scot Law Com No 256 ("the Law Commission Report"), para 15.96.
266 R 13 Election Petition Rules 1960.
267 R 13(2) Election Petition Rules 1960.
268 R 13(2) Election Petition Rules 1960.

5.130 In *Erlam v Rahman*,[269] the respondent unsuccessfully applied for dismissal and strike out on grounds that the petition failed to set out the facts with sufficient particularity as required by r 4(1)(d) of the Election Petition Rules 1960. The Divisional Court affirmed its power to order further particulars of the petition[270] and rejected an argument that r 4(1)(d) required a *"bare minimum of sufficient particulars"* for the court to order further and better particulars.[271]

5.131 See further, on strike out, under the subsections of 'How to start proceedings': paras 5.83-5.105 above.

5.132 In its March 2020 reform recommendations, the Law Commission stated *"Judges should continue to have regard to the needs of justice, striking a balance between access to the court and certainty in electoral outcomes"*.[272]

Trial

Place of trial

5.133 The trial must be within the constituency or electoral area for which the election was held, except that:

(i) If satisfied that special circumstances exist rendering it desirable to appoint somewhere else, the High Court may do so;[273]

(ii) PE: if the constituency is in Greater London, the High Court may appoint somewhere else in Greater London;[274]

(iii) The Election Court may adjourn the trial from one place to another within the constituency or electoral area.[275]

5.134 In *Erlam v Rahman*,[276] the petitioner applied for an order that the petition be tried outside the borough, on grounds of the likelihood of (a) voter intimidation during the challenged election, (b) the Election Court being surrounded by supporters of the respondent candidate, and (c) witnesses being likely to be intimidated. Supperstone J refused the application, reasoning:

> "The evidence, in my view, falls far short of establishing the special circumstances that would warrant moving the trial from the Borough. In reaching this conclusion, I agree with the observation

[269] *Erlam v Rahman* [2014] EWHC 2766 (QB) (DC).
[270] R 17 Election Petition Rules 1960; *Erlam v Rahman* [2014] EWHC 2766 (QB) (DC) at 36.
[271] *Erlam v Rahman* [2014] EWHC 2766 (QB) (DC) at 37.
[272] Law Commission Report, para 15.93.
[273] S 123(3)(a) and 130(6) RPA 1983; art 89(3) NAWRPO 2007.
[274] S 123(3)(b)
[275] S 123(4) and 130(7) RPA 1983; art 89(4) NAWRPO 2007.
[276] *Erlam v Rahman* [2014] EWHC 2767 (QB).

made by Mr Timothy Straker QC, for the Second Respondent, that the long-standing provision in primary legislation requiring local trials indicates that the concept of special circumstances is unlikely to embrace a concern about the number of attendees or the passion excited by political circumstances which creates potential for public rowdiness. Section 131(2) of the 1983 Act gives the Commissioner who hears the petition power to require "all constables and bailiffs [to] give their assistance to the court in the execution of its duties". The Commissioner can discuss issues of security and policing with the Commission of Police of the Metropolis so as to best ensure that witnesses who give evidence are not intimidated. Further, as Mr Straker points out, the Commissioner hearing the trial may request the Director of Public Prosecutions "by himself or by his assistant or by his representative", who may include a barrister or solicitor nominated by him, attend the trial if there are concerns, for example, about witness intimidation. (S.181(2))".[277]

5.135 The court's discretion to adjourn the trial from one place to another at any time, should greater evidence of need to do so arise, was further reason for the refusal.[278]

Proceeding in party's absence

5.136 Due to the partly inquisitorial jurisdiction, even if the petitioner decides not to take part in proceedings or submit evidence, the Election Court may consider it in the public interest to consider the allegations and scrutinise the respondents' evidence.[279]

5.137 For this reason, the trial of a petition must proceed notwithstanding:

(i) The respondent vacating their seat (PE and WAE) or ceasing to hold their office (LE); or

(ii) The prorogation of Parliament.

In public

5.138 Petitions must be tried in open court.[280]

5.139 A shorthand writer must attend the trial and be sworn by one of the judges to take down the evidence given at the trial and have it transcribed.[281] A copy of

---

[277] *Erlam v Rahman* [2014] EWHC 2767 (QB) at 15.
[278] *Erlam v Rahman* [2014] EWHC 2767 (QB) at 16.
[279] *Williams v Patrick* [2014] EWHC 4120 (QB) at 56.
[280] S 139(1) RPA 1983; art 95(1) NAWRPO 2007
[281] S 126(1) RPA 1983; r 18 Election Petition Rules 1960; art 91(1) NAWRPO 2007.

the evidence is then accompanies the certificate given by the Election Court to the Speaker (PE) or Presiding Officer of the Assembly (WAE).[282]

No need to first establish agency

5.140 Unless the court directs otherwise, it is not necessary to first prove a respondent candidate's agency before hearing evidence of corrupt practice. [283] In a LE petition, that applies to illegal practices too.[284]

Respondent may support petition

5.141 Where the petitioner claims a seat for some other person, a respondent (i.e. the RO or the successful candidate) may give evidence to prove that that other person was not duly elected or was incapable of being elected.[285]

Witness evidence

5.142 The summoning and swearing of witnesses takes place in the same way as in the High Court.[286]

5.143 The court may order any person appearing to have been concerned in the election to attend as a witness, refusal to obey being guilty of contempt of court.[287]

5.144 In a departure from normal civil procedure, the court can examine anyone in court irrespective of whether they are called by a party.[288] If it does, that person may then be cross-examined by or on behalf of the petitioner and/or a respondent. [289]

5.145 The DPP must (i) ensure the attendance of anyone who appears to them to be in a position to give material evidence as to the subject of the trial; and (ii) with the leave of the court, examine them as a witness.[290]

5.146 Witnesses may not rely on the privilege against self-incrimination or refuse to answer a question on grounds that answering may or would tend to incriminate their spouse or civil partner, but the trade-off for this is that statements to the court cannot be relied on in subsequent criminal or civil proceedings, unless the

[282] S 126(2) RPA 1983; art 91(2) NAWRPO 2007.
[283] S 139(4) RPA 1983.
[284] S 139(4) RPA 1983.
[285] S 139(5) RPA 1983; art 95(5) NAWRPO 2007.
[286] S 140(1) RPA 1983; art 96(1) NAWRPO 2007.
[287] S 140(2) RPA 1983; art 96(2) NAWRPO 2007.
[288] S 140(4) RPA 1983; art 96(3) NAWRPO 2007.
[289] S 140(3) RPA 1983; art 96(4) NAWRPO 2007.
[290] S 140(6) RPA 1983; art 96(5) NAWRPO 2007.

statements are false, in which case their statements may be relied on in proceedings for perjury.[291]

Conclusions open to the Election Court

5.147 At the conclusion of the trial, the Election Court must determine which of the following three conclusions to enter:[292]

(i) The person whose election was questioned was duly elected (the petition fails);

(ii) Some other person was duly elected (where a petitioner succeeds in showing that a winning candidate was unduly elected or their election was void on Grounds 2-6, above, and that some other person should have been); or

(iii) The whole election was void (where a petition succeeds on Ground 1, namely material breach of the rules rendering election not substantially in accordance with the law, with the effect that *"the election shall be declared invalid"*;[293] or WAE: where a regional candidate is declared not duly elected or returned).[294]

5.148 The circumstances in which another candidate to be declared duly elected where a petition succeeds on Grounds 2-6 is set out below:

(i) Where on a scrutiny and recount the winning candidate is shown to have in fact not had the majority of votes (Ground 2, above), the candidate found to have the actual majority is declared duly elected;

(ii) Where the winning candidate's election is declared void for their or their agent's corrupt or illegal practice (Ground 3, above) (this is not sufficient condition for a new election to have to be held, rather there is an additional condition, namely: that *"no other person has been declared elected in his place"*);[295]

(iii) Where the petition succeeds in establishing that the winning candidate had been disqualified or otherwise incapable of being elected at the time

---

[291] S 141 RPA 1983; art 97 NAWRPO 2007.

[292] Ss 144(1) and 145(1) and (1A) RPA 1983; s 99(1) NAWRPO 2007. In *Parkinson v Lewis* [2016] EWHC 725 (QB), at 35, His Honour Judge Saffman held *"There is no power granted by section 145 to declare that the successful candidates were not duly elected but that the petitioner is"*. The learned judge's statement should be read as confined to material breach of the rules decisions, ss 23 and 48 RPA 1983 (Ground 1 above), rather than all petitions.

[293] Ss 23 and 48 RPA 1983; art 17 NAWRPO 2007.

[294] Art 99(2) NAWRPO 2007.

[295] Ss 135(1) and 135A(1) RPA 1983.

they were elected (Ground 4), the candidate who secured the second highest number of votes is declared duly elected;[296]

(iv) Where a petition succeeds in showing that general corruption, bribery, treating or intimidation were committed for the purpose of procuring the election of a candidate and so extensively prevailed that they may be reasonably supposed to have affected the result (Ground 5, above), it is not the whole election that is avoided, rather *"his election, if he has been elected, shall be void"*;[297]

(v) Where a petition establishes that the respondent candidate or their election agent engaged as a canvasser or agent for the conduct or management of the election someone whom they knew or had reasonable grounds for supposing to have been found guilty of corrupt or illegal practice and within their disqualification period (Ground 6, above), this does not void the whole election, rather *"the candidate shall be incapable of being elected to fill the vacancy or any of the vacancies for which the election is held"*[298] and the principle of votes being thrown away then operates *"so as to entitle another candidate to be declared elected"*.[299]

5.149 The principle that the voiding of a candidate's election does not void the whole election for purposes of other candidates elected or seeking to be declared as such is further reflected by the statutory provision on the trial of the petition, which states: *"On the trial of a petition complaining of an undue election and claiming the seat or office for some person, the respondent may give evidence to prove that that person was not duly elected"*.[300] The principle was also enunciated by the Divisional Court in *Gunn v Sharpe*.[301]

5.150 Having made its determination, the Court must provide a certificate of the determination in writing to the Speaker (PE),[302] High Court and Minister for the Cabinet Office (LE),[303] or Presiding Officer of the Assembly (WAE).[304]

---

[296] *Beresford-Hope v Sandhurst* [1889] 23 QBD 79, p 95, per Lord Coleridge LCJ; *Re Bristol South-East Parliamentary Election* [1961] 3 WLR 577, p 609. The doctrine of votes thrown away is also accepted in commonwealth countries: see e.g. *Dabdoub v Vaz* [2008] CA 45/2008 (Jamaican Court of Appeal), at 42. The Law Commission has recommended abolition of the 'thrown away' rule: Law Com No 389, 13.10.

[297] S 164(1)(a) RPA 1983.

[298] S 165(1) RPA 1983; art 117(1) NAWRPO 2007.

[299] S 165(1) RPA 1983; art 117(4) NAWRPO 2007.

[300] S 139(5) RPA 1983; s 95(5) NAWRP0 2007.

[301] *Gunn and others v Sharpe* [1974] 2 All ER (QBD) (DC), p 818G-H.

[302] S 144(2) RPA 1983.

[303] Ss 145(2) and (5), and 199ZA RPA 1983.

[304] Art 99(3) NAWRPO 2007.

5.151 On a PE or WAE petition where there is a difference between the two judges as to whether the person whose election or return was challenged was duly elected or returned, the Court must certify that difference, with the effect that that person is deemed duly elected or returned.[305]

Report as to general corruption or candidate's corrupt or illegal practice

5.152 If a corrupt or illegal practice was alleged in the petition, in addition to providing the Speaker (PE), High Court (LE),[306] or Presiding Officer of the Assembly (WAE)[307] with a certificate stating the determination, the Election Court must also send them a report as to:

(i) Whether there is reason to believe that corrupt or illegal practices *"extensively prevailed"* at the election (i.e. on Ground 5, above);[308]

(ii) Whether a corrupt practice (other than undue influence or treating) was committed by a candidate, or with their knowledge and consent, such that they should be treated as personally guilty of that corrupt practice;[309]

(iii) PE and WAE: whether an illegal practice was committed by a candidate or with their knowledge and consent of the candidate, such that they should be treated as personally guilty of that illegal practice;[310]

(iv) Whether any of the candidates has been guilty by their agents of any corrupt or illegal practice during the election;[311]

(v) Whether a candidate found guilty by their agents should not be treated as reported guilty, nor their election void, because they have made out the statutory defence by proving that: (a) the offences mentioned in the report were trivial, unimportant and limited; (b) the offences mentioned in the report were committed contrary to the orders and without the sanction or connivance of the candidate or their election agent; (c) the candidate and their election agent took all reasonable steps to prevent the commission of corrupt and illegal practices at the election; and (d) the election was otherwise free from corrupt or illegal practice on the part of the candidate and their agents.[312]

---

[305] Ss 144(3) and 145(3) RPA 1983; art 99(4) NAWRPO 2007.
[306] S 144(4) RPA 1983.
[307] Art 99(4) NAWRPO 2007.
[308] Ss 144(4), 145(4) and 164 RPA 1983; art 99(5) NAWRPO 2007.
[309] S 158(1) RPA 1983; art 108(1) and (2)(a) NAWRPO 2007.
[310] S 158(1) RPA 1983; art 108(1) and (2)(b) NAWRPO 2007.
[311] S 158(3) RPA 1983; art 108(3) NAWRPO 2007.
[312] S 158(3) RPA 1983.

5.153 In any of the above scenarios, except where the defence is made out, the respondent candidate's election is void.[313]

5.154 *Erlam v Rahman*[314] provides an example of an illustration of an unsuccessful attempt to rely on the defence to a finding of guilty by agency. The Election Court found:

(i) The undue influence carried on with the petitioner's *"sanction and connivance"* and he gave no contrary orders, rather invited and approved the clerics' exhortations;[315]

(ii) The evidence was all against his asserting that he and his election agent took all reasonable means for preventing the letter;[316]

(iii) The offences were not of a trivial, unimportant and limited character';[317] and

(iv) The other findings of personation, other voting offences, making false statements, paying canvassers and bribery, meant it also could not be shown that the election was otherwise free from any corrupt or illegal practice on his part or that of his agents.[318]

5.155 Before naming anyone who is not a party to the petition or a candidate, the Court must give that third party an opportunity to be heard and to call evidence as to why they should not be reported.[319]

5.156 The report must be laid before the DPP.[320]

Special report

5.157 The Court may also make a special report to the Speaker (PE), High Court (LE), or Presiding Officer of the Assembly (WAE) as to matters arising in the course of the trial that it considers ought to be so submitted.[321] An example of this power being exercised is *Afzal v Jahan*.[322]

---

[313]Ss 159 and 164 RPA 1983; arts 109 and 116 NAWRPO 2007.
[314]*Erlam v Rahman and Williams* [2015] EWHC 1215 (QB).
[315]*Erlam v Rahman and Williams* [2015] EWHC 1215 (QB) at 570.
[316]*Erlam v Rahman and Williams* [2015] EWHC 1215 (QB) at 571.
[317]*Erlam v Rahman and Williams* [2015] EWHC 1215 (QB) at 572.
[318]*Erlam v Rahman and Williams* [2015] EWHC 1215 (QB) at 573.
[319]S 160(1) RPA 1983; art 110(1) NAWRPO 2007.
[320]S 160(3) RPA 1983; art 110(1) NAWRPO 2007.
[321]Ss 144(5) and 145(5) RPA 1983; art 99(6) NAWRPO 2007.
[322]*Jahan v Afzal* [4.4.15, Richard Mawrey QC sitting as a Commissioner]. Increase in the number of postal votes in two marginal Birmingham wards saw showed an increase in turnout of over 100% in one and 350% in the other.

Costs

5.158 The Election Court or High Court may apportion all costs of and incidental to the petition and any consequential proceedings in the manner and proportion it sees fit,[323] taking into account costs caused by vexatious conduct, unfounded allegations, unfounded objections, and any needless expense incurred or caused, whether or not they are successful.[324]

5.159 Where a petitioner established two of the 15 forms of corrupt and illegal practice he had alleged, the Election Court ordered that the respondent pay three quarters' of the petitioners' costs.[325]

5.160 After a decision on costs, the Election Court cannot reconvene to sit and clarify the meaning of its order.[326]

F. AFTERMATH

Court dissolved

5.161 After making its report, the Election Court constituted to hear the petition is dissolved.

5.162 Once a trial has concluded, the Election Court may not use the 'slip rule' power and slips may only be corrected by the High Court on application for correction.[327]

Receipt of certificate and report(s)

5.163 Upon receipt of the certificate and reports,

(i) PE: The House of Commons must order that the Election Court's certificate and reports (if any) be entered in its journals and give the necessary direction for (a) confirming or altering the return; (b) issuing a writ for a new election; or (c) carrying the determination into execution.[328] Where the Election Court has made a special report, the House of Commons may make such order in respect of that report as it thinks proper.[329]

---

[323] S 154(1) RPA 1983; art 104(1) NAWRPO 2007.
[324] S 154(2) RPA 1983; art 104(2) NAWRPO 2007.
[325] R *v Cripps ex p Muldoon* [1984] QB 686 (CA), p 696E-F.
[326] R *v Cripps ex p Muldoon* [1984] QB 686 (CA), 695B.
[327] R *v Cripps ex p Muldoon* [1984] QB 686; CPR 40.12(2).
[328] S 144(7) RPA 1983.
[329] S 144(7) RPA 1983.

(ii) LE: two or more High Court judges must certify a copy of the certificate to the proper officer of the council for which the election was held.[330]

Fresh election

5.164 PE: Following receipt by the Speaker of the House of Commons of the Election Court's certificate containing its determination as to whether the MP whose election or return had been complained of, or any other person, was duly returned or elected, or whether the election was void, the House of Commons must give directions for confirming or altering the return and issuing a fresh writ for an election.[331]

5.165 LE: Where an election has been declared void and no other person has been declared elected in their stead, a new election must be held in the same manner as on a casual vacancy.[332]

5.166 LAE: Where a candidate's return has been declared void and no other person has been declared elected in their stead, a new election must be held, per the casual vacancy process.[333] If the whole election (rather than just the return) is declared void, a new election must be held in the same manner as at an ordinary election.[334]

5.167 WAE: where the Election Court determines that a regional election was void, upon receipt of the Election Court's certificate determining that conclusion, the Presiding Officer of the Assembly must fix a date within three months for a poll to be held at another election in the same Assembly electoral region and notify the RO for that region.[335]

Prosecution

5.168 The Election Court's report naming anyone proven guilty of corrupt or illegal practice must be provided to the DPP.[336] The DPP is then under a duty to make such inquiries and institute such prosecutions as the case appears to them to require.[337] Persons reported may then be prosecuted[338] within one year after the

---

[330]S 145(6) RPA 1983.
[331]S 144(7) RPA 1983.
[332]S 135(1) RPA 1983. As to the filling of casual vacancies in the case of councillors, see s 89 Local Government Act 1972 (LE) or s 11 Greater London Authority Act 1999.
[333]S 135A(3) RPA 1983.
[334]S 135A(4) RPA 1983.
[335]Art 101(1) NAWRPO 2007.
[336]S 160(3) RPA 1983; art 110(1) NAWRPO 2007.
[337]S 181 RPA 1983; art 133(1) NAWRPO 2007.
[338]Ss 168 and 169 RPA 1983.

offence was committed,[339] or 24 months' on the DPP's application for extension.[340]

5.169 Following the finding of the Election Court in *Erlam v Rahman* that the respondent was personally guilty and guilty by his agents of the offences of making false statements as to candidates, bribery and undue influence, the police investigated but decided that there was insufficient admissible evidence to prosecute the respondent.[341]

Disqualification, mitigation and remission

5.170 A candidate or other person reported by an Election Court personally guilty of a corrupt or illegal practice is subject to incapacity, for five years for corrupt practices or three years for illegal practices,[342] from:

(i) Being registered to vote or voting at a PE or LE (but only if reported personally guilty of: (a) personation; (b) offences relating to applications for postal and proxy votes involving intent to gain a vote or deprive another of the opportunity to vote; or (c) voting offences);[343]

(ii) Holding any elective office (and must vacate any seat held);[344]

(iii) If subsequently prosecuted for the election offence that led to their disqualification, but then acquitted, then the Election Court may determine the extent to which the incapacity remains in place, whether fully in remission or merely mitigated.[345]

G. APPEAL TO THE COURT OF APPEAL

5.171 Appeal from the High Court's decision on a case stated lies to the Court of Appeal, but only on a point of law and with the special leave of the High Court, and there is no further appeal.[346]

---

[339] S 176(1) RPA 1983; art 128 NAWRPO 2007.
[340] S 176(2A) RPA 1983.
[341] *R (Rahman) v Local Government Election Court* [2017] EWHC 1413 (Admin) (DC) (Lloyd Jones LJ and Supperstone J) at 17.
[342] S 160(5) RPA 1983; art 110(3) and (5) NAWRPO 2007; *Erlam v Rahman and Williams* [2015] EWHC 1215 (QB) at 31.
[343] S 160(4)(a)(i) and (4A) RPA 1983; art 110(3)(a) and (4) NAWRPO 2007.
[344] S 160(4) RPA 1983; art 110(3)(b) NAWRPO 2007.
[345] S 174 RPA 1983.
[346] S 157(1) RPA 1983; art 107(1) NAWRPO 2007. This reflects the historical fact that the House of Commons could not permit the House of Lords to determine or alter its membership. S 12 Constitutional Reform Act 2005 took effect on 1.9.2009. This legacy was observed by the Law Commission's consultation paper [Joint Consultation Paper LCCP 218 / SLCDP 158 / NILC 20 (2014)], but its final report did not recommend making the Supreme Court the final court of appeal: Law Com No 389.

H. JUDICIAL REVIEW OF ELECTION COURT

Jurisdiction

5.172 The Election Court, even when a parliamentary Election Court featuring High Court judges, is an inferior tribunal and thus its decisions are susceptible to judicial review under s 31 of the Senior Courts Act 1981.[347]

5.173 The availability of the procedure whereby an Election Court may state a case for the High Court to determine a point of law does not delimit the availability of judicial review if (i) the point raised in the judicial review is an important one for the conduct of elections; or (ii) the point is not susceptible to consideration independently of the facts (by way of case stated rather than a challenge, generally, to the Election Court's decision).[348] Delay may lead to a refusal of permission on general judicial review procedural principles.[349]

5.174 Judicial review, rather than Court of Appeal appeal, is the correct means of challenging a commissioner's directions for trial.[350]

Parties

5.175 The defendant will be the 'the Local Government Election Court' or 'the Parliamentary Election Court', but is unlikely to contest the claim. Instead, the Divisional Court on judicial review will receive submissions from the interested parties, who will be the petitioners and potentially the DPP and the chief constable for any force that was involved.[351]

Grounds[352]

Insufficient evidence

5.176 In *R (Rahman) v Election Court,*[353] Lloyd-Jones LJ held, in respect to the error of law jurisdiction to judicially review an Election Court:

---

[347] R *(Afzal) v Election Court* [2005] EWCA Civ 647; R *(Woolas) v Parliamentary Election Court* [2010] EWHC 3169 (Admin) at 54; R *v Election Ct., Ex p Sheppard* [1974] 3 WLR 517 (D.C.), p 1323G, per Lord Widgery CJ.

[348] R *(Woolas) v Parliamentary Election Court* [2010] EWHC 3169 (Admin), at 51; R *(Rahman) v Election Court* [2016] EWHC 1280 (Admin) (DC) at 41 (Lloyd-Jones LJ).

[349] R *(Khan) v Election Commissioner* [2005] EWHC 2365 (Admin) (DC), at 39, per Scott Baker LJ.

[350] *Williams v Patrick* [2014] EWHC 4120 (QB), 2-3.

[351] E.g. R *(Rahman) v Local Government Election Court* [2017] EWHC 1413 (Admin) (DC) (Lloyd Jones LJ and Supperstone J).

[352] This section present example grounds from JRs in election law. The range of grounds of challenge in modern public is much wider and the reader interested in this area should look to a practitioner's text such as Auburn, Moffett and Sharland, 'Judicial Review' (OUP: Oxford, 2013).

[353] R *(Rahman) v Election Court* [2016] EWHC 1280 (Admin) (DC).

> "[A]n error of law would include a factual finding for which there was no evidential basis, that is circumstances in which a conclusion drawn by the Commissioner was not supported by evidence, or his conclusion was not reasonably open to him on the evidence."[354]

5.177 This ground is facilitated by the applicability of the criminal standard of proof to allegations of corrupt or illegal practices.[355] To find guilt by preferring one witness to another is a departure from the criminal standard.[356] In *R (Rahman) v Election Court*, the claimant challenged the Election Court's finding that he had paid canvassers on the basis that the Commissioner had preferred one witness over another. The challenge was nonetheless found unarguable because of the wider strength of evidence: (i) the preferred witnesses were several, (ii) they described three separate incidents of like nature (paid canvassers); (iii) they related what *"would have been an extraordinary story to have invented"*, and (iv) the witness who denied paying canvassers is found untruthful in comprehensive terms. In those circumstances, even evidence accepted by the Commissioner and the Divisional Court as being not *"particularly strong"* was sufficient to mean the conclusion was vitiated by error of law.[357]

Perverse findings of fact

5.178 The Administrative Court is not entitled to interfere with an Election Court commissioners findings of fact unless they are perverse in the *Wednesbury*[358] sense (outside the range of reasonable findings available to them on the facts before them when properly directing themselves in law).[359]

Procedural unfairness

5.179 In *R (Afzal) v Election Court*,[360] the Court of Appeal, having granted permission to appeal against refusal of permission to claim judicial review, quashed that part of the commissioner's decision that found the claimant councillor to have been guilty of corrupt and illegal practices and made an order enabling him to cast his vote in the pending PE. The Court did so on grounds of natural justice, specifically that the commissioner failed to recall for cross-examination a police officer witness whom the commissioner had invited to make a dock identification of the claimant and thereby omitted to consider a relevant point,[361] and thereby *"failed to ensure that [the councillor] had a fair opportunity*

---

[354] R *(Rahman) v Election Court* [2016] EWHC 1280 (Admin) (DC) at 15.
[355] R *v Rowe, ex p Mainwaring* [1992] 1 WLR 1059 (CA).
[356] R *(Rahman) v Election Court* [2016] EWHC 1280 (Admin) (DC) at 17.
[357] R *(Rahman) v Election Court* [2016] EWHC 1280 (Admin) (DC) at 18 (Lloyd-Jones LJ).
[358] *Associated Provincial Picture Houses Ltd. v. Wednesbury Corporation* [1948] 1 KB 223.
[359] *Mainwaring*, p 1066C-D.
[360] R *(Afzal) v Election Court* [2005] EWCA Civ 647.
[361] R *(Afzal) v Election Court* [2005] EWCA Civ 647, at 41.

to deal with the case that the Commissioner concluded had been made out against him. This was a fundamental requirement of a fair trial (see, for instance, Mahon v Air New Zealand Ltd [1984] AC 808, 821A-B)".[362] This decision is notable because the Court of Appeal was able to so find despite the art 6 ECHR ground not being developed and despite affirming that the Election Court proceeding were not 'criminal proceedings'.

5.180 *R (Khan) v Election Court*[363] is another example of judicial review brought on grounds of procedural fairness, where the claimant successfully challenged the Election Court's failure to give him proper notice of its intention to name him in its report as having been found guilty of illegal practices despite his not having been a party,[364] contrary to statutory protection of this principle of natural justice.[365] The Election Court considered the claimant to have had sufficient notice because he had had the opportunity to give evidence and had declined. The Divisional Court held that this did not constitute notice of intention to find illegal practices proved against the non-party.[366]

Error of law

5.181 Error of law by an Election Court in its interpretation or application of a provision of election law represents a potential ground of challenge. An example is *R (Woolas) v Parliamentary Election Court*,[367] where the claimant successfully argued that the Election Court had erred in its approach to s 106 RPA 1983 by interpreting it as permitting a false statement to relate to both to the personal and political character or conduct of a candidate. Another example is *R (Khan) v Election Court*,[368] where the Election Court failed to properly apply the s 160 RPA 1983 obligation to provide written notice to non-parties whom it proposes to name in its report of illegal and corrupt practices.

Incompatibility with the ECHR

5.182 The Election Court being a public body and as such obliged to act compatibly with the ECHR, ground of challenge will lie where it does not do so. In practice, this ground is a subset of the error of law ground, the claimant likely to argue that the Court erred by misdirecting itself as to the requirements of a given ECHR right. In *R (Woolas) v Parliamentary Election Court*,[369] a challenge to a

---

[362] R *(Afzal) v Election Court* [2005] EWCA Civ 647, at 42.
[363] R *(Khan) v Election Commissioner* [2005] EWHC 2365 (Admin) (DC).
[364] R *(Khan) v Election Commissioner* [2005] EWHC 2365 (Admin) (DC), at 13.
[365] S 160 RPA 183.
[366] R *(Khan) v Election Commissioner* [2005] EWHC 2365 (Admin) (DC), at 47-48.
[367] R *(Woolas) v Election Court* [2010] EWHC 3169 (Admin) (DC).
[368] R *(Khan) v Election Commissioner* [2005] EWHC 2365 (Admin) (DC), at 13.
[369] R *(Woolas) v Election Court* [2010] EWHC 3169 (Admin) (DC).

finding of s 106 RPA 1983 false statement, the Divisional Court granted judicial review where it found the Election Court to have erred by applying the relevant ECHR articles as a consideration subsequent to its finding of the s 106 illegal practice (i.e. whether to so find would be proportionate), rather than integral to the interpretation of s 106 in the first place.[370]

Procedure

Expedition

5.183 Because of the urgency (an election was in progress in which the claimant wished to take part), the Divisional Court may bypass the paper stage and go straight to the oral application.[371] A defendant or interested persons who do not make representations at that stage does not indicate lack of opposition.[372]

Permission

5.184 S 31(3) of the Senior Courts Act 1981 provides:

> "(3) No application for judicial review shall be made unless the **leave** of the High Court has been obtained in accordance with rules of court; and the court shall not grant leave to make such an application unless it considers that the applicant has a **sufficient interest** in the matter to which the application relates." (emphasis added).

5.185 *"Leave"* is now referred to as 'permission'. The *"rules of court"* are the CPR, Part 54 of which governs JR proceedings. CPR 54.5(1) requires a claim to be filed promptly and in any event not later than three months after the grounds to make the claim first arose.

5.186 S 31(3C)-(3E) of the Senior Courts Act 1981 provides:

> "(3C) When considering whether to grant leave to make an application for judicial review, the High Court—
>
> (a) may of its own motion consider whether the outcome for the applicant would have been substantially different if the conduct complained of had not occurred, and
>
> (b) must consider that question if the defendant asks it to do so.

370 R *(Woolas) v Election Court* [2010] EWHC 3169 (Admin) (DC), Thomas LJ at 95.
371 R *(Afzal) v Election Court* [2005] EWHC 721 (Admin) (permission decision), at 19.
372 R *(Afzal) v Election Court* [2005] EWHC 721 (Admin) (permission decision), at 19.

(3D) If, on considering that question, it appears to the High Court to be **highly likely** that the outcome for the applicant would not have been **substantially different**, the court must refuse to grant leave.

(3E) The court may disregard the requirement in subsection (3D) if it considers that it is appropriate to do so for reasons of exceptional public interest." (emphasis added).

5.187 In *R (Rahman) v Election Court*, [373] the Divisional Court considered the s 31(3C) question of its motion and determined the question as follows:

> "[T]he outcome for the claimant would have been substantially different had the Commissioner's decision of which complaint is made in ground 3 not occurred. He has been convicted of a further discrete allegation of corruption. The court is here concerned with a conviction for a corrupt practice, a very serious matter."[374]

5.188 Thus the fact that the claimant's other convictions for illegal and corrupt practices would remain undisturbed and he would remain disqualified from standing for public office for five years did not satisfy s 31(3D).

5.189 The Divisional Court also held, obiter, that it would have found that s 31(3E) applied, in that the point of law at issue required consideration by the court amounting to *"reasons of exceptional public interest"*.[375]

---

[373] R *(Rahman) v Election Court* [2016] EWHC 1280 (Admin) (DC).
[374] R *(Rahman) v Election Court* [2016] EWHC 1280 (Admin) (DC) at 38 (Lloyd-Jones LJ).
[375] R *(Rahman) v Election Court* [2016] EWHC 1280 (Admin) (DC) at 38 (Lloyd-Jones LJ).

CHAPTER SIX

ARTICLE 3 OF PROTOCOL 1 TO THE EUROPEAN CONVENTION

6.1 This chapters covers Article 3 of Protocol 1 to the European Convention on Human Rights ("**A3P1 ECHR**"), the *"right to free elections"*, which provides: *"The high contracting parties undertake to hold free elections at reasonable intervals by secret ballot, under conditions which will ensure the free expression of the opinion of the people in the choice of the legislature."*

6.2 In the foregoing chapters, A3P1 has been considered where it arises in relation to the statutory schemes. In this chapter, the rights protected and duties imposed by A3P1 are detailed as a separate field, in order that the reader can gain proper understanding of this important body of law.

6.3 This chapter will discuss A3P1 via the following sections:

A. General principles;

B. Free elections under conditions ensuring the free expression of the people;

C. Active aspect: the right to vote;

D. Passive aspect: the right to stand for election; and

E. ECtHR proceedings.

A. GENERAL PRINCIPLES

Scope

6.4 A3P1 applies to elections to the 'legislature', but not purely national legislatures: a regional government that is competent to enact administrative and town planning, local policy, public healthcare, education and agricultural laws in its region has been found to form part of the legislature.[1]

6.5 A3P1 does not apply to local authorities or regional elections, where they do not exercise a legislative function. Thus, parliamentary elections (PE) and Welsh Assembly elections (WAE) are within scope.

[1] *Vito Sante Santoro v Italy* (36681/97), 1.7.04, at 50.

6.6 A3P1 also does not apply to referenda[2] or the election or disqualification of a president.[3]

Principles overview: *Barclay*

6.7 In *R (Barclay) v Lord Chancellor and Secretary of State for Justice*,[4] Lord Collins JSC (with whom the rest of the court concurred and in a judgment described by Lord Neuberger MR as *"magisterial"*)[5] derived the following principles from the Strasbourg A3P1 jurisprudence as it stood by 2009:

> "53 First, article 3 of the First Protocol enshrines a characteristic principle of an effective democracy. It is of prime importance in the Convention system, of which democracy constitutes a fundamental element, and the rights guaranteed under article 3 of the First Protocol are crucial to establishing and maintaining the foundations of an effective and meaningful democracy governed by the rule of law...
>
> 54 Second, although article 3 is phrased in terms of the obligation of the contracting states to hold elections which ensure the free expression of the opinion of the people rather than in terms of individual rights, article 3 guarantees individual rights, including the right to vote and the right to stand for election...
>
> 55 Third, there is room for implied limitations on the rights enshrined in article 3, and contracting states must be given a wide margin of appreciation in this sphere...
>
> 56 Fourth, the content of the obligation under article 3 varies in accordance with the historical and political factors specific to each state; and for the purposes of applying article 3, any electoral legislation must be assessed in the light of the political evolution of the country concerned, so that features which would be unacceptable in the context of one system may be justified in the context of another, at least so long as the chosen system provides for conditions which will ensure the free expression of the opinion of the people in the choice of the legislature...
>
> 57 Fifth, article 3 is not (by contrast with some other Convention rights, such as those enumerated in articles 8 to 11) subject to a specific list of legitimate limitations, and the contracting states are therefore free to rely in general in justifying a limitation on aims which are proved to be

---

[2] *Paksas v Lithuania* (34932/04), 6.1.11 (GC), at 3.
[3] *Aksas v Lithuania* (34932/04), 6.1.11 (GC), at 72.
[4] R *(Barclay) v Lord Chancellor and Secretary of State for Justice* [2009] UKSC 9 [2010] 1 AC 464.
[5] R *(Barclay) v Lord Chancellor and Secretary of State for Justice* [2009] UKSC 9 [2010] 1 AC 464, at 120, per Lord Neuberger JSC.

compatible with the principle of the rule of law and the general objectives of the Convention…

58 Sixth, limitations on the exercise of the right to vote or stand for election must be imposed in pursuit of a legitimate aim, must not be arbitrary or disproportionate, and must not interfere with the free expression of the opinion of the people in the choice of the legislature…

59 Seventh, such limitations must not curtail the rights under article 3 to such an extent as to impair their very essence, and deprive them of their effectiveness. They must reflect, or not run counter to, the concern to maintain the integrity and effectiveness of an electoral procedure aimed at identifying the will of the people through universal suffrage. Any departure from the principle of universal suffrage risks undermining the democratic validity of the legislature and the laws which it promulgates…

60 Eighth, as regards the right to stand for election, the court accepts that stricter requirements may be imposed on the eligibility to stand for election to parliament, as distinguished from voting eligibility…

61 Ninth, the court takes account of the practice of members of the Council of Europe in assessing the compatibility of electoral rules with article 3, in particular in the area of qualifications to stand for election."[6]

Legality

6.8 A principle that merits presentation in addition to the summary in *Barclay* is that of legality, which is inherent in all the ECHR Articles and Protocols,[7] and takes on a particular importance for the application of A3P1. Unlike arts 5, 8-11, or Article 1 of Protocol 1 ECHR, the text of A3P1 does not contain an express reference to the *"lawfulness"* of any restrictions on the right, but the ECtHR has nonetheless confirmed that it is implied.[8]

6.9 The principle of lawfulness first comprises a formal element: breach of domestic legislation put in place to secure protection of A3P1 rights is likely to amount to breach of A3P1.[9]

---

[6] R *(Barclay) v Lord Chancellor and Secretary of State for Justice* [2010] 1 AC 464, at 54-61, per Lord Collins.

[7] See, e.g., *Amuur v France*, 25.6.96, at 50.

[8] *Abil v Azerbaijan (No. 2)* (8513/11), 5.12.19, at 66.

[9] *Paunović and Milivojević v Serbia* (41683/06), 24.5.16, at 65 (termination of applicant's parliamentary mandate not in accordance with the applicable legal rules).

6.10 Secondly, it involves a substantive conception of the rule of law that mirrors the common law principle of legality. This requires law to observe qualitative standards of foreseeability, precision, non-arbitrariness, and non-retrospectivity.

6.11 Thirdly, the lawfulness principle takes account of wider international law. The ECtHR has therefore held that A3P1 should be interpreted with reference to the relevant international and comparative law.[10] The ECtHR has had regard in particular to the Venice Commission's Code of Good Practices in Electoral Matters[11] when considering whether the conduct of the electoral process or the means of challenging such conduct are compatible with A3P1.[12] It is only a relevant consideration, however. For instance, the ECtHR has had regard to the Venice Commission's declaration that a 'duty of neutrality' is one of the preconditions to equal suffrage, and accepted that political pluralism is a pressing social need justifying some interference with freedom of expression, but nonetheless found that less than complete neutrality is sufficient to discharge the duty to put in place conditions enabling free elections.[13]

B. FREE ELECTIONS UNDER CONDITIONS ENSURING THE FREE EXPRESSION OF THE PEOPLE

Framework

6.12 A3P1 obliges contracting states such as the UK not just to avoid breaching individuals' subjective rights to vote or stand for election in free elections on a case by case basis, but to have in place a legislative framework that secures the obligation in the A3P1 text. This has been expressed as an "*undertak[ing] to hold free elections at reasonable intervals by secret ballot, under conditions which will ensure the free expression of the opinion of the people in the choice of the legislature.*"[14] This reflects the general principle of legality mentioned above, whereby lawful measures require foreseeability and not merely to have been made with lawful authority.

6.13 As a positive obligation requiring the state to expend money to create the structures and conditions for free elections, special importance attaches to the

---

[10] *Yumak and Sadak* (10226/03), 8.7.08 (GC), at 127; *Demir and Baykara v Turkey* (34503/97), 8.7.08 (GC), at 76 and 85; *Riza v Bulgaria* (42202/07), 15.3.12, at 71.

[11] Code of Good Practice in Electoral Matters (Guidelines and Explanatory Report) (CDL-AD (2002) 23 rev), adopted by the European Commission for Democracy through Law ("**the Venice Commission**") at its 51st and 52nd sessions (5-6.7.2002 and 18-19.10.02).

[12] *Namat Aliyev v Azerbaijan* (18705/06), 8.4.10, at 86; *Schindler v UK* (19840/09), 7.5.13, at 113; *Riza and Others v Bulgaria* (48555/10 48377/10), 13.10.15, at 177.

[13] *Communist Party of Russia v Russia* (29400/05) (2015) 61 EHRR 28, at 120.

[14] *Abil v Azerbaijan (No. 2)* (8513/11), 5.12.19, at 66.

role played by the national legislature in the choice and optimum use of national resources.[15]

Breach of domestic legislation

6.14 Once the state has discharged its duty to put in place the framework of legislation required by A3P1 to secure protection of its rights, if it then conducts procedures outside that framework, then that conduct is likely to amount to breach of A3P1. In *Paunović and Milivojević v Serbia*,[16] violation of A3P1 was found where an MP's mandate was terminated outwith the applicable statutory procedure.[17]

Voting system

6.15 So long as the voting system ensures the free expression of the opinion of the people, A3P1 does not require a particular type of voting system.[18] Adoption of single transferrable vote for Northern Irish elections (rather than the simple majority system used elsewhere in the UK) was held not to infringe A3P1.[19] This reflected the A3P1 principle of taking into account the historical context, here that Northern Irish voters tended to vote on ethnic or religious lines and one group was in a clear minority throughout all electoral districts, justifying a proportionate representation system and departure from the rest of the UK.

6.16 In a proportional representation system, imposition of a threshold of votes before which a party, even a party representing a country's ethnic minority, can take seats in the legislature is compatible with A3P1 read in conjunction with art 14 ECHR (the right to enjoyment of ECHR rights without discrimination).[20]

Composition of the legislature

6.17 The state's wide margin of appreciation under A3P1 takes into account historical and political context.[21] Measure of the importance of that principle

---

[15] *James and Others v UK*, 21.2.86, at 46; *Uzan and Others v Turkey* (18240/03), 29.3.11, at 83.

[16] *Paunović and Milivojević v Serbia* (41683/06), 24.5.16, at 65 (termination of applicant's parliamentary mandate not in accordance with the applicable legal rules).

[17] *Paunović and Milivojević v Serbia* (41683/06), 24.5.16

[18] Travaux Préparatoires, vol. VII pp.130, 202 and 210 and vol. VIII p.14; *Lindsay v UK* (8364/78) [1979] 3 C.M.L.R. 166 (admissibility), at 8; *Mathieu-Mohin and Clerfayt v Belgium* (9267/81) [1988] 10 EHRR 1, at 54.

[19] *Lindsay v UK* (8364/78) [1979] 3 C.M.L.R. 166, European Commission on Human Rights (admissibility), at 9.

[20] *Partei die Friesen v Germany* (65480/10) (2017) 65 EHRR 27, 43-44.

[21] R *(Barclay) v Lord Chancellor and Secretary of State for Justice* [2010] 1 AC 464, at 64, per Lord Collins.

was *R (Barclay) v Lord Chancellor*.[22] Here, the Supreme Court held that A3P1 does not require that all members of a legislature be elected, though that was desirable. The presence of two non-voting but unelected members within the legislature was held not to impair the essence of the people's right to choose the legislature, nor deprive that right of its effectiveness, nor frustrate the free expression of the opinion of the people in the choice of the legislature. That was because the legislature was the 30-member Chief Pleas of Sark, a Crown Dependency of 500 people.

Campaign conditions: spending limits

6.18 In *Bowman v UK*,[23] the ECtHR held that free elections and freedom of political debate are *"interrelated and operate to reinforce each other"*, and that *"it is particularly important in the period preceding an election that opinions and information of all kinds are permitted to circulate freely"*.[24] In *Bowman*, the applicant anti-abortion campaigner successfully argued that restricting unauthorised campaigners' campaign spending to £5 (in 1998) violated article 10 ECHR, read in conjunction with A3P1.[25] The spending limit for unauthorised third party campaigners is now £20,000 in England,[26] £10,000 in each of Wales, Scotland or Northern Ireland,[27] and £250 in each constituency.[28]

Campaign conditions: equal treatment and broadcasting

6.19 The obligation on the state to provide *"conditions which will ensure the free expression of the opinion of the people in the choice of the legislature"* implies the principle of equality of treatment.[29]

6.20 A greater margin of appreciation is afforded to measure limiting campaigners' participation in elections that individuals' right to vote,[30] which is discussed below, but not so wide as to permit exclusion of certain persons from participating in the choice of the legislature.[31]

6.21 In *Communist Party of Russia v Russia*,[32] the applicants claimed that, notwithstanding Russian law guaranteeing neutrality of the broadcasting

---

[22] R *(Barclay) v Lord Chancellor and Secretary of State for Justice* [2010] 1 AC 464.
[23] *Bowman v UK* (24839/94) [1998] 26 EHRR 1, at 42.
[24] *Bowman v UK* (24839/94) [1998] 26 EHRR 1, at 42.
[25] *Bowman v UK* (24839/94) [1998] 26 EHRR 1, at 47.
[26] S 94(3(a)(i), (4) and (5) Political Parties Elections Referendums Act 2000 ("**PPERA 2000**"). See chapter 1.
[27] S 94(3(a)(i), (4) and (5) PPERA 2000. See chapter 1.
[28] S 94(3(a)(ii), (4) and (5ZA) PPERA 2000. See chapter 1.
[29] *Mathieu-Mohin v Belgium* (A/113) [1988] 10 EHRR 1 at 54.
[30] *Yumak v Turkey* (10226/03) [2009] 48 EHRR 4 at 109.
[31] *Yumak v Turkey* (10226/03) [2009] 48 EHRR 4 at 109.
[32] *Communist Party of Russia v Russia* (29400/05) (2015) 61 EHRR 28.

companies viz a viz pro-governmental and opposition parties, and proclaiming the principle of editorial independence of the broadcasting companies, in practice five TV channels had been predominantly hostile to the opposition parties and candidates, and this was a result of political manipulation by the executive authorities or the governing party, United Russia.[33] The ECtHR accepted that the arrangements in place did not secure *de facto* equality of all competing political forces in terms of their presence on TV screens, but found no violation of A3P1 because:

(i) There was no direct proof of abuse by the government of its *"dominant position in the capital or management of the TV companies"*;[34]

(ii) The applicants did not explain how, in the absence of complaint of undue pressure by journalists, it was possible to distinguish between propaganda and journalists and editors' choice as to how to express or weigh an item of information;[35]

(iii) As to the positive procedural obligation, recalling from its art 10 caselaw that, where a state decides *"to create a public broadcasting system, … domestic law and practice must guarantee that the system provides a pluralistic service"*,[36] the ECtHR held that the applicants had obtained some measure of access to the nation-wide TV channels, free and paid airtime, with no distinction made between the different political forces.[37]

6.22 In *R (Liberal Democrats and another) v ITV Broadcasting Ltd*,[38] the Divisional Court held that a decision by ITV to include in its general election programming a television debate featuring only the Prime Minister and leader of the opposition, to the exclusion of the leaders of SNP and the Liberal Democrats, did not offend against A3P1.[39] Besides ITV not being a public body obliged to act compatibly with the ECHR, the claim that this inequality of treatment was incompatible with A3P1 was *"untenable"* because it satisfied legislation and statutory codes on the impartiality of election broadcasting:[40] *"Parliament has, for the purposes of broadcasting in the context of elections, made*

---

[33] *Communist Party of Russia v Russia* (29400/05) (2015) 61 EHRR 28, at 113.

[34] *Communist Party of Russia v Russia* (29400/05) (2015) 61 EHRR 28, at 120.

[35] *Communist Party of Russia v Russia* (29400/05) (2015) 61 EHRR 28, at 120.

[36] *Manole v Romania* (13936/02) 17.9.09, at 101. The ECtHR found disproportionate interference with art 10 rights of journalists who complained of undue pressure by their managers and the government during the elections; *Communist Party of Russia v Russia* (29400/05) (2015) 61 EHRR 28, at 126.

[37] *Communist Party of Russia v Russia* (29400/05) (2015) 61 EHRR 28, at 126.

[38] R *(Liberal Democrats and another) v ITV Broadcasting Ltd* [2019] EWHC 3282 (Admin).

[39] 117.

[40] See chapter 3 for discussion of this law.

provision by the broadcasting legislation" and *"a wide margin of appreciation is conferred on national legal regimes in this regard"*.[41]

The campaign: the right of the public to honest information

6.23 Besides the right of campaigners and the media to equal treatment, the state's positive duty to put in place the conditions of free elections is also relevant to how those campaigners and the media, as well as parties and candidates, are allowed to influence voters. In *R (Woolas) v Parliamentary Election Court*,[42] in the context of a petition alleging and establishing s 106 false statement, Thomas LJ held: *"[d]ishonest statements are aimed at the destruction of the rights of the public to free elections (article 3 of the First Protocol to the Convention) and the right of each candidate to his reputation: article 8(1)"*.[43] The future Lord Chief Justice held that art 10 ECHR (freedom of expression) does not provide a counterbalance where the publisher knows the statements to be false, because article 17 ECHR prevents reliance on ECHR rights to justify acts aimed at the destruction of ECHR rights.[44]

6.24 Far from opposing A3P1's protection of this public interest, art 10 has been found by the ECtHR to also protect the public's right to receive information.[45] Art 10 and A3P1 thus together suggest that the conditions of free elections require protection from disinformation.

Challenges to elections: procedure

6.25 A failure to ensure the effective examination of complaints as to serious electoral irregularities violates A3P1.[46] Therefore, faced with an arguable petition as to election irregularities, unreasonable and excessively strict procedural barriers on a petition will be incompatible with the state's obligation to hold free elections.[47] For instance, an overly rigid approach to the admissibility of evidence may infringe A3P1.[48]

6.26 To ensure the effectiveness of the remedy, the court may be required to request evidence and investigate, rather than dismiss a claim for lack of evidence, e.g. in

---

[41] R *(Liberal Democrats and another) v ITV Broadcasting Ltd* [2019] EWHC 3282 (Admin), at 116, per Davis LJ and Warby J.

[42] *Watkins v Woolas* [2010] EWHC 3169 (Admin) (DC).

[43] *Watkins v Woolas* [2010] EWHC 3169 (Admin) (DC), at 105, per Thomas LJ.

[44] *Watkins v Woolas* [2010] EWHC 3169 (Admin) (DC), at 105.

[45] *Von Hannover v Germany* (40660/08 and 60641/08) [2012] 55 E.H.R.R. 15 at 118.

[46] *Davydov v Russia* (75947/11), 30.5.17 at 335.

[47] *Namat Aliyev v Azerbaijan* (18705/06), 8.4.10, at 88.

[48] *Namat Aliyev v Azerbaijan* (18705/06), 8.4.10, at 85 and 87 (refusal to consider complaints because affidavits not duly certified and documentary proof of having applied to the election commission not attached to the appeal); *Davydov and Others v Russia* (75947/11), 30.5.17 at 332-335.

a complaint alleging large scale ballot tampering[49] or alleging display of election notices in breach of election law.[50]

6.27 To avoid delaying the electoral process, considerations of expediency and the necessity for tight time-limits are often justified. In *Erlam v Rahman*,[51] the Divisional Court stated, *obiter*, that the strict time limits for bringing a petition do not infringe A3P1 nor art 6 (the right to a fair trial).[52] The court had already (without recourse to A3P1) declined to strike out a petition for breach of the requirement in rule 4(1)(d) of the Election Petition Rules 1960 ("**the Petition Rules**") to set out the particulars with sufficient particularity.[53]

6.28 The justification for expediency cannot however justify undermining the effectiveness of electoral procedures, including procedures for questioning elections.[54] In *Scarth v Amin*,[55] Tugendhat J acknowledged this principle as being amongst the legislative aims pursued by the Petition Rules: *"the rules requiring timely and proper presentation of a petition are strict, because it is in the public interest that there should be early clarity as to who has been elected"*.[56] Nonetheless, applying A3P1, he rejected the respondent's application for strike out of a petition that had failed to comply with rule 4 of the Petition Rules by omitting to set out the votes given for each candidate, stating:

> "On the other hand, there is a countervailing public interest that there should be free elections "under conditions which will ensure the free expression of the opinion of the people": see article 3 of the First Protocol to the European Convention for the Protection of Human Rights and Fundamental Freedoms and Part II of Schedule I to the Human Rights Act 1998. This principle has long been recognised in English law, and goes back before article 8 of the Bill of Rights 1689 (1 Will & Mary, sess 2, c 2), ("That election of Members of Parliament ought to be free"). For there to be free elections there must be a procedure for determining what opinion the people have expressed in cases where an election is questioned, and for elections to be declared void in appropriate cases. It would be wrong in principle to adopt an interpretation of the 1960 Rules which placed conditions upon the presentation of valid petitions which were more restrictive than

---

[49] *Namat Aliyev v Azerbaijan* (18705/06), 8.4.10, at 89.
[50] *Abil v Azerbaijan (No. 2)* (8513/11), 5.12.19, at 81.
[51] *Erlam v Rahman* [2014] EWHC 2766 (QB) (DC).
[52] *Erlam v Rahman* [2014] EWHC 2766 (QB) (DC), at 40, per Supperstone and Spencer JJ.
[53] *Erlam v Rahman* [2014] EWHC 2766 (QB) (DC), at 26, per Supperstone and Spencer JJ.
[54] *Namat Aliyev v Azerbaijan* (18705/06), 8.4.10, at 81 and 90; *Orujov v Azerbaijan (4508/06)*, 26.7.11, at 56; *Abil v Azerbaijan (No. 2)* (8513/11), 5.12.19, at 75.
[55] *Scarth v Amin* [2008] EWHC 2886 (QB).
[56] *Scarth v Amin* [2008] EWHC 2886 (QB), at 16.

necessary to achieve the certainty that is required, and which obstructed the determination of what opinion the people had expressed."[57]

6.29 Tugendhat J returned to this balance in *Jim Miller v (1) Chris Bull (Returning Officer of Herefordshire Council (2) Benson Ferrari (3) DPP*,[58] to consider the preclusion of extension of petition time limits by r 19 of the Petition Rules. He held that, to the extent that r 19 meant that an arguable petition fell to be struck out, it was incompatible with art 6 and A3P1 ECHR and consequently fell to be read down pursuant to s 3 HRA 1998 so as to remove that incompatibility. Nothing in the primary legislation prevented that reading, so this s 3 interpretation was possible. He again reasoned according to A3P1 and its forebear in the Bill of Rights 1689:

> "43 It seemed to me that the major interest at stake in an election petition is not the private right of a petitioner, but the rights of the public. There is a public interest that there should be free elections held "under conditions which will ensure the free expression of the opinion of the people": see article 3 of the First Protocol to the Convention and Schedule 1 to the 1998 Act. This principle has long been recognised in English law. The Statute of Westminster 1275 (3 Edw 1, c 29) "elections ought to be free. . .") and article 8 of the Bill of Rights 1689 "That Election of Members of Parliament ought to be free") are both in force to this day. For there to be free elections there must be a procedure for determining what opinion the people have expressed in those cases where an election is questioned, and for elections to be declared void in appropriate cases. I suggested to Mr Lock that if there is any argument that could be advanced against the conclusion of the Court of Appeal in *Ahmed v Kennedy* [2003] 1 WLR 1820, then an argument based on that public interest might have a better prospect of success than an argument based on the private rights of a petitioner. He adopted that suggestion."[59]

6.30 In *Stoddart and Hume*,[60] the High Court rejected the argument that s 3 HRA 1998 enabled it to read s 136(1) RPA 1983 as giving it the power to extend time to pay security for costs. The court's reasoning was that, unlike in *Miller*, which concerned secondary legislation in the form of the Petition Rules, the security for costs rule was contained in primary legislation.[61] This decision led the High

---

[57] *Scarth v Amin* [2008] EWHC 2886 (QB), at 17.
[58] *Jim Miller v (1) Chris Bull (Returning Officer of Herefordshire Council (2) Benson Ferrari (3) DPP* [2009] EWHC 2640 (QB).
[59] *Miller v (1) Chris Bull (Returning Officer of Herefordshire Council (2) Benson Ferrari (3) DPP* [2009] EWHC 2640 (QB).
[60] *Stoddart and Hume v Garland and Little* [2014] EWHC 2817.
[61] *Stoddart and Hume v Garland and Little* [2014] EWHC 2817, at 26, per Supperstone and Jay JJ.

Court to reach the same conclusion in *Waghorn v Fry*,[62] on the same reasoning,[63] Slade J adding: *"As did the Divisional Court, Laws J, (as he then was) and Forbes J, in Absalom v Gillett [1995] 1 WLR 128 in respect of other formalities, I reach this conclusion with considerable regret"*.[64]

6.31 The regret may have been avoidable, as s 3 HRA 1998 applies to both primary and secondary legislation.[65] The only difference with primary legislation is that, if it cannot be read or given effect compatibly with ECHR rights, it must still be given effect, unlike secondary legislation.[66] The limits on the courts' power in s 3 HRA 1998 are to its interpretive power, limits famously described by Lord Nicholls in the following terms:

> "Section 3 enables language to be interpreted restrictively or expansively. But section 3 goes further than this. It is also apt to require a court to read in words which change the meaning of the enacted legislation, so as to make it Convention-compliant. In other words, the intention of Parliament in enacting section 3 was that, to an extent bounded only by what is 'possible', a court can modify the meaning, and hence the effect, of primary and secondary legislation."[67]

Challenges to elections: grounds

6.32 Amongst the positive duties on the state imposed by A3P1 is a duty to put in place a *"domestic system for effective examination of individual complaints and appeals in matters concerning electoral rights"*, which *"is one of the essential guarantees of free and fair elections"*, without which the other rights protected by A3P1 *"would be illusory"*.[68]

6.33 A3P1 is not concerned with whether an allegation of irregularity amounts to breach of election law, rather whether the election was held under free and fair conditions that ensured the effective exercise of voters and candidates' rights.[69] Thus A3P1 will not constitute a petition ground, additional to those provided by the statutory scheme described in Chapter 5.[70] Conversely, the limited

---

[62] *Waghorn v Fry* [2015] EWHC 744 (QB).
[63] *Waghorn v Fry* [2015] EWHC 744 (QB), at 32, per Slade J.
[64] *Waghorn v Fry* [2015] EWHC 744 (QB), at 34, per Slade J.
[65] S 3(1)(b) and (c) HRA 1998.
[66] S 3(1)(b) and (c) HRA 1998.
[67] *Ghaidan v Godin-Mendoza* [2004] UKHL 30, at 32, per Lord Nicholls.
[68] *Namat Aliyev v Azerbaijan* (18705/06), 8.4.10, at 81.
[69] *Namat Aliyev v Azerbaijan* (18705/06), 8.4.10, at 77; and c.f. *Communist Party of Russia v Russia* (29400/05) (2015) 61 EHRR 28, at 124.
[70] Discussed in Chapter 5.

function of an Election Court mean that it cannot, pursuant to s 3 HRA 1998, read down the statutory consequences of a finding of illegal practice.[71]

6.34 However, where A3P1 will be relevant to the Election Court's functions is to how it interprets the electoral law legislation engaged in the petition before it.[72] In *R (Woolas) v Parliamentary Election Court*,[73] the Divisional Court held that the Election Court had been right to take the ECHR (art 10) into account, but that the basis on which it did so was incorrect.[74] The Election Court had held that art 10's application was to the effect that the Election Court should only find an illegal practice in clear cases[75] and should determine whether the consequences were proportionate.[76] The Divisional Court held that any disproportionate consequence of the findings of the Election Court must be taken into account in its determination of whether it should find there had been an illegal practice (in the first place), not subsequently, as mitigation (which the statute, even by s 3 HRA 1998, does not allow).[77] Thus, in practice, A3P1's chief relevance is as interpretive lens to the legislation.

C. ACTIVE ASPECT: THE RIGHT TO VOTE

Franchise

6.35 A restriction of suffrage to persons with citizenship and resident in the country does not infringe A3P1.[78]

6.36 An indiscriminate removal of voting rights based on mental disability necessitating partial guardianship, without an individualised judicial evaluation has been held to violate the right to vote.[79]

6.37 Restricting the electoral rights of persons who have been the subject of civil bankruptcy proceedings for no other reason than their bankruptcy infringes the right to vote and does not pursue a legitimate aim.[80]

---

[71] R *(Woolas) v Parliamentary Election Court* [2010] EWHC 3169 (Admin) (DC), at 94.
[72] R *(Woolas) v Parliamentary Election Court* [2010] EWHC 3169 (Admin) (DC), at 95 per Thomas LJ.
[73] R *(Woolas) v Parliamentary Election Court* [2010] EWHC 3169 (Admin) (DC).
[74] R *(Woolas) v Parliamentary Election Court* [2010] EWHC 3169 (Admin) (DC), at 94.
[75] *Watkins v Woolas* [2010] EWHC 2702 (QB), at 74-75.
[76] *Watkins v Woolas* [2010] EWHC 2702 (QB), at 208-209.
[77] R *(Woolas) v Parliamentary Election Court* [2010] EWHC 3169 (Admin) (DC), at 95.
[78] *Alliance des Belges de la Communaute Europeenne v Belgium* (8612/79) [1979] 3 CMLR 175, European Commission on Human Rights (admissibility); *Re Expatriate United Kingdom Citizen* (8611/79) [1979] 3 CMLR 172, European Commission on Human Rights (admissibility).
[79] *Kiss v Hungary* (38832/06) 20.5.10, at 43-44.
[80] *Campagnano v Italy* (77955/01) 23.3.06, at 49.

6.38 A blanket disenfranchisement of convicted prisoners regardless of the nature of the offence or length of sentence has been held to be disproportionate.[81] By contrast, a system of disenfranchisement for a period of variable duration for prisoners serving three to five year terms, but permanent disenfranchisement for persons sentenced to more than five years and who failed to demonstrate prescribed rehabilitation whilst in prison has been held to have sufficient sliding scale not to violate A3P1.[82] In practice, this is the greater interference with the right to vote, but the element of variability and the fact that it was not a blanket measure was sufficient to persuade the ECtHR to find no violation.

6.39 The dissolution of parliament and postponement of new elections has been found to violate the entire voting population's right to vote.[83]

Registration

6.40 Registration, as a precondition to exercising voting rights, has the potential to engage A3P1 and to be incompatible with it where exercised unjustifiably. In *R (Robertson) v Wakefield MDC*,[84] the claimant challenged the refusal of an election registration officer ("**ERO**") to ensure that his details would not be supplied to commercial organisations despite his objection. The government had enacted regulations permitting EROs to supply a copy or copies of the register to any person on payment of a prescribed fee. The claimant challenged the refusal on grounds that he should not have to accept the sale of his data to commercial interests as a precondition to his registration, and in turn his A3P1 right to vote. The court held that the lack of a right to object was sufficient to render the refusal disproportionate with A3P1. Maurice Kay J held:

> "[I]f and to the extent that the 1986 and 2001 Regulations make the right to vote conditional upon acquiescence in the sale of the register to commercial concerns for marketing purposes, with no individual right of objection, they operate in a manner which contravenes article 3 of the First Protocol unless they are justifiable by reference to the criteria set out by the European Court of Justice in the *Mathien-Mohin* case."[85]

6.41 The regulation empowering the ERO to sell the register and list of overseas electors was subsequently revoked.[86] Legislation enabling regulations permitting sale of an edited form of the registers, excluding those who had objected, had

---

[81] *Hirst v UK (No 2)* (2005) 42 EHRR 849 (GC); and see, earlier, *Moohan v Lord Advocate* [2014] UKSC 67, at 69, per Lord Kerr.

[82] *Scoppola v Italy (No.3)* (126/05) (2013) 56 EHRR 19, at 103-106.

[83] *Russian Conservative Party of Entrepreneurs and Others v Russia* (55066/00 55638/00), 11.1.07, at 74, citing Commission report in the Greek case, Yearbook 12, pp. 179-80.

[84] R *(Robertson) v Wakefield MDC* [2001] EWHC Admin 915.

[85] R *(Robertson) v Wakefield MDC* [2001] EWHC Admin 915, at 42.

[86] Reg 3(1) Representation of the People (England and Wales) (Amendment) Regulations 2002.

already received royal assent, and regulations made thereto were amended to grant right to request exclusion.[87]

Overseas voters

6.42 In *Riza and Others v Bulgaria*,[88] the ECtHR held that A3P1 requires the implementation by the state of measures to allow expatriates to exercise their right to vote from their place of residence, as *"the presumption in a democratic State must be in favour of inclusion, [and] such measures are consonant with that provision"*.[89]

6.43 In *Shindler v UK*,[90] the 15-year condition in s 1(3)(c) RPA 1985, which allows non-resident British citizens to vote for 15 years after leaving the country, was held proportionate to the legitimate aim of not weighing interests on a case-by-case basis; namely: legal certainty and avoiding the problems of arbitrariness and inconsistency inherent in that alternative.[91] In *R (Preston) v Wandsworth LBC*,[92] the Court of Appeal reached the same conclusion, finding additional justification, *obiter*, from A3P1.

Choice

6.44 The free expression of the opinion of the people requires the participation of multiple political parties representing the different shades of opinion to be found within a country's population, but the right to vote does not guarantee that every voter should be able to find on the ballot paper the candidate or the party they had intended to vote for.[93] In *Russian Conservative Party of Entrepreneurs v Russia*,[94] it was alleged that refusal to register a party's list, due to substantially inaccurate information as to the candidates on it, violated its supporters' right to cast a vote for the party of their choice. The ECtHR held there was no violation of A3P1 because it was necessary to have regard to the broader context in which the right to vote could be exercised and that context featured more than 25 political parties and electoral blocs representing *"a broad gamut of political views and platforms"*.[95] If the applicant did not like any of

---

[87] Reg 93A RP (E&W) Regs 2001.

[88] *Riza and Others v Bulgaria* (48555/10 48377/10), 13.10.15.

[89] *Riza and Others v Bulgaria* (48555/10 48377/10), 13.10.15, at 140.

[90] *Shindler v UK* (19840/09), 7.5.13.

[91] *Shindler v UK* (19840/09), 7.5.13, at 116

[92] R *(Preston) v Wandsworth* [2012] EWCA Civ 1378, at 85-87, per Mummery LJ.

[93] *Russian Conservative Party of Entrepreneurs and Others v Russia* (55066/00 55638/00), 11.1.07, at 79.

[94] *Russian Conservative Party of Entrepreneurs and Others v Russia* (55066/00 55638/00), 11.1.07.

[95] *Russian Conservative Party of Entrepreneurs and Others v Russia* (55066/00 55638/00), 11.1.07, at 80.

them, he could vote *"against all candidates"*, as more than two millions others had.[96]

D. PASSIVE ASPECT: THE RIGHT TO STAND FOR ELECTION

Scope

6.45 A3P1 also applies to political parties, where they seek to present a list of candidates to participate in an election.[97] It also extends to the right of the candidate, once elected, to sit as a member of parliament.[98]

6.46 In addition to a right to be able to stand for election, this limb of A3P1 entails a right to do so freely and effectively, in fair and democratic conditions.[99] Illustrations of the parameters of this principle are set out below.

Application

6.47 Governments have broad latitude to establish criteria for declaring persons ineligible to stand for parliament,[100] but must avoid arbitrary disqualification and contain sufficient safeguards to protect candidates from unfounded allegations of misconduct.[101]

6.48 The following restrictions have been held not to thwart *"the free expression of the opinion of the people in the choice of the legislature"* protected by A3P1:

(i) Prohibitions on civil servants from standing for election;[102]

(ii) A residence requirement;[103]

(iii) The requirement to pay a deposit and making reimbursement conditional on exceeding a minimum of votes;[104]

---

[96] *Russian Conservative Party of Entrepreneurs and Others v Russia* (55066/00 55638/00), 11.1.07, at 80.

[97] *Georgian Labour Party v Georgia* (9103/04), 8.7.08, at 72-74; *Yabloko Russian United Democratic Party and others v Russia (18860/07)*, 8.11.16, at 66.

[98] *Sadak v Turkey (no. 2)* (25144/94, 26149/95 to 26154/95, 27100/95 and 27101/95), at 33; *Lykourezos* (33554/03), at 50; *Riza and Others v Bulgaria* (48555/10 and 48377/10), 13.10.15, at 41.

[99] *Namat Aliyev v Azerbaijan* (18705/06), 8.4.10, at 75.

[100] *Podkolzina v Latvia (46726/99)*, 9.4.02, at 33.

[101] *Abil v Azerbaijan (No. 2)* (8513/11), 5.12.19, at 70.

[102] *Ahmed v UK* [2000] 29 EHRR 1 (local authority solicitor); *Gitonas v Greece* [1998] 26 EHRR 691, 44 (secondee to position of deputy head of PM's office).

[103] *Melnychenko v Ukraine (17707/02)* [2006] 42 EHRR 39 (refugee from Ukraine living in the United States).

[104] *Russian Conservative Party of Entrepreneurs and Others v Russia* (55066/00 55638/00), 11.1.07, at 94.

(iv) A ban from standing as a candidate imposed on a former member of the Latvian Communist Party, who had actively participated in its activities before its dissolution with the fall of the USSR, on the basis that she could be presumed to be anti-democratic: *"While such a measure may scarcely be considered acceptable in the context of one political system, for example in a country which has an established framework of democratic institutions going back many decades or centuries, it may nonetheless be considered acceptable in Latvia"*;[105]

(v) A requirement that candidacy involve a single candidate and not a job share is compatible with A3P1;[106]

(vi) Exclusion of unaffiliated independent candidates from access to election broadcast transmissions (reserving this entitlement to national political parties).[107]

6.49 The following have been held to be a disproportionate interference with the right:

(i) Removal from a candidates list for insufficient knowledge of a country's official language, a disproportionate interference with the A3P1 right to stand of a candidate from a minority ethnic group;[108]

(ii) Delays in candidate registration, due to delays in determining challenges to nomination decisions, preventing them having as much time to campaign as other candidates;[109]

(iii) The permanent disqualification of an impeached president from standing not just for re-election as president but also as a member of parliament.[110]

E. ECtHR PROCEEDINGS

6.50 Following exhaustion of domestic judicial remedies, application may be made to the ECtHR under art 34 ECHR. To be considered, the application must satisfy the admissibility criteria at art 35 ECHR:

---

[105] *Zdanoka v Latvia* (58278/00) [2007] 45 EHRR 478, at 133. The ECtHR held: *"While such a measure may scarcely be considered acceptable in the context of one political system, for example in a country which has an established framework of democratic institutions going back many decades or centuries, it may nonetheless be considered acceptable in Latvia"*.

[106] R *(Cope) v Returning Officer for the Basingstoke Parliamentary Constituency* [2015] EWHC 3958 (Admin).

[107] *Oran v Turkey* (28881/07 37920/07), 15.4.14, at 73-75.

[108] *Podkolzina v Latvia (46726/99)*, 9.4.02,

[109] *Abdalov And Others v Azerbaijan (28508/11, 37602/11, 43776/11)*, 11.7.19, at 103.

[110] *Paksas v Lithuania* (34932/04), 6.1.11, at 110-112.

(i) The applicant must have exhausted all domestic remedies;

(ii) The application must be lodged within six months of the date of the final domestic court decision;

(iii) It may not anonymous, nor substantially the same as a matter that has already been examined by the ECtHR;

(iv) The application must be compatible with the ECHR and abuse of the right of individual application;

(v) The application must not be *"manifestly ill-founded"*;

(vi) The applicant must have suffered a *"significant disadvantage"*, unless the general interests of protecting human rights requires examination of the merits of the application.[111]

6.51 The application must comply with rule 47 of the ECtHR Rules of Court.[112] In 2016, 82% of applications were declared inadmissible, 51% of which were rejected as manifestly ill-founded.[113]

6.52 The ECtHR's jurisdiction in determining whether there was an unjustified interference in *"the free expression of the opinion of the people in the choice of the legislature"* is confined to establishing whether the decision given by the domestic court was arbitrary or manifestly unreasonable.[114] The ECtHR affords a margin of deference to the national authorities, legislative and judicial, based on *"their direct and continuous contact with the vital forces of their countries"*, considering them therefore *"better placed to assess the difficulties faced in establishing and safeguarding the democratic order in their state"*.[115]

---

[111]Article 35 ECHR.

[112]'Your application to the ECHR: How to apply and how your application is processed'.

[113]https://app.echr.coe.int/CheckList/?lang=eng&cookieCheck=true [accessed 14.5.2020].

[114]*Babenko v Ukraine* (43476/98), 4.5.99; *Partija 'Jaunie Demokrati" and Partija 'Musu Zeme" v Latvia* (10547/07 and 34049/07), 29.11.07; *Kerimli and Alibeyli*, at 38-42; *Riza and Others v Bulgaria* (48555/10 48377/10), 13.10.15, at 143.

[115] *Animal Defenders International v UK* (48876/08) (GC), at 111; *Oran v Turkey* (28881/07 37920/07), 15.4.14, at 75.

CHAPTER SEVEN
REFORM

7.1 This book goes to press at a time of proliferating calls for reform to election law, culminating in some commitments in the December 2019 Queen's Speech and the Government's response to some of the proposals.

7.2 Those reform proposals already adopted by HMG and some of those still awaiting adoption are presented in this final chapter, to give the reader a concluding view on the changes that may and will soon befall the body of law set out in the foregoing chapters. The reform proposals discussed below concern the following areas of election law:

A. Election integrity;

B. Online campaigning;

C. Consolidation and rationalisation of electoral law;

D. New electoral offence of intimidation;

E. The Commission;

F. Petitions.

A. ELECTION INTEGRITY

7.3 In its October and December 2019 Queen's Speeches, the Government announced plans to *"launch a consultation on electoral integrity that will consider measures to strengthen the provisions that protect our democracy from foreign interference and to refresh our laws for the digital age"*.[1]

7.4 In the Background Briefing Note to the December 2019 Queen's Speech, the Government declared its intention to implement measures designed to prevent ballot tampering, personation, and postal vote offences, including:

(i) Requiring an approved form of photographic ID at a polling station in parliamentary elections and local elections in England, building on the requirement already in place in Northern Ireland and piloted in 2019

[1]Queen's Speech, October 2019, p 105; Queen's Speech, December 2019, Background Briefing Note, p 127.

in England, and a proposal also made in the October 2019 Queen's Speech, citing the findings of the *Erlam v Rahman*[2] election petition;[3]

(ii) As to postal votes: *"banning campaigners from handling postal votes, introducing a power to limit the number of postal votes a person may hand-in, and establishing a requirement on those registered for a postal vote to re-apply every three years"*;

(iii) *"Limiting the number of people a voter may act for as a proxy to two electors, regardless of their relationship"*.[4]

B. ONLINE CAMPAIGNING

7.5 In February 2019, the House of Commons' Digital, Culture, Media and Sports Committee published the final report from its 18-month inquiry into disinformation and misinformation ("**the DCMS Report**").[5] It concluded:

(i) *"Electoral law is not fit for purpose and needs to be changed to reflect changes in campaigning techniques, and the move from physical leaflets and billboards to online, microtargeted political campaigning. There needs to be: absolute transparency of online political campaigning, including clear, persistent banners on all paid-for political adverts and videos, indicating the source and the advertiser; a category introduced for digital spending on campaigns; and explicit rules surrounding designated campaigners' role and responsibilities. ... Recipients should be able to identify the source, who uploaded it, who sponsored it, and its country of origin."*[6]

(ii) *"Political advertising items should be publicly accessible in a searchable repository— who is paying for the ads, which organisations are sponsoring the ad, who is being targeted by the ads—so that members of the public can understand the behaviour of individual advertisers. It should be run independently of the advertising industry and of political parties."*[7]

7.6 In the October 2019 Queen's Speech, the Government adopted the first of these recommendations, announcing plans to bring forward the technical implementation of an *"imprints regime"* for digital election material, in order to *"ensure greater transparency and make it clearer to the electorate who has produced and promoted online political materials"*.[8]

---

[2] *Erlam v Rahman* [2015] EWHC 1215 (QB).
[3] Queen's Speech and Associated Background Briefing, on the Occasion of the Opening of Parliament, 14.10.19, p 106.
[4] Queen's Speech, December 2019, Background Briefing Note, p 126.
[5] DCMS Committee Report, HC 1791, 18.2.19.
[6] DCMS Committee Report, HC 1791, 18.2.19, p 92.
[7] DCMS Committee Report, HC 1791, 18.2.19, p 93.
[8] Queen's Speech, October 2019, p 105.

7.7 By way of enforcement of this digital imprint requirement, the DCMS Committee and the Electoral Commission have also called for the strengthening of the latter's powers to compel social media companies to disclose information.[9]

7.8 On 30.1.2020, the Elections (Candidates' Expenditure and Nominations) Bill ("**HL Bill 78**") had its first reading. To the current list of matters constituting candidate election expenses,[10] which in respect to unsolicited material addressed to voters currently only covers material *"addressed to them by name or intended for delivery to households within any particular area)"*,[11] HL Bill 78 would add *"the cost of displaying digital advertising"* where it identifies the candidate, or is *"aimed at voters in the specific electoral area in which the candidate is standing and are aimed to promote or secure the election of that candidate"*.[12]

7.9 In its March 2020 final report, the Law Commission recommended the extension to online campaign material of the requirement[13] that printed campaign material be imprinted with the name and address of its printer, promoter, any person on behalf of whom the material is being published.[14]

C. CONSOLIDATION AND RATIONALISATION OF ELECTORAL LAW

7.10 In October 2019, the House of Commons Public Administration and Constitutional Affairs Committee ("**PACAC**") published a report[15] recommending the urgent updating of electoral law, stating:

> "Consolidation of electoral law would help make information on the requirements on candidates and their agents more accessible which is particularly important for people wishing to stand as independents and would help make it easier to comply with the law"[16]

and

> "Under the current body of electoral law, nearly everyone involved in a general election faces significant risks or challenges. A primary cause of this is the archaic and confusing state of electoral law. This is not an

[9]Electoral Commission, Reforming electoral law, p 4; DCMS Committee Report, HC 1791, 18.2.19, p 92, para 24.
[10]Sch 4A RPA 1983.
[11]Para 2 sch 4A RPA 1983.
[12]Cl 2(3) HL Bill 78.
[13]S 110 RPA 1983.
[14]Para 15.77.
[15]PACAC, 'Electoral Law: The Urgent Need for Review', 31.10.19.
[16]PACAC, 'Electoral Law: The Urgent Need for Review', 31.10.19, p 23, para 1.

acceptable state of affairs. The updating and simplification of electoral law must be seen as a pressing priority for the Government."[17]

7.11 In the final report from its 2012-2020 electoral law reform project, the Law Commission recommended that:

(i) *"[C]urrent laws governing elections should be rationalised into a single, consistent legislative framework governing all elections"*,[18] to address a legislative landscape featuring 50 pieces of primary legislation and 170 secondary, in which *"[e]ach type of election or referendum was governed by its bespoke piece of secondary legislation setting out its own election or referendum rules"* and *"The number of sources of electoral laws therefore grew with each newly introduced poll"*;[19]

(ii) Franchises for all elections should be set out in primary legislation,[20] the law on special category voters should be set out in a single regime,[21] there should be one electoral register,[22] a uniform set of rules to govern the postal voting process,[23] a single set of rules in primary legislation to govern the count at all elections,[24] a standard legislative timetable of 28 days should apply to all elections,[25] a single schedule setting out rules on all the prescribed expense limits and rules governing expenditure and donations,[26] restating the grounds for correcting the outcome or invalidating elections;[27] and

(iii) The rationalising of electoral offences: (a) the abolition of the offence of treating and the conduct prosecuted as bribery;[28] (b) the abolition of the offence of falsely stating that a candidate has withdrawn and the conduct treated as undue influence by deception;[29] (c) restating 'undue influence' as offences of intimidation, deception and improper pressure.[30]

---

[17]PACAC, 'Electoral Law: The Urgent Need for Review', 31.10.19, p 23, para 6.
[18]Law Commission and Scottish Law Commission, 'Electoral Law: a joint final report', HC145 SG/2020/35, Law Com No 389, Scot Law Com No 256 ("Law Com No 389"), paras 2.247 and 15.1.
[19]Law Com No 389, 2.10.
[20]Law Com No 389, para 15.7.
[21]Law Com No 389, para 15.9.
[22]Law Com No 389, para 15.13.
[23]Law Com No 389, para 15.30.
[24]Law Com No 389, para 15.55.
[25]Law Com No 389, para 15.65 and 15.66.
[26]Para 15.82.
[27]Para 15.88.
[28]Para 15.74.
[29]Para 15.79.
[30]Para 15.75.

7.12 The Electoral Commission has called for candidate election expenses be brought within its regulation of donations and spending by parties, non-party campaigners, office-holders, members, and members associations.[31] Currently it falls outside the Commission's investigative and civil sanctions auspices, leaving enforcement to the possibility of prosecution.[32]

7.13 Responding to the PACAC report, the Government stated: *"Whilst the Government agrees that the clarification of electoral law would certainly be beneficial, we are aware of more immediate challenges outside of the structure of electoral legislation, including operations, resilience, fraud and confidence"*.[33]

D. NEW ELECTORAL OFFENCE OF INTIMIDATION

7.14 Whilst not acceding to the PACAC report's recommendation that election offences be rationalised and restructured as summarised above (including undue influence becoming intimidation, deception and improper pressure), in its 13.5.2020 response to the committee's report, the Government nonetheless, expressed intention *"to attach electoral sanctions to existing criminal law offences of intimidation when they are committed against a candidate or campaigner during an election period. Nothing that is currently legal under criminal law will be made illegal. The individual found guilty of the offence would be prohibited from standing for any public office for up to five years."*[34]

E. THE COMMISSION

7.15 The Commission's draft statutory Code of Practice on qualifying expenses for political parties awaits approval by the Home Secretary,[35] whereupon it will be laid before both Houses of Parliament, which may resolve not to approve it or let it pass (the negative resolution procedure). Where a registered party treasurer, deputy treasurer, or third party campaigner uses the Code of Practice to determine the items and amounts of campaign expenditure to be entered in their spending return, and the total they arrive at is less than the relevant spending limit, they (and their party if they are a treasurer or deputy) will have a defence to any charge of breaching that limit.[36] There is thus strong incentive to follow it, as well as appreciable clarity being provided to stakeholders.

---

[31]Electoral Commission, Reforming electoral law, p 4.

[32]Candidates' election expenses are discussed in chapter 3.

[33]Government response to the Public Administration and Constitutional Affairs Committee's report Electoral Law: 'The Urgent Need for Review', p 2.

[34]PACAC, 'Electoral law: The Urgent Need for Review: Government Response to the Committee's First Report of Session 2019', HC 327, 15.5.2020, p 10.

[35]Paragraph 142 Explanatory Notes Political Parties, Elections and Referendums Act 2000 ("**PPERA 2000**").

[36]Ss 79(3) and 94(4A) and 94E(4) PPERA 2000.

7.16 Observing that the Electoral Commission's current maximum fine limit of £20,000 was a mere cost of doing business to some campaigners, the DCMS Committee and the Electoral Commission have called for it to be increased and changed to a fine based on a fixed percentage of turnover, in line with powers already conferred on the ICO.[37]

F. PETITIONS

7.17 In the mid to late 19th century, many of the cases that developed and now form modern election law were decided. In relation to local elections, many were brought by the Crown seeking a rule of *quo warranto* ('by what warrant'),[38] as a remedy against a person alleged to be improperly holding office, calling on them to show by what right they held that office and, if they were unable, because the court found them to have been improperly elected, the court could grant a writ of *quo warranto* to oust them from that office.[39] On the other hand, if the right person had been duly elected, and it was not shown that anyone else had been kept out of office nor the result of the election in any way affected, the Court would not allow the writ to issue.[40] Individuals too could apply for *quo warranto*.[41]

7.18 The procedure was then superseded by enactment of statutory provisions making election petitions the exclusive means of questioning elections,[42] though there was some judicial activity asserting *quo warranto*'s continued place.[43] This legislation brought local elections into line with Parliamentary elections, for which petitions had been declared the exclusive means of challenge by the founding statute transferring them from the House of Commons to the judiciary.[44]

7.19 In 1998, the Neill Committee, whilst recommending the creation of the Commission (*"a totally independent and authoritative Election Commission with widespread executive and investigative powers"*), in addition to recommending that it take over responsibility for the registration of political parties, stated that

---

[37] Electoral Commission, Reforming electoral law, p 3; DCMS Committee Report, p 92.

[38] Statute 4 & 5 W. & M. c. 18, s 2.

[39] *R v Blizard* [1866-67] LR 2 QB 55; *R v White* (1866-67) LR 2 QB 557; *R. v Parkinson* (1867-68) LR 3 QB 11; *R v Chester Corporation* 25 L J (QB) 61; *R v Tugwell* (1867-68) LR 3 QB 704; *R. v Oldham* (1868-69) LR 4 QB 290; *R v Plenty* (1868-69) L.R. 4 Q. 346; *R v Diplock* (1868-69) L.R. 4 QB 549; *R. v Cooper* (John) (1869-70) LR 5 QB 457; *R v Cousins* (1872-73) L.R. 8 Q.B. 216; *R v Harrald* (1872-73) LR 8 QB 418; *R v Welchpool Corporation*; *R v Beer* [1876] 35 LT 594, pp 693 and 700-701; *Forrester v Norton* [1911] 2 KB 953, p 956, per Channel J.

[40] R v Cousins (1872-73) L.R. 8 Q.B. 216, per Blackburn J.

[41] *Hindmarch, Ex p.* (1867-68) L.R. 3 Q.B. 12.

[42] S 87 Municipal Corporations Act 1882; *R v Morton* [1892] 1 Q.B. 39.

[43] *R v Beer*, p 698, per Lord Alverstone CJ, and p 700, per Channell J.

[44] S 50 Parliamentary Elections Act.

the Commission should have *"the right to bring cases before an election court for judgment".*[45]

7.20 In the modern era of election petitions, those appointed to try them have questioned the adequacy of leaving them to private individuals. Giving judgment in *Ali v Bashir*,[46] Commissioner Richard Mawrey QC stated:

> "The December order also required the parties to list the matter for further directions on a date to be fixed not less than 21 days from 20 December 2012. They did not. Indeed, apart from requesting amendments to the original order concerning the access of the parties and the Police to the original documents, nothing was done about directions for six months. Gentle prodding from me produced no results. As neither protagonist had access to litigation insurance or funds from his respective party, the Petition, as so often, was being conducted on a shoestring, thus emphasising once again, as in Birmingham and Slough, the utter unsuitability of the election Petition as a means of unmasking fraud and ensuring clean elections."[47]

7.21 In 2015, in his judgment in the petition *Erlam v Rahman*,[48] Commissioner Richard Mawrey QC went further, stating:

> "The Petition system is obsolete and unfit for purpose. It is wholly unreasonable to leave it to defeated candidates or concerned electors, like the present Petitioners, to undertake the arduous and extremely expensive task of bringing proceedings and pursuing them to a conclusion entirely at their own expense and with the risk of bankruptcy if they fail to surmount the Grand National sized fences placed in the path of Petitioners. We do not leave it to the victim of burglary or fraud (*a fortiori* the victim of rape) to bring civil proceedings against the perpetrator as the only way of achieving justice. Why do we leave it to the victims of electoral fraud to go it alone?",[49]

and

> "Furthermore, if they do win and are awarded their costs against the respondent, the latter, who is turned out of office and frequently then

[45]Fifth Report of the Committee on Standards in Public Life, 'The Funding of Political Parties in the United Kingdom', October 1998, Cm 4057–I, Volume 1: Report, S.10.
[46]*Ali v Bashir* [2013] EWHC 2572 (QB).
[47]*Ali v Bashir* [2013] EWHC 2572 (QB), at 101.
[48]*Erlam v Rahman* [2015] EWHC 1215 (QB).
[49]*Erlam v Rahman* [2015] EWHC 1215 (QB), at 665.

> prosecuted to conviction, is unlikely to be able to pay those costs. A petitioner's victory is often Pyrrhic."[50]

7.22 In its February 2019 final report, the DCMS Committee concluded that *"The Government should explore ways in which the Electoral Commission can be given more powers to carry out its work comprehensively, including ... [t]he ability for the Electoral Commission to petition against an election due to illegal actions, which currently can only be brought by an individual"*.[51]

7.23 In its October 2019 report, PACAC stated:

> "The election petition system for challenging elections is archaic, too complicated and not fit for purpose. It is in the public interest that meritorious election petitions are brought forward but the [sic] under the current system there is a risk that such petitions will not be brought forward, due to the complexity of the process and the level of potential cost. We agree with the Law Commission's recommendation that that the election petition system is brought into the modern court system. As part of any such reform, the Government must ensure the right balance is struck between ensuring access to justice for electors and also preventing vexatious attempts to challenge elections."[52]

7.24 On 16.3.2020, the Law Commission published its final report on electoral law, and demurred from recommending a public interest petitioner:

> "Despite support for the principle of a public interest petitioner, and the uncomfortable position of relying on private actors to test the validity and outcome of elections – at great financial cost and risk – we were not persuaded to recommend that there should be a public interest petitioner. The practical difficulties involved in introducing the concept – notably the question of who should be given that function, and how they might avoid having their political neutrality called into question - were grounds for caution."[53]

7.25 The Commission is already exposed to criticism of bias where it intervenes.[54] Yet where bias is alleged in legal challenge, the allegation has been given short shrift.[55]

---

[50] *Erlam v Rahman* [2015] EWHC 1215 (QB), at 666.

[51] DCMS Committee Report, p 93.

[52] PACAC, 'Electoral Law: The Urgent Need for Review', 31.10.19, p 23, para 4.

[53] Law Com No 389, para 13.50.

[54] R *(English Democrats Party) v Electoral Commission* [2018] EWHC 251 (Admin) [2018] 4 W.L.R. 54, at 51.

[55] R *(English Democrats Party) v Electoral Commission* [2018] EWHC 251 (Admin) [2018] 4 W.L.R. 54, at 51.

7.26 Instead of a public interest petitioner, the Law Commission recommended the use of protective costs orders to control the financial risk run by private individuals bringing petitions[56] and that returning officers ("**ROs**") have *"standing to bring petitions relating to any breach of electoral law in administering the election; they should in particular be able to bring a preliminary application to test whether a putative breach affected the result"*.[57] The Law Commission Report stated that 34 out of 36 consultees had supported this proposal.[58] The rationale for the proposal was that ROs *"have an interest in ensuring that the election they conducted was lawful"*.[59]

7.27 In so recommending, the Law Commission also *"acknowledged the risk that returning officers might be seen to succumb to external pressure when bringing a petition or a preliminary application to test the effect of a breach"*. They thought that risk controlled by the fact that *"judicial scrutiny of challenges brought by officers was a protection against unmeritorious claims"*. The Law Commission did not state why judicial scrutiny was sufficient guard against the risk of an RO improperly bringing a public interest petition but not if a totally independent and authoritative regulator did so.

7.28 In its May 2020 response to the PACAC report, the Government joined in with the chorus of statements as the cost and inaccessibility of the petition process, stating: *"the Government is aware of the difficulties with the current challenge system, notably the high cost and complexity of the process"*.[60]

7.29 Public interest petitioner aside, the Government has stated its agreement to the proposal, made by the Electoral Commission[61] and the Law Commission,[62] to bring election petitions within the normal court process, to increase accessibility, adding *"As part of any such reform, the Government must ensure the right balance is struck between ensuring access to justice for electors and also preventing vexatious attempts to challenge elections"*.[63] One implication of note is that this would make the pre-trial procedure more clearly subject to extension of time discretion according to the civil court's relief from sanction power.

[56] Law Commission Report, paras 13.54 and 15.96.
[57] para 13.57.
[58] Law Com No 389, 13.56.
[59] Law Com No 389, 13.55.
[60] PACAC, 'Electoral law: The Urgent Need for Review: Government Response to the Committee's First Report of Session 2019', HC 327, 15.5.2020, p 4.
[61] Electoral Commission, Reforming electoral law, p 5.
[62] Law Com No 389, paras 13.47 and 15.94.
[63] PACAC, 'Electoral law: The Urgent Need for Review: Government Response to the Committee's First Report of Session 2019', HC 327, 15.5.2020, p 4.

G. CONCLUSION

7.30 In June 2020, therefore, some consensus seems to have been reached between the government, the relevant select committees, the Law Commission and the Electoral Commission on the need for reform. To a degree, there is also consensus on much on what that reform should involve. How much of that will be done remains to be seen. Whether reformed or not, and whether moderately or substantially, the need for election law to be accessible and understood will remain of paramount importance. It is hoped that this book will contribute something to that end.

INDEX

More Books by Law Brief Publishing

A selection of our other titles available now:-

- 'Covid-19, Homeworking and the Law – The Essential Guide to Employment and GDPR Issues' by Forbes Solicitors
- 'Covid-19, Force Majeure and Frustration of Contracts – The Essential Guide' by Keith Markham
- 'Covid-19 and Criminal Law – The Essential Guide' by Ramya Nagesh
- 'Covid-19 and Family Law in England and Wales – The Essential Guide' by Safda Mahmood
- 'Covid-19 and the Implications for Planning Law – The Essential Guide' by Bob Mc Geady & Meyric Lewis
- 'Covid-19, Residential Property, Equity Release and Enfranchisement – The Essential Guide' by Paul Sams and Louise Uphill
- 'Covid-19, Brexit and the Law of Commercial Leases – The Essential Guide' by Mark Shelton
- 'Covid-19 and the Law Relating to Food in the UK and Republic of Ireland – The Essential Guide' by Ian Thomas
- 'A Practical Guide to the General Data Protection Regulation (GDPR) – 2nd Edition' by Keith Markham
- 'Ellis on Credit Hire – Sixth Edition' by Aidan Ellis & Tim Kevan
- 'A Practical Guide to Working with Litigants in Person and McKenzie Friends in Family Cases' by Stuart Barlow
- 'Protecting Unregistered Brands: A Practical Guide to the Law of Passing Off' by Lorna Brazell
- 'A Practical Guide to Secondary Liability and Joint Enterprise Post-Jogee' by Joanne Cecil & James Mehigan
- 'A Practical Guide to the Pre-Action RTA Claims Protocol for Personal Injury Lawyers' by Antonia Ford
- 'A Practical Guide to Neighbour Disputes and the Law' by Alexander Walsh
- 'A Practical Guide to Forfeiture of Leases' by Mark Shelton
- 'A Practical Guide to Coercive Control for Legal Practitioners and Victims' by Rachel Horman
- 'A Practical Guide to Rights Over Airspace and Subsoil' by Daniel Gatty
- 'Tackling Disclosure in the Criminal Courts – A Practitioner's Guide' by Narita Bahra QC & Don Ramble

'A Practical Guide to the Law of Driverless Cars – Second Edition' by Alex Glassbrook, Emma Northey & Scarlett Milligan
'A Practical Guide to TOLATA Claims' by Greg Williams
'Artificial Intelligence – The Practical Legal Issues' by John Buyers
'A Practical Guide to the Law of Prescription in Scotland' by Andrew Foyle
'A Practical Guide to the Construction and Rectification of Wills and Trust Instruments' by Edward Hewitt
'A Practical Guide to the Law of Bullying and Harassment in the Workplace' by Philip Hyland
'How to Be a Freelance Solicitor: A Practical Guide to the SRA-Regulated Freelance Solicitor Model' by Paul Bennett
'A Practical Guide to Prison Injury Claims' by Malcolm Johnson
'A Practical Guide to the Small Claims Track' by Dominic Bright
'A Practical Guide to Advising Clients at the Police Station' by Colin Stephen McKeown-Beaumont
'A Practical Guide to Antisocial Behaviour Injunctions' by Iain Wightwick
'Practical Mediation: A Guide for Mediators, Advocates, Advisers, Lawyers, and Students in Civil, Commercial, Business, Property, Workplace, and Employment Cases' by Jonathan Dingle with John Sephton
'The Mini-Pupillage Workbook' by David Boyle
'A Practical Guide to Crofting Law' by Brian Inkster
'A Practical Guide to Spousal Maintenance' by Liz Cowell
'A Practical Guide to the Law of Domain Names and Cybersquatting' by Andrew Clemson
'A Practical Guide to the Law of Gender Pay Gap Reporting' by Harini Iyengar
'A Practical Guide to the Rights of Grandparents in Children Proceedings' by Stuart Barlow
'NHS Whistleblowing and the Law' by Joseph England
'Employment Law and the Gig Economy' by Nigel Mackay & Annie Powell
'A Practical Guide to Noise Induced Hearing Loss (NIHL) Claims' by Andrew Mckie, Ian Skeate, Gareth McAloon
'An Introduction to Beauty Negligence Claims – A Practical Guide for the Personal Injury Practitioner' by Greg Almond
'Intercompany Agreements for Transfer Pricing Compliance' by Paul Sutton
'Zen and the Art of Mediation' by Martin Plowman
'A Practical Guide to the SRA Principles, Individual and Law Firm Codes of Conduct 2019 – What Every Law Firm Needs to Know' by Paul Bennett
'A Practical Guide to Adoption for Family Lawyers' by Graham Pegg
'A Practical Guide to Industrial Disease Claims' by Andrew Mckie & Ian Skeate
'A Practical Guide to Redundancy' by Philip Hyland

'A Practical Guide to Vicarious Liability' by Mariel Irvine
'A Practical Guide to Applications for Landlord's Consent and Variation of Leases' by Mark Shelton
'A Practical Guide to Relief from Sanctions Post-Mitchell and Denton' by Peter Causton
'A Practical Guide to Equity Release for Advisors' by Paul Sams
'A Practical Guide to Unlawful Eviction and Harassment' by Stephanie Lovegrove
'A Practical Guide to the Law Relating to Food' by Ian Thomas
'A Practical Guide to Financial Services Claims' by Chris Hegarty
'The Law of Houses in Multiple Occupation: A Practical Guide to HMO Proceedings' by Julian Hunt
'A Practical Guide to Unlawful Eviction and Harassment' by Stephanie Lovegrove
'A Practical Guide to Solicitor and Client Costs' by Robin Dunne
'Occupiers, Highways and Defective Premises Claims: A Practical Guide Post-Jackson – 2nd Edition' by Andrew Mckie
'A Practical Guide to Financial Ombudsman Service Claims' by Adam Temple & Robert Scrivenor
'A Practical Guide to Advising Schools on Employment Law' by Jonathan Holden
'A Practical Guide to Running Housing Disrepair and Cavity Wall Claims: 2nd Edition' by Andrew Mckie & Ian Skeate
'A Practical Guide to Holiday Sickness Claims – 2nd Edition' by Andrew Mckie & Ian Skeate
'Arguments and Tactics for Personal Injury and Clinical Negligence Claims' by Dorian Williams
'A Practical Guide to QOCS and Fundamental Dishonesty' by James Bentley
'A Practical Guide to Drone Law' by Rufus Ballaster, Andrew Firman, Eleanor Clot
'A Practical Guide to Compliance for Personal Injury Firms Working With Claims Management Companies' by Paul Bennett
'A Practical Guide to the Landlord and Tenant Act 1954: Commercial Tenancies' by Richard Hayes & David Sawtell
'A Practical Guide to Dog Law for Owners and Others' by Andrea Pitt
'RTA Allegations of Fraud in a Post-Jackson Era: The Handbook – 2nd Edition' by Andrew Mckie
'RTA Personal Injury Claims: A Practical Guide Post-Jackson' by Andrew Mckie
'On Experts: CPR35 for Lawyers and Experts' by David Boyle
'An Introduction to Personal Injury Law' by David Boyle
'A Practical Guide to Chronic Pain Claims' by Pankaj Madan
'A Practical Guide to Claims Arising from Fatal Accidents' by James Patience
'A Practical Guide to Subtle Brain Injury Claims' by Pankaj Madan

These books and more are available to order online direct from the publisher at www.lawbriefpublishing.com, where you can also read free sample chapters. For any queries, contact us on 0844 587 2383 or mail@lawbriefpublishing.com.

Our books are also usually in stock at www.amazon.co.uk with free next day delivery for Prime members, and at good legal bookshops such as Wildy & Sons.

We are regularly launching new books in our series of practical day-to-day practitioners' guides. Visit our website and join our free newsletter to be kept informed and to receive special offers, free chapters, etc.

You can also follow us on Twitter at www.twitter.com/lawbriefpub.

www.ingramcontent.com/pod-product-compliance
Lightning Source LLC
LaVergne TN
LVHW080027210926
848481LV00011B/3122